D0914044

John A. Logan
Stalwart Republican from Illinois

John A. Logan. *Illinois State Historical Library.*

John A. Logan

Stalwart Republican from Illinois

JAMES PICKETT JONES

A Florida State University Book

University Presses of Florida
Tallahassee

To Clare

ISBN 0-8130-0729-1   LC 82-2663

Copyright © 1982 by the Board of Regents of the State of Florida
Printed in the United States of America
All rights reserved

Library of Congress Cataloging in Publication Data is on page 292.

CONTENTS

ILLUSTRATIONS

ACKNOWLEDGMENTS

THE PREPARATION of this work has involved many individuals and institutions. I take pleasure in acknowledging some of the individuals and institutions who made this manuscript possible. The staff of the Manuscripts Division of the Library of Congress was most helpful in making available the library's huge Logan Collection as well as the collections of numerous other Gilded Age political figures. The staff of the Duke University Library and that of the Indiana State Library, Indianapolis, are also to be thanked for their kind assistance. I spent some time in Fremont, Ohio, working in the Rutherford B. Hayes Library, whose staff made available the library's extensive materials and gave me excellent advice on Ohio and national politics in the Gilded Age.

A large part of the manuscript material used in this work came from the collections of the Illinois State Historical Library, Springfield. It has always been a pleasure for me to work in the Illinois State Historical Library, and I would like to express particular gratitude to the late Paul Spence, head of the library's Manuscripts Division, for his never failing kindnesses and for his assistance over many years.

Finally, I am indebted to the staff of the Florida State University Library for its assistance.

Several Florida State University colleagues played particularly significant roles in the preparation of this work. Professor Joe M. Richardson gave me his encouragement and his good advice, especially on the Reconstruction chapters and on Logan's relations with black political leaders. The encouragement of Professor Darrell E. Levi must also be gratefully acknowledged. Professor Donald D. Horward gave me his support and his assistance in readying the manuscript for publication. To Professor C. Peter Ripley goes my deep gratitude for his close reading of the manuscript and for his excellent advice in revising the work.

To recently retired Professor William E. Baringer of the University of Florida I owe a long-standing debt that must be acknowledged once again. Professor Baringer guided me through my first work on Logan and over the years has remained a friend whose sense of humor I will always cherish.

None of these friends is responsible for mistakes that may remain; these are solely the fault of the author.

My deepest gratitude is reserved for my wife Clare. As I told her one beautiful Florida autumn afternoon, this is her book.

Preface

*J*OHN *A*. *L*OGAN: *S*TALWART *R*EPUBLICAN *FROM* *I*LLINOIS is the second volume of a two-volume biography of Logan—Union general, representative, senator, vice-presidential candidate, and champion of the Civil War veteran. The first volume *"Black Jack:" John A. Logan and Southern Illinois in the Civil War Era,* dealt with Logan's life from birth to 1867. It traced his rise as southern Illinois' leading political spokesman, focused on the volunteer general's Civil War career, and concluded with Logan's change of party, from Democrat to Republican, in 1867.

John A. Logan emerged from the Civil War a Union military hero. Taking advantage of his martial fame, Logan reentered Illinois politics and served in the House for four years before going on to fourteen years in the Senate. In 1884 he was the Republican nominee for vice-president in James G. Blaine's unsuccessful bid for the presidency. Logan's career from 1867 to his death in 1886 touched many of the most important developments in the United States during Reconstruction and the Gilded Age. He was a House manager in Andrew Johnson's impeachment and a friend and supporter of President Ulysses S. Grant. The Illinois senator figured prominently in the disputed election of 1876 as well as in the colorful election of 1884. In addition, Logan was a founder and longtime leader of the Grand Army of the Republic, that politically powerful veterans' organization.

This volume investigates some of the principal questions of the era. Reconstruction, the Negro's adjustment to freedom, patronage politics versus civil service reform, money problems, and congressional struggles with the executive are all parts of Logan's career.

No other scholarly biography of John A. Logan has been published. Most treatments of the soldier-politician are partisan campaign biographies written in the 1880s, the last published in 1887 by George F. Dawson. That work was read and edited by Logan and is biased and inaccurate. The most deceptive work on Logan was written by his wife. Mary

Logan's *Reminiscences of a Soldier's Wife* was helpful in research for this study, but it had to be handled carefully since the general's wife was chiefly interested in polishing her husband's "mail of untarnished integrity."

The most valuable research materials for a life of Logan are unpublished manuscripts. The Logan Collection in the Library of Congress is enormous, and the Logan Collection in the Illinois State Historical Library, while smaller, is also helpful. The Illinois political leader's letters to his wife give some clear insights into state and national politics as well as into the very special political relationship between John and Mary Logan. In addition, many other manuscript collections add to the picture. The papers of such Logan friends and foes as William E. Chandler, Shelby M. Cullom, Rutherford B. Hayes, Robert G. Ingersoll, Richard Oglesby, William T. Sherman, John Sherman, William Henry Smith, Lyman Trumbull, Elihu B. Washburne, and Horace White were particularly valuable. Newspapers, again friend and foe, tracked Logan's career. Four journals, the *Chicago Tribune* and *Inter-Ocean* (Chicago) and the *Illinois State Journal* and *Illinois State Register* (Springfield) were vital.

Many general works on Reconstruction and the Gilded Age as well as most of the biographies of Logan's contemporaries have pictured the Illinois soldier-politician in a similar manner. Logan has been characterized as one of the new breed of Radicals who, unlike Thaddeus Stevens and Charles Sumner, adopted the Negro issue out of political opportunism rather than moral conviction. He has also been portrayed as a corrupt politician who was an intimate of the inner coterie of the Grant administration and deeply involved in the scandals of the 1860s and 1870s. In *The Hero in America*, Dixon Wecter called Logan "an exceedingly crooked politician."

While Logan did support the "salary grab," he said he did so because poor men would be unable to serve in Congress so long as its members were woefully underpaid. There was no corrupt involvement with any of the Gilded Age scandals. Logan was a man of modest means, and there is no evidence that funds from dishonest transactions made their way into his pocket.

In an age of battle between patronage politics and civil service reform the Illinois boss was a foe of the merit system. While he cloaked his opposition in the usual rhetoric—fear of the creation of an elite class of civil servants and frustration of the will of the majority as expressed in elections—Logan's war against political reforms was, in reality, very simple. He needed patronage to keep his Illinois organization alive. And so he has been labeled one of the last great state patronage bosses. That label is accurate.

At the time John A. Logan fought civil service reform he stood as a constant defender of the rights of black Americans as well as one of the earliest congressional proponents of women's suffrage. There was no political profit to be made from his advocacy of black rights. The election of 1867 proved that, but Logan fought on. If he was merely an opportunist playing the issue solely for political advantage, then this shrewd politician was blind to the forces of racism at work in Illinois, midwestern, and American politics. His speeches in favor of black suffrage and black education were not going to win him widespread support. Indeed, if he was merely an opportunist, he fooled every black leader in the nation. In the last years of his career, no white American in elective office was more admired and none hailed more often as a staunch friend of black Americans than John A. Logan.

Logan's post–Civil War career is not the simple picture of "an exceedingly crooked politician" that is often presented. Here was a man who defended the patronage system and yet fought the Grant administration's grab for Santo Domingo. Here was a man who supported the salary grab as well as votes for women and rights for Negroes. A closer look at the Illinoisan's career has altered some time-worn ideas. This is a period in American life that needs further study. Perhaps other biographies and works on the economic, social, and political institutions of the final third of the nineteenth century will alter other notions of the way things were.

To many of his contemporaries John A. Logan was a reflection of themselves. He was a man from the frontier, a westerner who spoke a language many Americans understood. *Nation,* that voice of the elite East, said Logan's force "was much like the exuberant energy of a wild horse. What he lacked in the way of acquirements he made up by explosive earnestness." That "earnestness" in defense of the right of all to vote, in defense of the volunteer officer and enlisted man against the professional soldier, of the democratic West against eastern snobbery and caste gained Logan a wide following, unconcerned by his lack of "acquirements."

Massachusetts Senator George F. Hoar said: "He was a man of remarkable power, and remarkable influence, both with the Senate and with the people." The Illinois Radical-Stalwart was one of the best known Americans of his time—despised by those who saw in him the person-ification of the machine politician, adored by those who saw in him a man who defended them with words that they understood and with the "energy of a wild horse."

CHAPTER 1

Radical Reinforcement

Reinforcements have always been welcome. Republican leadership in Congress, fresh from victories in the election of 1866, followed by passage over Johnson's veto on March 2, 1867, of the First Reconstruction Act, the Command of the Army Act, and the Tenure of Office Act, welcomed the new recruits to be sworn in when the first session of the Fortieth Congress opened in Washington two days later on March 4. This new support ensured both the legislation necessary to continue congressional Reconstruction and the votes to override presidential vetoes. Perhaps even enough power to initiate presidential impeachment charges could be mustered. March 4, 1867, was a day of confidence for the Republican leadership on Capitol Hill. It was a day of further setback for President Andrew Johnson.

One new House Republican was John A. Logan of Illinois, a prewar Democrat who completed his move across the aisle on March 4. Once a highly partisan Democrat, Logan, in 1859, had boasted on the House floor: "I came here as a Democrat. . . . I have differed with the other side from my childhood and with that side I will never affiliate so long as I have breath in my body."[1] The Civil War and Reconstruction issues moved Logan, the ablest of the conflict's "political generals," to the "other side."

After Sumter, Logan had joined the fight to save the Union. In the war's first three years he showed little interest in other social, economic, and political questions the war had raised. Then, in the conflict's last year, he slowly began to shift his stance. Logan supported using black troops and, by 1865, had become an advocate of political and social equality for freedmen. After careful consideration in the year following Appomattox, John A. Logan had abandoned the Democratic party, moved away from presidential Reconstruction, and allied himself with Andrew Johnson's congressional foes. He embraced the view, strengthened by events of 1865 in Johnson's reconstructed South, that Congress was the sole body willing and able to protect blacks in their right to an education and their right to vote. Furthermore, Logan had become convinced that southern leaders had to pay for disunion and war. By 1866 he had joined those who demanded disfranchisement for many and prison for a few.

Logan's 1867 appearance in the House was remembered by Republican leader James G. Blaine, then a Maine congressman, as a "noteworthy addition." In a more personal portrait, Illinois Republican Shelby Cullom vividly recalled that Logan looked like "a natural soldier. His shoulders were broad, his presence was commanding; with a swarthy face and coal black hair, 'an eye like Mars, to threaten and command.'" [2]

From his election as Illinois' congressman-at-large in November 1866 to March 1867, Logan took every opportunity to widen his influence in his new party. He was active in the U.S. Senate contest in Illinois, which was won by Republican Lyman Trumbull. There was some support for the former general, but it was not sufficient and he wrote, "I got out of the race as I was determined not to be beaten and ruin my future prospects." [3]

After Trumbull's election Logan went to Washington to prepare for the session, then went to Connecticut to give the New Englanders an example of his bloody-shirt oratory. He called for universal suffrage and attacked President Johnson. The congressman also lost no time in writing influential Republicans in support of office for his friends. He succeeded in having an Illinois crony named House doorkeeper. [4] Logan was establishing his Republican credentials, performing political chores, and building his organization.

The highly partisan Prairie State press chronicled Black Jack's progress. Republican journals lauded their new convert and hailed his speeches as "bold and unequivocal." The Democratic press, whose bitterness toward the apostate would last all Logan's life, called him a "pot house charlatan" and excoriated him for "ventilating his vulgarity and bad grammar before the radicals of Connecticut." [5]

On the eve of the session's opening gavel Logan's possible role in the effort to impeach Andrew Johnson drew speculation. One Republican paper advised the congressman "be assured that the people are ready" to support impeachment, while a Democratic editor believed the Republicans would not be dragooned into impeachment by "men like Logan and [Ben] Butler, who are in the Republican Party only on probation." Ohio Republican Senator John Sherman wrote his brother, General William T. Sherman, Logan's Civil War commander, "the impeachment movement has so far been a complete failure—Butler and Logan are reinforcements but will effect nothing." [6]

The resumption of John A. Logan's congressional career came at a time when congressional power was approaching its zenith. On March 4 Speaker Schuyler Colfax declared the Thirty-ninth Congress adjourned sine die and immediately organized the Fortieth Congress. Never before had the outgoing Congress ordered the next session to convene immediately, and when the gallery doors were opened at noon a crowd rushed for seats. Ordinarily the new session, called by the president, began in December. At this juncture, however, the powerful Republican majority distrusted President Johnson; since it commanded a two-thirds vote in each house, it was able to force the change in procedure.

It was a time of new problems and new responsibilities for the Radical Republicans whom Logan had joined. Suddenly they were able to exercise substantial power. Yet serious questions about Radical effectiveness remained to be answered. Could Radical leadership retain the support of moderate Republicans? Could the Radicals themselves, united on the political issues of Reconstruction but divided on an entire range of economic issues, remain united? And finally, would the congressional leaders continue to overawe the president? Despite his defeats, Johnson still possessed the veto and the power to enforce legislation. But the chief executive could expect little support from congressional Democrats, a "hopeless, demoralized, and suspected minority." [7]

From his seat in the middle of the chamber's next-to-last row John A. Logan could see fellow Republicans Blaine, Butler, Thaddeus Stevens of Pennsylvania, and Ohioans Rutherford B. Hayes and James A. Garfield. Among Logan's fellow members of the Illinois delegation were Republicans Norman Judd, Shelby Cullom, and Elihu Washburne. Leader of the Prairie State Democrats was Scott Marshall, once Logan's close friend and political ally. When the vote for speaker was taken, Logan voted for Colfax as the Indianan defeated Marshall 127 to 30. [8]

Reconstruction dominated the new House and Logan's return to Washington. Early in the session he supported legislation to supplement the First Reconstruction Act as the measure easily passed. The supplement directed military commanders across the South to begin voter registration and to organize state constitutional conventions. On March 7 Ohio Republican James Ashley introduced a motion to impeach the president, and Logan voted with the minority against tabling.[9]

For the first week Logan said little, but on March 13 he made his maiden speech as a Republican. The occasion was a debate on a bill to spend $1 million for the relief of the destitute in the South. This measure had passed the Senate, but Logan and Butler fought it in the House. The Illinoisan attacked the resolution as a veiled attempt to provide pensions for ex-Rebel soldiers and their families. His opposition was based upon both bloody-shirt reasoning and a fundamental opposition to the appropriation of federal funds for state relief. Logan pointed out to the chamber that there were needy people in the Northwest as well and that they were loyal citizens. "Although there are many poor people in the Northwest," he continued, "we do not understand that we have a right to come to Congress to be fed." Both Democrats and Republicans opposed Logan. John Bingham, an Ohio Republican, said he was sorry to hear a member of his party opposed to the relief of the poor anywhere in the United States.[10] But Logan was set on finding a place in Radical ranks, and criticism from Democrats and conservative Republicans had no effect.

Debate on the southern relief bill was intermittent through the session's third week. Logan told the House that Freedmen's Bureau chief General Oliver O. Howard reported that ample relief funds were available. He also mentioned the opposition of Union veterans to the bill. Finally, Logan threatened to "offer an amendment to appropriate $1 million to assist the suffering people in the Valleys of the Mississippi and Ohio Rivers." Logan's opposition helped defeat the bill.[11]

On March 23 the president vetoed and returned the First Supplementary Reconstruction Bill to Congress. With Black Jack voting "aye," the House overrode by a vote of 114 to 25.[12]

During the session, debate also turned to military legislation, on which Logan was determined to play a major role. The volunteer nurtured an intense dislike of all professional soldiers, a dislike that remained constant throughout his post–Civil War career. On March 15 he regaled the House with stories of exorbitant ordnance costs, asking for a rigid check to see how the army spent its funds.[13] This brief speech served notice to the military that the "political general" intended to watch them closely.

At month's end adjournment until the summer was proposed. Logan fought adjournment, arguing "there is still a necessity for guards on the watch tower to see that no harm comes to the Republic." He believed Congress had passed only one valuable bill and urged a close watch be maintained on the administration. When the vote to adjourn was taken on the thirtieth, Logan voted with the losing side. The Senate remained in session until April 18. Indiana Radical Senator Oliver P. Morton was disappointed that the lower chamber departed before reporting out impeachment charges. The House would begin again on July 3.[14]

Throughout the first session impeachment was a subject of Capitol conversation. Republicans caucused to debate impeachment, with Logan joining Ashley, Butler, and Pennsylvanian John Covode as an outspoken advocate of charges against the chief executive. When no charges were forthcoming rumors circulated of a rapprochement between the Radicals and Johnson; but there was "very little prospect of such a result," according to Shelby Cullom. Logan's concern was revealed in a letter from one of his Illinois supporters to Ben Butler: "Logan wrote me that they [the House members] are cowardly and he fears impeachment has gone up."[15]

The Illinois press kept a close watch on Logan's congressional performance. Many Republican sheets printed in its entirety his speech against the relief bill. The oration was labeled "convincing and argumentative," by one paper and "honest and earnest" by another. Logan's constituents were told the remarks had made him a prominent national figure.[16] There were several requests for copies of the speech; Ben Butler asked for one hundred.[17]

Enemy journals, on the other hand, blasted the Republican for cowardice and cruelty for refusing charity to a vanquished foe. The *Illinois State Register* unfavorably compared Logan to Senator Trumbull, who had voted for the measure. Logan, the editor observed, was a "heartless demagogue," who became a Radical "because there was money in it." The *Chicago Times* called the Logan-Butler stand "Radical Christianity."[18]

When the session ended Logan remained in Washington for several days, deeply involved in politics. He took care of some patronage business back home and turned to the Republican Congressional Executive Committee, whose task it was to assist southern loyalists in the early days of congressional Reconstruction. This body met in April and Logan joined Senator Zachariah Chandler in trying to raise funds to aid those working in the South.[19]

After several days in the capital, Logan went to New York on business. Trying to parlay his recent fame and newfound political power into financial success, the congressman became involved in several enterprises. He joined Ben Butler as an incorporator of a land development venture called the Lower California Company of New York. The struggle to support his family adequately would be one of the great trials of Logan's life.[20]

That spring the Illinois Republican press boasted that "no man in the Union has more admirers" than Logan. Three Prairie State journals joined a Connecticut newspaper in endorsing the former general for president in 1868. The *Carbondale New Era* reprinted an article from the *Liberty Bell and Workingmen's Advocate* (Norwich, Connecticut) supporting Logan's presidential nomination. The *New Era* believed the next president "must be a soldier" and felt that no soldier was better prepared than Logan. The journal went on to write, "He is a live man, a progressive man, a Radical. He came from the people, he is one of the people, he knows the people." By late April a "Logan for President" endorsement ran over the mastheads of several Illinois papers. In its endorsement the *Freeport Journal* vowed: "We like him because he stands firm upon the broad platform that leading Rebels must be punished and that the rebellious states must be reconstructed upon the broad and eternal principles of right and justice to all men whether of high or low degree, whether black or white."[21]

Such support must have pleased the ambitious Logan, but he remained silent. Through April and May, Black Jack was so quiet that the acid Robert Ingersoll wrote his brother Ebon, one of Logan's Republican colleagues in the Illinois House delegation, "Logan has not been heard from. He never kept still so long before in his life." But politics was never far away and in May, Congressman Robert Schenck wrote to Logan and Zach Chandler to arrange a fall meeting of Radicals in Chicago.[22]

When Congress reassembled in July it continued the wrangle over Reconstruction. It was so "very hot and disagreeable" that even Radical members wanted to conclude their business with dispatch and adjourn until the fall.[23] A member of the administration predicted that the Radicals would hurt their cause by their extremism and conservatives would soon be aroused.[24] A picture of Logan during this session through an admiring constituent's eyes reported: "Logan is one of the handsomest members of the House. His hair is about two shades darker than the blackest hair ever seen, and with his black eyes and a very attractive smile that usually lurks about his mouth, form a combination that the ladies will admire." [25]

On opening day as Kentucky's representatives presented themselves to be seated, Logan challenged that right. He introduced a resolution calling for an investigation of the loyalty of all that state's members. He did not want the chamber "contaminated" by anyone who had supported the rebellion. "If they are loyal men," he felt, "they will pass through the ordeal and come out unscathed." John Bingham and Democrat James Brooks of New York disputed Logan's arguments. Scott Marshall joined them and told the House that disloyalty charges could be made against Logan himself. He revived stories of Black Jack's opposition to the war in the spring and summer of 1861. Logan hotly denied Marshall's allegation, but he did agree to limit the investigation to those Kentuckians against whom charges had been made rather than the entire delegation. Logan's resolution as amended passed the House. [26]

The depths of Logan's political ambition and his drive to surge to leadership in the Republican camp are revealed in his report to his wife of the debate over the Kentucky delegation. On the third he wrote, "I was engaged in a debate today . . . and got them excluded. (Victorious)." Four days later he boasted and threatened: "I may have gone too far, but I am in the boat, and I will have something to do with steering it or *it shall go under.* I know that I understand matters as well as any of them, and they shall follow as well as lead." [27]

Typically, Logan's outspoken comments drew a mixed response. Reviving the prewar nickname "Dirty Work" Logan, fixed on him by Republicans when he was a Democrat, the Democratic press attacked the turncoat. His speech was an "outrage" and Marshall's charges of the 1861 "treason" were spread across Illinois. Gideon Welles, Johnson's secretary of the navy, labeled the exclusion attempt nothing more than "Radical electioneering." [28] Praise came as well. Of his exchange with Brooks, the hometown *New Era* bragged that Logan "made the dirt eating New York Copperhead take water." Both Springfield's *Illinois State Journal* and the *Chicago Tribune* believed the investigation was fully justified. [29]

On July 9 debate on the Second Supplementary Reconstruction bill began in the House. This measure struck at Johnson and presidential Reconstruction when it authorized commanders of military districts to remove or suspend officials who refused to take the loyalty oath and to appoint loyal men in their places. These removals and suspensions had to be approved by the general of the army (Grant) and reviewed by Congress, not by the president.

Logan came to support such measures slowly. The previous winter he had serious doubts about military Reconstruction, but by summer these doubts had faded.[30] He not only supported the bill but intensified his efforts to "steer the Radical boat." Logan made his longest speech since his return to Congress in support of the Second Supplementary bill. He waved the bloody shirt at the Democratic opposition, reviewing that party's role in the late war. He admitted that he had been a Democrat until "shame" drove him from the party. Supporters of the pending legislation were simply "attempting to devise the most practicable and politic means to restore at the earliest moment to this whole land permanent and health-ful tranquility and prosperity." These men would not stand by, Logan said, while ex-Rebels and Copperheads joined to overturn all that had been done since 1861.

The question of the status of the ex-Confederate states was a major benchmark of Reconstruction thinking. From 1861 to 1867 Logan held the more conservative position that those states had never been out of the Union. Now he abandoned that view, linked arms with the early Radicals, and talked of the rebellious states as conquered provinces which should remain "subject to military rule at the hands of their conquerers, and so ought to remain until traitors shall learn how to blush for their crimes." Ghosts of Union dead and the horrors of Andersonville were paraded be-fore the listeners. Jefferson Davis was condemned as the chief traitor and the fiery former general vowed "had I captured Jefferson Davis and his disposal been committed to my hands, I would have organized an able court-martial and have given him a fair trial, just sentence, and prompt execution." He won loud applause from the floor when he concluded by saying that he would gladly welcome southern representatives who could demonstrate loyalty to the federal government.[31]

The supplementary bill easily passed both houses, but as Indiana Radical George Julian predicted, "Andy is going to devil us by delay and then blackguard us in his veto message."[32] The veto availed little and was quickly overridden. One effect of the veto message was to strengthen the hand of the impeachment party. The *Chicago Tribune*'s capital correspon-dent believed it gave them "new vitality."[33] General of the Army Ulysses S. Grant stood ready to enforce the new measure, advising Secretary of

War Edwin M. Stanton that he would show the secretary his orders before they were put in force.[34]

In the session's final week several more Reconstruction bills came to the floor, and Logan remained with the Radicals. Julian introduced a resolution condemning any effort to assume the Rebel debt. It passed with Logan voting "aye." On the eighteenth a bill was introduced providing that no one in the District of Columbia be denied the right to hold office by reason of race or color. Again the Illinoisan voted with the majority.[35] In spite of Radical efforts to bring Congress back on October 16, the body adjourned on the twentieth to meet again in November.

Logan's record in the summer session brought encomiums from his Illinois supporters. His long speech was published in full by a number of newspapers. It was praised as a "lively colloquy," and an oration "of great power and eloquence."[36]

One Illinoisan who did not offer praise was Scott Marshall. During the session President Johnson had nominated former General John McClernand to be minister to Mexico. Before the war Logan and McClernand had been close friends as Douglas Democrats in the Illinois House delegation. While Black Jack switched parties, McClernand remained a Democrat; a complete break resulted. Marshall wrote McClernand that Logan's active opposition helped prevent confirmation, and he vowed angrily: "We must fight our way up with the people and neither ask nor give quarter to the faction that now controls the country."[37]

When the House adjourned Logan went to New York on business. He cryptically told his wife that he was involved in a new enterprise about which he had said nothing, but he hastily assured her, "it is honorable and has nothing to do with my official position."[38]

An important battle in the political war of Reconstruction was awaiting the combative Logan in the fall of 1867. In October, Ohio would elect a governor and a legislature and ballot on a voting rights amendment enfranchising blacks. Ohio Republicans asked for the congressman's help and he answered the call at once. He agreed to make six speeches, but Buckeye State Republicans pressed him for at least twice that number.[39] Stumping Ohio, Logan gave the voters the first lengthy example of his bloody-shirt style since his conversion to Radicalism.

Like most bloody-shirt orators, Logan never failed to remind his listeners that both Confederates and Copperheads were Democrats and were responsible for the Civil War and its miseries. It was a short leap from that reminder of past Democratic iniquities to the conclusion that the party of 1867 was merely a continuation of that past evil. In time, the Democrats, and especially southern Democrats, developed their own bloody-shirt rhetoric, every bit as strident as that of the Republicans. Many politicians on both sides had interests in keeping emotional war issues alive well into the postwar world.

Logan's first speech in the Ohio contest, delivered at Hamilton on the twelfth, brought a premature boast that "Logan is carrying Ohio by storm."[40] Logan called the Democratic party a party of treason, and he struck hard at traitorous southern Democrats, Ohio Copperhead Clement L. Vallandigham, and Andrew Johnson. On the controversial subject of Negro suffrage the congressman challenged:

> Now I want some Democrat to give a reason why the Negro should not vote. I have read their speeches, and all they say is, "we don't want the nigger to vote" and turn up their noses as they say it. A gentleman in Congress from your state says the Negro does not belong to the human species. But they are made the same as you and I; but they are black—that is all the difference. If they were not made by the hand of God, I would like to know by whom they were made. . . . If you won't allow a man to vote because he has black skin, you have the right to say I shall not vote because I have black hair. I don't care whether a man is black, red, blue or white.[41]

He concluded at Hamilton, as he did in all his speeches, with a stirring appeal to veterans. He urged them to rally behind the party that stood behind them from Bull Run to Appomattox.[42]

Logan's transition from prewar Democrat to Ohio stump advocate of black suffrage is an amazing change of position. When strong midwestern racial prejudice is taken into account Logan's progress is even more astounding. One recent historian finds the Republican party's transition from prewar antiexpansionist party to postwar champion of Civil Rights "remarkable" in the face of northern racism. Logan's path was even far longer than that of his new party.[43]

When he moved on to Greenville, Ohio, on the seventeenth, a large number of Logan's former soldiers from the XVII Corps were on hand.

Special trains were run from Piqua to Greenville to swell the crowd to twenty thousand. The former general made a "powerful" speech and received a "handsome ovation." [44]

One week later "10,000 enthusiastic Republicans" heard Logan in Cincinnati. He spoke for two hours to a wildly receptive audience and that night appeared at the city's Burnett House, where he was visited by hundreds of members of the Grand Army of the Republic. [45] On the twenty-fifth Logan spoke in Dayton and then went by train to Cleveland for a major address on the twenty-ninth. The Cleveland meeting brought a number of special trains and the congressman's largest crowd of the canvass. Banners proclaiming "We Vote as We Shot" and "Welcome to the Soldier-Orator of the West" waved over the platform. Again Logan assailed Copperhead Democracy and "skinned them all over, clear to the bone." That night bonfires were lighted around his hotel and a large crowd surrounded the building insisting that Logan address it. He spoke briefly to loud applause. Black Jack's final speech was at Oberlin on the twenty-first, where he shared the platform with Rutherford B. Hayes, the Republican gubernatorial candidate. [46]

The Ohio press maintained a close watch on Logan's tour. He was hailed as "one of the finest rallying speakers in the country." One Republican editor believed: "The visit of General Logan at Cleveland has thrown more spirit into the canvass in this neighborhood than anything previously done. The electric fire of the Illinoisan communicates to all with whom he comes in contact." Another journalist wrote a campaign song to be sung to "The Wearin' of the Green." It went in part:

> The darkey won his freedom with bayonet and bullet
> Learned how to use the musket and the trigger how to pull it
> Where the hand and heart are loyal, caste and color it destroys
> And should vote, said John A. Logan, down South from Illinois
>
> Ohio too has boys in blue and proudly she can tell
> Of heroes, Grant and Sherman, and her glorious Little Phil
> But with tongue and pen and sabre, none a Copperhead annoys
> Dreads more than John A. Logan, he who hails from Illinois[47]

It is likely that Republicans who brought Logan, Colfax, and Oliver P. Morton into the state were afraid of losing the Republican stronghold, for some of the party's shrewdest midwestern leaders feared setback. Richard Yates warned Massachusetts Senator Henry Wilson of reduced majorities. Speaker Colfax predicted "ugly times this winter and it may try our backbone. We are probably to have a run of bad luck this fall, for in nearly every state we have side issues weakening us."[48]

The Ohio predictions were correct. Hayes won a narrow victory, while the voters returned a Democratic legislature. The latter outcome meant that Radical leader Ben Wade would be defeated for reelection to the Senate. In addition, the Negro suffrage amendment was rejected by thirty-eight thousand votes.[49] Democrats exulted in what they saw as the beginning of the end for congressional Reconstruction and for Radicals everywhere. All the election proved, believed Logan's staunchest supporters, was that a skirmish had been lost; but he predicted that better organization would win the battle of 1868.[50]

Through much of the eventful year of 1867 Logan was separated from his family. When the Fortieth Congress first convened he lived alone at the Willard Hotel. His wife, Mary, their eight-year-old daughter, Dollie, and their two-year-old son, Manning, remained at home in Carbondale. The congressman promised to come home after the session and plans were being made to bring the entire family to Washington before the year's end.[51] There was talk too of shifting the family's Illinois residence from Egypt to Chicago.[52] Black Jack's political ambitions were soaring and a residence closer to the state's center of power and population was important. The congressman and his Egyptian friend Isham Haynie invested in several acres in Cook County. In addition, Logan bought a lot on the corner of Wabash and Twenty-third streets and planned to build a residence there.[53]

In April, when the first congressional meeting recessed, Logan had gone home to Carbondale and his family. He hoped to spend a quiet time and rest for the summer return to Washington. The joy of the homecoming was tempered somewhat by the poor health of John Cunningham, Logan's father-in-law and old Mexican War comrade. Cunningham had been drinking heavily since his wife's death. The previous winter Mary had written the often absent Logan, "the family have caused me more *care and anxiety and labor* than even you know about."[54]

Logan's only public appearances in the period of rest in Illinois were lectures in Carbondale and DuQuoin. He contrasted Abraham Lincoln and Jefferson Davis, eulogizing Lincoln and branding the Confederate leader "grasping, tyrannical and selfish." Although the DuQuoin crowd was "large and appreciative," the *New Era* admitted the audience was "disgracefully" small. Never losing a chance to strike at Logan, the *Illinois State Register* concluded cynically, "We have a higher opinion of the people of Carbondale than ever before. We recognize them as people of taste." [55]

For the most part it was a quiet three months. Just before he boarded the train to return to Washington, Logan wrote Illinois Governor Richard Oglesby, "I have been at home all summer and have eaten large amounts of strawberries and had any quantity of rheumatism." [56]

Congress's second adjournment, in August, brought Logan back to Egypt. Illinois was sizzling and he took his wife and children to St. Paul for a month-long vacation in cooler Minnesota. It was a quiet time broken only by one speech. In September the Logans spent a week in Chicago. They discussed plans for their Wabash Avenue property and the popular politician acted as judge for a horse race. On the fourth Black Jack joined Zach Chandler, Richard Oglesby, and Ebon Ingersoll at a mass meeting of Republicans. The ever hostile *Chicago Times* dusted off its strongest epithets in calling Logan and Chandler "foulmouthed and drunken wretches." Later in the month the family returned to Carbondale while Logan went to Ohio to campaign. [57]

His labors in Ohio completed, Logan went to Carbondale to spend a month in his home district before entraining for Washington. This time the family went with Logan and he established his wife and children at the Willard, which Mary later remembered as having low ceilings, dismal halls, and a bleak dining room. The once fashionable hotel had declined in attractiveness yet remained popular because of its convenient location. Also staying at the Willard were the James G. Blaine family and Pennsylvania Senator Simon Cameron, and the Logan and Blaine children often played together. The ambitious Mary, eager to widen her social circle and to exert political influence, was pleased to be in the capital at last. [58]

Shortly after his return Logan was stricken with a painful inflammation of the lungs. He wrote Governor Oglesby, "My health is very poor . . . My trip to Ohio almost broke me down." The ailment was so severe that hearings of the House Ordnance Committee, to which the former general had been named, had to be postponed. [59]

Logan had returned to Washington to immerse himself in congressional business, but he kept a watchful eye on future prospects. Logan-for-president talk continued and a number of papers boosted him throughout the winter, although he had few illusions about his chances. The party was swinging to General Grant. Influential Egyptian Republicans wrote Congressman Elihu Washburne to advise him that despite support for "that great soldier, Logan" the Grant movement was gaining ground there. That consummate political manipulator Thurlow Weed also wrote Washburne trying to ensure Logan's support for Grant.[60]

Talk of Logan for governor in 1868 was more realistic. Daniel W. Munn, a Cairo Republican leader, wrote Black Jack asking him to seek the post and predicting easy victory for a ticket of Grant and Logan. But Logan knew better; there were others ambitious for the place on the ticket. Another former general, John M. Palmer, charged confidently that "Logan inspired great distrust" among the people. He felt that his own nomination would be "rather easy to obtain." Robert Ingersoll dismissed Logan and Palmer with a "plague on both their houses." He wrote outgoing Governor Oglesby: "I suppose Palmer is prepared to accept your seat as soon as you vacate and that Logan stands ready if possible to push him away and sit down himself. Man proposes and God disposes and maybe God will dispose of them both."[61]

On November 21 the final meeting of the Fortieth Congress's first session began. Congress met from the twenty-first to December 2. Little business was transacted and Logan played an insignificant role in these closing deliberations. Committees were named and the Illinoisan was happy to be placed on the powerful Ways and Means Committee. The appointment was pleasing to his supporters but offensive to the *Illinois State Register,* which reported Logan "has more mean ways than any other man we know of."[62] Horace White, able Chicago editor, confided to Washburne, "The appointment of Logan instead of Judd is a little provoking. . . . Judd is, I think, a better man than Logan for that committee."[63]

By the session's conclusion, Logan had begun to establish an efficient political operation in Washington. He had developed detailed records listing persons from Illinois who had come to the capital seeking favors. Arranged by county, he also listed newspaper editors, members of the Illinois assembly, businessmen, and sheriffs.[64]

When he served in the prewar House, Logan remained a relatively obscure back-bench Democrat. In 1867 he was a back-bencher no longer. He had gained military fame, he had joined the dominant party, and he had become a leader of that party. His political views placed him among that party's most radical faction. He and his fellow "Jacobins" believed that southern traitors must be punished, southern loyalists, black and white, must vote, and freedmen must be given social equality. Even black men in the North must have the vote. Logan's new party had saved the Union and with peace fought to preserve the gains of the war years from the machinations of the man in the White House. The Illinois Radical was hard at work for the Republic, the Republican party, and his own political future.

CHAPTER 2

Steering the Boat

LOGAN HAD a more prominent position on the floor when the roll was called for the second session of the Fortieth Congress. He sat on the aisle four rows back and listened as the president's message was read. Johnson, emboldened by the fall elections, attacked Negro suffrage, lashed out at military Reconstruction, and condemned Congress's "military force." Logan joined the hostile response and brought laughter when he proposed that the "corps of pages that now constitute the 'military force' of the House" be disbanded to ease Johnson's fears.[1]

But laughter passed quickly as the Radicals realized that Johnson still might have the power to delay black suffrage and to nullify the entire congressional plan of Reconstruction. That summer while Congress was recessed Johnson had taken the offensive. He pressed for Stanton's resignation and removed General Phil Sheridan from his southern command. Johnson's annual message "reinforced the radicals' opinion that his removal was a necessity."[2]

Reconstruction could be salvaged only through impeachment and a resolution charging impeachable offenses was introduced on December 7. Logan and Robert Schenck of Ohio led the floor debate, battling to prevent a vote when defeat of the resolution seemed certain. They failed to halt a roll call, and Logan voted with Thaddeus Stevens, Butler, Cullom, Julian, and Norman Judd to bring charges against the president. They failed by a vote of 57 to 108. Julian wrote his wife, "You will see how Congress backed down. . . . It is pitiful!" Logan agreed as did many of his supporters.[3]

Now that he was steering the boat, Reconstruction matters were never far from Logan's mind. On the sixteenth Johnson called for repeal of all Reconstruction laws passed by the Fortieth Congress. Logan responded

16

with a successful resolution that promised the House would never "consent to take one retrograde step from its advanced position of promoting the cause of equal rights."[4]

Logan's attendance record in the early days of the second session was excellent. Despite invitations to speak, he rarely missed a roll call. A New York Republican who tried to secure the congressman for a large rally was disappointed at Logan's absence and advised, "he escaped a *tremendous ovation.*"[5]

Just after Christmas, Mary and the children traveled to Illinois leaving Logan in the capital "working night and day to keep up, engaged on committees nearly all the time."[6] He voted for a resolution condemning the president for removing Sheridan, and he carefully watched the growing crisis surrounding Johnson's suspension of Stanton.[7]

In January the House debated two measures Radicals felt were vital to the future of congressional Reconstruction. Logan supported a bill taking certain jurisdiction away from the Supreme Court. He also stood with the majority on the Third Supplementary Reconstruction Act, which allowed a simple majority to implement a new constitution in ex-Confederate states regardless of the percentage of voters participating in the election. The bill cleared the House on January 21 and became law in March.[8]

Reconstruction was not Logan's only concern. He was always seeking new working parts for his political machine and new foundations for his political ambitions. Ever since its founding in 1866 he had been interested in the Grand Army of the Republic, and as one of the body's founders, he was pleased with the G.A.R.'s rapid growth.[9] In 1866 the veterans held their first national convention, urging benefits for soldiers' widows and orphans and electing Illinois General Stephen Hurlbut national commander.[10] That year Logan failed to win election as Illinois commander, and national leadership also evaded him.[11] Nevertheless he remained an active member through 1867 and in January 1868 the Grand Army elected Logan national commander at its Philadelphia encampment. Twenty states were represented at Philadelphia, but the Middle West remained the chief source of the organization's power and membership. Despite continued insistence that the organization was a fraternal one, its close affiliation with the Republican party was clear.[12]

But most of the G.A.R.'s political influence had been local, not national. It was a young organization, still feeling its way in 1868. Logan had different ideas. As national commander he moved its headquarters

John A. Logan with family. Left to right: Mary, Manning, Senator Logan, Dollie. *Reproduced from the collections of the Library of Congress.*

from Springfield to Washington and labored to centralize and control the society.[13] Shortly after his election as commander he received a letter from Surgeon B.F. Stephenson, one of the founders, which outlined methods of centralization that called for people close to Logan to be named staff officers in each department. Beyond the internal workings of the order, Logan issued orders urging local posts to support Republican candidates. Stephenson agreed and advised the congressman: "If a Republican president is elected it is the G.A.R. that will do it," but he later added that when asked the army's political role, "my invariable reply is the G.A.R. is not political."[14]

Later that year Logan gave firmer indication of the political role of the veterans' organization. In a September 19 letter to New Hampshire Senator William E. Chandler, marked "strictly confidential," the grand commander wrote: "The organization of the G.A.R. had been and is being run in the interests of the Republican Party."[15] Yet during Logan's three terms as commander he persisted in a surface show of nonpartisanship.[16]

John A. Logan's most enduring act as G.A.R. commander was his designation of May 30 as Memorial Day. The practice of placing flowers on soldiers' graves began with southern women. Northern troops observed the practice, and by 1865 the graves of Union dead were being similarly decorated. Occasionally Negroes placed flowers on the graves of their liberators.[17] By 1866 decoration ceremonies had invaded the North with Logan taking part in such an occasion at Carbondale. Nothing could keep before the public the late war and the need for a strong Republican Reconstruction like a reminder of the Union war dead.

In March 1868 when Mary Logan visited several Virginia battlefields she saw flags and faded flowers on Confederate graves. She described the practice to Logan and he shortly decided to make it G.A.R. policy. He issued General Order No. 11, which designated May 30 the day "for the purpose of strewing flowers, or otherwise decorating the graves of Comrades who died in defense of their country in the late rebellion." The idea was immensely popular from the first and over one hundred ceremonies were held in 1868.[18] By 1910 Memorial Day was a legal holiday everywhere in the United States except in nine former Confederate states.[19]

Logan received word of the early success of the idea from a legion of correspondents. Two brothers wrote from Olmsted Falls, Ohio, that they had strewn the graves of two old friends in "accordance with your orders." They included a poem written for the event. It concluded:

Sadly we gather yet willingly come,
We wait not the bugle nor the roll of the drum,
O'er the graves of our comrades fresh garlands we twine,
A tribute in memory almost divine.[20]

Although attentive to Reconstruction legislation and the steady construction of a political base among veterans, Logan was also mindful of needs at home. Early in the new year he introduced a resolution to provide improvements on the Illinois River and the Illinois and Michigan Canal. He also asked for the establishment of a marine hospital at Cairo. He was aware that some Illinois Republicans felt the party should turn away from Reconstruction and concentrate on inflation as the key issue for 1868. *Chicago Tribune* editor Joseph Medill wrote, "We can no longer take shelter behind the war, the Negro or Reconstruction. The first is ended, the second is 'played out', and the third will soon be completed." Logan's actions indicated strong disagreement with Medill's views.[21]

The winter brought the renewal of speculation about the Illinois Republicans' gubernatorial nominee. Black Jack received many communications on the subject. John Palmer would not seek the post, wrote one man, for Palmer believed that Logan's "stock is high." Isham Haynie wrote Logan that either he or Palmer should head the ticket "but as neither of you will . . . a general *'scrimmage'* seems to be imminent." Several other Illinois Republicans wrote the congressman-at-large that Palmer had indicated his preference for Logan. Some speculated that a plot was in the offing by which Yates would resign from the Senate with Oglesby appointing Palmer to the vacancy. This would account for the latter's reluctance. Stories persisted that Logan would not be a candidate chiefly because of his "deep interest" in the questions before Congress. Governor Oglesby, not eligible for reelection, was convinced that Palmer would be "finally induced to run."[22]

Business interests also took the congressman's time. On February 10, 1868, he agreed to purchase ten shares of Crédit Mobilier stock from Congressman Oakes Ames for a thousand dollars. Logan did not pay at once but held the stock until he had sufficient funds. Then too, he remained involved in the Lower California Company. The company's manager suggested in January that they turn the land into *"an American Liberia"* to which blacks would emigrate, establishing a "Negro state of their own which can enter the Union." Butler hotly retorted, "I am not rich, but I am not poor enough to cheat Negroes." There is no record of

Logan's response to the proposal. There was some time for pleasure; the Logans were able to attend readings given by Charles Dickens, who was on an American tour.[23] The former general remained much in demand as a speaker, but his duties in Washington often prevented him from leaving the city.[24]

On the House floor that winter a civil service merit system entered the lists in the form of a bill put forward by reformer Thomas A. Jenckes. Logan, a consistent foe of civil service reform throughout his career, tore into the Jenckes plan. The two men intensely debated the concept. In a letter congratulating Jenckes, Charles Francis Adams warned that "Mr. Logan wants to be able to put his best friends wherever he chooses and has no idea of giving up the privilege." [25] Adams was very close to the mark; Logan's Illinois organization could be wrecked by the Jenckes bill.

On February 5 Logan and Scott Marshall indulged in a rancorous exchange of the kind common to friends turned bitter enemies. Logan accused Marshall of significantly altering, in the *Congressional Globe*, remarks he had made on the floor. The two then traded insults. The Democrat said "I know my colleague is at times very irritable and sometimes troubled with what may . . . be called flatulency." As laughter rose, Marshall advised Logan to take Mrs. Winslow's Soothing Syrup for "such pains as have been agitating him this morning." Logan struck back, labeling his opponent's language "indecent" and doubting that Marshall was a gentleman.[26]

Suddenly, on February 21, only one issue seemed important. Andrew Johnson removed the suspended Stanton and appointed Lorenzo Thomas ad interim secretary of war. Radicals encouraged Stanton to "stand firm as the everlasting rocks," as one of Logan's constituents wrote. Massachusetts Senator Charles Sumner sent the secretary a one-word message that summed up this view—"Stick!" Stanton barricaded himself in the War Department.[27]

As G.A.R. commander, Logan, with the advice and cooperation of Michigan Senator Zach Chandler, planned to arm and use the organization as the crisis worsened. In a small, ragged note marked "confidential" the congressman sent General N.P. Chipman, administrator of the G.A.R., his emergency orders:

It seems that the city is filling up with a suspicious class of men, that may mean harm. Tho no demonstration has been made. The House will impeach A.J. and a row may ensue. I hope you will quietly and secretly organize all our boys so that they can assemble at a signal that you may agree upon to report at H.Q. and be ready to protect the Congress of the U.S. in the exercise of their lawful duties. This must be done quietly, and no indiscreet persons must understand or know anything about it, and no demonstrations of any kind must be made at all, if no necessity shall occur for us to act at anytime. Then the fact that we are on the alert must never be known as it would affect many of our boys that hold office.

Logan warned, "All of this must be done by verbal communications as no official orders must be made on the subject at present or until a necessity might arise to protect the Govt. again . . . be discreet, and come see me tonight." Mary Logan remembered G.A.R. sentinels in civilian clothing who patrolled the vicinity of the White House and the War Department throughout the crisis. As for Logan himself, he slept on a cot in the War Department "so that he could summon the Grand Army at a moment's notice." The contemporary press was aware of the situation, in spite of the precautions, and the *Illinois State Journal* reported Logan's offer of himself and 125 G.A.R. members as Stanton's praetorian guard. Calling the congressman a "braggart," the *Illinois State Register* laughed at the thought of Logan and his guards—"A pop gun would scare them out of their wits." [28]

At last the Radicals had their impeachment—the president had violated the Tenure of Office Act. Not only had Johnson violated the measure, he had also acted to threaten the entire structure of congressional Reconstruction. Impeachment became a political act to save congressional Reconstruction. Previously reluctant moderates would surely now join the advocates of removal. Michael Les Benedict adds: "By his decision to disregard the laws Congress had passed to circumscribe his power to obstruct Reconstruction, Johnson left them no choice." [29]

Washington seethed with excitement. George Julian had not felt such tension since First Bull Run. The Indianan was certain "the laggards would join us" and impeachment would carry the House. An Ohio representative wrote James A. Garfield that the question would carry by a "solid party vote." General Sherman hoped that would not happen and encouraged his brother to act as an individual, not as a partisan. [30]

On the evening of the twenty-second Logan addressed the House for thirty minutes. He believed the president had violated a penal statute, an act which easily qualified as a "high crime or misdemeanor." He reviewed the Tenure of Office Act and said that Johnson's ignorance of the law was no excuse. Laughter rang when he continued: "That may be a violent presumption in the case of Andrew Johnson, yet that is an axiom of the law." Logan argued that Johnson's intention was to "reinaugurate revolution" in the country much as the Confederates had done in 1861. He jested at Johnson's possible support and urged Congress to stand by the law. To those who said impeachment would wreck the country he answered that a nation that could withstand Civil War and presidential assassination "will stand the impeachment of as bad a president as Andrew Johnson." [31]

At five o'clock on the afternoon of February 24 John A. Logan answered "aye" as the House voted 126 to 47 to impeach the president. In a peculiar reversal of what might be the expected procedure, the House then named a committee of seven to draw up charges. Julian, Stevens, Bingham, George Boutwell of Massachusetts, James F. Wilson of Iowa, Hamilton Ward of New York, and Logan were selected. [32]

The seven-man panel included known Radicals who had announced their opposition to the chief executive. It also included Bingham and Wilson, two previously outspoken impeachment opponents. With Stevens and Butler, Logan voted to name Boutwell chairman. When an angry Bingham threatened to withdraw, Boutwell gave up the chair to him, knowing impeachment could not succeed if the conservative Ohioan left the committee. [33]

In the next week the committee put together nine articles of impeachment. They concentrated on Johnson's violation of the Tenure of Office Act. Thaddeus Stevens feared these nine were not enough and he urged Ben Butler to help him add two more before the trial began. The tenth article accused the president of attempting to bring Congress into "disgrace, ridicule, hatred, contempt and reproach." The eleventh was a catchall accusing Johnson of everything of which he could conceivably be convicted. One by one the charges were read and passed by the House. Following that action the body elected managers to raise the charges before the Senate. Bingham, Boutwell, Wilson, Butler, Stevens, Logan, and Thomas Williams of Pennsylvania were the choices. Ohio Democrat S.S. Cox knew that the choice of Logan, Butler, and Stevens "was a sign that no omission would be made in the presentation of the case in all its

... vindictive features." Once again the seven were weighed heavily against the defendant and once again Logan was selected; he was no longer a follower, he was helping steer the boat.[34]

The publicity that came to the managers must have pleased the ambitious Illinoisan. *Harper's Weekly* ran numerous drawings of the managers with Logan, whose mustache and long black hair make him easy to identify, prominent among the group. In March a flattering portrait of Black Jack was followed by words praising his military and legal abilities. On March 4 the House managers (except Stevens, who was ill) stood in the Senate while the articles were read. The Radicals were confident of success after a short trial.[35]

Yet as the hearing began Logan received a disquieting letter from *Chicago Tribune* editor Joseph Medill. The journalist reported that Illinois Republicans believed "that a grave and terrible blunder had been committed" in adding articles ten and eleven to the charges. "All hope of a speedy trial is now ended," he argued. "The chance of conviction is badly weakened. If Johnson can't be impeached . . . for violating the Tenure of Office Law he will never be put out for anything he said while swinging around the circle." Logan demurred. He contended that he never heard of a man failing to be convicted because there were too many counts in the indictment.[36]

Logan and his fellow managers faced five attorneys representing Johnson. Benjamin R. Curtis, former Supreme Court justice, had written a dissenting opinion in the Dred Scott case. Jeremiah S. Black had served as attorney general and secretary of state under Buchanan. William M. Evarts, perhaps the most outstanding member of the defense, was a New York lawyer. When the proceedings began Henry Stanbery resigned as attorney general to join the defense. Johnson's final attorney was Thomas A.R. Nelson, an old friend from Greenville, Tennessee. Black disagreed with defense tactics and was eventually replaced by William S. Groesbeck of Ohio.

Early in the trial the defense requested forty days to prepare its case. Logan spoke for the managers in opposition to the request. He denied any interest in unduly speeding up the action, but he told Chief Justice Salmon P. Chase that the defense had enjoyed the same opportunities for preparation as had the managers. Finally, ten days were granted and Medill, continuing as the voice of anxious support, wrote Logan, "we are all nervous about the delay." [37]

On March 30 the managers began presenting evidence. Boutwell,

Stevens, and Butler bore most of the burden for the prosecution. The latter's remarks brought a note of thanks from Stanton for "the mighty blow you struck against the enemy of the nation." [38] Senators reserved the right to interrupt, and their remarks, together with constant arguments over the admissibility of evidence, slowed the proceedings. It took twenty-three days to present the House case. An exasperated Julian wrote, "impeachment drags terrible." [39]

The defense began on April 9 and concluded on the twentieth. Two days later concluding arguments began. Boutwell, Stevens, Williams, and Bingham were chosen to speak for the prosecution with Nelson, Groesbeck, Evarts, and Stanbery for the defense. The orations ran well into May. Despite the trial's length, at least one Illinois Republican remained confident as he wrote that conviction of Johnson was certain. Yet by mid-April many Republicans suspected impeachment might fail. [40]

Logan was not chosen to deliver one of the summations. There was not time for every manager to speak at length. Senior members among the group, as well as a cross section of factions from the impeachment party, helped determine the choice. Logan played a minor role in the trial, but he did insert a long written argument in the record. In it Logan asked "what are impeachable offenses?" and quoted from American and British precedents. He concluded that removal could be accomplished for other than indictable offenses. Black Jack defended the constitutionality of the Tenure of Office Act and reviewed each article. Only at his conclusion did Logan wave the bloody shirt. He called Johnson "the great criminal of the age" and said, "his great aim and purpose has been to subvert the law, usurp authority, insult and outrage Congress, and reconstruct the rebel states in the interest of treason." He wrote emotionally: "Mercy to this criminal would be cruelty to the State." [41]

Many praised Logan's written summation. The *Chicago Tribune* felt it was "very strong and complete." In his memoirs James G. Blaine characterized it as "carefully prepared, well written, and throughout logical in its analysis." The congressman must have read with mixed emotion the congratulatory letter from his political ally Stephen Hurlbut. Hurlbut was "more than satisfied" after reading the argument. But he added, "There is a larger research than I had given you credit for, for I may as well tell you that I had not much faith in your studiousness. . . . To handle so grave an affair requires more than stump talent. I am glad that you have disappointed me so pleasantly." [42]

By May 16, when the vote on article XI was taken, Radicals were "in great consternation" that Johnson would evade conviction. The fifty-four senators had received constant pressure to vote conviction. As the trial began Illinois' Yates received a letter advising him "*Convict old Andy sure* if you have *any* hope of a hereafter." [43] Though the mock threat was playful in tone, the message was clear. But pressure on Yates could not compare with that on the seven Republicans who leaned toward acquittal. Typical of this pressure was that exerted on Republican Edmund Ross of Kansas, whose inclinations were unclear. As the roll call proceeded Ross remembered that everyone in the chamber peered "with an intensity that was almost tragic upon the face of him who was about to cast the fateful vote. . . . I almost literally looked down into my grave." Ross's answer to the chief justice's question was "not guilty." The tally was 35 guilty to 19 not guilty—Johnson was saved by one vote.[44]

A ten-day recess followed the initial vote. Adjournment allowed Republicans to attend their national convention in Chicago. Rumors spread that Ross would change his vote, but they were false. On May 26 the 35-to-19 alignment held on each of the specifications. Impeachment had failed.

There was little time to second-guess impeachment tactics; 1868 was an election year. Many speculated on the effect the failure to remove Johnson might have on state and national races. Elihu Washburne called the failure a "humiliation" but advised "the party is *not* dead, but will be stronger than ever." [45] Logan was not as sanguine. After branding the defection of the seven Republican senators "infamy," he remarked, "what will come of all this I can't tell, but hope for the best." [46]

The Chicago national convention raised the party's hopes for a rebound from the impeachment defeat as well as for control of the White House. Black Jack attended as a delegate-at-large and chairman of the Illinois delegation. On the nineteenth the former general addressed an enthusiastic Soldiers and Sailors Convention in Chicago. He attacked Johnson as a "renegade" and supported Grant as his party's best choice as standard-bearer. Logan "was devoted to General Grant and General Grant was very fond of him," wrote one observer. But Sherman, who had led Logan and followed Grant, could not believe his old commander would accept Butler and Logan as his party leaders and advisors.[47]

William Tecumseh Sherman was wrong. Grant, already firmly committed to support congressional Reconstruction, was ready to accept the Republican nomination. The convention met on May 20 at the Chicago Opera House with Carl Schurz in the chair. During a delay in the credentials report a cry of "Logan, Logan, Logan" rose throughout the hall. The congressman asked to be excused; he would have something to say later. Logan had "a face that is well known, and his erect form, dark complexion, coarse, jet black hair and mustache make him especially observable." [48]

On May 21 when nominations were entertained, Logan rose and was recognized. In the name of "loyal citizens, soldiers, and sailors," in the name of "loyalty, liberty, humanity, justice; in the name of the National Union Republican Party" he nominated Ulysses S. Grant. A storm of applause followed as hats and handkerchiefs waved across the house. From the gallery a pigeon dyed red, white, and blue was loosed to circle the hall. It was a great moment for Logan; his career too seemed to be soaring. [49]

The vice-presidential choice was a battle between Ben Wade and Schuyler Colfax. Before the convention an Illinois Republican had written Wade, "you have many friends in this state." Logan was one of them and he did his best for the Ohio senator. Fear of Wade's radicalism as well as his high tariff and soft money views had, in some measure, influenced the Johnson impeachment vote, and the party was not going to give second place to "Bluff Ben" from Ohio. After six ballots Colfax was chosen. Despite his support of Wade, Logan found that Colfax treated him kindly. [50] Black Jack regarded his party's ticket as a strong one and believed it would prevail against any Democratic slate. The opposition met and chose Horatio Seymour and Frank Blair.

While impeachment and national conventions dominated the news, Logan remained in close touch with Illinois political developments. The controversy over the gubernatorial nomination remained alive into the spring. Logan had taken himself out of contention and Palmer seemed to have the advantage. However, Robert Ingersoll actively sought the top place on the state ticket. The great orator wrote his brother often to divine Logan's intentions. The Ingersoll brothers also considered indicating to Logan that they would support him for Yates's senate seat in 1871 if he backed Bob in 1868. The latter wrote, "If L. wants to play fair and square I am willing to play with him. . . . I have always preferred a combination with L. He is the best of them all in my opinion." But Ebon disagreed. "I hardly dare trust Logan and shall let him rest for the present," he wrote an anxious brother. [51] One unfounded rumor had Robert Ingersoll interested in vying with Logan for the congressman-at-large post.

A former army associate of Logan's wrote in April concerned that

Black Jack was supporting his opponent. He went on in disbelief, "I cannot believe that you are using your high position and great influence among the people of Illinois to influence them in local elections." That was, of course, exactly what Logan was doing. He was determined to build a statewide organization that could influence all facets of Illinois Republican politics and that could be allied with the G.A.R. and patronage appointees as part of a national power base. If letters from politicians and editors were any indication, his efforts were succeeding.[52]

The Republican state convention met at Peoria, nominated John Palmer for governor, and picked Logan for congressman-at-large. Logan's choice by acclamation was praised by the *Chicago Tribune*. Opponents for the two Republicans were J.R. Eden for governor and an unknown, W.W. O'Brien, for Congress. The *Tribune* called Logan's opponent a "sneaking ally of rebellion." However, the Democratic press boasted that O'Brien would not be bullied by Logan and warned its readers that Black Jack was only for himself and was mostly interested in horse racing, cockfights, and "rotgut whisky."[53]

Before he could campaign Logan had to return to the House, which remained in session until July 25. First business concerned the admission of representatives from five southern states organized under the congressional plan. The measure passed with Logan voting "aye." Postimpeachment Washington was dull and Logan wrote Mary, who had returned to Carbondale, "this is the bluest time I ever saw in Washington . . . everyone moping around."[54]

If Logan had his way Washington would cease to be the nation's capital. Earlier in the year he voted for a bill to move the national capital to the Mississippi Valley, a position he would take for years. It failed to pass, and on June 15 he introduced another such resolution. The Washington of the late sixties had a southern atmosphere, and Logan attacked the citizens of the District of Columbia as disloyal persons who had "menaced and insulted" the people's representatives. Several members charged Logan with a "foul slander" against the people of the district and his measure was tabled.[55]

Military policy continued to be a Logan concern. Often in the second session he rose to comment on the way the nation's military was being run. As chairman of the select committee on ordnance Logan remarked that during the Civil War, Union shells killed more blue coats that rebels. That allegation brought a sharp retort from General Sherman. Also disturbing to Sherman was a Logan proposal concerning West Point. He wanted to distribute the number of cadets among the nation's colleges according each graduate the same rank as academy graduates.[56]

Military academy legislation also led to a two-day battle between Logan and Elihu Washburne. The northern Illinois Republican charged Logan with "striking" at West Point in his bill to end extra allowances for officers stationed at the academy. Black Jack denied the allegation. He said he was quite willing to praise professionals such as Grant and Sherman. However, he reminded his listeners that "traitors" such as Lee and Beauregard were also West Pointers.[57]

On one other occasion Logan struck at West Point as the sole center of military education. Blaine rose to defend the military and to accuse Logan of "jealousy." The Illinoisan denied the accusation and persisted, calling the bill "an effort to cut the throat of every civilian in the Army. . . . It is to help a class, an aristocratic class, at the expense of the unfortunate men who hold no commissions." Logan roared so intensely that Blaine brought laughter when he replied, "I think if the five minutes had not expired, the gentleman himself would have expired." Logan too drew smiles with "it would not have cost you a cent."[58]

The session's final consideration of army policy came on July 10. Logan and Garfield spent two days clashing over the bill proposed by the latter as chairman of the Committee on Military Affairs. Logan demanded a reduction in the number of general officers since the army was being cut to twenty-five thousand men. He accused Garfield's committee of only making a "pretense" of reducing the army. "When I say I am in favor of reducing the Army, I mean reducing the Army," he told Garfield. This included severe reduction of generals and colonels at the same ratio as private soldiers. Ben Butler offered a substitute reducing officers by one-half, those now retained to be mustered out by March 10, 1869. It passed 66 to 54 with Logan in favor and Garfield opposed. General Sherman complained to his senator-brother, "I did not like the spirit in Congress to cut down the army."[59]

Not much significant business was transacted through the final weeks of July, but on the evening of the sixteenth Logan gave what he considered his best speech of the session. The lengthy oration was called "Principles of the Democratic Party." It was a classic example of Black Jack waving the bloody shirt. A foretaste of his remarks was revealed in the introductory sentence: "the Democratic platform is a whited sepulcher, full of dead men's bones. It is a monument which is intended to hide decay and conceal corruption." He promised to show that his former party's promises for the future were "hollow and evasive." He again charged the Democrats with complicity in rebellion and he produced a ringing defense of the Reconstruction record of the Fortieth Congress. Democratic leaders were the "praters, croakers, and false prophets of the country." Toward the end of his remarks Logan said, amazingly, "I have no desire to keep alive old animosities or to recall the past with a view to let it rankle." It was a common disclaimer used by the most strident practitioners of the bloody-shirt technique. Logan's 1886 biographer, George F. Dawson, believed that this speech was the Republican party's "keynote" for the presidential contest. The congressman had a large number of copies separately printed in pamphlet form for wide distribution.[60] Logan's last act before adjournment was a vote to override Johnson's veto of a measure continuing the Freedmen's Bureau.[61]

Business took Logan to New York as soon as Congress adjourned. In July he had decided not to buy the Crédit Mobilier stock offered by Oakes Ames, but the Lower California Company was still "promising."[62] After a few days in New York, Logan joined Elihu Washburne in stumping Maine, a state with an early election date. Logan came at Blaine's request, which played to Black Jack's ego and to his need for money. "He will have a grand reception," predicted the Maine leader, and he "shall be liberally paid." While Logan was in New England he received a report from Mary warning against accepting a joint debate with O'Brien that fall. She added happily, "There is considerable excitement and enthusiasm among the Republicans here now. More than I ever saw before." Mary urged her husband to come home and vowed not to "stay away from you so long any more."[63]

In late August, Logan joined his family in Illinois. His respite was brief, however, for on August 27 he took the stump with a speech to a large meeting in Carbondale. Four days later he opened his speech at Morris, Illinois, with a promise: "We have preserved the Union and we will perpetuate it." The address was especially aimed at veterans. As he crossed the Prairie State Logan drew large and enthusiastic crowds and boasted to Mary, "I am making better speeches than I ever did, and doing great good as everyone says." Mary, in Carbondale, kept an eye on the opposition and reported that O'Brien spoke in Egypt blasting Logan. She believed that O'Brien's language had hurt the Democrats in southern Illinois. The Democrats used the race issue and Logan's endorsement of Negro suffrage. The congressman was called a "nigger Radical," and a Democratic group called the "White Boys in Blue" was created to counter the "black Republican" G.A.R.[64]

A large veterans' reunion was to be held in southern Illinois on September 17. Mary urged Logan to attend and promised to write General Sherman in hopes that he could come. The general, deluged by such invitations, was unable to join Logan in addressing the soldiers.[65]

Money is always a political problem, and Logan received an unexpected windfall in September. William E. Chandler, Republican senator from New Hampshire and national party chairman, wrote banker Jay Cooke in search of funds. Cooke begged to be "let off easy," but he did agree to send money to Logan, Bingham, and Robert Schenck. In early October, Black Jack received a check for a thousand dollars and a note from the financier enclosed in a letter from Chandler. Cooke wrote:

> My dear sir, we have never met and I heartily disagree with your financial views, but no man commanded more of my admiration during the war than did Genl. Logan and I have *full faith* that when you and I stand face to face some of these days you will at *least* give me credit for sincerity of views (as I do you) as well as for a true unselfish interest in my country's welfare.[66]

As the campaign drew to an end Logan took his florid oratorical style all over Illinois. His crowds continued to be large and his strength seemed to be growing. He concentrated primarily on bloody-shirt issues and was especially popular with old soldiers. His efforts were described as "spellbinding" and several touched off the "wildest enthusiasm" even though they lasted for three hours. Occasionally the congressman discussed monetary policy, agreeing with the party's platform. He denied the Democratic contention that the national debt must be retired at once.[67]

The election results gave Grant the presidency and his party control of both houses of Congress, although the Democrats gained seats in the House. Grant swept Illinois by a vote of 250,293 to 199,143. Palmer was elected governor and ten of the state's fourteen House seats were won by Republicans. In his statewide race, Logan defeated O'Brien 249,422 to 199,789. It was a solid victory, but the incumbent's majority was cut to 53 percent from his 57 percent in 1866.[68]

That decline was insignificant in a year of steady advance. Logan had been a national figure all year long and was widely identified as one of his party's chieftains. Grant's victory opened new possibilities for power and influence. In March 1869 the "criminal of the age" would give way to the "saviour of the Union." When Grant entered the White House Logan would not be far behind.

CHAPTER 3

Scourge of the Regular Army

BEFORE GRANT took office the lame duck session of the Fortieth Congress brought Logan back to Washington. His family came with him and again lived at the Willard Hotel. Illness prevented the congressman from answering the opening roll call on December 7 and continued into the dreary winter, keeping him from appearing in the House until January 5, 1869.[1]

With Colfax out of the House the Republican majority would choose a new speaker in March. Speculation centered on Blaine and Henry L. Dawes of Massachusetts; at least Blaine believed this to be the case. He wrote Logan praising him for his efforts in Maine the previous fall. Courting Logan's "sympathy and support," Blaine promised "to fully reciprocate any favor you may do me in the matter."[2]

It was a time of scramble for office and talk about the makeup of Grant's cabinet. Pressure on Grant and Colfax was persistent, but the incoming administration did little in the dying days of 1868. Beneath cabinet level, Republicans stood by to line the patronage trough with appointees who, in return for office, would give political labor and money. Patronage politicians would have one of their last unfettered opportunities to operate during the Grant years.

John A. Logan was one of the great defenders of this system and his opening shots in the third session were against Thomas Jenckes's civil service bill. Opposed to all such reform, Logan delivered a clarion call to spoilsmen to rise up and defeat the bill. The legislation was condemned as "the establishment of a favored class, ending in the establishment of a haughty and recognized aristocracy." He denied being merely interested in spoils politics and charged that Jenckes's plan was undemocratic and an assault on the Constitution. The measure, said Logan, was "bad in

33

theory, wrong in principle, opposed to the genius and spirit of our institutions and our people, and probably unconstitutional." The speech thinly cloaked Logan's determination to build a state machine out of the fabric of patronage. Now just at the point of great patronage favors flowing from a friendly president, Logan did not propose to see the institution of a meritocracy.[3]

His constituents were divided on his stand. A northern Illinois newspaper supported Logan's contention that the bill would establish a privileged class. On the other hand, a Springfield Republican, J.K.C. Forest, wrote Senator Yates that Logan had made a mistake in opposing the legislation. Even though Yates's term did not end for a year, Forest urged the senator to support the Jenckes bill to strengthen his chances for reelection. The Illinoisan advised Yates: "Logan and Palmer are your natural rivals, Oglesby is played out. . . . The fight with you will be Palmer, or Logan or Washburne." Bob Ingersoll also had his mind on the distant Senate struggle. He wanted to be district attorney of Chicago and told Oglesby: "I was told . . . that I was suspected of being for you for the U.S. Senate and that Logan was hardly for me on that account."[4]

As soon as the civil service measure went to committee the army appropriations bill reached the floor. All winter, military leadership had been concerned with growing congressional hostility led by Logan. General Sherman wrote his brother opposing the abolition of full general's rank, calling it a "mean" act. The senator reassured him that his popularity would prevent such a development. But Sherman was still fearful, advising John that if he did not succeed Grant as general of the army he would be in financial difficulty. The general also wrote Blaine, asking the Maine Republican's support in achieving the advance to general.[5]

Logan still felt the reduction provisions in the measure were a "humbug." He advanced the notion that a smaller army did not need highly ranked officers. Garfield retorted sharply when Logan told the House that anyone who was "afraid to touch the Army" was a "coward."[6]

Logan stepped from one controversy to another. On a gloomy, cold February 10, Congress assembled to hear the tally of electoral votes. Logan stood with the majority in rejecting Georgia's return because of voter intimidation. Because of the manner in which sixty-nine-year-old Ben Wade, Senate president pro tempore, handled the count, Ben Butler introduced a censure resolution in the House. Logan furiously rose to Wade's defense. He praised Wade's long service as "the vanguard of liberty and freedom," and opposed censure for an "unintentional" act. Black Jack's speech won prolonged applause. That night Wade appeared at the Willard and said, "Logan, God bless you. I have come here to thank you for coming to my rescue to-day." The retiring senator spent the evening with the Logans talking about old times.[7]

On February 20 the House, with Logan voting "aye," passed the Fifteenth Amendment. When the amendment had first been debated Logan moved to strike "or hold office" from "The right of citizens of the United States to vote or hold office shall not be denied. . . ." He argued that anyone who could vote could also hold office. The House disagreed, but the Senate concurred. A conference committee, including Logan, added the change and it was included in the final wording.[8]

Logan's last lengthy debate of the session concerned Indian affairs. The Illinoisan, reflecting the attitudes of many nineteenth-century Americans, showed deep hostility toward the Plains tribes. He ridiculed the idea of treaties with "wild and roving savages." He also opposed a large appropriation for these people, telling those who favored such a bill they should be sent to the Plains to enforce the treaties. Black Jack felt that buying clothes for "uncivilized" Indians was absurd. His stance provoked a hot blast from William Windom of Minnesota, who called Logan a "clown." Logan fired back by reminding Windom that the voters had retired him from the House and reelected the "clown."[9] On March 3 the Fortieth Congress, one of the most controversial in national history, adjourned sine die.

On the following day Grant and Colfax were sworn in and the Forty-first Congress assembled. For the first time in his political career John A. Logan was in Congress under a friendly administration. While great benefits would be forthcoming, Logan would have done well to have heeded Robert Ingersoll's warning to his brother: "From henceforth forward the Republican Party will have to be responsible for its own acts. The scapegoat will be gone and we will have to bear our own iniquities." At the first session Logan supported Blaine for speaker and the popular New Englander won.[10]

Early in the House term Blaine named committees. Logan was no longer on Ways and Means, but he appeared on the Committee on the Pacific Railroad. More important was his selection as chairman of the Committee on Military Affairs, a post he had eagerly sought. It was a grim day for William Tecumseh Sherman.[11]

The Military Affairs Committee acted at once. Logan reported out H.R. 237 to abolish the office of chief of staff to the general of the army. It passed. Then H.R. 238, preventing retired officers from receiving extra pay for temporary duty, was also passed.[12]

The session's final exchange over military matters was especially bitter. In an argument over the rank at which General S.P. Heintzelman should be retired Logan and Garfield snarled at each other. Garfield told Logan, "I have the law here, and will read it if the gentleman will yield." Logan replied, "I can read it as well as you can." "Very well," said Garfield, "let us hear the literary gentleman." Logan answered, "Oh, I do not claim to be a literary gentleman as the gentleman does." When a third member demanded the vote Logan roared, "the vote will not be taken until I sit down. I have as many rights here as you have." Logan was easily piqued by opposition and imagined insult and often engaged in such contretemps with other members. "He was at times impulsive and a little brusque in manner," volunteered an Illinois acquaintance of several decades, who also found the politician "usually courteous, genial and gracious."[13]

When Congress ended its work Logan remained in Washington through April and into May tending to G.A.R. business and working on patronage requests. At first he advised Mary, who had gone to Illinois, that he was getting along well with his appointments. He wrote influential Republicans in search of aid, but despite his efforts trouble developed. His potential senatorial rivals Yates and Trumbull, the latter not forgiven by Logan for voting against impeachment, fought some of his choices for office.[14] Yet Logan's influence with the president aided his efforts and perhaps caused Yates to complain in May, "Grant has been treating me badly of late."[15]

In May the congressman made a quick westward swing. He attended the G.A.R. encampment in Cincinnati, tightening his grip on the organization. Then he joined his family in southern Illinois. In May he spoke at the Carbondale Methodist Church and drew from an opposition journal a cynical gibe. The paper called it going "from the sublime to the ridiculous for the rattling political stumper to become a bible-banger." While in Egypt Logan also reminisced about his youth in a speech at Southern Illinois College and waved the bloody shirt at a Memorial Day address at DuQuoin. In the latter speech the former general hailed Union veterans as men who "fought not only for the protection of our flag, but also for the preservation and perpetuation of Christianity in this land, for Christianity cannot long flourish where liberty is destroyed." [16]

Logan's Methodist church membership, often mentioned positively by his supporters and cynically by his detractors, as well as his insistence that the Republican party was fighting for Christianity, was of significance in a state and section in which religious affiliation had a powerful effect on voting behavior. Organized religious bodies in which members worshipped together and discussed politics after church led to great political cohesion within their ranks. Midwestern Methodists voted Republican by a wide margin, thus giving Black Jack an additional hold on the allegiance of his numerous and influential codenominationists. However, Logan rarely took part in politicoreligious struggles between Protestant Republicans and Catholic Democrats over such issues as prohibition and parochial schools. Anti-Catholicism was absent from his speeches and letters. Logan's chief use of religion was a bloody-shirt variety to assure the voters that his party was the nation's true moral voice. [17]

A return to Washington in June took Logan from the fight to "preserve" Christianity to the battle for patronage. His pressure on the administration led one of Trumbull's confidants to report, "I had seen . . . enough at the White House to satisfy me that Logan and company were *against* everybody that was not *for* them." [18] After a brief business trip to New York, Logan returned to Illinois to spend a placid summer.

Except for an occasional local speech Logan spent his time with his family in Carbondale. Through August, September, and October he addressed himself to family matters long neglected during his absences. He enjoyed good health and in October advised a friend, "I have been buried in the country, know nothing of the political or financial world except newspaper *news*." [19] Nevertheless the Logan-Palmer-Oglesby-Yates-Trumbull political scrimmage remained very much alive during this bucolic interlude. In September, Governor Palmer informed Oglesby that the latter's trip to California with Trumbull and Norman Judd looked suspicious to Logan. Black Jack feared a combination against him was materializing, wrote Palmer. [20]

That winter the Logans returned to the capital and to a new residence. They rented a large brownstone near the corner of New York Avenue and Fourteenth Street, a few blocks from the White House. Ben Butler, Zach Chandler, Blaine, and Garfield lived in the neighborhood. [21] On December 6 Logan answered the roll call for a session that was to last seven months.

Reconstruction legislation was still on the docket. Logan voted for the readmission of Georgia and joined the intense debate over the admission of Virginia.[22] That state had drawn up a new constitution and ratified the Fourteenth and Fifteenth Amendments. Grant wanted the Old Dominion admitted and its representatives seated. Some Radicals feared that once admitted Virginia would alter its constitution to deny Negroes their civil rights, something Georgia had done earlier. Butler's Reconstruction Committee reported out a bill that included a test oath for Virginians in which they would vow not to change their organic document. John Bingham rose to oppose the Butler bill and Logan supported the Ohioan. Black Jack pointed out that once Virginia became a state it would have all the rights of statehood, including the right to amend its constitution. The Bingham amendment narrowly passed, 98 to 95. Logan voted with Scott Marshall and James Brooks, Democrats with whom he had exchanged insults in the past, as well as with Banks, Cullom, Garfield, and Ingersoll. The complete bill passed the House 142 to 49 only to run into Charles Sumner's insistence that some kind of oath be enacted by the Senate. Eventually the Senate version prevailed and Logan voted for it when it was resubmitted to the House.[23] Logan and Cullom shared the view that Reconstruction should be completed as soon as possible. Still later in the session both men voted for the admission of Texas and Mississippi.[24]

In late January, Logan tilted at windmills. He once again strongly supported the removal of the capital to the Midwest, preferably St. Louis. He also introduced a resolution asking the granting of belligerency status to the Cuban rebels who had been involved in a fifteen-month war with Spain. The Grant administration was keeping its hands off of the situation and the resolution was an embarrassment. Congressional salaries were debated in February and the Illinoisan defended the proposed increase. He felt the members were underpaid and urged them to stand up for their rights.[25]

"Let me congratulate you on the energy as well as the sagacity with which you have prosecuted the disreputable characters who have done so much to bring Congress into contempt," wrote *New York Tribune* editor Whitelaw Reid after Logan had forced the expulsion of Representative B. Frank Whittemore of South Carolina from the House. The Military Affairs Committee probed evidence that Whittemore sold appointments to West Point and the Naval Academy. The congressman told the House he had not profited; the money had gone to the needy of his district. Ben

Butler and Congressman Luke Poland of Maine thought Logan's insistence on immediate removal too hasty but Black Jack persisted. However, before the Carolinian could be expelled, he resigned. Further investigation revealed that John T. Deweese of North Carolina and Roderick R. Butler of Tennessee had also taken money in return for appointments. Deweese told the body he thought the practice was common; nevertheless, he resigned from the seat he believed he had "disgraced." A two-thirds vote could not be mustered to expel Butler and he was merely censured.[26] The sales had been to persons outside of the members' districts. Logan introduced a bill to restrict appointments to those who had lived in the district for one year, which passed by voice vote.[27]

A patronage battle between Logan and Trumbull raged through the early months of 1870. Despite opposition from Palmer and congressmen Shelby Cullom and Jesse Moore, as well as Logan, the senator forced the removal of the U.S. marshal for southern Illinois. There had been minor malfeasance in the office and not even Grant could halt the removal. Palmer protested to Logan, "Genl. Grant cannot humiliate us all . . . merely to gratify Trumbull." Moore saw in Trumbull's motivation "a chance to pay John A. for reading him out of the party at Chicago." For the moment the potential Senate rivals, Logan and Palmer, were allies.[28]

It was military affairs that especially concerned Logan in this session. For months tension between Logan's committee and the army command had been building. In October 1869 General Sherman labored over his first report "with great precision" so as to give Logan's committee "my idea of the form and strength of the army." He sent the report to General Philip Sheridan, who found it satisfactory. In January word of the House bill began to leak and Sheridan called it "imperfect" and warned that the army was "concerned." Sheridan next wrote Logan urging him not to insist on its adoption. On the basis of his long experience in the West, Sheridan maintained that the army was not too large. "Little Phil" then denounced the proposed pay reduction on grounds that general officers could not maintain themselves on a salary less than that of railroad superintendents. The Civil War hero believed that taxpayers were willing to support an adequate army. The secretary of war also wrote to tell Logan of his success in cutting military expenditures.[29]

None of the arguments deterred Logan; he pressed on with his bill, which reached full floor debate in March. Logan proposed to reduce the number of major generals from five to three and brigadier generals from sixteen to six, to abolish the brevet rank, to reduce all officers' salaries, and to dismiss unemployed officers. The committee chairman advised the House that Congress had just reduced the number of infantry regiments from forty-five to twenty-four but had done nothing with the 509 officers left without commands. These men, Logan felt, should be dismissed. Black Jack then introduced salary figures. With food, clothing, and housing allowances Sherman received over $18,000, Sheridan nearly $15,000, and the major generals between $9,300 and $9,800. Logan proposed a fixed salary with no additional compensations. This would leave Sherman at $12,000, Sheridan at $10,000 and the major generals at $8,000. The Illinoisan reminded the House that the speaker and vice-president were paid only $8,000.[30]

The press applauded the committee for eliminating the brevet rank but was less enthusiastic about the measure's other provisions.[31] The military leadership was outraged. General George H. Thomas, commanding at San Francisco, wrote Sherman to ask if passage could be prevented. He called it "more heartless" than he thought Congress capable of. Sherman, who it was reported could not mention the bill without two or three oaths, wrote his brother his opinion of the measure and of the motivation behind it. The "Logan Bill" took the form it did because Logan would "never forgive me for putting Howard in McPherson's place."[32] "Logan was always full of prejudice and always running to the rear to make speeches and political capital," continued the general-in-chief. Sherman added that at war's end Logan had expected to be retained as a regular army general and for failure to receive the post "he feels sore at Grant."[33]

During the controversy Sherman wrote Senator Henry Wilson, chairman of the Senate Military Committee. Logan was shown the letter and had it inserted into the record. He labeled it "remarkable" and went on to protest what he called Sherman's effort to "dictate" his own legislation and to "stifle" Congress. He demanded that the legislative branch be free and unfettered from military dictatorship and concluded with a ringing eulogy of the Civil War's volunteer soldiers and of enlisted men still in the army: "They are the boys who made generals and presidents and I shall stand up here as the defender of these boys." The *Globe* indicated "long continued applause upon the floor and in the galleries."[34]

The bill passed the House only to be altered in the Senate. The pay rate and number of generals remained the same, but immediate discharge of generals with no commands was changed. These men were allowed to retain their ranks until resignation, retirement, or death. A conference worked out a few minor changes and the bill passed.[35]

John A. Logan's record in the postwar Congress was as a rigid economizer. Slashing governmental expenditures was on his mind when he composed the army bill. On the other hand, personal venom toward Sherman in particular and professional officers in general was also a major force behind the former general's actions. Logan would never completely forgive Sherman for failing to give him permanent command of the Army of the Tennessee after its commander, General James B. McPherson, was killed at Atlanta in 1864. The Logan-Sherman clash was a classic example of the difference between professional and volunteer soldier. Sherman's contempt for the volunteer's abilities caused him to refuse Logan the command in the first place. This contempt intensified in the postwar world as Sherman faced the frustration of having the man he had passed over move into a position of power that allowed him to play a role in determining army policy.[36]

Turmoil gripped the army in the wake of Congress's action. Major General E.O.C. Ord wrote Sherman from California making urgent requests to move him to headquarters in the face of reduced pay. Sherman remained especially bitter. He grumbled that the bill had "reduced my office to a sinecure and the next step will of course be disbandment." He went on, "our country is . . . governed by its meanest people and soon no honest man will be tolerated." Sherman vowed bitterly, "The extension of the franchise don't elevate the ignorant, but pulls down the educated." When John McClernand wrote from Illinois urging Sherman to go to Europe to observe the Franco-Prussian War, the general said he could not afford to because of the slash in funds. In the summer Sherman asked to move army headquarters to St. Louis, which he thought would be more economical. Grant denied the request.[37]

While he checked the regulars, Logan was alert to the needs of the former volunteers. He often introduced relief bills for individual veterans, and he fought for a more favorable pension policy. Logan also sought an alteration in the Homestead Act so as to make land distribution easier for veterans, but he steadfastly opposed any benefits for Confederate veterans.[38]

In the spring the House engaged in a long tariff debate. Black Jack spoke for farmer consumers and, unlike the majority of his party, fought continued high levels of protection. He wrangled with Pennsylvania's

William "Pig Iron" Kelley, disputing the protectionist's argument that tar-
iffs benefitted the laboring man. Kelley, whom Logan called "The Iron
Duke," advised Logan that he was hurting his party by his opposition to
the tariff. The combative Illinoisan shot back: "In my section of the country this is not regarded as a party question." Several times during the
debate Logan engaged in insulting exchanges with Ways and Means
Chairman Robert Schenck. Schenck implied that Logan did not fully understand the tariff question and Logan retorted "the gentleman takes occasion all the time to 'pitch into' me, because I have . . . offered amendments to the bill." Several days later Logan called the tariff an "atrocity"
and vowed again to defend his constituents' interests. Schenck then accused Logan of dilatory practices and said his method of opposition was
as if the bill was being "kicked to death by grasshoppers." [39]

The position of the congressman-at-large was followed closely by
Chicago journalists. Joseph Medill questioned Logan's free trade lean-
ings, but he was also opposed to the excessively high duty levels sought
by Kelley and other eastern representatives. On the other hand, from the
Tribune staff Horace White wrote a letter of appreciation. Furthermore,
he told Logan he would use his influence in the upcoming Senate race to
secure the election of a candidate "opposed to the arrant heresy of protection." [40]

Caribbean policy interested Logan as the session dragged on into the
summer. Once again he insisted on belligerency status for the Cuban rebels and he castigated the administration for not rallying to support a
neighboring people fighting against tyranny. He was particularly distressed that the government had not been more active in protecting U.S.
citizens in the combat zone. Another island, Santo Domingo, came to the
House's attention at about the same time. Sentiment for annexation was
strong in the Grant administration and among Grant's aides. As he had on
the tariff, Logan bucked party leadership. He attacked the annexation
movement and denounced the addition of "naked and half-savage people
like those of Santo Domingo." [41] Although he was widely thought of as a
close Grant confidant and supporter, the Illinoisan did not hesitate to take
an independent stand when he believed the administration to be in error.

The Grand Army of the Republic met in May and Logan was pleased
to be elected commandant for the third consecutive year. Black Jack discovered a plan to make General Alfred Pleasanton commandant and to
move headquarters to New York. The attempt failed and Logan was re-

turned to the post. The encampment resolved to publicize Memorial Day, to urge all posts to endorse legislation in support of pensions, and to petition Congress to donate public lands for veterans. Memorial Day was more widely observed that year as Quartermaster General Montgomery Meigs ordered his department, in charge of national cemeteries, to decorate graves.[42]

Mary and the children left steamy Washington for Illinois in May, leaving John to moan that he was "lost and lonesome." However, he did tell his wife that he was up early every morning trying to secure appointments for his friends. The military bill, as agreed to in conference, passed the House and was going to the Senate. Logan thought that it would pass but remarked that he "cannot say what those old fogies may do as you know how easy they are influenced." As the busy session drew to a close Logan said he had worked enough and was through taking an active part in the deliberations. He added, "I am feeling very well, but am entirely *too fat* for the weather." [43]

Logan spoke too soon. In mid-June B. Frank Whittemore, reelected by his constituents, appeared to be seated. Logan fought acceptance of his credentials and carried the House of Representatives with him.[44] For the last month of the session Logan lived up to his vow of inactivity. He bought a library of Sir Walter Scott and Charles Dickens and read for relaxation. But the political scene was never long out of his correspondence. An investigation of the Santo Domingo question had begun and Logan told Mary that Grant and Orville Babcock, Grant's secretary, had been injured by the revelations. "I am not glad of it, for the reason that we will have it to bear in our next canvass and it will be hard to defend," he stated.

On July 4, alone and bored, Logan wrote a most uncharacteristic note to his wife. He mused, "I am some times almost determined to quit political life altogether, and I think what can I do. I am not fit to do anything else and hardly that." The thought quickly passed and Logan headed home that summer with his eye to the future and fixed on the United States Senate.[45]

CHAPTER 4

"A High Place in the World"

THERE WOULD be little time in the summer of 1870 for John A. Logan to rest. His political future would be decided in those first warm months of the new decade. Logan had labored as congressman, as G.A.R. commander, and as active orator to build a political reputation. At the same time he had worked just as diligently to create a legion of loyal supporters across Illinois. Offices received and offices promised were the bricks and mortar of an organization he hoped could dominate the Prairie State to his advantage. The events of the summer, fall, and winter of 1870 would test the effectiveness of his work since the war's end. Success meant an advance to the Senate; failure could mean a return to private life.

It may not have been regarded as a political axiom in 1870, but it is generally true that the party in power loses ground in midterm elections. In addition, the Republican party had been in control of the executive (with the exception of the confusion of the Johnson years) and legislative branches for a decade. Would a reaction sweep the longtime incumbents out, and how would such a reaction affect Logan in Illinois?

Many were ready to assess the year's political portents. Vice-president Schuyler Colfax, Radical Congressman George W. Julian, and journalist Horace White predicted political squalls ahead for the Republicans. Colfax saw a "hard fight" for control of the next House and suggested a reason for Republican troubles might be "the removal of the strong cohesive power of the Reconstruction issues." Julian saw his party's difficulties resulting from a lack of discipline and a rise of corruption. Three men he specifically charged with "thieving" and a lack of "political honesty" were Ben Butler, Illinois' John Farnsworth, and Logan. Julian's list was an indication of the divided Radical camp, for though the Indiana representative voted with the trio on Reconstruction issues, he felt they were morally tainted even if he made no specific charges against them. White, a free trader, believed Republicans would have to abandon their protectionist stand if they were to win.[1]

For months, speculation over the Illinois Senate race had been rife. Congressman Jesse Moore wrote Richard Oglesby, one of Logan's potential rivals, that Joseph Medill, powerful editor of the *Chicago Tribune,* believed the contest would be a three-way battle between John M. Palmer, Logan, and Oglesby. He implied that Medill leaned toward Oglesby since Palmer was a states' righter and Logan "could not be trusted." Concerned about the *Tribune*'s choice, Logan had written Horace White, who had disappointingly refused to commit himself. By early summer Palmer's partisans were growing concerned about Logan's vigorous early efforts and they urged the governor to become more active. Some springtime press speculation rumored that Logan would not seek reelection as congressman-at-large; other newspapers exhorted him to stand again for the House. By the summer Logan had determined to win renomination and reelection to his congressional seat, but it was only to be a first step to the Senate—his real interest was elevation to the upper house by the Illinois General Assembly in January 1871.[2]

After a brief July rest in Carbondale Logan swung northward to Chicago to build support and to tend to business. He spent two weeks in Cook County and was able to report gains on all fronts. He conversed with city leaders and came away feeling certain that Chicago Republicans would support him strongly. The results made him feel "first rate." Logan especially courted Horace White, and after a day with the journalist he wrote Mary, "He feels kindly towards me I am sure." She was encouraged by the news of White and told her husband that she realized it was an "important time" for him and that she prayed for him. While he was in Chicago, Logan sold a lot for $26,000, the cash to be used in his upcoming race.[3]

For some reason, perhaps his refusal to support administration policies, Logan and President Grant had become somewhat estranged, a situation that continued through the year. Grant was in Chicago when Logan was there, and Black Jack bitingly wrote Mary, "Grant looked as stupid as ever, no one hardly called on him." General Sherman was unaware of this strained relationship and he observed with concern Grant's acquiescence to the demands of Butler, Logan, and "men of that stripe" who would sell out the chief executive. But Senator Trumbull was attuned and wrote an Illinois friend: "Grant I find is not for Logan. He told me that Logan seemed to be complaining all the time. From what Grant said there is evidently no good feeling between him and Logan."[4]

Springfield followed Chicago on Logan's trail. There was little interest in politics when the congressman arrived to prepare for the state convention. It was a slack political year without presidential and gubernatorial contests and Logan found the atmosphere "dull." Yet virtually every major political figure in the state regularly received mail speculating on the 1871 contest.[5]

The Republican State Convention assembled on September 1. The conclave was so beautifully orchestrated by Logan that his every appearance produced "wild and boisterous applause." On the other hand Governor Palmer walked into the hall and onto the platform almost unrecognized. The hostile *Illinois State Register* was both appalled and impressed by the Logan organization: "It is not many men who can get together two hundred office-holders and office-seekers, cut and dry the programe, and have it carried out to the letter as was done yesterday." The congressman-at-large was nominated by acclamation. His acceptance speech was an hour-long oration "repeatedly and vociferously applauded." It was an impressive show of power, which he hoped would influence those soon to be elected to the state legislature.[6]

On convention eve Logan received an invitation from Ben Butler to attend a September encampment of the Massachusetts G.A.R. Convinced it was wise for him to remain in Illinois, Logan declined. This brought an "annoyed" response but the "Beast" resignedly submitted with *"sara, che sara."* He went on to congratulate Logan on his renomination and added, "I suppose that was only a prelude to your election to the Senate."[7]

As soon as the convention adjourned Logan began stumping central Illinois with appearances in Jacksonville and Atlanta. Then he went to Chicago, to Galesburg, and back to Chicago. As Black Jack crisscrossed the northern counties the opposition grew alarmed. On the eighth Palmer warned Oglesby, "Logan is on the move. Lookout!" Five days later, Lincoln's old friend Supreme Court Justice David Davis wrote Oglesby, "Logan is canvassing . . . you must turn out."[8] A lackluster Democratic convention chose William B. Anderson of Jefferson County, a former Union brigadier, legislator, and a greenbacker, as Logan's challenger. There seemed little doubt that Logan could defeat this unknown. In an expansive mood Black Jack wrote Mary "things look well," and "I have met great success so far," but he warned, "I have not a day to spare until I am sure of victory." [9]

An unusual bit of news arrived in September, one most welcome to a man with Logan's thirst for fame and recognition. Frederick V. Hayden, a member of a mapping and exploring team in the West, wrote from Ft. Bridger that he had named a snow-covered 12,000- to 15,000-foot mountain "Logan Peak." The peak was visible to travelers on the Union Pacific Railroad. Hayden also promised the Logans a photograph of "Camp Logan," one of his party's bivouacs. Logan had encouraged Hayden's work, and the explorer indicated, "I am more than anxious to see you in the Senate." [10]

Evidently the pressure on Richard Oglesby to act quickly to head off Logan moved the ex-governor to action. Former Grand Army leader Stephen Hurlbut informed Logan that Oglesby was touring the North, "which means that Dick the Second wants to take the place of Dick the First." Logan was aware of this increased activity in the enemy camp, but he remained confident. The opposition, which knew of Logan's confidence, reported in October Black Jack's boast that a majority of the legislature was already committed to him. Trumbull commented skeptically, "I guess that is hardly so." The confrontation between Logan and Oglesby, one-time friends and allies, became bitter as the race progressed. [11]

Logan spent early October in Chicago, still fairly confident of his hold on Cook County Republicans but unsure enough to continue his contacts. By the fifth the rigors of the campaign had begun to take their toll, and the candidate reported being "almost worn out." He complained one day that he had no help and then three days later happily boasted of addressing a very large political gathering. To his chagrin Democrats purchased the *Chicago Republican,* once his devoted friend, and the first editorial under new management attacked Logan. However, he believed the attack could be turned to his advantage since it indicated that Logan, not Oglesby, was the candidate of whom the Democrats were most afraid. From Aurora Black Jack reported strong support and complained that he was far stronger in northern Illinois that he was in Egypt. At the same time he confidently told his wife that Oglesby's campaign was making little headway. [12]

Mary and the children remained in Carbondale during the canvass. John and Mary wrote each other almost daily; Mary, admitting to loneliness, thanked him for his letter, which she "feasted upon." Most of Logan's notes to his wife were political reports with a few words of affection for his family. On October 4 he rather uncharacteristically wrote: "You are so good to write me all the time. I only live for you and our children and I hope that I may have your love and assurance that you do not feel that I am neglecting my house while I am battling my life away for our success. I want to give my family a high place in the world." [13]

Republicans from other states asked Logan to appear on their behalf and he did make a junket into Iowa that fall. He spoke in Waterloo, Newton, and Des Moines, waving the bloody shirt to crowds of screaming veterans. Iowans admired Logan more than any other public figure in America, wrote one Hawkeye sheet. Also on hand in Iowa was a *New York Sun* correspondent, who predicted Logan's imminent Senate triumph because "he is a man of great vigor and originality of mind. His course upon the Cuban question has been such as to render him a great favorite with all friends of universal freedom." [14]

Back in Illinois, Logan spoke in Springfield before going to Egypt to conclude his campaign. He drew large crowds in his native section, but when he returned to vote in Carbondale he was an exhausted politician. [15]

It was a contest in which organization was more important than issues. Logan gave his standard bloody-shirt harangues, praising veterans and the Republican party and denouncing the Democratic party as a nest of traitors. These words drew opposition fire. The *Quincy Daily Herald* called Logan's speeches "bombast and blatherskite" and the *Illinois State Register* defended Anderson as a "true man, brave soldier, and irreproachable citizen." Occasionally Logan mentioned monetary policy, speaking against Democratic inflation. He advocated paying off existing greenbacks and issuing no new paper. [16] The lack of issues and Anderson's inability to seriously challenge Logan meant that most political talk centered on the Senate race ahead, not the congressional contest.

The outcome of the November balloting was predictable. The Republican slate swept Illinois; Logan won by 168,862 votes to 144,190 for Anderson. Logan's party took nine of fourteen congressional seats, a net loss of one. Thirty-three percent fewer voters cast ballots in the at-large race than voted for the same office in the presidential election year 1868. Logan's vote percentage climbed from 53 percent in 1868 to 55 percent in 1870. The smaller turnout was due not only to the midterm election de-

cline but also to the lack of a real contest for the post. Overall, Illinois
Republican majorities were down from 1868. Nationwide the results
were the same. There was growing evidence that the tariff and monetary
issues were cutting into the effectiveness of the bloody shirt. The Republicans held on to the House of Representatives, but their previously huge
majority was substantially reduced.[17]

A month after his victory Logan would have to return to Washington
for the final session of the Forty-first Congress. Meanwhile, he continued
to scramble for legislative votes. Once again he walked the streets of Chicago buttonholing members of the large Cook County delegation. He enlisted friends there to work for him while he was absent. By November 25
he felt "very sure" of his majority; nevertheless, he continued to organize. He put together a committee in Springfield to maintain his strength
and prepare for new gains once the session got under way. "All in the
future is staked on this fight," Logan wrote his wife.[18]

On December 4, alone, the congressman arrived by rail in Washington. Logan did not intend to stay through the entire session and he was
granted a leave on December 16. But before he left, Black Jack turned his
volunteer's eye on the regular navy. As if to indicate that the army and
Sherman were not his only targets, the Illinoisan moved to abolish the
rank of admiral at once and vice-admiral as soon as it fell vacant. In dis-
cussing his measure he defended the "lopping off" of useless ranks. It
was his opinion that the admiral's rank had been created to honor David
G. Farragut and not to be passed on endlessly. Banks and Butler joined in
to blast David D. Porter, the current vice-admiral. Logan never mentioned Porter by name, and for once eschewed personalities and name-
calling, as the House passed the bill.[19]

"My friends write to me to come at once, they are scared about something," Black Jack wrote to his wife as he hastily left Washington. He had
heard rumors of Oglesby gains and concluded with "I am sure if I am
beaten there is no confidence to be placed *in man*." When he reached
Chicago he discovered that the rumored Oglesby inroads were real, yet he
remained hopeful. "This world is a funny piece of machinery and I am
learning more of its meanness every day," he mused philosophically. During the last two weeks of 1870 the ambitious congressman bobbed back
and forth between Chicago and Springfield. He was regularly informed of
Oglesby's efforts in the various counties by informants who clearly hoped
to gain from their support. One week before Christmas the candidate sent
Mary plans for her role in the final push to victory. She was to bring their

son, Manning, and one of Logan's brothers to Springfield and take rooms at the city's finest hotel, the Leland.[20]

In making the race for Richard Yates's Senate seat, Logan was challenging most of Illinois' Republican leaders. The incumbent, first Civil War governor of Illinois, was completing an undistinguished first term. He had generally followed party leaders, supported congressional Reconstruction, and voted for Johnson's conviction. But Yates had developed an alcoholic problem that was a political liability often discussed in the state press. There seemed little chance Yates could hold his seat, but he was quoted in the summer vowing: "Palmer and Logan think they have the inside track, but I will show them that the Republican party still lives. I am not to be beaten by any galvanized democrat. I was a Republican from the start."[21]

Senator Lyman Trumbull was openly hostile to Logan and was skeptical of Black Jack's strength throughout the contest. Governor John Palmer, like Logan a former Democrat, agreed that Logan had "overrated his strength." He wrote Richard Oglesby that he had talked to many legislators who were for Oglesby. Oglesby thanked Palmer for his assistance and agreed that he was steadily gaining strength. He believed that if the election was held that December he would win. Of Logan he felt, "his place [congressman-at-large] is good enough for him, he sought it, let him keep it." Oglesby emerged as Logan's chief competitor, and he was in regular correspondence with Palmer. However, Congressman Jesse Moore, an Oglesby confidant, warned that "Palmer will take the thing if he can get it." Nevertheless, he went on to advise Oglesby, "You and Palmer will of course work together. You would prefer Palmer to L." Justice David Davis also lined up on Oglesby's side. He wrote from Washington to inform Oglesby that the impression there was that Logan would win, but he hastened to add that he did not consider it all that certain. Davis felt Logan had lost ground in the last six weeks and he urged Oglesby to keep his temper under control. The only state leaders for Logan seemed to be Congressmen Norman B. Judd and Shelby Cullom. Oglesby and Moore were convinced Logan had promised both men to support their quest for his abandoned place as congressman-at-large. With the incumbent governor, his immediate predecessor, both Illinois senators, and the only Illinoisan on the U.S. Supreme Court in opposition, Logan's organization faced a severe test.[22]

Another Logan opponent was the outspoken German-American Gustave Koerner. He had lived in southern Illinois and since he remembered

it is you are neutral." The president, said Trumbull, responded that he knew nothing of officeholders' electioneering and denied it had been done with his knowledge. But he made no commitment to any candidate.[28]

One of the most revealing insights into not only this contest but also the interplay of politics, journalism, and personality is found in a note from Joseph Medill to Oglesby. The editor of Illinois' most prestigious Republican paper apologized to his friend Oglesby for his failure to work for the former governor. He wrote:

> An immense pressure was brought to bear on our firm to deflect it for L. An office consultation was held . . . and it appeared that one was for L., one for O., and two others leaned to P. or [William] Lawrence. It was imposed as a compromise that the *Tribune* should remain silent. . . . But you know that a strong tinge has pervaded our Springfield dispatches in your favor. L's special tactics have been severely criticized, exposed, and in effect censured. He is many votes weaker than he would be but for those dispatches. He feels it and complains of it.

The editor added: "Mrs. L and my wife and self are warm friends and I have not moral courage enough to face Mrs. L and tell her I am working against 'John'. It is a hard thing to fight a woman."[29]

All the forces operating against him could not deny Logan the victory he had labored for months to gain. On January 13 the Republican legislators caucused. Since the party controlled the legislature the caucus nominee would go to the Senate. On the first ballot Logan received 98 votes to a slim 23 for Oglesby, 8 for Koerner, and 1 for Palmer. Oglesby's forces had badly miscalculated; it was a Logan landslide. Five days later the assembly confirmed the action giving Black Jack a 131-to-89 victory over Democrat Thomas J. Turner, a former congressman.[30]

A legacy of bitterness followed the Logan triumph. One observer called it an example of the decay of Republican political principles and an indication that "mere boldness and unscrupulousness" can decide the outcome. Another believed Logan's election was a severe setback for Prairie State Republicans. Congressman Jesse Moore informed Oglesby that Republican congressmen favored the former governor because Logan was not "really personally popular." He lauded Oglesby for fighting to the end and in summing up attributed victory to organization alone. A Yates supporter agreed, adding that no candidate's partisans could match Logan's *"sans culottes."*[31]

When Logan took his seat in the Senate in March he joined Lyman Trumbull, whose term did not expire until 1873. For some time relations between the two had been cool. Logan had opposed Trumbull's election in 1867 and relations had worsened when the senator refused to vote to convict Johnson. Now, as Logan joined the Senate, new sources of hostility appeared. Trumbull was disgruntled at the "bragging, blowing, and bluster" from Logan's faction. Besides, he had heard that all Illinois Republicans were to be made subservient to Logan and he angrily swore "This will not do." Furthermore, the senator, when told that Logan had made deals about federal patronage appointments in Chicago in order to win, pledged to block them. "I mean to see Grant and tell him what I have heard," he wrote, and then added, "I think he will object decidedly to having the offices parcelled out to secure Logan's election. The truth is Grant is not much for Logan, thinks he is a fault finder." [32]

In spite of the bickering John Logan was immensely pleased by his elevation and by the success of his organization against such an array of foes. Through January dozens of letters poured in from G.A.R. posts across the nation congratulating him.[33]

Before he took his place in the Senate, Logan had the lame duck third session of the Forty-first Congress to complete. He took his family back to its Washington brownstone. The first business Logan handled was a Military Affairs Committee investigation of the expulsion of three West Point cadets. Logan must have reveled in the difficulties of a place he disliked so much. He got in a few verbal jabs at the professional officers teaching at the academy for permitting lapses in discipline. Finally, an investigation was ordered by the House.[34]

During the session Logan spoke strongly for homesteads for veterans, endorsing the measure not only to aid veterans but also to help settle the West. His proposed bill passed 186 to 2. Another militarily related proposal was one to raise the pay of soldiers guarding the frontier of Texas. Logan fought it on grounds that all troops deserved the same pay. An angry exchange occurred when Logan attacked the bill's proponent, Congressman Edward Degener of Texas, for bypassing the Military Affairs Committee. Degener replied that he had tried to find Logan, but he had been absent most of the session.[35]

Logan's last day in the House was spent in acrimonious wrangling. First there was renewed debate over removal of the capital. Then the House discussed its power over money bills. Logan argued that the House gave in too often to Senate amendments. When asked how he would feel when he went to the Senate, Logan said his position would not change. Aaron A. Sargent of California attacked Logan for "lecturing the House," whereupon the Illinoisan accused him of wanting to "knife me." Sargent retorted in disgust that Logan's "imagination was diseased." The quarrel continued with Logan accusing his opponent of sarcasm, sharp words, and conceit. Sargent told Logan "if the gentleman does not mend his manners they will probably be mended for him by the Senate." In debate later that day Logan ended his interrupted seven-year career in the House with his final words in that chamber, "I object." [36]

CHAPTER 5

The Senator Stands for Grant

THE YEAR John A. Logan took his Senate seat was his calmest and most uneventful in more than a decade. War had been followed by Reconstruction tensions, then impeachment, and finally the intense campaigning of 1870. Logan found himself a freshman in the upper house, assigned to a rear seat and insignificant committees, and given few responsibilities. Black Jack had made a reputation in the House for his outspoken Radical views, his strident oratory, and his cantankerous ways in debate. He had considered himself a powerful member of the House, but on March 4 he found himself seated in the last row of the Senate. When committees were named Logan was placed on the Mines and Mining, Public Lands, and Military Affairs committees; he was lowly ranked on all three. The last named, chaired by Henry Wilson, was the most to his liking.[1]

In addition to Wilson and his fellow Illinoisan Lyman Trumbull, the Senate contained some of the most famous names of the nineteenth century. The irascible Parson Brownlow of Tennessee, wealthy Matt Carpenter of Wisconsin, and former Vice-President Hannibal Hamlin of Maine were there. So were men who had put together powerful state organizations of the kind Logan had worked to create: Zach Chandler of Michigan, Oliver P. Morton of Indiana, Simon Cameron of Pennsylvania, and the imperious Roscoe Conkling of New York. Also in the chamber was the original Radical, Charles Sumner, as well as reformers George Edmunds of Vermont and Carl Schurz of Missouri. In the Senate Logan's attack on the military would come face to face with General Sherman's brother, John, Ohio's senior senator.

Reactions to Logan's arrival in the Senate were varied. John G. Nicolay, Lincoln's private secretary and biographer, asked, "Will [Logan] go for Grant or set up for himself?" Illinois patronage appointees were in a panic over Logan's "large calculations about change." Some, including America's most famous black man, Frederick Douglass, welcomed the new senator with accolades. Douglass called Logan "an indefatigable worker, a keen political strategist and popular stump speaker." He also mentioned "pertinacity" and "courage" in his description of the new member from Illinois.[2]

The spring session lasted twelve weeks with Logan playing a minor role in debate. His first Senate act was to introduce several private relief bills. On March 10 Logan became involved in his first Senate controversy. The Republican leadership, supported by the administration, acted to remove Charles Sumner as chairman of the Foreign Relations Committee. Sumner had fought annexation of Santo Domingo and a more pliable Simon Cameron was named in his stead. Logan did not follow administration dictates and joined Trumbull, Sherman, and Schurz to defend Sumner. It was Logan's opinion that Sumner was still a man of energy, ability, and principle, and the only reason for Sumner's removal was his difference with the cabinet, a reason not adequate according to the Illinoisan. Black Jack reminded his listeners Sumner "led the army of liberty in this country." When Logan rose to make his maiden speech "there was a general stretching of necks in the galleries and every senator fixed his gaze on the successor of Yates. He did not assume the commanding air to which the House is accustomed, but spoke slowly, calmly, and in distinct, but not loud tones." The *Chicago Tribune* hailed the effort as "skillful and forcible." At his conclusion the new senator was warmly congratulated by fellow solons. However, the effort was to no avail and the Massachusetts senator was removed. Logan's first Senate act continued his unpredictable, on again–off again relations with the Grant administration.[3]

Over the next several weeks Logan was quiet, often not voting. He seemed to be feeling his way and abstaining when unsure. His remarks, infrequent at first, were much more temperate than they had been in the House. He spoke on several minor military matters, once suggesting an appropriation reduction on grounds that the army's requests were always extravagant.[4] In April when the Senate took up the Ku Klux Klan Act, aimed at halting southern terrorism, Logan, as he had done in the House, supported this force act giving Grant power to send troops to secure civil rights.[5]

Although he differed with Logan on the force bill, Lyman Trumbull

Roscoe Conkling. *Reproduced from the collections of the Library of Congress.*

found the former general a surprising colleague. "Logan talks and acts pretty independently," he wrote a friend. He and Logan had voted together more often than had he and Yates, and Trumbull continued to find that "there is not much love between Grant and Logan."[6]

Logan was inactive during the last month of the session. He went to see a doctor about his rheumatism and stopped in New York on business after consulting a Boston physician. Both his health and his business went well, but he found New England hostile toward Grant and his friends. When the session ended on May 27 Logan returned to New York before joining his family in Illinois.[7]

It was a busy summer for the Logans. The senator had decided Chicago was a residence more befitting his position so the family left its long-time home in Carbondale to move to the city of 300,000. Logan bought a house at 61 Calumet Avenue and complained all through August of the slowness of work on the place. He spent the time speculating on land, making $20,000 from one sale and promptly investing $26,000 in five Cook County acres. Mary spent the summer in Egypt preparing family and possessions for the exodus. July was a sad month for her. Hibert Cunningham, her brother who had fought in the Confederate army, died.[8]

By September 1 boxes and crates began arriving in Chicago, followed by Mary and Manning a week later. Dollie had been sent to school in Cincinnati, and her father wrote urging her to study and to try to improve her penmanship and spelling. An Irish cook was engaged to help Mary, and by month's end the family was settled at 61 Calumet Avenue. In moving northward Logan left the section with which he had been so intimately connected all his life. The young Egyptian, who had been advanced to political and military power by southern Illinois, had socially and politically outgrown his downstate residence. As he left Egypt one Republican there believed the move would destroy Logan's prestige in the region of his birth.[9]

One month after the Logans moved, the great Chicago fire ravaged the city. Although the October 9 holocaust did not reach their new home, the street and yard were filled with refugees, and Mary spent several days helping homeless people while the senator offered his services to the city. General Phil Sheridan was sent to Chicago to command the troops who maintained order and aided recovery, whereupon a heated controversy raged between Sheridan and Governor Palmer. The general believed Palmer was trying to strike at Grant through him, and one Illinois Republican felt the governor had foolishly injured himself by his actions. Logan could only have been pleased that controversy surrounded a potential rival.[10] The junior senator led efforts to restore his newly adopted city and promised every effort possible when he returned to Washington.

In late November John, Mary, and Manning traveled to Washington. Dollie was at school in Cincinnati, but plans were made for the twelve-year-old to spend Christmas with the family in the capital. Through the fall Mary warned her daughter to stop playing and start studying. The girl had gotten into trouble for untidiness and her mother administered a sharp lecture.[11]

When the Senate convened, the reticence of Logan's first session had passed and he took a greater part in debate. His increased affluence and power may have prompted his more outspoken record. However, in spite of increased income, Logan still did not employ a secretary to handle official correspondence. While many of his colleagues sent beautifully written notes, Logan, and sometimes Mary, continued to write the letters.[12]

The Senate began its deliberations on December 4 and Logan immediately introduced a bill he shepherded throughout the session. It provided relief for those devastated by the Chicago fire. From personal observation he described the "blackened, smouldering ruins of the Prairie Queen of the West." After lengthy debate the Senate passed the bill.[13] When new committees were announced on the seventh, Logan remained on the Military Affairs and Public Lands committees while he was added to the Committee on Privileges and Elections and the Committee on Pensions. Both new posts were of great interest to the G.A.R. leader.[14]

Early in the session civil service came to the floor for consideration. Logan had opposed the Jenckes Bill in 1868 and he continued to speak out against such legislation. However, there had been a change in Republican attitudes as a result of the 1870 vote decline. Grant had asked for changes in the method of appointing officials; and, though Congress did not enact a reform bill, it did allow Grant to appoint a civil service commission. Logan even opposed that concession.[15] In December, Grant gave Congress the commission's report recommending merit examinations, job classification, and an end to assessment of officeholders. The president asked Congress to fund the new system. Many believed the administration was moving to placate reform sentiment in time for the elections of 1872.

Logan, who had risen to the Senate on the strength of patronage politics, fought the imposition of a merit civil service. He labeled the bill a "humbug" (one of his favorite words) and returned to the argument that a meritocracy would result in a vested aristocracy. He was not convinced that examinations were the right way to determine who should serve the people. "I do not believe that any one can tell . . . the qualifications of men in that way, except so far as their mere learning is concerned," he said. Continuing, Logan told the chamber what he would recommend: "Wherever a man performs his duty . . . he should be left alone, and wherever a man does not, turn him out." Logan's philosophy was that of rural, midwestern America, which had formed his heritage and his political base. Early in the controversy spoilsman Oliver P. Morton confidently felt reform would be beaten after "lively discussion" in the Senate.[16] He was correct; the nation was several years away from an effective civil service act.

Logan constantly embraced the idea of reform but never developed affection for the specific measures that came before the Senate; nor did he have any acceptable alternative. What Logan was certain of—but never admitted—was that his political career was too heavily dependent upon patronage for him ever to compromise on civil service.

After clashing with Grant over civil service he next tangled with the Republican senatorial caucus. He was angry because it ignored men like Sumner and Trumbull—and probably himself, although he did not say so. The freshman attacked the group for its tyranny and for its refusal to accept dissent, likening it to boys who lost playing marbles and took their marbles and went home. Sumner called Logan's remarks "admirable."[17]

Logan also challenged some of his Radical allies over bills that paraded through the Senate to remove disabilities from former Confederates. In general, Logan favored easing these restrictions and therefore often found himself opposite old Radicals like Morton and Chandler when the roll was called. Black Jack's stand brought what must have been an uneasy letter of thanks from an old enemy, Zeb Vance, the wartime governor of North Carolina, who praised Logan in the name of the "unhappy people of the South."[18]

Tariff schedules concerned Logan in March. He had opposed protection in the past and continued generally to follow that course in the Forty-second Congress.[19] Late in the second session the Illinoisan challenged high duties on iron and produced an angry retort from the Pennsylvania senators when he said: "Whenever you touch iron everybody squeals."

He did defend protection for goods such as lead and tobacco, both Illinois products.[20]

The Senate was difficult going for Logan in the first two sessions. He had trouble bringing his matters before the body and often seemed confused and frustrated. In bewilderment he once mused, "I am very much surprised at the different character of movements that are made here. I do not know what we are doing, and I don't think anybody else does." In spite of this Logan remained patient and courteous, often bringing laughter from floor and galleries. He did manage a steady stream of private pension and other measures benefitting veterans.[21]

Logan's most widely noted remarks during this assembly came on May 31 and June 3. On the thirtieth Charles Sumner, put aside by his party and near the end of his life, furiously lashed out at President Grant. The veteran senator attacked the seizure of his party by those who had "exalted the will of one man." Black Jack rose to challenge the man he had defended in March. He called Sumner's words "brutal, vile and malignant" and not fit for any deliberative body. He admitted Grant had "shortcomings" and informed his auditors, "I do not endorse everything that has been done by this administration." But he felt the nation owed Grant a great deal and he provoked applause with his recital of the president's Civil War career. He said it was unfortunate that Sumner's speech would aid the Democrats in 1872. Logan commented sadly that Sumner's learning and statesmanship from which "we have all received nourishment and that has prepared us for the good work—from that tall estate the Senator fell yesterday!"[22] Logan considered the speech, given as it was on the eve of the Republican convention, a "big splash." *Harper's Weekly,* in an editorial, called it "a little speech of genuine eloquence."[23]

It was a tumultuous year for American political parties. Deep dissatisfaction with the Grant administration and a drive to end governmental corruption combined to start tremors inside the Republican party. Also involved was a demand for the end of Reconstruction; the South must control its own affairs. A rebellion had developed in 1870 led by Missourians Carl Schurz and B. Gratz Brown. In time Logan's colleague Lyman Trumbull, the deposed Sumner, and Illinoisans John Palmer and David Davis joined the Liberal Republican movement.

Through 1870 and 1871 Logan's refusal to follow the straight administration line puzzled these men. His positions on Reconstruction and civil service were repugnant to them, but they could use help from any quarter. In 1871 Trumbull believed Logan could capture Illinois from Grant "if his friends are let alone." The senior senator appreciated Logan's power and warned that a clash with Black Jack would not be advisable.[24] Trumbull was willing to wink at Logan's patronage vices in return for Logan's voice in behalf of Liberal Republicanism.

Through the winter of 1871–72 Trumbull received letters from his constituents reporting Egyptian Democrats, veterans, and German-Americans, as well as other groups, willing to join to fight Grantism. The senator, who nourished hopes of a presidential nomination from such a coalition, cautiously watched Logan. In January he reported to Horace White that Logan was "much dissatisfied" with the administration but concluded: "what he will do I cannot say."[25]

In February, before the Senate, Trumbull finalized his break with the Republican party. He had convinced himself Grant would not win since the party's "best elements" would not follow the chief executive. He wanted to break up the present organization so that the people could choose a president because he was fit and not because he would reward "political bummers." However, Horace White warned against trouble in Illinois since many liberals thought they could still control the regular state convention against the Grant men.[26] By the spring, Trumbull, Judge Davis, and New York Tribune editor Horace Greeley had emerged as leading liberal presidential possibilities.

All of this rumbling among Illinois Republicans, partially obscured by distance and unclear intelligence, was disturbing to Logan. Even though he had just defeated a coalition including most of the widely talked about Illinois liberals, so much reform sentiment sweeping the prairies could be dangerous. Logan received word that Oglesby was still a regular, clinging to hopes of taking Trumbull's seat in 1873. Palmer was reported to be riding the fence with Davis, a dozen other state leaders, and the Chicago Tribune in the liberal camp. Horace White, who had convinced a number of Republicans to bolt, wrote Logan that the "heft" of the party in Illinois had embraced liberalism and that the state delegation to the liberal convention at Cincinnati would be enormous.[27]

There is no evidence to indicate that John A. Logan ever considered supporting the 1872 bolters, but the first five months of the year were quiet ones for him. As he had been in 1861, 1865, and 1866, Logan was unusually silent and contemplative as he assessed his next move. Logan's popularity in Illinois had been amply demonstrated and his support could

influence the fall returns there. In late April, Trumbull received disturbing information: "Grant is being prevailed upon to smother his repug-
nance for Logan—to send for and *consult* with him—how to save Ill!"
This correspondent asked, "Is Logan for sale; or, can he sell Ill?"[28] Two
weeks later veteran Illinois politician Jesse K. Dubois predicted a hard
fight in the state. Without mentioning Logan's name he fretted, "Grant
seems to have a strong grip on some men of our state that I was in hopes
would have been with us."[29]

Logan swung toward Grant as the congressional session ran its course.
Yet he must have been tense since he admitted in May, "I came to the
Senate and was nervous all day." His family returned to Illinois and John
spent the final weeks in Washington alone. The "big splash" of his defense of Grant was the final signal that Logan had rallied again behind his
former commander's standard. He attended the national convention in
Philadelphia and praised the party's nominees, Grant and Henry Wilson,
chosen to oppose Horace Greeley and B. Gratz Brown, candidates of the
liberal Republican-Democratic coalition. At Philadelphia Logan stated
that Grant had been "faithful over a few things, we will make him ruler
over many." The Illinois senator was named to the executive committee
of the party's congressional campaign committee.[30]

As soon as Congress adjourned on June 10 Logan boarded the train
for Illinois. He rested for most of June before taking the stump. Grant did
almost no campaigning, admitting, "I am no speaker and don't want to be
beaten."[31] Instead the party wheelhorses were sent out to laud the president and decry the uneasy alliance of Greeley and the Democrats. Despite
Logan's tardy enthusiasm for Grant he was much in demand. His first
efforts were in Illinois, where to no one's surprise the bloody shirt waved
again. Logan admitted that Grant had made some unfortunate appointments but he told the voters that was preferable to Greeley and Tammany
Hall. Liberals, including William Jennings Bryan's father, Silas, afraid of
Logan's influence, begged Trumbull to appear to counter the popular former general.[32]

The party's mightiest leaders asked Logan's aid. Since Maine voted
before most states, Blaine wanted the Illinois senator to speak there in
late August so that his state's success could influence other states. Logan
was unable to go to New England. Simon Cameron also petitioned; he
wanted Black Jack to tour Pennsylvania.[33]

Kansas, Nebraska, and Utah drew Logan in July. His speeches went well, but he complained of traveling in open wagons through clouds of dust.[34] Back in Egypt in torrid August weather Logan spoke in Cairo and Murphysboro. A letter from Secretary of War W.W. Belknap awaited the senator on his return to Chicago. Belknap had encouraging news from across the country and praised Logan for "laying them out" in Illinois. He cautioned against overconfidence and appealed for Logan's support in Pennsylvania.[35]

In September the Logans traveled in different directions. Mary went by rail to Provo, Utah, to see her invalid father, who now lived there. John spoke in Ft. Wayne and Indianapolis before finally answering Cameron's call to come to Pennsylvania. The occasion was a Soldiers and Sailors Convention at which the former general, sharing the platform with Garfield and Henry Wilson, received a rousing ovation.[36] On his return trip to Illinois Logan joined Rutherford B. Hayes and Ben Butler in stumping for votes in Cincinnati. Despite John Sherman's plaint, "I cannot awake any enthusiasm for Grant," his fellow Ohioans lustily cheered the Republican orators.[37]

After a brief stay in Chicago during which he shared a platform with James G. Blaine, Logan stumped Illinois. He spoke to German-Americans in an attempt to woo them away from the liberals and Gustave Koerner. Crowds in cities and small towns heard the senator contrast the Republican party with the enemy alliance. William E. Chandler made one final attempt to convince Logan he should tour the East, only to be turned down since the Illinoisan had already agreed to speak in Wisconsin for Senator Carpenter.[38] War and Reconstruction were never far from Logan's mind as he circled the country. He defended Grant's record and told voters the reason for all the talk of corruption was an administration crackdown on malfeasance.

The Republicans won an easy triumph over the weak Greeley combination. Many Republicans agreed with Secretary of State Hamilton Fish's estimate that "the expurgated Republican Party is stronger on account of those who have gone out from it." Grant won by 286 to 66 in the electoral college while carrying Illinois by 241,237 to 184,772, as the Republicans retained the governor's mansion and took fourteen of the state's nineteen House seats.[39]

The third session of the Forty-second Congress brought Logan back to the Senate. He was the only Illinois senator to answer the opening call; Trumbull was at home fighting for his political life. Black Jack was concerned only with minor veteran-related matters through December. It was not until January 6 that he participated in a lengthy colloquy. On that date the Indian Appropriations Bill came to the floor with Logan attacking provisions to sell arms to Indians, especially to the "fierce" Sioux. Continuing his unsympathetic stand he said: "If we feed them and keep them quiet, it is a great deal better than to allow them to hunt and roam the prairies." Logan wanted to christianize the red men so as to "mollify their savage nature." He tangled with Iowa Senator James Harlan, who asked if Logan wanted them to go back to the bow and arrow. Advocate of a paternalism that would break the Plains warriors to the white man's way, Logan replied that he simply wanted them to go to the plow, to churches, and to school.[40]

Debates on army and navy appropriations consumed Congress during the session. Logan did not move to reduce seriously military funding this time, fixing his attention more on economies in the naval arm. He thought the navy had too many officers and believed the number should be reduced. It was perhaps this spirit which led Admiral David D. Porter, navy commander, to complain to Sherman the previous year about the "very foul" political atmosphere in Washington.[41]

On March 4 the Forty-third Congress assembled for the swearing in of the new senators and to listen to Grant's second inaugural address. Richard Oglesby had taken Trumbull's seat and Logan accompanied his former friend and more recent foe to the swearing-in ceremony. Logan also was one of three members of the committee on arrangements who escorted Grant into the chamber and then onto the east portico for his address. The special session lasted only from the fourth to the twenty-sixth and accomplished little. New committee designations were made with Logan remaining on Oliver P. Morton's Committee on Privileges and Elections. The most important step forward for the Illinoisan was the assumption of the chairmanship of the Military Affairs Committee. Henry Wilson, the former chairman, described by one senator as "kindly disposed, but as muddy as Potomac water after a hard rain," now presided over the Senate.[42]

During the brief Senate session a California visitor, accompanied by a friend, walked into the Senate chamber. The westerner saw a dark-haired, dark-skinned member on the floor and assumed he was a Negro legislator from the South. He asked for an identification of the "colored gentleman" talking to Senator Schurz. His friend burst out laughing and told the visitor that he had pointed out General Logan.[43]

Spring and summer was a time of rest for the Logans, but it was also a time of sorrow. John Cunningham, Mary's father, died in Utah in March. Logan, detained in the capital, wrote, "I feel the great loss of your good father and deeply feel with you in your grief." By April the couple was together in Chicago, but after a short stay there John went to Springfield and Carbondale to visit his family. He found his brother, Tom, an alcoholic, "in great trouble," and his mother was ill. With tongue in cheek he wrote Mary from Egypt, "I have a great notice to come here and practice law again. (Joke)."[44]

Through June and July, Logan was in and out of Chicago while Mary, with Dollie home from school, spent most of her time at 61 Calumet Avenue. In August the senator took a two-week fishing trip to Torch Lake, Michigan, to get away from "even the post office" and "enjoyed it immensely."[45]

In the autumn Logan went to Indiana to speak and then on to Ohio to attend the seventh annual meeting of the Society of the Army of the Tennessee. In Toledo, General Sherman introduced Logan, who gave the society's annual address. It was a speech that denied that the society engaged in politics, referring entirely to the social nature of the reunions.[46] For the most part Logan rested that fall, even refusing to accept official documents in Chicago. He ordered them sent to Washington where he would attend to them when he arrived in November.[47]

It was a chaotic fall for the United States and it was an anxious one for Logan. On September 18 the prestigious Jay Cooke banking firm failed and the country awoke to find itself in a serious depression. Agricultural and business overexpansion, stock frauds, and a worldwide depression ended the nation's war and postwar boom with a sickening crash. Businesses failed, factories closed, construction halted, and unemployment increased. For someone of modest wealth who counted on extra income from occasional investments, it was a trying time. When he returned to the capital Mary remained in Chicago. John wrote that he was having trouble sleeping and confided that "things look rather blue." He hoped for a "peaceful session," but did not know what to expect.[48]

Economic catastrophe had swept away much of the appeal of war-related issues. Inevitably currency, tariff, and banking legislation would find their way to the Senate agenda. Logan had little experience with these issues and he began to inform himself. Not far into the new year he would become embroiled in a great battle over national economic policy. Although John Logan would continue to speak out on issues related to the Civil War, he would increasingly have to look forward to the new issues facing postwar America.

CHAPTER 6

The Paper Money Trinity

DEPRESSION and scandals shook the Grant administration in the mid-seventies. "Grantism" became synonymous with corruption as Vice-President Schuyler Colfax, presidential secretary Orville Babcock, and Secretary of War William W. Belknap were forced from office. Logan, who often boasted that no taint of corruption appeared on his public record, staggered through several accusations but emerged without positive evidence against him although his name was linked with the Salary Grab and the Crédit Mobilier.

As a member of the Senate, Logan voted for a salary increase from $5,000 to $7,500 per year for members of Congress. More controversial was the clause that made the increase retroactive for two years—a $5,000 gift in back pay. The act was introduced in the House as an amendment Ben Butler added to the general appropriations bill. The Massachusetts representative felt that his personal wealth allowed him to introduce the measure without being suspected of bad motives. "In his eyes the increases were so obviously a matter of justice and good administration that he advocated making the pay raises retroactive," writes a Butler biographer. James A. Garfield opposed the amendment's provisions and, looking beyond the salary increases, saw in the measure an effort by Butler to exploit "the scandal in order to discredit and then supplant the party leadership in the House." [1]

In the Senate as well, prominent Republicans were arrayed against each other. Strong opposition was voiced by two wealthy men, Michigan's Zachariah Chandler and Roscoe Conkling of New York. Chandler infuriated Logan when he "argued that if a man could not get along on five thousand dollars for five months' work it would be better for him to resign." Men of more modest means, including Logan, angrily retorted that Chandler could afford to live on the paltry five thousand since he was a rich man.[2]

There was a national outcry of protest against what was instantly dubbed the "Salary Grab," and when the Forty-third Congress met, repeal of the raise was debated and passed. Some senators proposed a return of the retroactive $5,000, a proposition Logan fought vigorously. He defended his original vote for the bill, certain that congressmen deserved the amount for their hard work. His conscience, Logan said, did not hurt him a "particle."[3] Some congressmen eventually returned the extra pay, but a majority, including Logan, did not. Throughout December he complained of the "low down arguing" in the Senate over the salary bill. He cynically wrote Mary, "they all seem to be patriots and will . . . take no pay whatever for their services. . . ." He labeled repeal advocates "demagogues" who only voted in the affirmative because of public opinion. It was clear that he did not regard the action a corrupt one. After repeal passed Logan assured his wife, "You will get along on our salary and I will sell some property."[4]

The scandal surrounding Congress and the Crédit Mobilier construction company involved Colfax and a number of congressmen, including Garfield and Logan. Massachusetts Congressman Oakes Ames, employed by the company, sold over three hundred shares of stock to influential legislators. The paper was offered either at a discount or with the understanding that the original purchase price could be paid for with dividends from the stock. John A. Logan, along with a number of other senators and representatives, bought Ames's offerings—Logan in February 1868. Ames was interested in influencing the solons to act favorably toward the company.[5]

When Ames's activities were revealed, the Congress launched an investigation. Logan was called to testify and he readily acknowledged his initial purchase of ten shares. He further stated that there had been no legislation before Congress concerning Crédit Mobilier, but if there had been he would have supported it since his constituency was "favorably disposed" toward the company's enterprises. Supported by Ames's testimony, Logan explained that he had never paid Ames; but in June 1868 he was told by the New Englander that the dividend had not only paid for the shares but also had netted a $329 profit. Ames gave Logan a check for that amount. Then Logan was told by a friend that there was potential trouble in holding the stock. He promptly went to Ames, returned the stock, the $329 dividend, and $2 in interest for good measure.[6]

The investigators exonerated Logan. After being libeled for his connection, Logan's exoneration brought praise. The *New York Tribune* wrote that Logan "comes off much better than any other Congressman who took Mr. Ames' fascinating stock." A Chicago constituent informed Logan that he and his friends were "highly gratified" at their senator's innocence, and the *Chicago Tribune* absolved Logan of all blame.[7]

While weathering two scandals in one year, Logan went on with the usual business of his office. He wrote numerous letters, visited Washington departments in search of information and jobs for his constituents, and in December 1873 reported being in good health. He remained the most visible source of sympathy for veterans and as such received a large volume of mail from disabled soldiers. Among his correspondents was James Tanner, a double amputee and an active crusader for veterans' benefits. The man who would one day become national pension commissioner petitioned the Illinois senator for an increase of support for men such as himself.[8]

But the legislative branch was not primarily interested in veterans' legislation, for the Forty-third Congress began its course in the middle of the most serious depression in sixteen years. Money talk consumed the Senate. A bewildering collection of currency bills ranging across the economic spectrum was introduced. The Illinois senator, not a fiscal expert, worked long hours to learn the subject and compose a speech that would reflect his views and what he hoped were the views of a majority of the citizens of Illinois.[9]

During the Civil War the Union had printed greenbacks to finance increased expenditures. At war's end over $400 million in greenbacks were still outstanding. In 1866 Congress gave the secretary of the treasury power to retire some of these greenbacks, and he gradually withdrew $44 million in paper. However, protests against this policy mounted. Greenback circulation had inflated the money supply, raised prices, increased wages, and eased credit. Debtors, including many midwestern farmers, supported continued inflation; business interests, especially in the East, were in favor of contraction. When Logan entered the House he voted against further contraction of the currency the first time he had an opportunity to do so.[10] He was joined by most midwestern representatives. On

Mary Logan. *Illinois State Historical Library.*

the other hand, midwestern Democrats, led by Senator George Pendleton of Ohio, suggested an issuance of several billion dollars in greenbacks. Though Logan opposed contraction, he could not support Pendleton's "Ohio Idea" and spoke against such proposals.[11] Through the first two and one-half years of the Grant administration Logan was rarely involved in currency debate. In February 1870 he did join midwestern congressmen, regardless of party, in voting for increasing the currency by $50 million.[12]

The panic increased the outcry for expansion of the currency. New converts, wrecked by the crash, hurried into the expansionist camp. Many looked to the treasury for instant relief, and Grant and Secretary of the Treasury William Richardson wavered. Finally, in October they agreed to reissue some greenbacks, circulating $26 million in retired paper by mid-January.[13]

Early in the depression Logan spoke out for currency expansion, asking for the return of the $44 million in greenbacks retired by the Johnson administration. Additionally, he demanded more elastic currency facilities for the South and West, sections he believed were purposely held at a disadvantage by the banking East.[14]

Because of illness and financial problems Mary did not accompany John to Washington. When Senator William E. Chandler wrote to her he was sorry she had not come since it was a "very social season," she must have regretted her absence.[15] Logan wrote his wife regularly and an excellent record remains of his day-by-day reflections during this lengthy currency debate.

Minor matters were a prelude to the currency battle. In December Logan introduced numerous private pension bills and read a number of petitions to the Senate. One of the latter was from a group of Illinois women asking "equal protection with colored men in exercising the right to vote." The Illinois senator opposed a long Christmas recess because of the "great crisis . . . when the whole country is trembling upon the very verge of ruin." He voted with the minority on the question and Congress went home until January 5.[16]

On the ninth Logan sent his wife the currency speech he had written for Senate delivery. He worried that both the *Chicago Times* and the *Chicago Tribune* would oppose his Salary Grab stand and several days later Mary confirmed the latter's "dirty fling" at him. Logan reported working until midnight every night to prepare himself for the fray.[17] Because of their outspoken views, Logan, Oliver P. Morton, and Thomas W. Ferry of Michigan were dubbed the "paper money trinity." On January 19 the Illinois member of the trio made a long speech against resuming specie payments. In his recital of monetary policy he asked if specie payments were necessary to currency stability and answered in the negative. Then he asked if a moderate currency increase was wise at that time and answered "yes." Logan tangled with specie champion John Sherman, who had earlier urged Grant to support his position. In debate, despite the seriousness of the matter, Logan's remarks occasionally brought laughter. Once when he was accused of being an "inflationist," he denied the charge on grounds that a moderate increase was not inflationary. Besides, he added, Webster defined inflation as "to puff up" and "to swell out." Gentlemen, said Black Jack, might be inflated, never money.[18]

Logan was proud of his speech and believed he would be sustained by his constituents. He worked on the publication of his speech and boasted that though the *New York Herald* opposed his views it complimented him on his handling of the subject. John confided to Mary that he had studied currency thoroughly that winter and was not alarmed in debate. Furthermore, he boasted of receiving a wide correspondence supporting his stand. "I am right and time will bring the country to its sense," he hoped.[19]

From Illinois came a mixed reaction to the currency address. The unswervingly loyal *Illinois State Journal* hailed the remarks as an accurate reflection of western sentiment and reproduced the entire speech. The *Inter-Ocean* also praised Logan and defended him from attacks by "shallow newspapers" like the *Chicago Tribune*. That sheet tore into the Illinois senator, saying he "slashed around as usual." Black Jack's knowledge of finance was scoffed at by both the *Tribune* and the *Chicago Times*. In *Harper's Weekly,* Thomas Nast bitingly caricatured Morton, Logan, and Carpenter, provoking the Illinoisan to exclaim "Little Nast thinks he can teach statesmen how to run the government."[20]

From late February, through March, and into April the Senate droned with statistics and rang with emotional arguments for and against a currency increase. Logan won the plaudits of inflationists and the scorn of those who would contract the money supply. He grew close to Morton, a comrade of the "paper money trinity," and vowed "I will always be the friend of old Morton, he has stood up night and day with me and made the fight."[21] As the opposition rallied Logan grew depressed at its extent:

"We are fighting against all the large papers, all the bankers, all the importers, and aristocrats, for the people." The *Chicago Times* called Logan and Ferry "windbags" and regularly decried Black Jack's knowledge of economics. One Logan speech was entitled "Ignorance in the Senate," by the *Times*. Logan singled out Schurz as the leader of the Senate opposition and saw the Missourian backed by the Treasury Department "crowd" and a strong bankers' lobby. He advised Mary that this coalition was "bringing all kinds of pressure on Grant to have him take sides against us." With little confidence in the president, Logan continued, "He may do it. It is just like him." [22]

Senate Bill 617, the end product of the expansionists, was not an extreme measure. It included a $46 million increase in circulation. [23] On March 26 Carl Schurz, who was convinced that many senators would support sound money "were they not afraid of their constituents," tried to reduce the limit, but his amendment was beaten 40 to 18. [24] The following day Logan and Schurz exchanged bitter words. The Illinoisan accused the minority of arrogance and intellectual conceit. Schurz castigated Logan for impolite language and said he would not be bullied. Logan replied that he had not bullied anyone nor would he be bullied. George Edmunds joined Schurz, patronizingly remarking: "We all understand the manner of the Senator from Illinois. He can no more help his manner than I can mine." Instantly Logan struck back:

> My manner is my own. It may be gentle or it may not be. It may sometimes be belligerent or it may sometimes not be. We all have our own peculiarities. It is not a crime that I know of. My manner is earnest; I mean what I say; and if every other Senator meant always what he said, perhaps we should understand each other better. [25]

After this exchange one of Logan's constituents congratulated him on his chastisement of Schurz, Sherman, and the "selfish cold blooded capitalists" they represented. But Schurz received a note from another Illinoisan praising his retort to Logan. [26]

John kept Mary closely informed of the situation and his role in it. He remained confident of victory and defiantly wrote that the *Chicago Tribune* could "howl" if it wished. He called his clash with Schurz "letting off steam" and told of "demolishing his stuff." [27]

The senator also reported Charles Sumner's sudden death. He was deeply affected by Sumner's passing "because of his real loneliness." Logan added, "To think that so great a man should be so little loved." He predicted a battle between Ben Butler and George F. Hoar for the now permanently vacant chair.[28]

From Chicago came replies replete with information and encouragement. Mary praised her husband's speeches and reported that he was gaining strength all over Illinois. A friend called Logan "the people's leader in the Senate."[29]

After Senate Bill 617 passed, speculation and pressure focused on the president. It was generally believed that Grant favored the bill, but with the law in hand he vacillated. Bankers descended on the president and on one occasion found Logan, Ferry, and Carpenter talking to Grant. On April 18 John told of "running to the president and everywhere else" to counter "the 'money bags' of New York who are now howling to get the president to veto the bill." Eight days after the bill passed, Grant, aware of the power of the expansionist Republicans, told the cabinet he would sign it into law. Overnight he reversed himself and on April 22 sent the veto to the cabinet and to Congress.[30]

The veto was a thunderbolt. The "paper money trinity" and their followers were at first amazed and then angry. The three, joined by Simon Cameron, talked of a manifesto denouncing the president. They would save themselves by disassociating themselves from Grant. Eventually the idea of a manifesto was rejected. Logan thought the veto would cost Grant support. He vowed to say nothing further "unless driven to it by insult." Logan spent most of his time in his rooming house reading newspapers that told of his anger at Grant's decision. "I am the especial mark now of the press," complained Logan. He saw in Grant's action the beginning of a third term push. When she heard the news Mary "could not help crying." She praised her husband for fighting a good fight in the best interests of his constituents, but she urged him to remain silent until the vote to override and then defend his views with "dignity and calmness." She knew him too well and warned "don't lose your temper no matter how exasperated you feel. . . . Don't for heavens sake accuse the president of dishonesty because it would only gratify persons who would like to array the president and all his cohorts against you."[31] On April 28 Logan conceded failure as the vote to override was taken. When debate on the question began, the senator said he hoped the vote could be taken without talk which had already explored every facet and could only lead to "aroused feelings." Logan likened further debate to kicking a dead dog. He brought laughter when he said that extended debate could only serve to demonstrate to the dog that "there was punishment after death." Aaron Sargent of California said he wanted to talk to prevent resurrection, to which the Illinoisan retorted:

I am in good humor about this thing; I am not mad with anybody; I am not going to get in a bad humor about it, especially when I am beaten. That is the time when I am always in good humor. But if you commence this debate, you who make yourselves responsible for it will have to take the responsibility. We have no disposition to do it, and you had better let it alone. No good can come out of it, no benefit to the country, no benefit to the Senate, and no benefit to any one individually.

He added that he would be silent and vote, but he delivered one final warning to the opposition "not to commence a war."[32] As Logan had predicted, the override move failed by a vote of 34 to 30. The great currency battle was over.[33]

Although it could not compensate for defeat, the senator must have been pleased by the volume of correspondence from Ohio, Indiana, and Illinois praising his efforts. Grant was roundly condemned and Logan and Morton praised. A Bloomington, Illinois, Republican told Logan that the president was politically dead in the West and "you are the man out here. . . . You are now mentioned as our next President."[34] But Logan's opponents also received an outpouring of congratulations for their victory. Many were happy the Republican party had maintained what they believed to be a sound fiscal policy. One man urged Schurz to "sting" the expansionist leaders so as to provoke a response that would drive them irretrievably away from Grant.[35]

Logan reserved his special venom for Grant. He was certain the president had his eye on a third term and would do anything to "break down" possible rivals—which he considered himself. Logan seethed at the flattery heaped on Grant by "the aristocrats of the country": "The money of the country wants a strong Government, and the poor and weak, it seems, must always be poor and weak." As he often did when faced with failure, Logan became despondent—"I am tired to death with . . . Washington and almost so with political life as there is nothing but treachery in it." [36]

During the battle Mary watched her husband through the eyes of an enemy. Senator William E. Chandler, who wrote her often over the years, told her in April that Logan was "behaving well" except that he "has gone crazy" over the currency issue. "I tell him we New England people can take care of the whole business, but the Western folks will continually interfere," a jest Black Jack might not have found amusing under the circumstances. He told Mary of his differences with Logan, but despite them his warm attachment to his colleague was obvious. Logan, the New Englander observed, was "able, courageous, eloquent, and full of zeal for his cause and for his friends." "Our politics needs more such men," the hard-money senator added. For her part, Mary was pleased with the kind words. She guessed that if Chandler had been a westerner he would have agreed with Logan on financial policy. "I am certain even now," she wrote, "you half agree with him (for he is *always* right)." [37]

Although the currency debate dominated the session, military affairs also concerned Logan. Further talk of troop reductions was in the air, but Logan was not a major advocate this time. He did insist, however, that if reduction came it should be done at the same rate among private soldiers as among officers. Generals Sherman and Ord, believing the 1869–70 cuts were final, were horrified. Proposals to further reduce his staff Sherman called "personal, invidious, mean." [38]

Disgruntled at the direction the session had taken, Logan took little part in Congress's closing deliberations. He did argue for banking reforms to benefit the South and West, but his vigor had been expended earlier. Mary and Manning (who now insisted on being called John, Jr.) joined him in late May, making life more pleasant. [39]

Increasingly Logan's thoughts turned to Illinois politics. He feared the continued defection of Illinois German-Americans from his banner, which would make the state "close" politically. The fear was realistic. Gustave Koerner, long a Logan foe, believed the senator's inflationary ideas were only assumed to ensure his reelection in 1877. But the German-American leader predicted Logan would only succeed in shattering the Republican party in the Prairie State, paving the way for Democratic victory. Logan was concerned that his split with Grant would cost him heavily in patronage, thus weakening his machine, for "the people are wont to follow where power and patronage is." Trying to encourage him, Mary felt that the people would still support him no matter what office-seeking "spaniels" did.[40]

On June 23 Congress adjourned but without Logan, who was already in Illinois assessing his power. He attended the state convention in an attempt to maintain his position and to prevent the body from endorsing Grant's veto. But inflationary sentiment did not control the convention, and when the body went on record in support of a resumption of specie payments Logan agreed to tailor his position to that of his state party's views. The senator conceded that he had wrongly estimated public opinion on this issue.[41] While in the state the Logan family visited friends and relatives in Egypt before Mary and the children settled for the summer at 61 Calumet Avenue in Chicago.[42]

The panic had cut into Logan's finances, affecting his investments. To recoup some of these losses the general spent August and September in Colorado investigating the possibilities of investing in a silver mine. The trip mixed politics with business as Logan spoke several times along the way. Mary feared that money problems might force the sale of their Chicago home and she confided to her husband, "It would break my heart to part with it." To avoid that, John sold some of his Cook County real estate and invested part of the proceeds in a one-seventh share in the East Dives Mine near Georgetown, Colorado.[43]

On his return to Illinois the senator joined in the fall canvass, speaking in the Prairie State as well as in Indiana. Rising in the Midwest was a new independent political movement whose "plague on both your corrupt houses" attitude was winning support. Logan denounced the move because it would overawe the party that had saved the union and brought progress—the Republican party. It was a grim fall for the Grand Old Party. For the first time in fourteen years the Democrats took control of the House of Representatives. In the upper house, however, Logan would still sit with a majority. But the days of a solid Republican majority in the Midwest and the nation seemed over.[44]

Talk of the 1876 presidential race had already begun. Democrats were hopeful and Republicans speculated on their possible standard-bearer. Talk of a third term for Grant persisted, and James G. Blaine was seen as the president's most serious challenger. Elihu Washburne, Oliver P. Morton, and Roscoe Conkling were also mentioned. Blaine, seeking to widen his base of support, wrote Horace White to discover the *Chicago*

Tribune's preference. The journalist did not believe Washburne was a viable candidate, and, speaking for editor Medill, he thought the *Tribune* would simply back "the strongest candidate."[45] Some talk of General Sherman for chief executive began to circulate but the army commander scotched it at once. To his brother he wrote of the reasons he saw for the Republican decline. Sherman called it a party "without meaning" controlled by a narrow, selfish clique. The army, he was certain, was not favorably inclined toward the Republicans. Although denying that he would become a Democrat, the general lashed out:

> I feel not the remotest sense of gratitude to the Republicans as a party. They have allowed themselves and their Military Committees to be used to bolster up and sustain this fungus; that has fastened themselves on Washington and eaten up the sustenance that should go to sustain the soldier that works on the frontier. Grant has listened to them . . . but even he will learn that they love him *less* and themselves *more*.[46]

Logan, who rarely figured in presidential speculation and who was the cause of much of the general's indignation, would have bitterly disagreed with Sherman.

On the eve of the new congressional session Logan was ill. Yet together with Mary and their son he arrived for the December 7 opening and, seated in the chamber, impressed Kansas Republican John Ingalls as one of the "magnates," a designation in which Black Jack would have delighted.[47] Throughout the session Logan was relatively inactive. He was quiet through December, but one of his end-of-the-year actions marked a turnabout. After all the impassioned speeches of the spring, the senator voted to resume specie payments. Senate Republicans, considering upcoming elections, had decided on a resumption measure that included some compromise provisions to please inflationists. A caucus that brought together the soft-money trinity with contractionists like George Boutwell, George Edmunds, and Conkling and moderates like John Sherman hammered out the compromise.[48] It was agreed that all congressional Republicans would support this legislation regardless of their earlier views. The bill passed 32 to 14 as Morton and Ferry joined Logan. One historian has written: "In view of the many bitter wrangles among Republicans on the resumption question since the end of the Civil War . . .

the bill's managers maintained remarkable discipline over their unruly troops." Another student of the act suggests the basic reason for this "remarkable discipline." "The bill, it is clear, was at heart political in origin," writes Irwin Unger. But the reasons for the bill were clear to contemporaries. In December, *Nation* commented that the measure was "got up to produce both an appearance of union where no real union exists and an appearance of doing something where nothing is done." [49]

Black Jack's reasons for the switch were varied. He had backed inflation as a partial remedy for the depression; and although hard times still gripped the nation, he seemed to feel that the most severe phase had passed. Two factors helped to change his vote: the actions of the Illinois State Convention and the losses suffered in the fall elections by other congressmen who had supported expansion of the currency. In May Logan had written "the people are wont to follow where power and patronage is"—and both were with the administration. [50]

Logan may also have been moved by his new interest in Colorado silver mining. Evidently the Illinoisan wrote the bill's section providing for the redemption of fractional greenbacks with subsidiary silver. Although he never openly acknowledged authorship, his mid-seventies interest in silver and Senator Edmunds's speculation that Logan wrote it are significant evidence. [51]

In January, Louisiana politics generated a new oratorical flare-up in the Senate. In 1874 a violent state election led to a New Orleans race riot that resulted in the deaths of a hundred people, mostly black. On the fifth Logan rose to chastise Democrats for sitting in silence and acquiescing in the murders. He brought applause from the galleries when he warned Democrats, "Your friends have got to stop their bloodshed and murder. If they do not . . . they will be made to do it." When a southern senator called the reports "mere electioneering stories" Logan declared "men who jeer at the talk about murders . . . are seared with iron and have no sympathy for human life." Eight days later the Illinois senator gave a lengthy speech decrying the Louisiana outrages. He had an angry exchange with Georgia's John B. Gordon, a former rebel general, as Black Jack blasted southern concepts of "chivalry," "truth," and "right." He stoutly defended black men's civil rights before he sat down pleading that he was "weak and feeble." The next day Logan resumed, defending Grant against southern charges of oppression. All the president desired, explained Logan, was "that these men should quit their every-day chivalric sport of gunning upon negroes and republicans." To those who might find his support of Grant surprising, Logan explained that he disagreed with the president when he thought him wrong and supported him when he was right. Once again the galleries exploded with applause.[52]

Telegrams of support poured in to Logan from across the North. An Illinois jurist called the speech "fearless and able," the *Inter-Ocean* thought it was Logan's "ablest," and the *Chicago Tribune* acclaimed the words "bold, defiant, aggressive, calm, and logical." After opposing Black Jack for a year the *Tribune* hailed his attack on the white leaguers. But two Prairie State Republicans, John M. Palmer and Gustave Koerner, as well as the Democratic *Illinois State Register,* dissented. The *Register* believed Logan's speech had made him the "laughing-stock" of Washington.[53]

On March 3 the Forty-third Congress adjourned. Normally the Forty-fourth Congress would have begun in December, but an election dispute led to an eighteen-day special session in March. Louisiana political chaos was the center of the argument once again. The question involved the seating of P.B.S. Pinchback, a Republican cohort of Governor W.P. Kellogg. The governor wrote Morton to urge support for Pinchback and Logan joined the Indianan in insisting on his certification. The Illinois senator reasoned that if Pinchback's election stood, "quiet and peace" would come to the troubled Pelican State.[54] The Senate, unready to decide, postponed the question until December.

Perhaps the most dramatic moment of this brief session was Andrew Johnson's appearance in the Senate. On March 5 the former president took his seat among men who had voted him guilty in 1868. Also across the aisle were two House managers, Boutwell and Logan. As Johnson walked to his seat Boutwell stared straight ahead and Logan looked into space.[55]

Leaving Mary in Washington John went to New York on business and to have his portrait painted. Then he swung westward to Chicago. The Logans had rented their home and the senator stayed at the Grand Pacific Hotel. John told Mary he would work hard that summer to increase their income. In mid-April he traveled to Springfield, where he consulted with Governor John Beveridge and Republican legislators. Already on Logan's mind was reelection twenty-one months away. Egypt was next on the agenda: Logan went to Carbondale to see his invalid mother.[56] For a month he bounced back and forth between Carbondale and Chicago. He began to work among the Cook County legislative delegation, writing Mary that he had found a solon whose wife wanted flower seeds. *"Send him all sorts ... a great quantity,"* asked the senator. Logan's trips to Egypt were to sell land. He complained that prices had fallen so low there were no profits to be made. Back in Chicago, at the Grand Pacific, Black Jack vowed never again to rent the house in the summer.[57] Patronage appointments kept him busy, but Grant did not cooperate and Logan angrily charged the chief executive with breaking his word.[58]

In May the senator returned to Colorado and his silver mining ventures. Reports from the Rockies were not encouraging. Miners from his mine and the nearby Pelican Mine drilled into the same vein and clashed over rights; one man was killed. Litigation tied both mines in knots and Logan reported profits would be a long time in coming. He began to consider withdrawing his financing altogether. It was freezing in the mountains, but the senator was content just to be away from politics for the summer.[59] In late June, Logan traveled to San Francisco for the G.A.R. encampment. While in California, Logan found "the people an arrogant set, they think they have all ... the brains." In August he was in Colorado again, trying to gain a profit from the East Dives Mine. However, he was able to report making only a modest income.[60]

No matter how much John Logan talked about trying to avoid politics, he could not escape; and truthfully he did not want to. He found support all over the West and received much encouragement to seek the Republican presidential nomination. But he advised Mary that any such move would bring "the whole Grant and Washburne crowd down on me with a vengeance." And yet, he thought, solid support from Illinois Republicans would give him a good chance.[61]

Logan remained in Colorado until mid-September, when he joined Mary in Chicago. He took little part in the few fall campaigns, missing an Ohio appointment to speak for Rutherford B. Hayes, who was running for governor. He did play a part in local races and worked for Republicans in Chicago city elections.[62]

By 1875 various Civil War leaders had begun to write memoirs and reminiscences. That summer Appleton's published General William T. Sherman's *Memoirs* in two volumes. The general reported the work was selling "like hot cakes." In defending what he said of others he added:

Of course I could not tell the truth without treading on some-body's toes and I have no intention to be disturbed by any amount of criticism. I tried to deal in praise or censure as little as possi-ble, only to account for my own conduct. Logan did not make the march to the sea at all, but was in Illinois making speeches, and he was peculiarly obnoxious to Thomas.[63]

Of Logan and General Frank Blair, Sherman wrote: "I regarded both . . . as volunteers that looked to personal fame and glory as auxiliary and sec-ondary to their political ambition, and not as professional soldiers." When Sherman wrote of the battle of Atlanta and his refusal to give Lo-gan command of the Army of the Tennessee after the death of its com-mander, General James B. McPherson, he said:

General Logan had taken command of the Army of the Tennessee by virtue of his seniority and had done well, but I did not consider him equal to the command of three corps. Between him and Gen-eral Blair existed a natural rivalry. Both men were men of great experience, courage, and talent. Both were politicians by nature and experience, and it may be that for this reason they were mis-trusted by regular officers like Generals Schofield, Thomas, and myself.[64]

No doubt thinking of the effect of such words on the chairman of the all-important Senate Military Affairs Committee, John Sherman thanked his brother for giving him a copy of the general's book but referred to it as a "dangerous task." "By publishing now you assumed a serious risk of offending many of your associates and contemporaries," wrote the Ohio senator. He later added that it was unfortunate that the general had not confined himself to more kindly comments on certain individuals.[65]

There is no record of Logan writing to Sherman, but the author did receive comments from other Civil War leaders. General Grenville M. Dodge thought that Sherman did not know the entire story of Logan's ac-tions after McPherson's death. Grant wrote and commented at great length on the *Memoirs'* treatment of Logan and Blair:

I think you made a mistake in attributing selfish motives to Blair and Logan for going into the war. You may be right, but who has the right to judge other men's motives when their actions are right? In your Memoirs you speak highly of their services, deservedly—but wind up with a 'fling' at the inducements that actuated them to the course they pursued. Both were members of Congress when the war broke out. Both were Democrats at that time, a party that . . . was not then giving much support to the Government. How much better it would have been to let "History record itself;" and said nothing about motives. How still better it would have been to have stated that these two former Generals were members of Congress when the war broke out, that they left their seats to enter the field in their country's cause, thereby illustrating a patriotism which was so general that it enabled the government to suppress a rebellion such as the world never witnessed before.[66]

Sherman believed that an unnamed group of Grant's political followers had tried to retaliate by conveying the impression to the president that the *Memoirs* had been unjust to him. On meeting Grant, the general was pleased to discover that his old commander had not taken offense.[67] The decade-long hostility between Logan and Sherman was intensified by the *Memoirs*. The two volumes had done little to ensure friendly consideration of the army's problems by the Senate chairman of the Military Affairs Committee.

The rigors of summer travel took their toll on Logan. Cold Lake Michigan winter winds found the senator laid low with inflammatory rheumatism. It was Logan's most serious health crisis since he stopped several Confederate balls at Ft. Donelson. On December 4 Mary wrote her daughter, "Papa . . . can't walk alone on account of the rheumatism in his limbs." Nine days later she informed Richard Oglesby that he was recovering but "has never been so weak in his life." He was confined to a room at the Palmer House for much of late November and early December. Mary remained in constant attendance and the press reported that the senator was "at times incoherent from the effects of the powerful opiates." Letters and telegrams requesting information and praying for a speedy recovery poured into the hotel.[68] Logan was unable to attend the opening of the congressional session. He remained in Chicago until the new year, when he, Mary, and Manning finally reached the capital.

The new session and the new year looked like a time of trial. The decline in Republican fortunes everywhere, the end of Grant's reign, and the uncertainty surrounding the Grand Old Party's presidential nominee were dangers ahead. Most of all, the next year was a time of new testing for Logan's Illinois organization. Was the party strong enough to return the senator to office or would the independent political winds sweeping the Prairie State break its hold on the voters and the legislature?

CHAPTER 7

The Organization Is Defeated

BEFORE THE 1876 campaign and his own struggle for reelection began, Logan had to survive another political scandal. Through 1875 and 1876 evidence of fraudulent collection of whisky taxes and illegal relations between distillers and politicians was uncovered. The "Whisky Ring" was concentrated in the Midwest, its epicenter running from St. Louis to Chicago. Grant's reformer Secretary of the Treasury Benjamin Bristow organized an assault on the ring and launched a swift series of arrests at St. Louis, Chicago, and Milwaukee. More than two hundred persons were indicted.

Suspicion fell on many Republican politicians in the Midwest, including virtually every prominent Illinois Republican. Although Logan was not indicted and there was no proof of his connection with the fraud, some of his friends and appointees were implicated and he was thought guilty because of his association with them. The *Illinois State Register* was convinced that if "this crooked whisky business is pushed far enough Johnny Logan will come marching home also."[1] Prosecutor Bluford Wilson accused Logan of being connected with the ring. Wilson charged that Black Jack did nothing to assist in the removal of his friends even after "rascality" and "inefficiency" were proved. The reason, thought Wilson, was the long service these men had rendered the Logan "machine." The *Chicago Tribune* countered Wilson by averring that since Logan had once tried to remove Wilson, the official was merely seeking revenge. The journal also reported that Secretary Bristow had told one of its reporters, "there is no evidence; and has never been, which in any way implicates Logan in the Whisky Ring, and I don't believe there will be."[2]

One reason Logan appeared uncooperative was his serious winter illness. The prosecutor wrote Bristow that the illness was mere sham

brought on by the ring prosecutions. There is no doubt that Logan's illness was serious; but it also seems probable that the machine politician
was not zealous in routing out the wrongdoers either before or after his
bout with rheumatism. Logan clearly regarded Bristow as a man ambitious for the presidency and a bitter personal enemy, who was determined to destroy him politically. In the spring of 1876 Logan received a
letter from Shelby Cullom also denying involvement. "Any man who
states it states that which is false in every particular," vowed Cullom in a
declaration that Black Jack echoed. C.H. Fowler, president of North-
western University, wrote to defend Logan, commending him for his
"courage and patriotism and *efficient* service." The educator decried the
"Satanic Press" and told Logan that the country was sick of "so much
falsehood and slander."[3]

On January 6, 1876, Logan answered his first roll call of the Forty-
fourth Congress. Although he was still weak, he worked hard—Mary
thought harder than ever before. In addition to his chairmanship of the
Military Affairs Committee and service on the Privileges and Elections
Committee, Logan was put on the Finance Committee, chaired by John
Sherman.[4]

Indian affairs came to the Senate's attention, and Logan demanded
that courts convict red men for stealing timber and for other crimes. Proposals had been made to turn the Indian Bureau over to the War Department but Logan opposed them. He urged that Indians not be attacked,
rather that they be educated, christianized, and taught to "fear our laws."[5]

A controversy over West Point arose late in the month. The Appropriations Committee suggested a reduction of pay for academy instructors,
but the former general fought the slash. He was convinced that such a cut
was illegal since pay by rank throughout the army was fixed by law. Logan also fought an economy measure that would have killed the Military
Academy band. "Music excites and incites patriotism," said the veteran.
"But the latter-day saints of economy want to drive music from the land. I
presume they would like to drive poetry out from the land." Jokingly
Black Jack thought he knew the reason for these Democratic measures:
"They do not need wind instruments." Laughter swept the galleries only
to rise again when Missouri's Lewis Bogy replied: "We are not given to
blowing our own horns."[6]

P.B.S. Pinchback's disputed election to the Senate from Louisiana returned to the agenda in March. Logan again spoke for Pinchback's admission, arguing that his color had much to do with opposition to his admis-

sion. The mulatto was being expelled because laws were not upheld equally for whites and blacks although "God knows they ought to be," said the Illinoisan. Despite some support, Pinchback was not seated.[7]

It was a slow-moving session with little significant legislative action. Everyone cautiously eyed the election ahead, unwilling to deal with controversial subjects. Minnesota's William Windom admitted: "We are not likely to kill ourselves by hard work in Congress this session. Was there ever anything like it? Nearly five months . . . gone and nothing done."[8]

During those five months, presidential speculation steadily mounted as party men thought more about the race ahead than about lawmaking. The Republican front-runner seemed to be James G. Blaine and for a time Grant considered a third term. Some feared a certain victory for the old war hero despite the scandals of his eight years in office.[9] Eventually Grant bowed out and Roscoe Conkling assumed the mantle of leadership of the administration forces. Indianan Oliver P. Morton shared some of that following and was more popular in the West than was Conkling, but Morton's poor health was a handicap. Benjamin Bristow was the darling of the reformers, including many 1872 Liberal Republicans who had returned to the party. For a time Elihu B. Washburne, congressman and lately ambassador to France, pursued the presidency. There were several favorite sons, of whom Ohio's recently elected Governor Rutherford B. Hayes was the most prominent. By the spring, Shelby Cullom had assured Logan that Washburne had no chance. Illinoisan John Hay promised Blaine his support and pompously reported "the nomination of Morton is positively dreaded by the best men in the party." Another Illinoisan, William Henry Smith, Associated Press general agent at Chicago and close intimate of Hayes, gauged the situation in the Northwest. He had found no deep commitment to anyone, with support divided between Blaine, Washburne, and Bristow. The reformer, he felt, was weak and Washburne's supporters were hoping for a Blaine-Morton deadlock to pave the way for their man's selection. All of this, Smith was certain, was favorable to Hayes's chances.[10] Logan kept his own counsel and made no open commitment during the winter and spring.

Regular congressional business was interrupted on April 5 when the Senate began sitting as a jury in the impeachment trial of Grant's Secretary of War William W. Belknap. Accused of malfeasance in office based on evidence of graft from sales to army posts, Belknap had suddenly resigned. Grant's quick acceptance probably saved his secretary. It was argued by those opposed to Belknap's conviction that when the House presented its impeachment charges the former secretary was a private citizen and thus could not be impeached. The trial dragged on through the spring and summer. Logan asked only a few questions in the course of the proceedings, refraining from lengthy expostulations. After several delays and recesses the Senate voted on the five articles of impeachment on August 1. Citing the illegality of the process since Belknap was no longer a "civil officer of the United States," Logan voted "not guilty" to all charges. He told the chief justice when called on: "I condemn the conduct of the respondent as strongly as any one . . . [but] it was never contemplated by the framers . . . that private citizens should be arraigned and tried before the Senate." Two-thirds of the Senate failed to vote guilty and Belknap was acquitted. The further evidences of corruption and of Republican division were embarrassing in these first months of the presidential campaign. Logan was joined by such Republican Senate leaders as Conkling, Boutwell, Thomas Ferry, Hamlin, and Windom in voting not guilty. On the other side were Simon Cameron, Morton, Oglesby, and John Sherman.[11]

After spending most of April and May on the Belknap case, the Senate was prevented from further deliberation by the opening of the Republican National Convention in Cincinnati on June 14. On opening day, Logan joined *Nation* editor George W. Curtis in speaking to the delegates. The orations could not have been more dissimilar. Reformer Curtis assailed corruption in general and Roscoe Conkling in particular, while Logan denounced the redemption of the South by rebels.[12]

The Illinois Republican party was not solidly committed to any candidate. The convention delegation contained little sentiment for Bristow, Morton, or Conkling; it leaned toward Blaine. Illinois state Republican chairman Charles B. Farwell worked diligently in Blaine's behalf. The *Chicago Tribune,* which favored Bristow, feared Logan's opposition to its man and reported that Black Jack was strongly in favor of fellow machine-chieftain Conkling. Logan's support for Blaine, thought the *Tribune,* was merely surface affection, a charge bitterly denied by the *Inter-Ocean.* By the time the convention opened the *Tribune* appeared to have changed its mind: it reported Black Jack working hard for a solid Blaine vote from the Illinois delegation, which it dubbed "Logan's lambs."[13]

Midwestern observers viewed the prospects differently. Barring a "midnight trade" John Hay was certain Blaine would sweep the Prairie State votes. Smith saw Blaine well ahead but reported the Illinois delegation could not be counted for certain because many of its members were special friends of Senator Logan. Chauncey I. Filley, a shrewd St. Louis Republican and Morton leader, saw only Blaine and Morton with midwestern strength. The Illinois state Republican convention had met in May and had nominated Logan's old House colleague Shelby Cullom for governor. It had urged the party's national platform committee to endorse the present currency system and to defend the civil rights of all Americans.[14]

Nominations at Cincinnati were made on June 15, but a gas failure darkened the hall and halted balloting until the sixteenth. The gas was rumored to have been turned off by anti-Blaine men, who feared that Blaine would be nominated that night on the first ballot.[15] On the sixteenth Blaine led the first roll call with 285 votes, followed by Morton's 124, Bristow's 113, Conkling's 99, and Hayes's 61. With 378 votes needed to nominate, Blaine was still 93 votes short. Little change occurred until the fifth ballot, when Hayes's total jumped to 104. But on the next roll call Blaine began to pick up votes and climb toward victory. To stop a Blaine majority, those opposing the speaker concentrated on Hayes. Blaine's rumored involvement in a railroad fraud convinced many he would not appeal to Americans tired of the Grant scandals. Hayes, on the other hand, was eminently available. Governor of a key state, he had supported sound money and specie resumption, and he had an excellent Civil War record. Most important of all, Hayes's public record was spotless. On the seventh ballot Hayes received 384 votes to nip Blaine, whose total had risen to 351. William Wheeler, a New York congressman, was chosen as Hayes's running mate.[16]

Logan had not supported Hayes, preferring Morton to maintain Radical leadership in the White House, yet working for Blaine in the Illinois delegation to avoid a swing to Bristow. When the convention finally acted, Logan lauded the ticket as a "very good one." The Illinois senator was particularly pleased that Bristow had not been nominated and rather absurdly boasted "if I had not been there I am not so sure that Bristow would not have been nominated." Mary had gone to Chicago during the convention and her husband wrote, "I never had so hard a week's work as at Cincinnati." He told of Joseph Medill's opposition there and he feared that the *Chicago Tribune* was determined to "wreck" him.[17]

After the convention Black Jack returned to the Senate and to an intense debate on Indian policy. A House appropriations bill persisted in

attaching the Indian Bureau to the War Department and Logan was adamant in his opposition. On June 20 he delivered a long speech on the
history of Indian treatment, reciting a record of brutality and fraud on the
part of the army. Logan recognized some Indian outrages but pointed out
much "unnecessary" bloodshed directly traceable to the army. When
Bogy argued that only the bayonet kept Indians peaceable, Logan disagreed and said it was because they had been "taught to be peaceable."
Furthermore, the Illinoisan told the Senate he was more afraid of Missouri's James brothers than of Indians. Moreover, Logan saw Indian wars
started mainly "for the purpose of getting promotion." The moment officers knew they could be promoted for attacking Indians they would do
so. "It is human nature," added Logan, who wanted the granting of bre-
vets for attacks on Indians halted by the Senate.[18] The Senate refused to
agree to HR 3478's provisions on the transfer of the Indian Bureau to the
War Department. The deadlock kept Congress in session through the
summer and Grant reported to Hayes on July 4 no indication of an immediate solution. In July, Logan was appointed a Senate conferee and eventually the transfer was carved out of the bill.[19]

In late June, Logan was attacked for not reporting out of his Military
Affairs Committee a House bill to reduce the army. He heatedly argued
that it took the House seven months to get the bill together and it would
take more than two weeks for his group to study it. Since it came late in
the first session he proposed to hold the bill over until December. Besides,
Logan thought it was a "bad time" to cut the armed forces. Sioux attacks
on the northern plains made it necessary to increase cavalry forces there.
Logan introduced and maneuvered to passage a bill authorizing volunteer
enlistments for that force. He also shepherded through a bill to employ
Indian scouts.[20]

While Logan remained in steamy Washington, Mary and the children
traveled to Philadelphia to see the Centennial Exposition before going to
Chicago. As the session dragged on, the Illinois senator, now an investor
in silver mines, introduced a bill to make silver dollars legal tender. He
called the 1873 repeal law a "trick" and clashed with Senator Morrill
of Vermont. When Morrill charged such a bill would help only western
silver-mine owners, Logan denied the charge and pointed out that it could
be argued that the protective tariff benefited only New England industrial-
ists. The proposal was tabled.[21]

The Illinoisan's final speech of the session was an endorsement of Morton's resolution to print ten thousand copies of Grant's speech on the Hamburg, South Carolina, race riot. Waving the bloody shirt, Logan told the Senate a "conspiracy exists to-day as much as it did before the war." The conspiracy, he continued, included the "murder of Negroes, intimidation of voters, slander, and falsehood." On August 15 the first session of the Forty-fourth Congress finally went home. It was about time, thought Logan, who was in good health though "worn out." [22]

After a short rest Logan took the stump both for the national ticket and for himself. Although Logan was not an enthusiastic Hayes supporter, a Republican president was still necessary. A Hayes friend reported Logan had called the civil service remarks in the nominee's acceptance speech "dead stuff." Despite such reservations, Logan spoke for the ticket in Pennsylvania and Indiana as well as in Illinois. [23] Ohio concerned national leaders, but Indiana and Illinois seemed sure for Hayes. [24]

More immediately in Logan's thoughts was his own fight for reelection. Republican strength in Illinois had been slipping and failure to elect a majority to the General Assembly could return Logan to private life. Gubernatorial candidate Shelby Cullom had long supported Black Jack as had a majority of Illinois Republicans. But the press concerned him. On September 25 Mary wrote that the *Chicago Tribune* was surprisingly complimentary, and the editor of the leading German-American journal, the *Illinois Staats-Zeitung,* informed the senator of his newspaper's support. But Democrats and Independent Greenbackers hoped for an uprising that would end Logan's career. [25]

One great imponderable in 1876 was the Independent-Greenback movement. If it elected any members to the Illinois assembly they could become the balance of power and would probably side with the Democrats. In July, *The Great Campaign,* a Greenback sheet, began publication in Chicago. The journal appealed directly to poor veterans not to be turned by the bloody shirt from more important economic issues. *The Great Campaign* urged repeal of the resumption act and vowed to join the Democrats if they endorsed Greenback ideas. The party nominated Peter Cooper for president and blasted equally "Hooinhells" Hayes and "Slippery Sam" Tilden. Cartoons often graced the newspaper's pages and Logan was easily recognized in them as portraying the bloated Grant corruptionists. [26]

When the Democratic state ticket was announced it was applauded by the Greenbackers—to Logan's distress. *The Great Campaign* left little doubt of its opposition to the senator, linking him with the Crédit Mobilier and the Salary Grab.[27]

To counter *The Great Campaign* as well as the *Chicago Tribune,* Logan needed to keep the *Inter-Ocean* solvent and active. He believed it to be the "leading Republican paper of the Northwest." But the *Inter-Ocean* was in financial trouble and Logan wrote Zach Chandler in search of national party funds to keep the journal in print. Such funds were "absolutely necessary and *must be* given." [28]

On election eve Illinois looked as if it would return a narrow Hayes majority, but it was shaky for Republicans on the local level. The German-American vote, usually Republican, was uncertain. William Henry Smith warned his friend Hayes that the "greenback folly" would cut into his majority and make the legislature very close.[29]

Smith's prediction was accurate. Hayes polled 278,232 votes to 258,601 for Tilden and 17,207 for Cooper. Cullom won the governor's race by less than 7,000 votes, and the Republicans lost seven of their nineteen House seats. However, it was the legislative return that alarmed Logan. The Republicans claimed 100 seats to 89 for the Democrats, but 15 seats were held by Independents. The "greenback folly" had indeed threatened the Republican hold on an Illinois Senate seat.[30]

Hayes's election nationwide was as uncertain as was Logan's in Illinois. At first appearance Tilden had been elected; but Republican leaders William E. Chandler and Zach Chandler cited vote frauds in South Carolina, Florida, and Louisiana and claimed victory for Hayes. Logan was immediately catapulted into the national dispute. Grant telegraphed a request for him to go to New Orleans to witness the Louisiana vote count. Zach Chandler wrote of the importance of the count, and Black Jack received a number of telegrams shouting fraud and claiming victory for the G.O.P. Hayes was assured that Logan and Chicago Congressman Charles Farwell would protect his interests in the Pelican State.[31] Plagued by doubts at home due to the legislative division, Logan turned down Grant's request and did not go to Louisiana. But he did telegraph many political allies across the South to help prevent a Democratic attempt to carry the state "by force." [32]

In December, Logan returned to Washington for the meeting of Congress. Mary remained in Chicago working actively for her husband's re-election. The disputed presidential election caused the greatest excitement in the capital. Logan confessed that he was so excited he could not sleep well. On December 21 Logan was appointed to the Senate Committee on Counting the Electoral Votes. It was recognition of his position in the chamber that placed him alongside Republicans George Edmunds, Morton, and Frederick T. Frelinghuysen and Democrats Allen Thurman, Thomas F. Bayard, and Matt Ransom in this vital assignment. But Black Jack, facing his own crisis, again declined a role in the disputed presidential election. He vacated only when assured that a Republican of similar views would replace him; Roscoe Conkling was named to the vacancy.[33]

The greatest cause of John A. Logan's sleepless nights was the rapidly approaching election in the Illinois assembly. On December 6 he admitted "I fear the action of the Independents." He even heard of some Republican defections in concert with the Independents. Logan remained convinced the third-party men would as soon vote for him as for any Republican. He vowed not to give way to a Republican supposedly more acceptable to the Greenbackers. By mid-December, Black Jack had written friends all over Illinois and promised to continue this correspondence until election day. A letter to J.H. Oakwood was typical. In it Logan expressed doubt of the election outcome, but he requested Oakwood's aid promising to "feel under many obligations to you for such kindness." Logan concluded: "I have been pursued and persecuted until I feel that I am entitled to some vindication at the hands of my friends and sincerely hope to find it in the action of the next legislature."[34] Logan was also again promised support by the editor of the *Staats-Zeitung*. He warned Mary to hold this endorsement under cover until the "proper time." On the seventeenth he received a note from Grant promising to render any assistance Logan suggested. Since there had been proposals that Illinois send Grant to the Senate, his assurance of support removed one question mark. The *Inter-Ocean* quoted the outgoing president as saying, "In such critical times as these it would be a national calamity to have Logan defeated."[35]

When the legislature assembled on January 3, 1877, Logan would need all the support he could muster. He was easily accorded his party's nomination while, after a fight, the Democratic caucus chose John M. Palmer, former governor and a Liberal Republican in 1872. The Independents named William B. Anderson. As he had done in 1871, Logan brought Mary to Springfield to court the solons. She was assisted by Dollie, a striking teenage brunette, in greeting and entertaining the legislators.[36]

Despite the makeup of the assembly the *Chicago Tribune* predicted Logan's success. The newspaper found the Republicans solidly behind the senator and mentioned his favorable consideration by one or two Independents. But the *Tribune* commented on a problem peculiar to this contest. Since the presidential victor was unknown, no senatorial aspirant had certain patronage to barter in return for votes.[37] As the Thirtieth General Assembly began its first day the members were haggard from all-night caucuses. Some rumbling was reported at once. A Cook County Republican boycotted the caucus since he knew Logan would be chosen even though he could not win. On the other side, Palmer was denounced by the Independents.[38]

On the eighth, Governor Cullom addressed the assembly as Logan listened from the platform. The legislature conducted normal business as rumors flew around Springfield. One after another Democrat was suggested and ruled out by the all-important Greenbackers. Palmer, Trumbull, and John Farnsworth were rejected. There was also talk of a Republican dark horse who could claim the allegiance of the powerful fifteen. On January 11 Supreme Court Justice David Davis was first mentioned as a man who could win with Democratic and Independent votes. As the deadlock continued the *Tribune* stopped predicting a Logan victory and began to question the "Logan or nobody" tactics that Black Jack was insisting upon. The editorial page reported that as long as the G.O.P. clung to Logan it had no bargaining power with the Independents. Although the *Tribune* defected, the *Inter-Ocean* and *Illinois State Journal* remained faithful to Logan throughout the session. Both Republican journals condemned the *Tribune* for not giving Black Jack its undivided support.[39]

The introduction of David Davis into the senatorial race threatened Logan. Chicago lawyer W.C. Goudy wrote Davis to sound him out; on the tenth he reported Logan beaten but refusing to surrender. Goudy believed an alliance to elect Davis only waited on word that the justice would accept if elected. He warned, however, that some Democrats feared his place on the electoral commission and on the court would be filled by a Republican and thus might be reluctant to vote for him. The attorney asked Davis to reply quickly since Logan was trying to buy Democratic votes and might succeed if not headed off at once.[40] There is no record of Davis's reply to Goudy, but Lincoln's old friend later insisted that consideration for the Senate came to him unsought and unexpected. He accepted the nomination in part because he "never believed in the Electoral Commission as a mode of determining the presidential election." [41]

A severe winter storm did not stop all legislators from attending the January 16 session when the first ballot was taken. Logan received 96 votes, Palmer 89, and Davis 7, and 10 others were scattered among several men. [42] Palmer men were convinced the incumbent could not win; however, former Senator Orville H. Browning was certain neither Palmer nor Logan could win. As early as the seventeenth Browning predicted a Davis victory. [43]

Over the next week, indecisive ballots showed little change. On the fourth roll call, Logan received the votes of all 100 Republicans, but no Independents joined Black Jack's cause. By the thirteenth ballot on January 20, Logan, holding at 99, tried to cheer his supporters by claiming several Democrats would vote for him as soon as Palmer withdrew. It was an empty boast, for the ballots following Palmer's withdrawal saw no Logan victory or even any increase in his total. On the twenty-third the *Chicago Tribune* called a Logan victory "no longer even a theory." The *Inter-Ocean* reluctantly agreed and believed the cause in large part was betrayed by the "*Tribune* Serpent." [44]

Telegrams of encouragement from political friends were some consolation in the struggle. "You have stood by the right and have been faithful to the principles of the Republican Party," wired Oliver P. Morton, Hannibal Hamlin, and John Sherman as they added their best wishes for Logan's success. James G. Blaine spoke of his "warm personal interest" as he "anxiously" awaited each ballot. Green B. Raum saw Grant and sent on the president's strong support and continued offer of help. [45]

A stormy, long Republican caucus was held on January 22, but nothing changed. Logan refused to withdraw. The following night, the party finally dropped Logan in favor of Illinois Supreme Court Judge Charles Lawrence. The *Tribune* reported that Logan had blocked Elihu Washburne's nomination since he thought Washburne could win but knew Lawrence could not. To the *Tribune* it was characteristic of the "rule-or-ruin" attitude of Logan, the "Republican Jonah." [46]

On January 25 the fortieth ballot brought the protracted contest to an end. David Davis picked up a majority, left the bench, and joined

Oglesby in the Senate. Following Logan's defeat the Illinois attorney general told a *Tribune* reporter that Black Jack had taken his defeat as "philosophically as a man can, though he is naturally somewhat chagrined. . . . He is plucky and looking forward most hopefully to the future." [47]

Keith Ian Polakoff has written: "The election of Davis is most remarkable for the lack of communication it reveals within the Democratic party." The Illinois press had mentioned Davis as a possible candidate for weeks, "and still the national party leaders were uninterested in what was happening in Illinois." The decentralized structure of nineteenth-century parties played a major role in creating the "inertia" which led to Tilden's defeat. It also led to Logan's defeat. [48]

Logan's retirement was noted by many. One of Oliver P. Morton's Indiana friends attributed the defeat to a plot by rebels and Copperheads. Former Congressman George W. Julian reported that Judge Davis "is cursed by all parties and many of his old friends refuse to speak to him." But reform Republican Walter Q. Gresham admitted he was glad Davis had replaced Logan. An Illinois Democrat was "exuberant" because his "long subjugated state" had thrown out John A. Logan. [49]

William Henry Smith, as usual, reported the Illinois news to Hayes. He felt sure the party's loss of the Senate seat was unnecessary, made possible only because of Logan's selfishness. By his actions Black Jack had dug his own political grave in Illinois, estimated Smith. His selfishness combined with the loss of patronage would permanently retire Logan. The *Illinois State Register* did not mourn Logan's passing. His defeat, cheered the Springfield newspaper, "is one of the grandest political successes ever accomplished in this state." In New York, the *Nation* hailed the outcome as a victory for good government and bade adieu to Logan as a public figure. [50]

As soon as he withdrew from the contest Logan returned to Washington. "Everyone here seems seriously to regret my defeat," he informed Mary. He added that he had become reconciled to leaving the Senate. To the people who had stood by him Logan sent notes of thanks which concluded: "The steadfast friendship of so many of my party makes the disappointment more endurable." [51]

In the two months Logan had remaining in the Senate he attended sessions regularly but played little part in debate. To the end he fought for veterans' benefits and for an equitable reduction of the army. Grand Army members must have mourned his departure, while Sherman, Sheridan, and the officer corps could only have been pleased. Logan's final remarks as a senator came on a Roscoe Conkling patent bill to aid a man who was trying to develop a chemical that was more effective than yeast. "If he can improve bread, very well," agreed the outgoing senator from Illinois.[52] The prospect of buying his own family's bread was Logan's chief concern as he cleared out his desk, shook hands with his colleagues, and walked out of the Senate chamber.

CHAPTER 8

"The Fiery Furnace"

J OHN A. LOGAN'S senatorial defeat secured the presidency for his party and for Rutherford B. Hayes. When independent David Davis left the bench, he was replaced on the electoral commission by Republican Justice Joseph Bradley. On each set of contested electoral returns the commission decided 8 to 7 along partisan lines. Hayes won the disputed electoral vote count 185 to 184. The irony of his indirect contribution toward returning a Republican to the White House was small comfort for Logan.

Although he retained his Senate seat in the final session of the Forty-fourth Congress, Logan's greatest concern through February and March was the possibility of an appointment in the Hayes administration. Mary was convinced her husband would be given a cabinet post or a foreign mission "worthy of your past labor." She preferred Russia, England, France, Belgium, or Spain: Logan moved with alacrity to round up support and direct it at the incoming president. In a note marked "Confidential," the defeated senator wrote a friend:

> You can readily see that I am a defeated individual, but it is not necessary for me to go into the details. I merely wish to say that if you feel that I would be a proper person to take a position in the cabinet of President Hayes, you can do me good in that direction, but I do not wish you to engage in this enterprise unless you can feel in your conscience that it is a proper thing to do.

How many such letters Logan sent out is unknown, but he hoped to start an avalanche that Hayes could not ignore.[1]

The "Logan to the cabinet" movement gained momentum as February passed. Ex-governor John Beveridge of Illinois and western politico

Jerome B. Chaffee urged Black Jack's selection. Chaffee claimed to talk for the "great majority" of western Republicans as well as for James G. Blaine. Senator Oglesby and five members of the Illinois House delegation asked for the War Department as a fair reward for Logan's "unswerving devotion to Republican principles." Twenty-four House Republicans from Alabama to California joined in the campaign, specifically mentioning the War Department. Illinois Governor Cullom sent a request in the name of all Republican state officers, senators, and representatives. The former general and military affairs chairman, they believed, was eminently qualified for the War Department. The Illinois Democratic press jeered cynically at the idea of "Logan for secretary of war! Hurrah for civil service reform" and added that Black Jack was the very man to go into "his fraudulency's cabinet as a fence for stolen goods."[2]

While Logan's friends campaigned to put him in the cabinet, strong opposition to the appointment developed. One of Hayes's closest friends, William Henry Smith, reported that liberal Republicans were disturbed over reports Logan would be named. Smith said he had "laughed them out of their fears." Joseph Medill opposed Logan and called the pressure in his behalf "bold bulldozing." A reformer told Hayes that Logan's appointment would "shock the better elements of the party"; a minor post was enough for a man whose "moral tone is low." "No such man must be near you," he urged. Several leading Republicans had advice for their new leader. Carl Schurz sent his suggested cabinet list, pointedly ignoring his late Senate opponent. John Sherman thought Logan deserved "the highest consideration," but he was convinced he did not have "the qualities of caution and deliberation requisite in a cabinet officer."[3]

By February, Hayes had eliminated three types of Republican from cabinet consideration. Excluded were "holdovers from the Grant administration . . . presidential candidates" and appointments to "take care of somebody." At least one and perhaps two of these categories eliminated Logan.[4]

As Hayes's inauguration grew near, Logan's friends made a final effort. Oglesby gathered signatures from eight other senators on a petition. F.W. Palmer of the *Inter-Ocean* asked for the Interior Department if War was not possible. Logan himself was active and twice called upon Garfield to ask the Ohioan's support in his quest for the War Department. On March 2 the Illinois congressional delegation and a group of fifty supporters went to Senator Sherman's home, where Oglesby made a speech and presented Hayes with a written supplication bearing 117 names. The president-elect assured the Illinoisans he recognized Logan's services, yet despite this supplication and Hayes's words, George McCrary of Iowa was named to the War Department and Logan got nothing. To add to the disappointment, Black Jack was not invited to Grant's last state dinner.[5]

John and Mary Logan were bitter at Hayes's refusal of cabinet office. Mary bemoaned the shattering of the "serene future" they had imagined, and in her *Reminiscences* she recalled this as the "most unfortunate time of our lives." She argued that John should leave politics, convinced he could make a good living elsewhere. For his part, Logan felt "sold out" by the president's "base ingratitude." He predicted an administration worse than Andrew Johnson's and announced that he could not "honorably" accept any post from its hands. Finally, he agreed with Mary that the time had come to abandon politics forever.[6] Yet within days of his departure from elective office Logan was petitioning the despised Hayes for office for a friend, Ward H. Lamon, an old associate of Lincoln's.[7] Politics had been Logan's life and talk of never again seeking office was merely a product of temporary depression.

Logan's political friends joined the couple in their condemnation of Hayes. Alluding to the president's reform, conciliatory administration, one Illinoisan told the former senator why he had not been chosen: "You did not fight at the head of a Rebel regiment, neither did you liberalize in '72, neither did you live in Ohio, three sins unpardonable in you." Another, looking to the man who had dispensed patronage in the past, mentioned talk of a diplomatic post for Logan. He urged Logan to turn down such a mission since the time for his return to office could not be far distant. But some Illinoisans were gratified by Logan's rejection. Former Senator Browning was pleased with the repudiation of machine leaders and senatorial usurpation. He pleaded for an end to trafficking in offices.[8]

When the session ended, Logan sadly returned to Illinois. He went to Springfield and was warmly welcomed by old friends. After a talk with Cullom the former senator reported "all is right." He made a quick trip to Egypt and rejoined Mary and their son in Washington. At a meeting of the Republican National Committee that April, Logan joined William E. Chandler in attacking the administration's betrayal of Louisiana and South Carolina Republicans.[9]

Despite the harsh criticism of Hayes, the Logans did not end their efforts to gain appointive office. On May 9 Mary approached the problem directly—she went to the White House. There is no record indicating whether or not John knew of her meeting with the president. Mary was received cordially and she pressed Hayes in her husband's behalf. She seems to have abandoned either hope of or interest in a foreign post and concentrated instead on the collectorship of the port of Chicago, a potentially lucrative job. Mary reviewed Logan's lengthy service to country and party and promised he would turn the collectorship into a "model office." Evidently she also told the president of their desperate financial straits. Several days later Hayes's friend William Henry Smith wrote from Chicago of Logan's economic problems. He said the ex-senator was very poor and had recently borrowed money to pay a $40 bill. In spite of his information Smith cautioned against putting Logan in the customhouse. The president was "much moved" by the story and felt something should be done. He reported to Smith, "Soon after coming here I was led to think that some good men would oppose him, but in view of the facts you name, ought not such opposition to cease or to be disregarded? Think of Logan's services in 1861–1865." [10]

Nine days after Mary Logan's supplication Hayes disregarded the "good men" and named Logan ambassador to Brazil. The limited prestige of a minor diplomatic post which would take him far from Illinois politics was unappealing; Logan declined.[11] Dom Pedro would never receive credentials from General Logan. His reasons for refusing had already been set forth in a letter of May 5 to House Clerk Edward McPherson. McPherson had suggested a foreign mission, but Logan wrote:

> I am poor. When I came home from Washington I did not have enough money to pay my expenses. The panic . . . left me very much embarrassed. What property I have may pay my debts, but will leave me to start again without anything. I have spent my all for the party and in politics which was foolish I admit. These facts show you that I could not go abroad. I *couldn't* afford it. . . . I shall leave for the far west very soon to see if I can strike something that will give me a start again.[12]

The Chicago collectorship was more lucrative and much closer to home. Through May and June, forces supporting and opposing Logan made their opinions known. Green B. Raum, an old Illinois friend of Logan's, went to Senator Sherman, Hayes's new treasury secretary, and reported that Sherman favored Logan. The Illinois state G.A.R. commander wrote to ask Logan's appointment as a reward to veterans. In early June, David Davis received a letter backing Black Jack and painting a sad (and perhaps exaggerated) picture of the ex-soldier's financial affairs:

> Logan is . . . poor. . . . He told me last night he had but fifty cents in money. He has some real estate but largely mortgaged. He is really in a bad fix. He feels badly, says he sits all day at home and reads to keep his mind from distraction. . . . He says he has been out of the practice of law for 16 years and don't feel that he can get back.[13]

Opponents seemed unmoved by Logan's rumored poverty. Editors of three Chicago newspapers, the *Chicago Tribune*, the *Post,* and the *Inter-Ocean,* fought a Logan appointment. He was condemned as the state's leading salary grabber and opponent of civil service reform. Hayes was advised that naming Logan would hurt the Hayes administration in Illinois and demoralize those who endorsed the struggle for merit in office. William Henry Smith, Hayes's friend who was eventually named to the Chicago collectorship, reported an intense feeling of disgust at the mention of Logan's name. Many believed, wrote Smith, that the new administration represented "a new and improved order of things." "To put the chief of sinners" into such a responsible office would be the height of inconsistency, he added.[14]

Oddly enough Logan wrote Hayes to endorse other men for the collectorship. He strongly endorsed ex-governor of Illinois John Beveridge and joined Senator Oglesby in backing the senator's old law partner, Sheridan Waite. Logan brought up his friends' efforts in the president's behalf and told him, "I hope [my name] will not be considered for a moment. . . . I feel sure it is not suited to me at all, and I do not desire it, nor could I take it." An obviously pleased Smith quickly reported Logan's lack of interest to Hayes.[15]

Was Logan truly disinterested? Or was his disclaimer an indication that he was not seeking the post in hopes the president would offer it to him? The day after he told Hayes he would not take the post he wrote Richard W. Thompson, the new secretary of the navy, and again brought Beveridge's name forward, complaining that old-line Republican officeholders were being ignored. He blasted Carl Schurz but reported "kindly" feelings toward Hayes, the man he had denounced and would continue to denounce in private correspondence. Even more amazing was Logan's hope, expressed to Thompson, that Hayes "make a good . . . sweep" of officeholders. Again there was a disclaimer: "At present I do not wish any position for myself. I could not in honor accept anything here in Chicago after making recommendations that I have for others." [16] Perhaps he considered the collectorship beneath him, perhaps he hoped to make a new financial start in Colorado silver; but he may also have been attempting to counteract his reputation as a greedy office-seeker and pave the way for a future position of a kind he could accept.

In June, taking Dollie with him, Logan abandoned the quest for office and took up the quest for silver. He roamed Colorado, often reporting something promising in the offing and forecasting a number of get-rich-quick schemes that never developed. He asked Mary to sell some bonds and he disposed of some real estate, but the returns were disappointing. Once Mary wrote her husband that he had a job offer from the Chicago Life Insurance Company, which he declined at once, denouncing "nearly everybody" for their past duplicity. [17]

Political comments ran through Logan's letters. He found the Rockies swarming with anti-Hayes sentiment and predicted the Ohioan would be "the most unpopular president ever in the White House." He also attacked the *Chicago Tribune,* vowing to "get even." As to his political future, all Logan promised was to "move slow, and do nothing that will embarrass me." [18]

In August, Logan employed a mining expert certain to discover a big vein. Logan worked hard and was in good spirits and good health. Mary constantly cautioned him against robbery, fraud, and drinking, and she anxiously urged him to come home soon. She went to Egypt in August and discovered that people there thought the Logans were wealthy. She told them otherwise. Mary beseeched her husband never to return to Carbondale to live no matter what their financial condition. Finally, she asked Logan to return for the national G.A.R. encampment at St. Paul. "Sherman is *not to be* there," she pointed out. [19]

Together with Colorado Governor John L. Routt, Logan went by wagon through the San Juan Mountains looking at placer sites. At Oro City and Fairplay he saw prospects for rich veins, and finally at summer's end he invested in a "good buy." [20]

After a brief stop in Chicago, where he discovered Smith's appointment as collector, Logan went to the nation's capital. He used his limited legal experience and his great political influence to represent those doing business with the federal government. Black Jack had no good words for the administration that had called him "sinner" and shut him out. "Hayes ... will have to come down from his high perch before long," thought Logan. He called the regime a muddle of inconsistencies replete with grumbling and slander.[21]

Despite the denunciations Mary still sought a place in that administration. She wrote Raum to solicit his and Secretary Sherman's support and was informed that a major mission was possible. When she urged her husband to take the English mission, he rebuked her: "My dear wife they have no thought of offering it to me." Logan eventually decided that all those associated with Hayes would be "forever damned politically," and he determined to remain aloof.[22]

In November, Logan began a case out of which he predicted a $1,000 fee. Money was needed that fall since Dollie was to be married to William F. Tucker of Chicago. Logan hoped for enough funds to provide for the event, but he cautioned Mary not to "make any show, but have a quiet wedding." In the end he left everything to her and Dollie. On November 27, the twenty-second anniversary of her parents' marriage, Dollie became Mrs. Will Tucker. She and her husband lived in the Calumet Avenue home when the Logans returned to Washington for the winter. John, Jr., also remained in Chicago. The twelve-year-old was a student at Morgan Park Military Academy.[23]

As the year ended, Republican leaders were preoccupied with the state of midwestern politics. Some thought Hayes was gaining strength among party leaders there. The president, however, was concerned that his removal of the old Chicago collector, J. Russell Jones, and his nomination of Smith had offended Illinois party magnates. He reported that Davis and Oglesby were both upset. Logan, whose anger at the change was unbounded, called on Oglesby to work to defeat Smith's confirmation. Governor Cullom, concerned over the party split, wrote Hayes urging him to tender the Berlin ambassadorship to Logan. He advised the chief executive that western Republicans would be "satisfied" and the appointment "would heal up much soreness that now existed among Republicans toward him."[24]

There was little chance Hayes would make another offer to Logan.

From the customhouse Smith struggled with the Logan forces and was not in a conciliatory mood—he poured out his rage to both the president and to Secretary Sherman. He had tried to take the lead in harmonizing the discordant elements of the Illinois G.O.P., he said, only to run into Logan's demand for "unquestioning recognition of his supremacy and the taking of an oath to help him punish his enemies." According to Smith, Logan's enemies included the Chicago newspaper editors, Elihu Washburne, Oglesby, and Chicago Representative Charles Farwell. Smith called Black Jack's methods "base and corrupt" and patterned on those of Aaron Burr, Martin Van Buren, and Roscoe Conkling. Smith met with Logan in late 1877 and the latter asked for the removal of the U.S. marshall for northern Illinois. The former senator was enraged at Smith's refusal. That refusal unleashed the Logan "hounds," according to the collector. It also brought about an effort to discredit Smith with the president. Although seen entirely through the eyes of a bitter enemy, this picture of Illinois Republican politics indicates grave factional division that the Hayes administration had not healed in its first year. It also indicated that Logan was busily at work winning the allegiance of enough Prairie State Republicans to return him to office in the near future.[25]

The Logans lived in a boardinghouse at 812 Twelfth Street in Washington in the winter of 1878. John continued his legal activities before various federal departments. He handled some state business in Washington and Governor Cullom promised "liberal compensation" for his labors. The former senator got a fee in early February, which he thought would pay that winter's expenses. Mary wrote Dollie and Will regularly, notifying them that Logan was well and working hard. She was glad 1877 had passed and looked forward to better things ahead. "We have passed through a fiery furnace and can begin life together on the bottom round," she rather dramatically observed. That winter there was more time for attendance at social affairs, and Mary established friendly relations with first lady Lucy Hayes, in spite of the president's refusal to give Logan a suitable post. The Logans also spent much of their winter reading aloud to each other, a favorite recreation.[26]

Mary went to Chicago in March, leaving a lonely Logan to plow on with his legal work and lobbying. He was associated with W.W. Wilshire in representing Illinois before a federal claims commission. Logan handled a number of cases that spring, but he made little income from them.[27] Frustrated after five months of hard work and low income, Logan was depressed at his future prospects. He saw nothing ahead but "hard work and only a fair living" and exclaimed, "You know how I have struggled to try and be somebody."[28]

The "somebody" Logan wanted to be was a United States senator once again. He remained acutely sensitive to every development. He accurately sensed a growing hostility from Oglesby, who heard tales of a Logan challenge for his Senate seat in January 1879. Although some Chicagoans mentioned Logan as a Cook County candidate for the House of Representatives, he responded cautiously, believing that it was simply a move to lure him away from the Senate race. In March Logan began contacting Illinois legislators and former legislators. Leaving little to chance, he went to work early. "I have been reminded that the campaign in our state was near at hand," wrote Logan coyly, as if anyone had to remind him of such an event. He urged one former member and "faithful friend" who had voted for him in 1877 to stand for the assembly. Logan explained:

> If . . . I can help you let me know. I have not forgotten how you stood by me through that long struggle. We shall have a hard fight. I know Republicans are used to that and our principles are worth fighting for. If we have been sold out more than once we must be more careful about the men we nominate for *every position* and we can win the victory. I am sure.[29]

In June Logan returned to Illinois, ostensibly on business but in reality to sample grass-roots political opinion. He went to Springfield and on to Carbondale. In Egypt he did concern himself with the farm managed by his brother, Tom, and owned by the two brothers jointly. He reported crops were good but Tom was grumbling as usual. On July 4 Logan made a speech widely published in the state press; but feeling little could be done in peak summer heat, Logan returned to Colorado, the cool mountains, and the search for silver. His bonanza had not yet come in, nor did it that summer.[30]

Logan's early move toward the Senate drew comment. One of Dick Oglesby's friends labeled Black Jack's conduct "ungenerous." However, he was convinced the masses would deny Logan success. Influential Chicago lawyer Isaac Hitt made Hayes aware of the Logan-Oglesby clash and urged that administration power be used to return Logan to Washington.[31]

After returning from the West, Logan sought support from Cullom and then went to Washington, where he saw the president. There is no indication of the response of either man, but Logan was leaving no possible source of support untested. By October Black Jack was back in Illinois stumping the state. William Henry Smith first reported an "uncertain" contest, but by November 12 he had to estimate that Logan was "undoubtedly the strongest." The collector was trying to create an anti-Logan combination, but he doubted its chances. "Can you suggest anything?" he queried the president. Through November, Logan remained confident of victory.[32]

As the time for the legislature to convene approached, several Illinois journalists offered Logan advice, information, and assistance. Good words also came from outside the state. P.B.S. Pinchback's New Orleans newspaper was certain Logan's "brilliant record and personal magnetism," which had given him the largest personal following in Illinois, would return him to the Senate. However, Logan also received some discouraging words. Clark Carr, a Republican author who had backed Logan for reelection in 1877, informed Black Jack he believed Oglesby deserved to succeed himself this time.[33]

Unknown to the Logan camp, Oglesby was receiving his share of disheartening news. A McLeansboro legislator wrote that he held the senator in high esteem, but since the Republicans of his district were "almost unanimous for General Logan" he felt it his duty to follow their will. Oglesby, in his canvass for legislative votes, received a number of negative and uncommitted responses. The incumbent's bitterness grew as the canvass proceeded, for he thought his record merited his reelection. One encouraging bit of news was the *Chicago Tribune*'s strong endorsement, which gave Oglesby the optimism "to struggle on."[34]

The exhausting canvass Logan and Oglesby waged that fall aided in returning a Republican majority to the General Assembly. For the first time in six years Republicans controlled both houses.[35] Both men also stumped to win the support of a majority of those Republicans sent to Springfield. At the same time the two candidates vied for newspaper support. Logan claimed more than thirty journals including the *Inter-Ocean* and *State Journal*. Oglesby won Springfield's *Illinois State Register* in addition to the *Chicago Tribune*. The former was really more anti-Logan than pro-Oglesby, but it believed that Oglesby was at least "a decent man." The *Register* greatly enjoyed the incessant bickering between the *Inter-Ocean* and the *Tribune*.[36]

There was last-minute talk that the Democratic minority might join dissident Republicans in support of Oglesby. One Logan man pointed out the necessity for a first-ballot victory to prevent such an occurrence. Logan also received a promise of influence among Democratic solons if it was necessary.[37]

Hayes maintained a low profile in the Illinois race. Nevertheless, Green B. Raum, acting for Logan, and Smith again attempted to influence the president. Raum saw Hayes and wrote that he wished Logan to be reelected. On the other hand, Smith described Black Jack's "disreputable" campaign and his boast that once in the Senate he would "make things 'hot for Hayes'." Smith reported his own trip to Springfield, which had led to the charge that he was representing Hayes in Oglesby's behalf. In the state capital Smith found Logan announcing to some followers that he had "made up with the Administration," while boasting of his implacability to others. To the end Smith predicted a Logan defeat. So did the *Chicago Tribune,* which reported that Black Jack had once promised Oglesby he would never oppose him. The *Tribune* predicted Republican legislators would not be swayed by the Logan "gang" in spite of its grand promises of patronage. As late as January 15 the newspaper estimated only 35 caucus votes for Logan.[38]

The predictions by Smith and the *Tribune's* editors were far from the mark. On January 17 the Republicans caucused and Logan won a surprisingly easy victory over the incumbent, 80 to 26 on the first ballot. Four days later Logan defeated John C. Black, the Democratic nominee. The Democratic-Oglesby coalition did not materialize.[39]

Congratulatory letters and telegrams poured in from all over the state and nation. Many were pleased at the *Tribune's* defeat and denounced Medill's "blackguard" behavior. Schuyler Colfax congratulated Mary and berated Oglesby for "unjust" charges against Logan. Raum was overjoyed at the victory and pleased with Logan's campaign, which was so "nobly" conducted as to leave no "wounds." Former House colleague Godlove Orth wrote from Indiana celebrating Logan's "vindication from foul aspersions" of his enemies. Senator Matt Carpenter wired "Bully for you dear friend," and Chicago businessman Potter Palmer roared "Damn the Tribune" in his note of congratulations. Accepting thankfully, Logan proclaimed it a "glorious victory" and found "vindication" from the "misrepresentations" of the *Chicago Tribune* especially sweet.[40]

The angry and disappointed Oglesby received consolation from those who were sure the "Peoples' voice was not heard." But a DuQuoin Republican produced a reason for his support of Black Jack that may have played a role in Logan's triumph. He held Oglesby in high regard, but:

> I am alarmed when I see both Houses of Congress crowded with Rebel brigadiers and a solid South. It seems to behoove us to send as many of the Old Hickory Hells fire and brimstone fellows right now as possible and we have all talked the matter over and most of us . . . who are Republicans from *principle,* came to the conclusion that it is best to send Logan back now and supercede old Davis by yourself when the time comes.[41]

In the White House, Hayes received a complete election analysis from Smith. It was, of course, stridently hostile toward Logan, revealing the depths of Republican factionalism during the Hayes administration, and it indicates some of the basic components of a successful nineteenth-century political organization. Smith said the events were almost "ludicrous" had they not been a "disaster" to the party. He believed Logan had once promised not to run against Oglesby but had gone back on that promise. Smith was convinced that Post Office and Internal Revenue employees, all loyal to Logan, labored diligently for him to the neglect of their jobs. Illinois distillers were also a strong element in the Logan campaign—an attempt once again to implicate Logan in the Whisky Ring. Furthermore, the *Inter-Ocean*'s support, Smith charged, had been purchased by a group of Logan's friends, who offered to invest $40,000 in the financially shaky journal in return for an endorsement. William Penn Nixon, the editor, declined at first but in desperation eventually acquiesced.

"Mrs. Logan was the greatest power," continued Smith. She visited legislators, entertained their wives, and worked "with an earnestness that was irresistible." To carry the caucus, she begged members for "just one vote for darling," and the vote was delivered.

Logan used his own version of the carrot and the stick. Smith reported numerous stories of promises of patronage for support coupled with threats of revenge for noncooperation.

Hayes's informant summed up what he saw as the election results:

> The Republican party through its misrepresentatives has retired to private life an honest man with a clear record who was one of the

Fathers of the party. . . . Elected to be his successor, the author of the infamous Black Laws of Illinois, a salary-grabber . . . and a lobbyist. He has never ceased to be a Democrat; and [his election] has placed Illinois among the doubtful states in 1880.

In conclusion the disgruntled Smith warned that Logan was an incorrigible Hayes-hater, who, with Roscoe Conkling, Simon Cameron, and Matt Carpenter, would lead a "reaction against reform and decency." Smith had been told that in a room full of Illinois Republicans Logan had exclaimed: "Hell, I can tell you why I am opposed to Hayes. It is because he is a G___d d_____d liar." [42]

Logan's Illinois organization had again been able to control the Republican legislative caucus. Mary Logan was certain victory had been possible because the dissident "mongrels" who defeated the senator in 1877 had since been retired to private life. [43] The Logans had passed through the fiery furnace of private life and decreased income.

While Black Jack had been out of office, President Hayes's efforts at reform had alienated Conkling and many other Republicans who had adopted the designation "Stalwart." The party was divided among the Stalwarts, the Hayes reformers, and a large number of Republicans who hoped for the 1880 nomination of James G. Blaine; these last were dubbed "Halfbreeds." [44] Since Hayes had already announced he would not seek reelection, the three factions had begun an early scramble that would end at the party's 1880 national convention. Within months Black Jack would be identified as a Stalwart chieftain. Hayes and reform had no friend in the new junior senator from Illinois.

CHAPTER 9

Return of the Stalwart

THE WASHINGTON railroad depot and surrounding streets were crowded with people as the Baltimore and Ohio train shuddered to a stop. A smiling John A. Logan, his drooping mustache making him instantly identifiable, waved from the cars and stepped to the platform. The throng, accompanied by music, fireworks, and booming cannon, escorted Black Jack to the Willard. The hotel was a festive scene as Civil War veterans, congressmen, and old friends hailed the Illinoisan's return. No one close to the administration was on hand. Despite that absence, Logan thought the demonstration was the greatest Washington had accorded any man save Grant.[1] Since the January triumph Logan had been hailed everywhere he traveled. A trip to southern Illinois brought a "splendid reception," followed now by the capital welcome organized by Green B. Raum and other old friends. In February, Logan had celebrated his fifty-third birthday, an occasion that caused Mary to exclaim: "I thank God for sparing you to me all these years that we have been together."[2]

As soon as Logan settled at the Willard he returned to the business of politics. One Republican politician observed that Hayes was anxious to establish friendly relations with Stalwarts like Carpenter, Chandler, and Logan. The Democrats possessed a Senate majority for the first time since 1861, and Hayes needed all Republican votes regardless of faction. On the twenty-fourth Logan visited "Hayes & Co. to see what they are going to do." Within days he was deluged with petitions by mail and in person begging his assistance. He had already begun to collect recommendations for the removal of unfriendly officials and the appointment of loyal Stalwarts. Everything did not run smoothly, and Black Jack complained that Oglesby was trying "to get all he can before going out."[3]

On March 18 Logan was sworn in as the Forty-sixth Congress began

113

its deliberations. Mary joined him in Washington shortly after the session began. Financial problems remained serious, for when Dollie requested $300 her father informed her he had only just begun to receive his salary and after paying for board and clothing had only $25 left. "I have no money on deposit in Chicago to draw on nor anywhere else," he explained.[4]

The Forty-sixth Congress found Logan a junior member of the Senate minority. Republican division and economic unrest had helped create a Democratic House and given Black Jack's former party a small Senate majority. His seniority gone, the Illinois senator was placed last on the committees of Military Affairs, Indian Affairs, and Territories. Democrat Theodore F. Randolph of New Jersey held Logan's old post as chairman of the Military Affairs Committee.

The makeup of the upper house had changed in other ways as well. Many of the old faces were gone. Logan joined Zach Chandler, Conkling, Carpenter, and Simon Cameron's son, Don, as leaders of the dwindling Stalwart aggregation. Blaine had reached the Senate as had former Union General Ambrose Burnside, and Republicans George F. Hoar, William Windom, George Edmunds, and Justin S. Morrill were still members. A Radical like Logan was dismayed by the presence of so many former rebels and Copperheads at the seat of power. Daniel Voorhees of Indiana and George Pendleton of Ohio sat together with Zeb Vance of North Carolina, Wade Hampton of South Carolina, and John B. Gordon of Georgia. If he wandered over to the House he could have found Joseph E. Johnston of Virginia, Alexander H. Stephens of Georgia, and John Reagan of Texas. The possible effect of this invasion of former Confederate leaders worried Black Jack, and the men from the South would soon hear the roar of the bloody shirt.[5]

Logan took up where he had left off in 1877 and submitted a number of private relief and pension bills in March. He was relatively quiet, however, until April 11, when he tangled with Virginia's Robert E. Withers over the Army Appropriations Bill. The measure included a pay increase for officers detached for special duty in the War Department. Too often "soft places" had been given to persons by special act, declaimed Logan, as he dismissed a letter Withers produced as one written by an ambitious officer and merely passed on by the secretary of war. Pay discrimination within the same rank the former general found abhorrent.[6]

On April 15 John returned to the legislative battles in earnest. In a lengthy speech he opposed a rider to the Army Appropriations Bill that was particularly obnoxious to him. The Democratic majority sought to repeal the law authorizing the use of the army "to keep the peace at the polls," arguing that troops were not necessary and sometimes interfered with elections. Black Jack saw the Democrats as grasping for control of the government. The Illinoisan regarded the rider as a blackmail attempt to force Hayes to accept its terms or run out of money if he vetoed the act. If this tactic should destroy the balance of power, then, as the Roman general said, "*Actum est de republica*—It's all over with the Republic." Logan believed the change would be applauded only by white leaguers and rifle clubs who used violence against blacks. Logan pointed out that when troops had been sent into northern states to hunt runaway slaves, southerners had been pleased; therefore, "I ask in the name of conscience, in the name of justice, in the presence of humanity, what there is in that principle that will follow and starve and persecute a man in slavery that will not protect him when he is a freeman?" The nation's answer to the Negro, he said, was: "No, we hunted you when you were a slave; we will still stand by and see you murdered now and shot down in cold blood; we have clothed you with the rights of an American citizen and we feel that we have no power to protect you! My God what a Government that is!" When Democrats guaranteed the protection of all voters by the states, Black Jack laughed and called free elections a "dead letter" in the South. Southern whites "have never . . . accepted the decision of the war," and they treated with scorn what they called the "nigger amendments." If blacks could freely vote, queried the Prairie State Stalwart, why, out of a black population of four million, was Mississippi's Blanche K. Bruce the only black in Congress from a southern state? Logan predicted a mass exodus of blacks from Dixie until whites there "sadly moralized over deserted cities and uncultivated fields and mourned their stupidity and selfishness."

The conclusion of his oration indicted the Democratic party and warned its leaders of the dangers inherent in their proposed course. Logan vowed that they were "sowing the wind" and should "beware of the harvest": "I make the open charge that the democratic party is tampering with the gravest interests of a people who are vigilantly awake." He decried the opposing senators' eulogizing of the "arch-traitor" Jefferson Davis and charged his opponents with responsibility for whatever discord existed in the nation. Republicans, he assured the nation, would:

Shelby Collum. *Reproduced from the collections of the Library of Congress.*

never permit a modification of the rights of the 4,000,000 blacks of the South. They, after having been liberated from slavery and elevated to the full rights of citizenship, shall not be remanded to a condition as bad or worse than serfdom or peonage.[7]

Logan supported a number of amendments aimed at making the bill more palatable or at least slowing down its passage. Seven of these alterations were tabled by the Democrats as Black Jack cast his vote against tabling. When the bill passed, Hayes exercised his veto and the majority was too small to override it.[8] Logan was pleased to be supported in his actions by Governor Cullom, but the parliamentary battle found his colleague David Davis on the other side. Predictably, Logan's constituents took opposing views of his indictment of the South. The *Inter-Ocean* believed the speech "glistened with many telling points," while the *Illinois State Register* saw "Logan parade the decayed remnant of the ensanguined shirt."[9]

The gauntlet Logan hurled at the South in his speech of the fifteenth angered many southerners. Alabama Congressman William W. Lowe spoke for his fellows when he struck back at the Illinoisan, reviving the charge that Logan had raised troops for the Confederacy and was guilty of hypocrisy. Lowe denounced what he felt were the midwesterner's slanderous and degrading remarks about his section. The Alabaman's ultimate reaction was to challenge Logan to a duel. Black Jack's response was to treat the challenge with "silent contempt." His verbal assault and his refusal to become involved in the "code duello" brought a shower of praise from Logan partisans. He was praised for exhibiting moral courage in the face of a southern braggart and for treating the entire issue of the military's relations with the civil government in a "most masterly manner." So many letters came in that John and Mary spent fourteen hours writing 150 letters to well-wishers. Most pleasing were the resolutions endorsing Logan's stand passed by the Republican Congressional Caucus and by the Illinois Republican legislative caucus in early May.[10]

For the remainder of April the Army Appropriations Bill was the center of Senate debate. In May the seemingly never-ending question of election frauds in Louisiana resurfaced; William Pitt Kellogg, a Republican who had been seated, had his election challenged. In the discussion Logan became embroiled in a sharp exchange with Democrats Ben Hill of Georgia and Eli Saulsbury of Delaware. He denounced the Georgian for

imperiously cutting him off with a wave of the hand and accused Saulsbury of soaring conceit. "The great state of Delaware should not be complimented" at being served by Saulsbury, said Logan. Not long after that
clash Logan and Zeb Vance verbally sparred. Vance objected to continued
derogatory statements about former Confederates now sitting in Congress; they were there in obedience to the Constitution and the laws. In a
lighter vein, he remarked that after all the Senator from Illinois had come
to North Carolina, "with such a numerous retinue and they were so urgent in their solicitations that I, for one, found it impossible to resist so
weighty an invitation." Logan shot back "when I got there I did not find
you." As the chamber erupted with howls, Vance told Logan, "but I came
as soon as I could." [11]

The first session dragged on through June, ending on July 1. Many of
the *Record*'s pages are filled with the continuing confrontation over appropriations. Logan was not very active but he did rise occasionally to
defend equal suffrage and insist that troops were needed to curtail the
depredations of "ku-kluxers." Just before adjournment Vance introduced
a letter from two North Carolina legislators of "dark complexion" denying the Republican claim that blacks had been kept from voting there.
William Windom skeptically asked "About how dark? were the two
men." Black Jack drew laughter when he snapped, "About as dark as I
am." Vance concluded that they were "Fully dark enough to belong to the
republican party." [12]

Spring was a pleasant time for the Logans. In April, Mary wrote Dollie, "Papa's prospects for realizing something from an unexpected quarter are good." The couple went to Fortress Monroe for a weekend and
seemed to be more relaxed and less careworn than at any time in years. In
mid-June, Mary took the B & O to Carbondale, where she was to supervise farm affairs before joining the senator in Chicago when the session
concluded. [13]

Although he was secure for five more years and 1879 was not an election year, Logan closely observed the undercurrents of Illlinois political
life. He was closeted with Governor Cullom in Washington, and the two
men pressured Hayes for personnel changes that would aid them. They
were especially interested in the position of U.S. marshall for northern
Illinois. The hostile William Henry Smith urged Hayes not to remove the
marshall merely to please Logan by replacing him with one of Black
Jack's political allies. The man Cullom and Logan had in mind Smith

branded a "cunning manipulator." Such a move, reported Smith, would convince reformers the president had capitulated to the Stalwarts. Smith seemed convinced that Black Jack need not be truckled to, especially since he had no support in Chicago. "In this city," he wrote, "Gen. Logan's following is insignificant and uninfluential. Most of the businessmen have no confidence in him and are opposed to him; the potent social influences are against him and his wife." The only strength Black Jack could muster, felt the elitist Smith, came from "county politicians . . . who hope for, and are content with, small things; and who do not, for lack of education, distinguish between real and simulated statesmanship."[14]

For some reason Smith's tactical view changed drastically by early summer. He traveled to Washington and while there had a "full, free and altogether pleasant interview" with the senator he had excoriated so often. The two men agreed to "harmonise" the party in Illinois to achieve success. Logan promised to send Smith copies of any speeches he made during the summer and fall. Perhaps an earlier comment that "I can appreciate the suggestion made, that it is wise policy to do something for Senator Logan's friends," had finally become his policy. However, in April, when he wrote those words, he questioned the wisdom of giving further influence to a "pronounced opponent" of the administration. To do so would mean "the Fox would be in possession."[15]

There is much evidence that 1880 presidential politics was involved in this spring rapprochement. Ohioan John Sherman, friend of Smith and Hayes, had his eye on the Republican nomination. Sherman reported Logan very friendly in what seemed to be a sincere manner. The secretary of the treasury urged that some concessions be made to Logan and believed "it is better for you [Smith] to cooperate in a friendly way with Logan rather than to antagonize him." In an insight into Logan's character shared by many, Sherman wrote:

> I have always found that, while Logan is exacting and suspicious, yet by a frank and easy way with him, yielding nothing but good humor, he is tractable enough. He naturally complains when his requests are not granted and criticises, sometimes abuses his friends, but if they can patiently bear his temper, there need be no serious difficulty with him.[16]

Sherman's pleas may well have altered Smith's stance. The collector reported in May that Logan had assured Sherman he would not be a presidential contender and, furthermore, thought Grant should not be a candidate. In April, Smith had been convinced Logan was one of the leaders of the Grant third-term movement and Sherman could expect no support from Black Jack. Smith's earlier reaction was correct. Logan was a Grant man but not yet so open as to lead Sherman to abandon any hope of convention support from Illinois.[17]

That summer and fall Logan toured Illinois, spending some time in Egypt. When Dollie and Will Tucker vacationed in the West in August, John, Mary, and John, Jr., remained in Chicago. In September, Logan addressed the G.A.R. national encampment at Des Moines. Following the appearance he remained in the West, speaking at state fairs and soldiers' reunions in Iowa, Kansas, and Colorado. As summer gave way to fall, Logan left few doubts as to his choice for 1880—Ulysses S. Grant.[18]

During the Grant administration Logan's attitude toward the president had been mixed. One reason for criticism was the Illinoisan's realization that he was not a member of Grant's inner circle. The passage of time, however, had removed some of Grant's intimates and Logan saw an opportunity to move closer to the seat of power in a new Grant administration. This would be a virtual certainty if Logan played a key role in the general's nomination and election. Furthermore, what were the alternatives? Sherman and Blaine did not offer the possibilities for intimacy and power offered by Logan's old Civil War comrade.

As Logan clarified his position the summer "harmony" began to break down. Sherman accused Logan of "meddling" and reported that friends had assured him Logan would "not have things all his own way." The secretary observed "Logan . . . seems to be opposed to everybody but himself and is a general complainer." Yet Sherman concluded, "I feel a real kindness for him, have respect for his courage and abilities and want to be friendly." By November, Sherman was growing more disturbed and wrote Smith, "It will be necessary to have a frank conference" with the Illinois senator. Ex-senator Richard Oglesby had even greater reason to fear Logan's activity. The patronage whip wielded by Logan and Cullom seemed to be destroying any chance to revive his fortunes.[19]

By November 1 a real scramble had developed in Illinois. For several years Elihu B. Washburne had been estranged from his old friend Grant, and in 1878 and 1879 he began to develop his own candidacy for the 1880 nomination urged on by a number of Prairie State politicians. But in 1879 a rise in Grant's popularity convinced Washburne he had no chance, and he realigned himself behind Grant. William Henry Smith, who despised Washburne, was pleased with the withdrawal yet he feared a third term for Grant would endanger the Republic. Smith met several times with Logan to counter Washburne's influence and with blind overconfidence thought that "in time through good management . . . I hope to see Logan openly advising against the renomination of Grant." [20]

Smith believed Logan would join him against Washburne and Grant, but nothing was farther from the truth. Logan and Washburne wrote often to compare notes on the upcoming contest. Black Jack once even specifically warned Washburne to watch out for the opposition of "Smith & Co." in Chicago. Logan feared that a large number of anti–third-term candidates would enter the battle, thus hurting Grant's cause. For his part, Washburne had found no Sherman strength and predicted a Blaine victory if Grant did not run. But he was confident the party would be "so overwhelming for Grant that Blaine would get out of the road." [21]

On December 13, in reply to a note from Smith, Logan quieted the collector's fears that the Republican congressional delegation was hostile as had been rumored. The senator urged that his suggested appointments be made and threatened to fully inform the voters who was responsible if the appointments were not made. "The same thing was done with me during our other administration," he recalled, "but it only made me stronger with the people." Logan also told Smith he was trying to be friendly to all potential candidates but that Sherman "has had his ears filled" and was not very cordial. "I can stand it," bragged Logan. The senator had seen a letter written by Smith in which he had labeled Logan a "selfish politician," a sentiment "that was not very kind." After Logan's four-page letter of the thirteenth Smith made little effort to "manage" Logan. [22]

The second session of the Forty-sixth Congress brought the Logans back to Washington and to their boardinghouse on Twelfth Street. The senator did little in the three-week pre-Christmas meeting. In early January he read petitions asking for votes for women and for stiff enforcement of antipolygamy laws in Utah. Logan promised to exert himself in the latter cause to settle it on the "basis of pure Christianity." [23]

Late in 1879 Zach Chandler, visiting in Chicago, had died suddenly. Logan had shared a platform with the Michigan senator the night before, and the Logans were at breakfast in the Palmer House when they were informed of his death. On January 28 Black Jack eulogized his longtime colleague. "There was an indescribable something that attracted me and caused me to like the man," said Logan, who, almost inevitably, differed with Shakespeare's "The good is oft interred with his bones," certain that Chandler's good would live on. At a time when the Stalwarts were pushing for a return to the White House, the loss of one of their leaders was serious. Even in his eulogy Logan did not fail to remind his listeners that Chandler had been a "model of stalwart mold" and that his death was "the fall of the stalwart oak." [24]

The central event of the second session for Logan was the attempt to exonerate Union Major General Fitz-John Porter from charges that had led to his court-martial and conviction. At the battle of Second Bull Run in August 1862, Porter had disagreed with an order from his superior, General John Pope, and had failed to move in accordance with that order; for his disobedience he had been court-martialed. After a forty-five-day trial, Porter was convicted in January of 1863 of "willful failure to obey his orders [which] prevented the capture or destruction of the rebel army under Jackson on the 29th of August, 1862."

For more than two decades after his conviction the case remained a subject of controversy. For years Porter sought a rehearing, only to be rebuffed. Finally, in 1878 Hayes ordered a court of inquiry, and that body recommended reversal of the verdict. [25]

Porter's congressional champion was Senator Theodore F. Randolph, a Democrat and chairman of the Military Affairs Committee. All through 1879 Porter labored to win Hayes's support and, when that was achieved, to win exoneration, restoration of rank, and back pay from Congress. The former general vowed, "It is an open fight, and the best way is to stand out open and claim the rights directly." He appealed to Blaine for support and was in regular correspondence with Randolph. The New Jersey senator advised delay through December, promising to bring it to his committee as soon as possible. [26]

Randolph moved cautiously through January despite Porter's prodding. The general heard rumors of a Republican plot against him and denounced Garfield, a member of the original court-martial, as an "arrant coward." He wrote some leading Republicans, including Richard Oglesby, soliciting support, or at least a fair hearing. Randolph polled Senate Republicans but found little inclination on their part to plow through the vast amount of documentation. In mid-January the senator felt the bill would clear the committee and be reported out by month's end.[27]

Senate Bill 1139 reached the floor on January 27. The measure annulled the court-martial, restored Porter's rank, and gave him back pay amounting to about $60,000. When Randolph had finished, Logan rose and told the chamber, "I dissent *in toto*." He denied the president's legal authority to organize the board of inquiry, especially since no error had been found in the court-martial. Porter believed Logan's reasons were weak but recognized that they did "give a hold to the enemy." He greatly feared the case had become a political fight, though he thought some Republicans would support him. All through February, Logan used every parliamentary device possible to block debate.[28]

If Porter had read Logan's correspondence, he would have had greater reason to believe his case had become a partisan issue. Most people attached a definite political significance—the struggle of loyal unionist Republicans against the ever traitorous Democrats. The situation was made to order for a bloody-shirt Stalwart like Logan. The contrast between his candidate, Grant, the savior of the Union, and the Democrats' support for the court-martialed Porter would not be lost on northern voters.[29]

A disturbing question for Porter was the extent of his Democratic support. There was some question that the Democrats would vote the money needed to provide him with back pay. That fear was partially offset by Randolph's assurance that despite Logan's actions, there was no concentrated opposition on the Republican side. Most G.O.P. senators would dodge the issue, and Blaine was even friendly, reported Randolph.[30]

Black Jack would not dodge the issue, and he certainly was not friendly. On March 2 the Illinois Stalwart began the longest congressional address he had ever given. Occasionally interrupted for other business, Logan held the floor until the fifth in a heavily documented oration which takes up forty-five pages in the *Congressional Record*.[31] A reversal would be a dreadful precedent, began Logan, who praised the members of the original court-martial board as men of fairness and courage. Why overturn the verdict of nine honorable officers who had the evidence before them eighteen years earlier, asked Logan. The volunteer general insisted that the president had illegally opened his board of inquiry and that Congress had no power to reverse the court. Not far into his remarks the senator compared Porter to Benedict Arnold.

On the fourth, as Porter listened form the gallery, Logan dealt with the former general's failure to move because of darkness and recited examples from Washington to Grant of commanders who marched at night. The galleries applauded as he swore, "But, sir, we were willing to fight. We loved our country, and we believed in obeying orders." He reminisced of night marches during the Vicksburg campaign when his men had gone into battle singing "John Brown's body lies mouldering in the grave." The galleries burst into mixed applause and hisses.

Porter's actions aided the enemy and prolonged the war, asserted Logan. The volunteer reminded his listeners of those who served well and protested against rewards to one who "faltered in duty." In conclusion, Logan reaffirmed his belief that the bill would set an "evil precedent." The enactment:

> overrides statutes, and is the exercise of unconstitutional power. . . . Its tendency is to applaud insubordination. Its effect will be to encourage derelection of duty. . . . Upon every motive for the public good, without one impulse personal to myself against the subject of the bill.

Reaction to his address was pleasing as an avalanche of letters and telegrams poured into Logan's office. Former general John Pope labeled it the ablest speech delivered in the Senate in years and believed the facts were now "stamped . . . on the public mind and history forever." He added his personal debt of gratitude. Washburne called it a great service to the cause of loyalty, and the president's son, Robert Todd Lincoln, called for congratulations from every loyal American. Generals Manning Force, Stephen Hurlbut, and Benjamin Prentiss hailed the stand and General Irvin McDowell, commanding in California, numbered himself among "the great multitude who admired the masterly way you handled the subject." McDowell, who was involved in the 1862 action, was deeply indebted to Black Jack for his defense. The Republican man in the street, especially those supporting Grant, saw the speech as a pivotal campaign document. "Old Fitz" got just what he deserved, wrote a New Jersey Republican; an Illinoisan called Logan's words "crushing political thunder." [32]

Politics and politics alone motivated Logan, claimed Senator Randolph. Moderate Republican Senator George F. Hoar informed Porter's advocate that the case had become the "pivot" of the congressional boom for Grant. Logan's speech abounded with contrasts between Porter and Grant, included solely to gain gallery applause. If those disgusted by the Stalwart game were to save Porter, wrote Randolph, they would have to act with alacrity. He took heart from indications that all Republicans did not favor the Illinois senator's "brutal zeal." One old-line Stalwart, Simon Cameron, was reported to be upset at the attack on Porter but counseled delay since he would not rise to defend the cashiered soldier until the presidential canvass was over.[33]

General John M. Schofield, who had been involved in Hayes's court of inquiry, was unconvinced by Logan's arguments. He wrote General William T. Sherman that Logan had used only anti-Porter evidence. Once the speech was fully digested, argued Schofield, it would open Logan to ridicule. The general regretted that the matter had become a partisan issue.[34]

The Illinois press reaction to Logan's involvement in the Porter case was mixed. The *Illinois State Register* called Black Jack's speech a "tirade" against a "gallant officer" who should be reinstated. The Democratic paper was convinced Republicans were chiefly attempting to make "political capital" out of the Porter bill. On the other hand the *Chicago Tribune,* often a Logan critic, attacked the Porter bill as "outrageous and audacious" and hailed the senator's "eloquent, valuable, and effective service." The *Illinois State Journal* joined in the praise, calling Logan's long effort "the most masterly speech of the session."[35]

Matt Carpenter followed Logan and endorsed the Illinoisan's stand, making even more pointed comparisons between Grant and Porter. In the next few weeks Black Jack clashed with Randolph and Delaware's Thomas Bayard over the facts of Porter's wartime service as well as the Senate's right to handle the matter.[36]

When the session adjourned on June 16, Porter's bill had not passed. In resignation the former general was glad it had gone as far as it had and hoped for a better reception next winter when, with the election over, he felt "the field will be more fair." Randolph consoled Porter with a report that Logan's venom had embarrassed his party in a presidential year. But he cautioned that the political situation being what it was, a delay would be wise. Randolph also discovered that Logan would probably not be able to distribute his lengthy remarks because of cost. One Porter partisan reported, however, that the Illinoisan had attempted to have the speech distributed free of charge under G.A.R. aegis. The permission was re-fused.[37]

From early April until mid-June John Logan was absent from the Senate. The Porter case had given the Illinois senator and his Stalwart friends a valuable opportunity to advance the Grant candidacy. For months a movement centering in Illinois, New York, and Pennsylvania had been working to align national, state, and local Republicans behind the Grant banner. Mundane legislative work did not claim Logan's time once the attack on Porter had been made. This was the time to take the field and battle to return the Republican party and the United States to true Republicanism.

CHAPTER 10

The Immortal 306

Stalwart Republicans had found four years of Rutherford B. Hayes too long a time to be out of touch with the White House. They resented the administration's attack on patronage citadels in the Treasury and Interior departments. Furthermore, they opposed the abandonment of southern Republicans, which had been the price of Hayes's disputed victory. "When I think of this contest," wrote Maine Republican Thomas B. Reed, soon to become famous as the "Czar" of the House of Representatives, "I cannot help thinking of what Logan says about Grant. 'Wherever we were we knew he was thinking of us and would look out for us.' Wherever *we* find *ourselves* we know that R.B.H. is thinking of us and will look out for himself." [1]

Roscoe Conkling, Don Cameron, and Logan commanded the Stalwart campaign to return the general to the White House. For most of the Hayes administration Grant was out of the United States, touring the world and being honored by heads of state from England to Japan. He returned to the United States in November 1879 and was welcomed to Illinois with great fanfare. Logan joined Shelby Cullom in making welcoming speeches at Galena on the fifth. Black Jack told the enthusiastic gathering that Grant's "usefulness to the people has not ended." Six days later the former president swept into Chicago, where he was feted for several days. On the thirteenth a massive banquet was held with Grant at the head table flanked by Sherman, Sheridan, Logan, and Cullom. [2] After a brief sojourn in Illinois, Grant was urged to take another trip, this time to Florida, the Caribbean, and Mexico. The former president refused to talk about the presidency. While his friends organized, Grant projected the image of an elder statesman who was seeking no public office.

Throughout 1879 John A. Logan worked quietly, taking political soundings and coyly maintaining contact with the Sherman and Washburne forces as well as with the administration through William Henry Smith. On December 13 Logan predicted for Smith that the national convention would meet in Chicago and that Don Cameron would win the Republican national chairman's post. That winter both predictions, considered great victories by the Stalwarts, came true. The Blaine camp was outraged by Cameron's triumph. William E. Chandler, a Blaine leader, believing Sherman had acquiesced in the choice of Cameron, complained: "We can't fight third term, Sherman, and all the sneaks who beat us before."[3]

Among the sneaks was Elihu B. Washburne. The former congressman, whose presidential ambitions Logan had opposed in fear that Washburne might control Illinois politics, persisted in assuring Logan that he had completely abandoned such ambitions. Reports that he remained interested were "devices of the enemy" inasmuch as he was for Grant "first, last and all the time." Washburne closely watched Sherman's candidacy, reporting "herculean efforts" and a rumor started by the Ohioan's followers that Logan would drop Grant and endorse Sherman in return for a patronage payoff. However, Sherman, clinging to a hope Logan could be lured away from the third-termers, reported in late January that the administration's refusal to give the Illinoisan the appointments he wanted "may be the turning point with him."[4]

In late January, Logan at last made his position public in a letter to the *Inter-Ocean*. From that time forward his speeches, including the attack on Fitz-John Porter, were part of a national pattern aimed at promoting Grant. In February, Logan and his Prairie State agents went to work to ensure that the Illinois convention delegation would be solidly for Grant. A meeting of Cook County Republicans on the twenty-fifth was hailed as an "overwhelming success" by two Chicago Stalwarts. One of them circulated the story that two Blaine men were hired attorneys for Jay Gould's railroads and "their usefulness for Blaine was soon gone." The *Inter-Ocean* endorsed Grant while the city's *Times, Journal, Staats-Zeitung,* and *Tribune* fought the third-term bid, with the last named strongly for Blaine. When the *Chicago Times* asked Robert G. Ingersoll if he thought Logan could deliver Illinois for Grant, he replied in the negative: "Illinois is as little 'owned' as any state in this Union." F.W. Palmer of the *Inter-Ocean* informed Logan, still in Washington, that contrary to the senator's instincts he had "no confidence in the sincerity of Washburne's professions for Grant." [5]

Those professions continued, but they were interspersed with warnings. Early in the month Washburne feared an anti-Grant boom in northern Illinois and reported bad news from Indiana. He thought Logan might counter the latter since "you are very strong there." Later Washburne was sure the situation had improved and "our old chief will go through." [6]

While he was sending on this information, Washburne received notes urging him to remain in the race. Thurlow Weed was skeptical of Grant's chances of victory, and former Indiana Congressman John Coburn flatly denied Grant could be nominated. The Hoosier advised Washburne "all [Grant's] friends will rally to you in a mass and with enthusiasm." Several Illinoisans urged Washburne to remain available and ready for a transfer of support at the convention. Perhaps Palmer's warning to Logan was not an empty one; this flattery could erode Washburne's loyalty. [7]

James G. Blaine remained in the shadows as the quests for the nomination began. Tempered by defeat in 1876, he and his followers cautiously avoided outward activity while keeping a close eye on Illinois and the third-termers. A Chicagoan boasted "we will have no Cameron or Conkling own this state" and saw a Blaine victory as the first step in Logan's slide to oblivion. Jerome Chaffee, however, feared that a Grant triumph in Illinois would clear the way for the former president's nomination. Logan's state was the "pivotal" one for Blaine, thought Chaffee, but he admitted his chances were minute. [8]

Badgered by the Chicago press for years, Logan had one lone voice of support—the *Inter-Ocean*. The newspaper had backed him in the past and it editorialized in favor of Grant in 1880. But Black Jack was a vexing friend, and relations between Logan and *Inter-Ocean* editor William Penn Nixon were strained that spring. The journal, in a perpetual financial crisis, needed funds and Logan and his friends had provided none since 1878. In addition to money problems, Nixon was afraid the Grant tide would shortly ebb. Logan replied, protesting that he had no money and attempting to buoy Nixon's spirits on the nomination question. The senator promised redoubled efforts in favor of Grant and restated his personal friendship for Nixon. [9]

As Illinois counties chose delegates to the state convention scheduled for May, Grant fell behind Blaine. By April, the third-termers had only

Don Cameron. *Reproduced from the collections of the Library of Congress.*

27 of 85 chosen delegates, and Logan suddenly left Congress to work in Illinois, telling the *New York Times,* "General Grant is in the hands of his friends, and they will not withdraw him until he is beaten, no matter how many ballots are taken. That is the whole case." The departure came in response to forecasts of a Blaine upsurge and an appeal for unity and assistance. Mary alerted Will Tucker that his father-in-law was *"coming on business"* and asked that he muster their Cook County allies, telling no one else the senator was coming home. As Logan left the capital, Washburne confidentially assured him Grant's stock was on the rise. When he reached Chicago, Logan closeted himself at the Palmer House with Dan Shepard, F.W. Palmer, M.L. Joslyn, and "Long" Jones, four of his closest Illinois Stalwart advisors. They "went to work on the all absorbing topic." Soon after he arrived Logan addressed a large gathering at the Music Hall. He entered the hall to a rising crescendo of cheers, and his address was often interrupted by applause. This enthusiasm notwithstanding, the *Chicago Tribune* reported Logan was "very much scared over the situation" in Illinois, and the senator admitted Blaine had strong support in the state.[10]

Immediately after his Chicago speech Logan and Will Tucker went by rail to Egypt to work for delegates from the southern and central tier of counties pledged to the general. Their efforts were so successful that Logan wrote Mary on the nineteenth, "matters improving and will be all right." Logan returned to Chicago late in April and established a headquarters for the delegate push. Daily telegrams from across the state poured in generally indicating an improvement in their position, occasionally requesting aid or protesting against political chicanery by Blaine men. Washburne, who remained in close touch with Logan, was growing confident that Grant would win easily, perhaps even by *"acclamation."*[11]

A letter Logan sent to Henry W. Draper, a Hancock County Republican, was typical of his courting ritual.

> I have been advised of an effort that is being made to carry your county in the convention to be held to elect delegates to the State Convention against Genl. Grant. Now I have no interest in Genl. Grant personally any more than I have in any other good Republican whom I believed could and would properly administer the affairs of government. But I want to see Ills. stand by her own distinguished son and I further believe that he can be more certainly

elected than any of the other candidates. . . . I think Ills. can ill afford to be led by the gentlemen and papers that are making the fight against Grant into yielding the leadership to a man in no sense interested in us or the West. And particularly when we remember the records of these men and their organ the 'Chicago Tribune.' The Stalwarts have always had to fight this paper and these men to sustain true republicanism. Trusting your county will send a sound Grant delegation to Springfield.[12]

Logan's protestation of only passing interest in Grant as no more than a favorite son was surely transparent. The attack on Blaine as an easterner uninterested in the West was a common tactic employed by the third-termers in Illinois.

The various third-term enemies watched the reported improvement of Grant's fortunes with a mixture of trepidation, disbelief, or cynical pleasure. An Illinois Democratic congressman was pleased that Grant would be nominated since he would be easiest to defeat. John Sherman remained confident of his own chances, believed Ohio would stand solidly behind him, and refused Logan's April request that he endorse Grant. From an Illinois friend Sherman received a warning that it would be useless to try to carry that state against the *"machine."* Blaine would not be deterred, however, and he told Schurz on April 28 that he still maintained a lead over Grant in Illinois delegates selected to that point. One enemy Logan, Conkling, and Cameron faced was Republican war-horse Thurlow Weed. As the prospect of a Grant nomination grew, Weed wrote leading Republicans identical letters warning that the former president could not carry New York whereas Washburne, Blaine, or Sherman could. Finally, the *Illinois Staats-Zeitung*, while denouncing the third-termers, believed that Black Jack did not really care who won as long as he remained Republican state boss.[13]

May was showdown time in Illinois. Some county delegates, including Cook County's, were still to be chosen before the state convention met on the nineteenth. Early in the month Logan, who was briefly confined to bed with a high fever, reported steady Grant gains outside of Chicago, and by the seventh his confidence in victory was high. On May 8, Cook County Republicans chose among delegates pledged to Grant, Blaine, or Washburne. They returned 70 Grant men, 63 for Washburne, and 45 for the Maine senator. Black Jack was pleased that Blaine had trailed and condemned Washburne, who he believed was still a candidate despite his vows of support for Grant. He was confident that the vote statewide would give Grant a clear victory over both Blaine and Washburne. The opposition *Illinois State Register* agreed and warned the Blaine-Washburne forces that they were no match for the "sharp and timely tricks" of Logan and A.M. "Long" Jones.[14]

When the Cook County delegates elected on the eighth met on May 10 there was a division between third-termers and Blaine-Washburne forces. The opposition's thirty-eight-vote lead made it appear that only anti-Grant delegates from Cook County would go to Springfield. When the anti-Grant majority began to investigate some credentials disputes, Logan, in a rage at the insult, staged a bolt. The Grant men assembled at the Palmer House and carried on independent deliberations. The Stalwart leader was convinced that the state convention would settle the dispute by accepting all or at least part of the Grant slate. Thus, by bolting, Logan felt he had averted a complete shutout and had ensured Grant's statewide triumph. "Don't be alarmed about it. It is all right and will be sustained," he wrote Mary, who remained in Washington. He also told her to reveal the strategy to Conkling. The senator himself wired Don Cameron the results, which he felt had "settled Illinois for Grant now till Gabriel calls."[15]

Expecting a "hard fight" the senator left Chicago on the sixteenth for the May 19 state convention. The convention drew the largest number of visitors in its history. All hotels were packed and even cot space was at a premium. When it assembled, the convention showed a Grant majority outside of Cook County, and Logan was able to place key Stalwarts on the Credentials Committee. That body finally decided to split the Cook County votes, giving Blaine and Washburne 56 and Grant 36—another Logan coup.[16]

An even greater victory lay just ahead. The Illinois Republicans usually selected national convention delegates by congressional district. These men were traditionally bound to support a chosen candidate for only one or two ballots, after which time they were free to act as they wished. On May 20 Black Jack proposed a procedural change. He suggested that the entire Illinois delegation be picked by a committee of the state convention. Logan reasoned that only then would the state convention be certain that the delegation truly reflected the state body's majority view. He further proposed that the selection committee be named by the convention's presiding officer, in this case a good Stalwart and a long-time friend, Green B. Raum. Logan's remarks touched off what the *Chicago Tribune* called the "most exciting session probably ever known in a Republican State Convention in Illinois." [17] Blaine and Washburne men protested, and a heated debate ran far into the night. At 2 A.M. on the twenty-first the Logan proposal came to a vote. It passed 309 to 304. The next move was an instruction that all Prairie State delegates vote as a unit for Ulysses S. Grant. The vote was 399 to 285 in favor of the enforced unit rule. The enraged *Chicago Tribune* reported that at the point of victory Logan turned to his followers and "winked." Then he said to Raum, "That ends the business." [18]

The Grant victory was a masterpiece of political manipulation managed by John A. Logan and his lieutenants. Logan was elated at his victory and his confederate A.M. "Long" Jones crowed to Mary: "Glory. Genl. Logan at the head of the Illinois delegation solid for Grant. Will cast forty-two votes for Genl. Grant, the next president." [19]

Anti-Grant men viewed the Illinois Republicans' turbulent May with dismay and revulsion. The ever vigilant William Henry Smith met often with Black Jack and reported him cordial and, more interestingly, not at all sure Grant could win the nomination. He also found Logan friendly to Sherman, who, the Illinois senator said, might "with good management" be nominated. Whether the pessimism over Grant and friendship with Sherman were genuine or shrewdly stated to disarm Smith is impossible to determine. Hayes's Illinois friend gave grudging praise to Logan for his work in Illinois. Smith was sure that "but for the energy of John A. Logan and the devotion of the machine at his back Genl. Grant would not have received one-fifth of the Republican support of the state." On May 15 Smith wrote, "I believe the 'machine' will be able through sharp practice to make the delegation to the National Convention practically solid for Grant." After meeting with Black Jack, Smith told Hayes that the senator had little hope for a Grant nomination; rather he "is really fighting for his own political existence. He has in view a candidate that will be friendly to him." Was this an overture to Sherman or indeed any potential Republican candidate who would, in return for Logan's backing, provide unquestioned patronage and leave the Illinois machine alone? When the Springfield convention had concluded, Smith agreed with Hayes that the "popular will had been disregarded." [20]

For his part, John Sherman agreed that it was best for him to assume a watch-and-wait attitude, being prepared to "take advantage of events." Coolness and moderation were to be his policy. On May 15 Sherman promised to confer with Logan as soon as possible.[21]

Washburne's tactics are puzzling. His letters to Logan had slowed and then stopped altogether. Smith believed the Washburne men in Illinois did not believe in a Washburne nomination; his candidacy was merely a tactic to stop Grant. Through May, Washburne received requests for a clarification of his position as well as requests from third-termers for an unequivocal statement of support for the man he had called "our old chief." But he silently let events run their course.[22]

Washburne was also playing a tricky game. Either he could not control his Cook County friends or he made no effort to control them. *New York Times* editor George Jones and Chicago third-term supporter Emory A. Storrs urged Washburne to work for Grant, but he remained silent. William Henry Smith was convinced Washburne had been nursing a grudge against Grant for several years, and Adam Badeau, Grant's close friend, wrote that the general always believed that Washburne had betrayed him.[23]

Blaine men in Illinois were frustrated. They were convinced Grant would still fail and urged large anti–third-term demonstrations in Chicago during the national convention. The members of the Logan-Conkling-Cameron triumvirate were branded "political devils," but it was admitted they were a difficult combination to defeat. The greatest hope of the Blaine men seemed to lie in breaking the unit rule at the national convention.[24]

Some reformers were so disturbed at the drift of events they seemed ready for another bolt. Horace White wrote fellow journalist Murat Halstead that Schurz counseled immediate action after the Chicago nomination "in order to arrest public attention and show people that the iniquity is to be resisted." White added, "On reflection I think he is right." A Grant nomination might bring a split similar to the Liberal Republican movement of 1872.[25]

The labors of the Grant triumvirate gave Grant a lead in pledged delegates when the Chicago convention met in June. The trio was determined to force the unit rule on the party, thus holding all anti-Grant votes in their three states and delivering those votes for the former president. The sixty-three votes involved could be the difference when the roll was called. The tenacious, aggressive Stalwarts, through parliamentary maneuver and spellbinding oratory, were certain of success. Two of their greatest dangers were their overconfidence and ruthlessness. Conkling especially was so imperious that it was thought he might force the opposition to coalesce.[26]

The national committee, chaired by Cameron, could be pivotal in deciding the manner of voting. Anti–third-termers claimed a committee majority, but the chairman maintained the body had no power over the convention's rules. He refused to entertain any motions dealing with rules. Since it was the prerogative of the national committee to name the temporary chairman, who would preside over the convention, Grant leaders feared the selection of an opponent. In that event a pro-Grant candidate would be nominated from the floor and Cameron would rule that the unit rule was to be used for this contest. Once established, the unit rule would prevail throughout the convention.[27]

On May 31 those opposed to the Stalwarts tried to get a resolution through the national committee to reject the unit rule. Cameron sat in silence refusing to hear the motion. This deadlock might have been resolved by the committee's removal of Cameron from the chairmanship. Instead, rather than alienate the powerful Stalwarts, whose aid would be needed against the Democrats, the anti-Grant members suggested a compromise. They proposed Massachusetts Senator George F. Hoar, pledged to no candidate, as temporary chairman, and a convention roll call on the unit rule. Cameron continued to resist, but under renewed threats of the Pennsylvanian's removal the Stalwarts finally agreed. The convention then rejected the unit rule; sixty-three votes were freed. Grant's chances for victory dimmed.[28]

The seventh Republican National Convention met to the accompaniment of mass meetings for and against the third term. Logan joined black leader Frederick Douglass in addressing a crowd that the *Inter-Ocean* estimated at twenty thousand in Grant's behalf. A counterdemonstration of ten thousand met to urge the election of anyone other than the hero of Appomattox. The Illinois delegation's headquarters at the Grand Pacific swarmed with senators, state legislators, officeseekers, and the usual flotsam and jetsam of American politics, drawn to one of the nation's greatest political and social rites.[29]

Six men were placed in nomination by the Republican party. Grant, Blaine, Washburne, and Sherman were joined by William Windom and George Edmunds. Logan gave the first speech for Grant, but the principal effort was by Conkling. With 379 votes needed to nominate, Grant polled 304 on the first ballot, 20 more than Blaine in second place, and far ahead of Sherman's 93. Again and again the roll of the states was called and the deadlock continued. Grant held above 300 but was far short of the necessary 379, while the others could not combine on one of their number so as to push through to victory. The third-term triumvirate was accused of a Fabian policy of delay aimed at wearing the convention down, thus assuring a Grant victory by default and exhaustion. But delay helped little. For thirty-three ballots Grant's vote hovered between 303 and 309. For twenty-nine of those ballots the Illinois vote held at 24 for Grant, 10 for Blaine, and 8 for Washburne. Then, as the clerk reached the thirty-fourth ballot, Ohio Senator James A. Garfield began picking up votes. On the thirty-fifth ballot the former schoolteacher and Civil War general became a serious threat, and one roll call later he mustered 399 votes and the nomination was his. To the horror of the reformers, the vice-presidential place went to Conkling's political crony Chester A. Arthur.[30]

Thrusting back disappointment, Logan rose to second Garfield after his selection was assured. "In union and harmony there is strength," asserted the Stalwart. "Whatever may have transpired in this convention . . . I hope that in our conclusion it will pass from our minds." Prolonged cheers greeted Logan's concluding vow: "The men who stood by Grant's banners will be seen in the front of this contest on every field." As an Illinois delegate Logan had fought for a Grant nomination, proudly telling the convention, "I am a steadfast Stalwart Republican and never scratched a ticket." Now he intended to honor that pledge. The senator was chosen Illinois' national committeeman and was also named to the committee to notify Garfield of his selection.[31]

The Stalwarts had failed; never again was this faction to come as close to a Republican nomination. Within a year, Conkling would retire to private life, and Don Cameron would never match his father's power and longevity. Logan was left to lead the Stalwart remnant in the face of civil service reform, southern redemption, and eventual Democratic victory. The 1880 convention was the last great moment of those men who thought they alone understood and represented true Republicanism. Even at that moment chances of victory were not good. Arthur's biographer said, "Stalwart hopes were based on arrogance and fantasy," and neither were winning political tools. Those who fought for Grant to the last thought of themselves as men apart, a special breed. Conkling's fellow

New York Senator, Thomas C. Platt, listed the names of all 306 men who voted for Grant on the final ballot when he wrote his *Autobiography.* Badges were printed and subsequent meetings saw aging party members reminisce over the 1880 battle. In 1893, long after Logan's death, the governor of Pennsylvania invited Mary Logan to a dinner for members of the 306 still living. They toasted their fallen leaders, Grant, Conkling, and Logan, and boasted with pride that they belonged to the "Immortal 306." [32]

In June 1880 there were no cheers or toasts. An angry band of Stalwarts was not placated by Arthur's nomination. Some, led by Conkling, stalked away determined to do nothing for the ticket. For most of them a time to think and perhaps some overtures from the nominee would have to precede active campaigning.

The anti-Grant men were relieved. William Henry Smith at first had feared the convention might do to the Republicans what the Charleston convention had done to the Democrats in 1860. A civil service plank in the platform and the defeat of the unit rule revived his hopes, and he was certain Conkling's high-handed manner had hurt his faction. Without naming Logan, Smith told President Hayes, "The promises made to me in advance . . . by some of the [Grant] leaders, when the time for action came, were disregarded, and I was convinced deceit had been in their hearts from the first." [33]

In June the Logans parted, Mary going to Chicago and then on to Carbondale to see a coal mine which had been opened on their land. John went to New York on business. While there he went to Coney Island, which he found "the most lovely spot I have ever seen." He promised Mary that if they did not go to Europe the following summer, they would spend some time at the New York seaside resort. [34]

It did not take Black Jack long to rally behind his party's nominee. When he returned to Illinois in June, he found a letter from one of his Stalwart friends in the revenue service indicating readiness to contribute to a campaign fund and to work for Garfield. On July 20 Logan wrote Garfield that political prospects looked good in Illinois. "I opened the campaign in Southern Ills. last Thursday and had a good meeting," he observed. The senator predicted, "You will run . . . ahead of our state ticket. The Stalwarts here will do their duty and . . . I will move matters as best I can." Three days later Garfield replied, thanking Logan for sending a speech, which the nominee called "able, thorough, and comprehensive." Garfield asked Logan for his choice of speaking engagements in Ohio and concluded, "There are many things in the management of the campaign about which I should be glad to talk with you more fully. . . . Why can't you make me a visit soon?" Iowa Senator William B. Allison also reported seeing Logan and finding him hard at work for the ticket.[35] Target of the Republican campaigners was an able former Union general, Winfield Scott Hancock, the Democratic nominee.

Logan was also convinced that Garfield could capture several southern states if the party sent "several of our leading statesmen, men of national reputation whom the cutthroats would not dare molest." Although he did not say so, perhaps he thought of himself as one of those who could regain the South for Republicanism.[36]

August, a bustling month for Logan, began with a request from Garfield that Black Jack accompany the presidential party to New York. The Illinois senator did so and he made a speech at the August 5 strategy conference. Logan was upset to discover that the sulking Conkling had still not taken the campaign trail. "Lord Roscoe" did not join the Garfield party in New York, and he was severely criticized. By the tenth, Logan was speaking in Portland, Maine; he was pleased with his response, but upset over the length of his journey. Mary was "disgusted" with Conkling's stance and feared Hancock might take New York. "I am afraid of defeat some times," she quaked. Grant too feared a Democratic victory and the general agreed to join Logan in speaking for Garfield since "it will not do to be beaten now."[37]

Logan joined Conkling's lieutenant Thomas C. Platt and Don Cameron as Stalwart representatives on the Republican campaign executive committee. Marshall Jewell was chairman of that body and Stephen W. Dorsey secretary. Dorsey's appointment was a "sop to the Stalwarts" and came after Logan threatened to pull out of the campaign unless the Illinoisan was permitted to name the secretary. Among other members were Chauncey I. Filley, Stephen W. Elkins, and William E. Chandler. When a Western Executive Committee headquarters was established in Chicago Logan was named chairman. Jewell talked over money problems with Logan while Dorsey heard from Charles Farwell, who decried Logan's boast that he would carry Illinois. Logan's tactics would probably "crush out as many Republicans as he could," thought the hostile Farwell.[38]

In September, Black Jack took his stump style to Indiana. On the fifth at Indianapolis he gave the oration he considered his best speech of the year. A deeply appreciative Garfield sent Logan warm thanks for his efforts. Chester A. Arthur also wrote Logan begging for his return to the East on election eve. "I am particularly anxious that you should speak," wrote the dapper Arthur, "I beg you to come." Busy in the West, the senator could not accede to the vice-presidential candidate's plea. Numerous lesser lights begged for Logan's voice all over Indiana and Illinois. Pleading a rapidly weakening voice and a full schedule, Logan had to refuse many. He did participate in the conference at Garfield's farm in Ohio that brought Conkling into the campaign.[39]

Although Republican candidates were optimistic in the fall of 1880, Logan warned his party not to relax before November. As an active speaker and as chairman of the western division of the National Campaign Committee, Black Jack labored until the votes were counted. Garfield defeated Hancock 214 to 144 in the electoral college and, narrowly, 4,449,052 to 4,442,035 in the popular count. In Illinois, Garfield wound up with a lead of 318,037 to 277,321. Logan was pleased that another Republican would sit in the White House. Roscoe Conkling had joined the campaign late in the day, but the Illinois senator had vigorously spent himself in Garfield's behalf throughout the canvass. Such support would surely be rewarded, and Logan hoped for four more years of patronage power. Perhaps such loyalty would bring even greater reward. After the general election an Illinois state's attorney congratulated Logan on his role in the triumph and asked, "Why should not Illinois furnish the President in 1884?"[40] Logan might have replied rhetorically, "Why not indeed?"

Chapter 11

A Hornet's Nest in the Senate

Weakened by his exertions on the long campaign trail and crippled by his persistent rheumatism that winter, John A. Logan was sent to bed. He was in Egypt tending his coal-mining venture at Murphysboro when bitter early winter blasts stopped work on the mine shaft and slowed the senator's recovery.[1]

Logan's illness prevented his answering the opening Senate roll call on December 6. He and Mary did not arrive in Washington until the eleventh, and the senator made his first appearance in the Senate two days later. During this final session of the Forty-sixth Congress Black Jack held his appointments on the committees of Privileges and Elections, Military Affairs, Indian Affairs, and Territories.[2]

The Fitz-John Porter case reached the Senate floor again on December 13; Logan, protesting he was "not physically able" to join in the debate, made few remarks. Senator Theodore F. Randolph and the other Porter defenders believed (as the cashiered general had forecast in 1880) that the preelection hysteria had passed; consequently they brought forward another relief bill. The Illinois senator reminded his listeners of his earlier remarks, which had satisfied "a great many gentlemen." Logan repeated his denial that a court-martial could be overturned in this manner. Lamenting that he was "feeble," he nevertheless remained in the chamber rather than accept a pair: if a vote was to be taken, Logan insisted on answering the roll call with a vigorous "no!" The following day Black Jack told Porter's advocates that the only way the former soldier could be returned to the army was by a presidential pardon. The Illinoisan accused Randolph, chairman of the Military Affairs Committee, of trying to obviate Porter's appeal for a pardon because he knew that none would be forthcoming. Once again Logan mentioned the unhealthy precedent

that reinstatement by the Congress would set, and once again he alluded
to his earlier speech:

> I exhausted my physical strenth on this bill before us trying to
> demonstrate to the country that this man was an unfit man to go
> into the army. I am not able to do it again, but I will take time
> enough before it does pass to expose it.

"Whom the gods wish to destroy they first make mad," warned the Stalwart. Finally, Randolph accepted an amendment that put Porter on the
retired list as a colonel but gave him no money to cover the period from
court-martial to reinstatement. With Logan voting with the minority, the
amendment passed 36 to 21. Then the entire bill passed 38 to 20. Logan,
joined by most Republicans and by his Prairie State colleague David
Davis, again stood with the minority. Then, to Logan's delight, the House
refused to pass the bill.[3]

In December, Logan, through Conkling, received a plea from Frederick Douglass to prevent his removal as U.S. marshall for the District of
Columbia. Southern prejudice was behind the move, declared Douglass,
who asked Conkling to alert Logan—who, the black leader was certain,
would "unite with yourself in any effort you may make in my behalf."
Grant also wrote late in the year asking Logan's support for a measure
retiring E.O.C. Ord as a major general.[4]

Ironically the first business of the new year was a bill to place Grant
on the army retired list. When Logan introduced the measure, the Stalwarts joined to remind the Senate of Grant's "eminent public services."
Randolph objected to a hasty consideration of the bill only to draw a spir-
ited response from the Illinoisan. Black Jack reminded the New Jersey
Democrat that many similar bills had been passed and that current opposition was based on personality. Missouri's George Vest could not
"consent to provide places for generals, no matter how distinguished,
who like ourselves have taken the chances of political life and have been
beaten." Logan jumped to his feet and chastised Vest for refusing Grant
what had been given to lesser men. Through the remainder of the session,
Logan tried to get the bill onto the calendar, only to be blocked by objections. When the Forty-sixth Congress ended the bill had not been passed.[5]

Despite Logan's contention that many bills like the Grant bill had
passed, this one was slightly different. Grant was to be retired at full rank

and pay rather than the usual three-quarters pay given those on the army's retired list. Army Commander Sherman opposed the action, writing his brother, John, that he regarded it as a measure that might prejudice the interests and harmony of the service; Sherman also wrote to Logan in the same vein. Denying anything but the highest regard for Grant, the army chief again asserted that the army would be "harmed" and the situation among Grant, Sheridan, and himself would be made "uncomfortable." Logan acquired a copy of the letter General Sherman sent to his brother and sent it, together with the letter he had received from the general, to Grant. The former president was sure General Sherman's letter to his brother was "an afterthought." He continued:

> He feels ashamed of his first course and has written to his brother to hedge. He is not looking after the interests of the Army, nor do I believe he represents their feelings in regard to the bill.

President Hayes supported the bill and for a time was estranged from General Sherman because Sherman opposed it. Sherman wrote Hayes to tell him that Logan was the source of the conflict. He dredged up Logan's frustration of 1864 and maintained that "ever since Logan has moved heaven and earth to revenge himself on me; and has labored to make a breach between Grant and me."[6]

The first quarter of 1881 was a period given over to forming a new cabinet—and of scrambling for appointive offices in the new administration. Garfield hoped to placate the Stalwarts by naming some Grant men to his cabinet. Logan's name was prominently mentioned, and the president-elect wrote the Illinois senator for advice on "several subjects connected with the organization of the new administration." Black Jack replied that he preferred the Senate; instead he pressed Robert Todd Lincoln as his choice for secretary of war. Lincoln thanked Logan for his support, saying he was uncertain he wanted the spot but urging Logan to "argue" him out of his doubts. Grant joined Logan in the search for a cabinet post for some Illinoisan, and when Lincoln's name was mentioned he supported him even though he doubted the president's son could financially afford a cabinet seat. Somehow Logan's persuasion overcame Lincoln's reservations, and Robert Todd Lincoln was chosen Garfield's secretary of war. Other Illinoisans coveted cabinet posts, and Chicago Stalwart attorney Emory A. Storrs was angry at Logan when the senator refused to support him for attorney general. When the president's choices were finally announced, Grant was not pleased. He sent Conkling his complaints and urged the New Yorker to round up Logan and Cameron for a meeting at the Willard as soon as he got to the capital.[7]

Garfield's appeal for advice was one evidence of Logan's increasing role as a Republican power broker, and there were others. Pennsylvanian John Cessna, running for the Senate, petitioned Logan to join with Conkling "and a few more of the 306" in influencing Don Cameron in his behalf. Shelby Cullom joined the senator in bombarding Garfield with demands that Logan's political supporter A.M. "Long" Jones be named marshall for northern Illinois. So adamant was Logan about this appointment that William Henry Smith cautioned Hayes that it would be unwise to press his own choice on Garfield. It was a time for Illinois Stalwarts to be rewarded and to freeze out Blaine men. One member of that group would not even ask for office since he knew Logan would move to block him. Nevertheless he felt his time would come since "Genl. Logan will never dare to carry such a high hand again in this State for any man as he did for Grant." The Halfbreed politico would soon learn that Logan could be just as high-handed for himself as for Grant.[8]

The pressure of the horde of office-seekers combined with winter colds tired the Logans. The senator had little rest and was "nearly crazy with the pressure," and financial worries still plagued them. Because the coal mine had not yet proved profitable, the couple, living at Mrs. Lockwood's boardinghouse at 812 Twelfth Street, had to practice rigid economies. Mary feared her husband might "break down" and she coveted either a drastic change in his life style or a lengthy rest. But there were social pleasures. They attended a diplomatic reception and accepted the Hayes's invitation to a presidential reception on February 24.[9]

That winter Oliver O. Howard, who had succeeded Logan as commander of the Army of the Tennessee, became commandant of West Point. Logan praised the choice, and the general sent his thanks. For some time the Illinoisan had wanted an oath administered to cadets in which they swore primary allegiance to the United States government. Howard informed Logan that such an oath was being required and a lecture on the "folly of state sovereignty" was being given the entire corps. The senator was very gratified with Howard's regime; past management having been so poor, Logan thought that the academy might have been abolished altogether. He applauded the oath and lecture since West Point correctly should instill national loyalty and eradicate thoughts of rebellion and states' rights. Always opposed to West Point's aristocratic snobbery, Logan wanted Howard to "set aside this disgusting aristocracy and overbearing spirit," stop hazing, and wipe out the "immoral tendencies of West Point." [10]

Logan, complaining that Congress was doing very little, ran into opposition to his bill restoring the franking privilege, which had been done away with some years earlier. He believed the frank facilitated official business and properly took the burden of postage off of solons, some of whom, like himself, could not bear it. George Edmunds and David Davis supported Logan, and Henry Gassaway Davis of West Virginia led the opposition. The bill was sent to committee, reported out, and blocked from consideration by Democratic maneuver. [11]

The final business of the session was a Democratic attack on Civil War pensions. West Virginia's Davis charged widespread fraud and wanted to investigate the use of the funds. Logan snorted that it was not the Senate's right to follow the recipient to see how he used his money. The great champion of the Civil War veterans assailed Davis's language as "common and vulgar" and labeled his remarks "very thin." He challenged Davis and later Iowa's Samuel J. Kirkwood to prove their charges of several million dollars' worth of fraud. The figure was purposely inflated to scare the public, claimed Logan. He defended the veterans:

> The soldiers generally are poor men. This country was not entirely saved by the wealthy men of the country. The majority of the men who carried the muskets, and whom I stand here to defend to-day, were poor men. [12]

That session Logan found time to defend an old foe and sorrowfully bury an old comrade. His defense of the Interior Department's Indian policy during Carl Schurz's term brought "particular gratitude" from the reformer since the two men had not "been in accord" on past political issues. When Wisconsin Stalwart Matt Carpenter died in February, Logan was named to the committee to supervise the funeral. With a projected party deadlock in the new Senate, Mary Logan called Carpenter's death "a great loss to the Senate." [13]

The new Senate met on March 4 to attend the inauguration and confirm the president's appointees. Veterans Allen Thurman, Theodore F.

Randolph, and Hannibal Hamlin, along with the lone Negro member, Blanche K. Bruce, were gone; but John Sherman had returned. Most significant, Matt Carpenter's death and the resignation of Senators Blaine, Windom, and Kirkwood to join Garfield's cabinet temporarily left the Republicans with four places unfilled, which encouraged the Democrats to challenge them for Senate leadership. George Pendleton presented the Democrats' committee choices, which the opposition refused to accept. A large crowd jammed the galleries to watch the "Bourbon" Congress give way to the Republicans, but they were to be disappointed. Until the four Republicans were replaced, the Democrats could hold up committee assignments, Senate organization, and confirmation of Garfield's appointees. Early in the session David Davis, who maintained an independent posture on most votes, announced he would vote on organization with the Democrats. When the four G.O.P. replacements arrived the Republicans would equal the Democrats, putting control of the chamber in the hands of Virginia independent William Mahone. Rumor placed Mahone in the Republican camp, but his vote was uncertain. On the fourteenth Georgia's Ben Hill "taunted and abused" Mahone in a scathing attack on the Virginian. Later that day, as tension gripped galleries and floor alike, the diminutive Virginian with the iron-gray beard cast his first vote in a routine procedural matter: he joined the Republicans.[14]

The deadlock, however, was not to end quickly. Until the newly elected Republicans took their seats the Democrats filibustered. For weeks the Senate did nothing but argue, engaging in some of the bitterest acrimony heard in the chamber since the Civil War. Logan, now seated in the first row, was in the center of several of the most heated exchanges. On March 24 he sparred with Joe Brown of Georgia over the two men's political careers in general and change of party in particular. Logan concluded the contretemps remarking, "I do not think our former history is very interesting anyhow."[15]

On March 30 Brown's Georgian confrere, Ben Hill, attacked Logan as an 1861 secessionist. The gallery roared its approval when the swarthy senator with the drooping mustache flatly called the charge a falsehood. Hill announced his acceptance of Logan's word. Black Jack then damned the Democrats for continually digging up already disproved accusations and blasted them for waving the bloody shirt as hard and as often as his own party did. The *New York Times*, disgusted with the aimless, unproductive debate, called Hill's attack "stale and dull." In the Prairie State the *Illinois State Journal* called Logan's response to the "hair-brained" Hill "firm and forcible," and the *Chicago Tribune* agreed. But the *Illinois State Register* was pleased with Hill's remarks and advised its readers that the remarks were very close to the truth.[16]

As the session staggered into April, the fiery Illinoisan battled Indiana's Dan Voorhees and South Carolina's Manning Butler. Political violence was the subject, and Logan reviewed the record of southern attacks on Negroes and Unionists. He presented General Sheridan's report on outrages only to draw Voorhees's and Butler's replies that it was all a lie. When he assailed the report, Voorhees snarled at Logan "now make the most of that." Butler sat directly across the aisle from Black Jack and he charged that there were as many deaths in Illinois as in South Carolina. Quick to retort, the Prairie State senator told the difference: in Illinois authorities were accustomed to suppressing riot and disorder; in the South "ku kluxers" used force to deny civil rights. Applause and hisses swirled around the gallery, and it had to be cleared. Butler leaped to his feet; when Logan asked not to be interrupted, the Carolinian said he would not have Logan dictate to him. The much calmer Illinoisan passed this off as meaningless "bravado" and said excited behavior was no substitute for brains. At one point in the nasty and intemperate debate Logan said, in an audible aside, "This is a hornet's nest, is it not? They are swarming it seems."[17]

Logan accompanied Senator Carpenter's body to Wisconsin and was absent from the chamber for two weeks. When he returned he made a long speech fully reviewing his pre–Civil War career in an attempt to silence his critics forever. As a part of his evidence he read an unsolicited letter from Mississippi's L.Q.C. Lamar testifying in the senator's behalf. Lamar had served with Logan in the 1861 House; he wrote: "You expressed the deep regret you felt at my proposed action [in support of secession] and deplored the contemplated movement in terms as strong as any I heard from any Republican. . . ." After a passionate appeal for fairness and an end to this shadow over his record, Black Jack asked that "these vile slanders" be laid to rest.[18]

In early May the Republicans finally broke the filibuster and the new committees were named. Logan returned to the chair of the Military Affairs Committee and remained on Indian Affairs. He gained two new assignments, both significant, the Appropriations and Judiciary committees. The Senate confirmed several of Garfield's nominees, but in May an explosion between the president and New York Stalwarts Conkling and Platt ended the frail postelection party harmony. The Senate adjourned on May 20 after a profitless session, which ended with the G.O.P. perilously divided.[19]

A patronage battle between Conkling and his New York Halfbreed and Reformer opponents, many of whom had supported Garfield's nomination, led to a crisis. The new president had, at first, appointed only men acceptable to the Stalwarts. Under fire from the press and from Halfbreed leaders, including Secretary of State James G. Blaine, Garfield changed his selections, including his nominee for the powerful New York collectorship. William H. Robertson, Conkling's greatest New York foe, was Garfield's nominee. Fearing a debilitating party split, many Senate Republicans tried to persuade Garfield to drop Robertson. But the president held his ground, provoking a shocking reaction by the New York senators: on May 16 Conkling and Platt suddenly resigned and returned to Albany to seek vindication from the legislature. For once, "Lord Roscoe" had overplayed his hand; the legislature retired the two men to private life.[20]

Fellow Stalwart Logan had no forewarning of the New Yorkers' action and was at first puzzled by their reasoning. He advised Mary that he would have no public comment "as I have concluded to take care of myself." The press, closely following the clash, observed that the Illinois senator had not endorsed Conkling's actions. As if echoing Logan's vow to "take care of himself," the *Register* reported that Logan and Cameron had established a working relationship with Garfield and would not jeopardize it by rallying to the side of the New Yorkers. Ten days before the resignations Logan had become convinced Blaine was the power behind Garfield; the Robertson appointment was his proof. The open fight between Blaine and Conkling, Logan believed, would hurt both men. The Illinoisan, already looking forward to his own presidential nomination in 1884, thought both potential rivals had been removed from contention.[21] In Conkling's case Garfield agreed. He branded his actions "suicide" and wrote Hayes "I was sorry to have a row; but it probably was inevitable—and better come now than later."[22]

Senator Logan's vow to take care of himself paid off handsomely. Rather than open contention and quick political oblivion, Logan, who would never have resigned under such circumstances, remained in touch with the White House and received most of the appointments he had asked for. Chief among these was A.M. "Long" Jones's nomination as marshall. Almost all the Illinois congressional delegation, led by the senators, went to the Justice Department to press Jones's case. Then a large Halfbreed delegation, led by Logan's foe Charles Farwell, went to Garfield to oppose Jones only to return "chagrined and demoralized" when Garfield picked Logan's man. William Henry Smith observed that the Jones appointment had alienated the anti-Grant Republicans of Illinois. An Alton, Illinois, Democrat agreed. He found Prairie State Republicans drifting apart, "the Logan-Cullom coalition being odious to thousands in the party." Although some Illinois Republican journals were pleased with the choice, the *Chicago Tribune* despairingly called it the "complete triumph of the Stalwart wing." An open feud raged, Smith informed Hayes, fueled by Logan's "bossism" and Garfield's surrender to Black Jack. "It is to be regretted that this should be turned against the president," wrote Smith. He concluded with a prediction: The New York contest was far more significant; once it ended in a presidential victory, the "'Boss' system disappears from our politics." [23]

While his political activity brought success, business results were mixed. Logan went to New York in April, bought some stock, and by early summer had made $1,200. He reinvested and hoped to continue his profits. In Egypt, however, the Murphysboro mine produced nothing. Will Tucker was supervising the mine, which through April was a disappointment and by June had to be abandoned. Logan sold two acres for $700 as well as the drilling machinery to help pay off the debt incurred in prospecting. He advised Mary to use money from wheat grown on their Carbondale farm to pay taxes and went back to the market, buying two hundred shares of rail stock. [24]

John and Mary traveled to Illinois in June and were staying at Chicago's Grand Pacific Hotel when, on July 2, they received a telegram from Robert Todd Lincoln telling them that Garfield had been seriously wounded by an assassin. The secretary of war thought the president could live only a few hours, but later that day he reported encouraging improvement. Lincoln telegraphed Logan the latest daily information on the changes in the president's condition. In mid-July the Logans went to Washington to show their concern and to be on hand in case the worst happened. Garfield defied early predictions and lived on through July and August. [25]

It was soon discovered that the assailant, Charles J. Guiteau, was a Chicago Stalwart whose words when he fired were, "I am a Stalwart and

Arthur will be president." Guiteau, who was mentally ill, was usually described as a disappointed office-seeker. He had briefly stayed at Mrs. Lockwood's, and Logan was embarrassed by the coincidental connections between the deranged Guiteau and himself. The senator made every effort, in interviews with the press, to characterize Guiteau as an insane man with whom he had no dealings. The landlady supported Logan's denials, adding that he had been a great nuisance to the senator, who advised her to get rid of him at once. Although many papers sought to blame the assassin's act on the malign influence of patronage politics, not even those most hostile to Logan attempted to implicate him.[26]

As the summer passed and the nation watched the White House bulletins, Logan played the stock market. He spent late July and much of August in New York with Jerome Chaffee and Don Cameron speculating, principally on railroads. Due in large part to Garfield's condition, the market fluctuated wildly. Logan reported a rally one day and a panic the next and complained, "I am sweating." In August he split five hundred shares of Missouri, Kansas, and Texas with Chaffee and two thousand shares of Union Pacific with Cameron. On August 24 he reported making $500 the previous week and on September 6 he sold some shares and "cleaned up" $3,000.[27]

On September 19 Garfield died. Logan rather callously philosophized, "He died in the best time for him that his name may be made immortal, but 'tis sad. Official life is a bubble after all." He went to Ohio for the funeral.[28]

As soon as the ceremonies ended the Illinois senator returned to New York. The new Stalwart president was there, and a rising market offered a chance for a killing. At the end of September, Logan gleefully wrote Mary he had already made $6,000 "clear" and stocks still unsold could bring as much as $15,000. His political profits also seemed secure. The Illinois Stalwart talked to Arthur several times and found him "all right." "I will have no trouble with Arthur," he said confidently; "anything I want done in Chicago he will do." However, the incoming president would not make immediate commitments, and the greedy senator found him "worse than Grant," adding, "You can get nothing out of him about anything." Nevertheless, there was nothing to fear for "he trusts me exceedingly . . . and I think I can get along with him all right."[29]

Arthur's elevation to the presidency was followed by a renewed stampede for office. Even before Garfield's death one observer told David Davis that Washington was filled with Stalwarts holding their collective breath waiting to trample each other in the rush for office. When the president died Logan received a bale of requests. *Inter-Ocean* editor William Penn Nixon, vowing renewed devotion, "earnestly" sought the Chicago collectorship. It was a matter of augmenting the *Inter-Ocean*'s "political prestige" as well as a reward for his "unselfish services" to the Stalwarts. Along with the petition, Nixon sent Logan thirty shares of *Inter-Ocean* stock that the senator had purchased. They were issued blank since Black Jack wanted no record of his name on the company's books that might indicate undue influence in running the sheet.[30] Nixon's efforts were to no avail. Although he was supported by Chicago Congressman Charles Farwell, and by a continuous campaign in the *Inter-Ocean,* the choice fell on Jesse Spalding. The *Inter-Ocean* contended that Logan's first choice had been his former secretary, Dan Shepard, and that the Spalding choice was a defeat. The *Chicago Tribune* denied Logan's support of Shepard and praised Spalding while railing at the grasping Nixon. On December 27 the *Tribune* published a long interview with Logan in which he praised Spalding and denied any campaign for Shepard. Nixon had become a "laughing stock," thought the *Tribune,* which lauded Logan's interview as "fresh and interesting." Spalding's designation ended the controversy; it also ended the collectorship of the controversial William Henry Smith. The affair began a long battle between Logan and the *Inter-Ocean,* whose columns lost no opportunity to attack the senator.[31]

Logan's name was mentioned for Arthur's cabinet, but once again the Illinoisan preferred the senate. He did press Arthur to put his Colorado friend Jerome B. Chaffee in the cabinet. Chaffee in turn thought Whitelaw Reid's *New York Tribune* could be "induced" to support the new president if Chaffee was appointed.[32]

Chaffee and Logan maintained close contact through the winter. As Arthur composed his cabinet, retaining only Lincoln from Garfield's group, the Coloradan was not tapped. Hypocritically he criticized the president, calling him a "politician." Chaffee hoped Arthur would construct his administration so as to dictate either his own renomination in 1884 or to influence the choice of his successor. Logan's fellow speculator also attempted to close the chasm between the senator and Charles Farwell. He revealed a confidential Farwell note advocating Orville Babcock for Chicago collector as a harmony gesture. A show of solidarity in Illinois was possible and would "be appreciated by Blaine men," advised Chaffee.[33]

At first Arthur counseled with Grant, Conkling, Logan, and Cameron and seemed to open his administration to Stalwart influence. Halfbreeds and Reformers were alarmed by this development. An Ohioan reported word from a Logan confidant that Black Jack and his allies, with Arthur's aid, were already working to implant the unit rule in the party's next national convention. However, the president's cabinet was not filled with Stalwart cronies, thus allaying some fears.[34]

On December 5, when the first regular session of the Forty-seventh Congress began, Logan placed the Grant retirement bill before the Senate. This time the Illinoisan shepherded it to final passage. George Vest attacked the bill again but Logan countered, reiterating its similarity to all other retirement bills, which paid three-fourths of active duty pay. Bayard wanted a special pension for former presidents, but Black Jack insisted that the nation's greatest soldier should receive military retirement. Vest had championed Porter, and Logan accused the Missourian of being willing to restore Porter while he refused to aid Grant, "to whom we owe more for the salvation of this country than to any other military man." On February 23, after two years of haggling, Logan's bill passed by a bipartisan vote of 35 to 17.[35]

At this session Illinois' junior senator held his Military Affairs, Appropriations, and Judiciary Committee appointments but asked to be excused from Indian Affairs. The Stalwart was one of the senators who eulogized Matt Carpenter, remembering his deceased colleague's "generosity and kindness." [36]

When a proposal to organize a select committee to investigate women's suffrage reached the floor and was derisively received by some, Logan supported a committee that would include friendly legislators so as to give women's suffrage advocates a fair hearing. The proposal passed.

It was during this congressional term that the Illinois Republican produced a bill to provide federal tax revenue for public education. About $65 million a year was collected in taxes on "distilled spirits," and Logan proposed using this money for state public education on the basis of proportional population. Some proposed apportionment based on rates of illiteracy, but the midwesterner believed that such apportionment would unfairly punish his state and section. The South, he averred, had poorer education because southern states refused to pass adequate tax measures. Even on a proportional basis, Logan announced to the Senate, this proposal would greatly aid in the elevation of the South's educational standards. Alabama's annual share would be four times what that state had spent in 1880. This argument prompted one Alabaman, who described himself as a stranger, a rebel soldier, and a Democrat, to thank the Yankee senator for his education bill.[37]

Logan's proposal stirred up opposition both in and out of Congress. Temperance men called the money "tainted" and felt funds from the sale of something "wicked and demoralizing" should never be used for education. The *Inter-Ocean* was quick to report a meeting of Chicago's Methodist ministers, including Logan's own pastor, which denounced the bill. Yet Joseph Medill of the *Chicago Tribune,* long estranged from Logan, supported the measure. He derided the clergy's opposition as a "narrow, sentimental view to which the Almighty is not a party." Although it was not reported, another reason for opposition was surely southern distrust of federal funds for education. Federal funds proposed by a Stalwart might have been followed by demands for equal education for the races. At least one black newspaper in Alabama supported Logan's plan. The bill was sent to the Committee on Education and Labor but was never reported back to the floor. Nevertheless, Logan persisted in his concept, publishing an article on the subject in *North American Review* in April 1883.[38]

The seemingly endless Fitz-John Porter imbroglio broke upon the Senate again this session, but with a slightly different twist. Late in 1881 Porter had appealed to Grant to thoroughly examine the facts in his case. Grant agreed and after "careful consideration and much thought" he wrote President Arthur that he was "thoroughly convinced . . . that for these 10 years I have been doing a gallant and efficient soldier a very great injustice in thought and sometimes in speech." As chief executive Grant had refused to review the court-martial, and some critics (not including Logan) said the only reason for the change was to influence Democrats to vote for passage of his own retirement bill. Grant continued into early 1882 to intercede in Porter's behalf to aid the government in "reaching a just and practical solution" of the case. Grant's change of course did not sway Logan. However, President Arthur was moved to pardon Porter and remove the disability clause that denied him the right to hold any office. Following the pardon the Military Affairs Committee once again took up a bill to restore Porter's rank and provide back pay. The majority reported favorably, but Logan, Porter's bête noire, filed a minority report. Congress was evenly split and the session adjourned without action.[39]

Logan's steadfast position was cheered by many. The *Chicago Tribune* supported Logan editorially. Medill thought after thorough investigation that Porter "ought to have been shot." The journalist branded Porter a "Copperhead scoundrel" who had been determined to wreck the Union cause. "Don't let up an inch," he encouraged the senator. A number of Civil War veterans wrote that despite Grant's switch they believed Logan was right. Illinois Democrats did not agree and they saw only a "dull-brained" vindictive senator who "never rises above a prejudice."[40]

In January tragedy struck the Logan family. Dollie Logan Tucker, who had given her parents a grandson named Logan, lost a daughter in childbirth. Mary rushed to Chicago to comfort her, but the senator stayed in the capital. He wrote, "I hope Dollie will not make herself sick, she must bear her trial." One month later the senator had some good news for the bereaved couple. He was able to have Will confirmed as a major in the army paymaster's department to be stationed in Santa Fe, New Mexico.[41]

Debate on army appropriations concerned Congress in the spring and early summer, and for once Sherman agreed with the bill's general features. The most hotly argued portion of this measure dealt with military retirement, which was fixed at age sixty-two. Although it would not apply to present generals, Sherman just happened to be sixty-two that year. The general must have bristled when he read Logan's argument that sixty-two was too old to lead men into battle. Black Jack strongly supported the provision, arguing in a lengthy dissertation on military history that no great generals had been sixty-two or older during their most notable campaigns. Logan fought Thomas Bayard's amendment to raise the age to sixty-five, but it carried 28 to 22. Other efforts to amend, including the complete exemption of the general-of-the-army, were defeated. Finally, Logan reported from a House-Senate conference that the age had been altered, at House insistence, to sixty-four, to which the Senate conferees had agreed. The bill passed in that form on June 26. The final wording made no difference to Sherman, who informed Sheridan, his successor, that he would retire in December 1883.[42]

That April and May an exhausted John Logan left Mary in Washington and traveled to Hot Springs, Arkansas, in an attempt to shake off a lingering illness. Throughout the winter rheumatism had stiffened the senator and he had been reported confined to his room on several occasions. At the spa he bathed daily and the waters, together with his medication, markedly improved his condition. He returned in "first rate" condition ready to face the rigors of a session that might linger well into the torrid Washington summer.[43]

Logan centered his efforts on internal improvements, veterans' pensions, and the naval appropriations bill during the session's final three months. Early in the year he had joined several midwestern congressmen in organizing a meeting of those interested in improving waterways in the interests of *"cheap transportation."*[44] In response to appeals from their constituents these men advocated construction of a canal connecting the Mississippi River and Lake Michigan. This Hennepin Canal had been proposed earlier and a survey had been made. In spite of protests from railroads, Logan spoke for the waterway on grounds that the competition would allow his constituents to market their goods more cheaply. Some senators challenged the proposal's constitutionality while others demanded that a new survey be made since the earlier one was outdated. The new survey was agreed to even though Black Jack argued that the old one was quite adequate and that construction should begin immediately. Because of his failure to have canal construction included, Logan voted "no" to the entire rivers and harbors bill of which the Hennepin Canal was a part. Arthur vetoed the bill on grounds of excessive "pork," but the Senate overrode. Logan stood with the defeated minority in voting to sustain the president.[45]

Pension debate brought up the criticisms of the previous Congress and found Logan defending the pension recipients. When one senator proposed to list on post office walls all those receiving money, the veterans' champion indignantly roared that it would make them seem to be "pirates or plunderers."[46]

Reporting for the Appropriations Committee, Logan brought the naval bill to the floor near the session's end. There were immediate complaints that the committee was interfering with the rights of the Naval Affairs Committee. Logan, who had made the same charge in behalf of the Military Affairs Committee earlier in his career, now passed the remarks off as unnecessary "growling and grumbling." Furthermore, he continued, the reorganization provisions contained in the statute were put in because the Naval Committee would not act. The greatest stumbling block to passage was abolition of the commodore's rank. The Illinoisan maintained it was a relatively new rank whose abolition was being pro-posed in the name of economy since the service was top-heavy with of-ficers. In addition, all present commodores were exempted and might serve out their careers. Charles W. Jones of Florida and John F. Miller of California fought with Logan, the latter eventually proposing the estab-lishment of a commission to investigate the rank's deletion. The amend-ment passed with Logan in opposition. On July 31 the entire bill cleared the Senate.[47]

While Congress rambled on, Logan kept a close watch on state and national Republican politics. A powerful state base was a necessary first step in Logan's soaring ambitions which were now fixed on the White House. He also needed to maintain accurate information on the plans of potential rivals across the nation. The senator received regular reports from Prairie State appointees. They discussed the political tenor of their districts, asked for small favors, and swore undying allegiance. Logan's position on the Porter case and pension legislation drew applause. As the year passed more and more of the correspondents mentioned the presi-dency. A Peoria friend took a survey of "commercial travelers" he met in Illinois and reported their feeling that Black Jack was strong in Indiana, Wisconsin, Minnesota, Kansas, Pennsylvania, California, and through-out the Southwest. Chicago lawyer Richard Tuthill, a loyal Logan confi-dant, reported pro-Blaine activities among Cook County Republicans and vowed to report regularly. Jerome B. Chaffee also continued to send ad-vice. He wrote that some of the party faithful were upset at Blaine for too openly coveting the 1884 nomination two years early.[48]

The Illinois press remained a vexing subject for the ambitious and overbearing Logan. He had refused to back William Penn Nixon of the *Inter-Ocean* for the collectorship, thus forfeiting the journalist's support. At the same time the *Chicago Daily News* grew more hostile. M.E. Stone, editor of the six-year-old journal, regretted the estrangement, re-minding the senator of his past support in spite of the "bossism" tag fixed on Logan by some. Stone, who had endorsed Nixon's candidacy, told Lo-gan he had been warned that Black Jack regarded any opposition as an "impertinence," and events had substantiated the charge. He added: "if you regard it as the sole duty of your friends to render a servile and un-questioning obedience then you and I can never agree."[49]

The Illinois Republican State Convention met in June; Logan's agents A.M. "Long" Jones and Dan Shepard together with Shelby Cullom's leaders were very much in control. The Halfbreeds, led by Charles Far-well, were there trying to wrest control of the party machinery from the Stalwarts. Farwell, observed Jones, wanted to end "one-man rule" so he could establish himself as the "boss." The Chicagoan's tactics failed, he was accorded a cool reception, and Jones was chosen convention chairman with Shepard secretary, a result styled "distasteful" by the *Inter-Ocean*. For a time a rift in the Logan-Cullom alliance seemed to be opening when some of the senator's associates tried to give the impression that Black Jack preferred Green B. Raum for senator. Jacob Wheeler, marshall for southern Illinois, was convinced Logan should advance Cullom to the Senate in 1883 in return for Cullom's support for Black Jack's presidential bid. The crisis passed and the effective cooperation continued. Further evidence of Republican bickering occurred when, after the convention adjourned, Jesse Spalding, Arthur's new collector, asked Logan to block "Long" Jones's selection as chairman of the state central committee. Spalding believed Jones, more than any Illinois Stalwart, could not bring unity to the Republican slate in 1882.[50]

But the Logan steamroller could not be halted. The senator wrote Republican committee members from all over Illinois in behalf of Jones and Shepard, and many took his advice. Jones garnered the chairmanship and Shepard was chosen secretary despite an effort by Spalding and Farwell to defeat the Logan ticket "at all hazards." Spalding "died hard and foolishly," reported the new chairman as he declared "the battle is over and the victory is upon your side." Since Jones regarded his enemies as Arthur men, he believed this 1882 victory strengthened Logan for the 1884 contest.[51]

The occasional rifts in the ranks of Republicans were minor worries in the face of the overwhelming triumph of Logan's forces. Two years before the national convention chose a presidential nominee, Black Jack seemed assured of a solid bloc of Illinois votes. A popular congressional record and an expanded campaign outside the Prairie State could provide a real challenge for Blaine and Arthur in 1884. Even if Logan's presidential hopes were unfulfilled, the solidity of his Illinois machine made his reelection to the Senate in 1885 look almost certain.

CHAPTER 12

A Household Word

"JOHN A., you never was in as good shape in your life before" were consoling words from one of Logan's best sources of information on Illinois' grass roots. He went on to report strong newspaper support, including that of some *Chicago Tribune* correspondents.[1] Cheered by that news, John and Mary Logan returned to Illinois in late summer. After meeting Jones and the other Chicago Stalwarts and traveling on to Springfield, the couple wound up in Egypt. They remained there briefly before going to Santa Fe to visit the Tuckers. For almost two months the couple remained in the Southwest so Logan could rest in an attempt to recover from painful sciatica. Interrupting his rest now and then, Logan became involved in some copper and gold prospecting near Santa Rita and Silver City in western New Mexico.[2] The other member of the family, seventeen-year-old John, Jr., entered Pennsylvania Military Academy at Chester that autumn. After the boy's first term the school reported he had passed every course except Latin. The report went on to laud the senator's son for his gentlemanly manner while expressing reservations about his academic work. John had "an excellent mind but lacked application" was the verdict.[3]

In October the Logans went northward to Colorado and east to Kansas. At Fort Leavenworth they were joined by General and Mrs. Phil Sheridan, who traveled with them to Chicago. Upon arrival, the senator was greeted by a "regiment" of Cook County politicos anxious for the support of his voice in the election only two weeks off. On November 3 Logan was feeling "blue" about his party's prospects but hoped to carry the state legislature. The Illinois General Assembly did remain in Republican hands, but elsewhere results were discouraging. In state after state Democrats won state houses and governors' mansions while the G.O.P.

was routed in the race to control the House of Representatives. Fortunately for Logan, the Republicans increased their Senate majority. The Logans did not seem too depressed by the results, for just after the election they joined Mr. and Mrs. George Pullman, General and Mrs. Sheridan, and Robert Todd Lincoln at the Pullman's village for an excursion that Mary called a "lovely day." [4]

On December 4 Logan answered the initial roll call of the Forty-seventh Congress's winter term. Its early business included Logan's reporting of a host of petitions asking an increase of pension benefits for one-armed and one-legged ex-soldiers. He spoke strongly in favor of legislation to benefit the ten thousand men in these categories. Mary left John alone for several weeks as she went to Chicago on business, but she returned before Christmas. On New Year's Day, in response to the president's invitation, Mrs. Logan assisted at the annual White House reception. [5]

Before the holidays arrived the Illinois senator had a vigorous legislative month. Civil service reform, Indian affairs, and, inevitably it seemed, Fitz-John Porter's relief bill jammed the agenda. Garfield's assassination by a patronage hound triggered increased support for a merit system. Ohio Democratic Senator George Pendleton introduced a bill establishing a civil service commission, which would advise the president in making and executing rules dealing with federal appointees. Even die-hard patronage defenders like Logan, sensing a rising tide of popular support on the eve of an election year, gave their voices and votes in approbation. The Illinoisan was deeply involved in the debate, offering several amendments. He insisted in one that examinations be entirely "practical" so as to test fitness for the specific job for which the person had applied. He provided in another amendment for a bona fide oath to establish the residence of each applicant. Both these amendments were agreed to. Logan also suggested a raise in the salary of Civil Service commissioners from $3,500 to $4,000. This proposal was defeated. On December 27 the Pendleton Act passed the Senate 38 to 5 with longtime civil service reform foe John A. Logan voting "aye." [6]

During the summer of 1882 Logan had visited a number of Indian reservations while traveling in the Southwest. When the Indian appropriations bill reached the floor the senator spoke out on Indian education. He reported touring Indian school buildings that were not in use and interviewing illiterate Indian children. Logan believed the only answer was to educate Indians away from the reservation among whites so as to have them "absorbed in the white people as good citizens." An end to Indian separatism and total amalgamation remained Logan's solution for the problems of native Americans. He did believe that once educated in this manner Indians should be sent back to reservations to run their own businesses rather than have Indians remain prey to white traders. "We have got to deal justly with the Indians," stated the dark-complexioned Logan—of whom Indian ancestry was often inaccurately alleged. Before the session ended, Black Jack was named to a five-man commission to investigate the condition of the Sioux on the northern plains.[7]

The Illinois Stalwart's greatest activity of the session was his skirmish against Fitz-John Porter. Grant's change of heart and Arthur's pension had won the general new advocates, and when New Jersey Senators William J. Sewell and John R. McPherson introduced the bill on December 11 the latter guessed Logan might be the only voice in opposition. While vowing to make a "few feeble remarks," Black Jack immediately acted to block the measure's consideration but failed. Concerning Porter's renewed appeal, he informed the Senate, "Persistence in a wrong does not make it right."[8]

That winter, Logan and Grant presented their conflicting views to the American people. Black Jack wrote a detailed account of the facts, the court-martial, and the Senate's past actions. In a *Chicago Tribune* column he demonstrated that Grant's new view was based on some faulty assumptions, and Logan held to his opposition to any bill of exoneration. In the *North American Review* article "An Undeserved Stigma," Grant expressed the opinion that Porter could not have carried out the order that he refused to obey. The former president did not want to restore Porter to the army, but he did plead for a restoration of Porter's military reputation.[9]

Through the final week of 1882 and the first two weeks of 1883 the debate rambled on. Almost alone, Logan carried on the fight. Time and time again he tried to postpone the bill indefinitely only to lose by narrow margins. When Grant's ideas were mentioned, Logan, denying any lack of respect for Grant, told the senators he had given facts whereas Grant had not. When McPherson persisted with Grant's stand, Logan accused him of "bad grace" in trying to turn Grant against his former military and political lieutenant. The Illinoisan made several lengthy speeches, reading much of the court-martial testimony into the record. With several Republicans (including Don Cameron) joining most Democrats, the Senate, for the second time, passed the bill. The vote was 33 to 27. Logan might have been pleased by the bill's omission to provide any back pay, but he was far more pleased when the House refused to pass any bill at all.[10]

As they had in 1880, volumes of laudatory letters poured in. Veterans, including many who had served either under Porter or at Second Bull Run, or both, praised the Illinois senator. General John Pope hailed both the *Chicago Tribune* article and the speeches as irrefutable. "It is useless for me to discuss this matter with you," wrote Porter's Civil War commander; "You know it even better than I." Connecticut Republican Augustus Brandegee was "electrified," and Mortimer D. Leggett, one of Logan's Civil War division commanders, proclaimed his 1880 and 1883 orations the two best in the Senate since the Civil War. From the home front the publisher of the *Chicago Evening Journal*, an assistant U.S. attorney, and numerous politicians sent their thanks. The attorney thought of the affair as "the cause of the people against caste," a sentiment with which Logan was in wholehearted agreement.[11]

The Logan-Grant disagreement affected Mary's attitude toward Julia Grant, with whom she spent some time in January. The senator's wife found it difficult to be pleasant. "I was so mad all the time to think how we have worked for them and then to have Grant abuse Papa so outrageously," she confided to Dollie. Mary would not forgive or forget; neither Logan tolerated opposition very well.[12]

January also brought hard work on the West Point appropriations bill and on general army funding. Academy money was reduced about 9 percent as the Illinois Republican guided the measure through committee, floor debate, and House-Senate conference. The Army appropriations bill moved through the legislative process with less difficulty and rancor than usual.[13]

Polygamy and pensions also concerned Logan during this session. He branded the former "a cancer on the body politic" that had to be removed. One method of eradication Logan suggested was to deny all polygamists the right to vote or hold office. When accused of interfering with freedom of religion, the Illinoisan denied the charge, reminding his accusers that his proposal would only affect persons guilty of a crime. Throughout the winter, Logan spoke for increased pension grants, especially for disabled veterans. He also submitted an amendment placing black veterans on the same bounty and pension schedules as white soldiers. When the pension bill came to a final vote, Logan said he preferred

John A. Logan. *Illinois State Historical Library.*

the higher House version but he voted "aye" nonetheless.[14] For once, winter blasts did not lay Logan low. His daughter heard "Papa has kept up remarkably well this winter and is looking splendidly."[15]

One congressional action filled with political significance was the passage in March 1883 of the Mongrel Tariff. Many protectionist Republicans, including President Arthur, had joined revisionists in pressing for tariff reform. Logan was not in that group and was relatively silent on the whole tariff controversy. In 1882 Congress had created a nonpartisan study commission, which Logan had voted against. Although packed with protectionists, the commission recommended cuts of up to as much as 20 percent. Arthur supported the findings and urged Congress to act.[16]

After hacking through the forest of protected items, the Congress passed a tariff bill just prior to the March 3 adjournment. However, massive logrolling kept the reductions small, many too slight to have any real effect. After laboring to retain protection for Illinois industries, Logan voted in favor of the entire tariff package. The senator fought the extension of the free list to include tobacco and whisky and stoutly opposed a significant reduction in duty on glass products. The latter, he maintained, would ruin glass manufacturing in the United States.

Other Illinois businesses such as glue manufacturing, flax milling, and vinegar distilling found a guardian in John A. Logan. Generally his efforts to lessen the impact of reduced protection on Prairie State industries was successful, but it did contribute to the "mongrelization" of the commission's proposal.[17]

With spring's arrival the Logans went to Illinois. The senator left Mary at the Grand Pacific Hotel in Chicago while he visited the legislative session in Springfield and tended to business in Carbondale. Stalwarts all over the state had to be encouraged and listened to by the man who would lead them into the 1884 fight for the presidency. Perhaps he heard, as former President Hayes had, that Blaine's stock had fallen in Illinois. He was certainly pleased that the assembly had advanced his ally Shelby Cullom to the Senate that winter. Although the *New York Times* once reported that Logan supported Robert Todd Lincoln for the seat, the senator had remained neutral in what eventually became a Cullom-Raum battle. Cullom had promised support in the past, and the increased power that accompanied his elevation to the Senate would aid Black Jack's presidential ambitions. When the newly elected senator arrived in the capital Logan took him on a tour of the departments. However, in his memoirs,

Cullom complained that Logan did not aid in his securing important committee assignments.[18]

For the first half of 1883 information, advice, and encouragement came in and had to be sifted, weighed, and either used or discarded. A Kentucky Stalwart, veteran of the third-term battle, offered encouragement; and long-time Chicago political supporter Merritt Joslyn, now employed in the Department of the Interior, reported that Indiana reformer Walter Q. Gresham had been made postmaster general in order to deny the Hoosier State to Logan. Chaffee sent some good advice to his Illinois friend. He urged Logan never to be goaded into exchanges with the press. Arthur "is jealous of you" he added. Blaine's game of noncandidacy Chaffee believed was insincere, and he predicted the Maine senator would be beaten if nominated. In conclusion Chaffee cautioned Logan against trusting Cameron. When all factors were considered, the Colorado Republican wrote, "it looks to me you stand as good a chance as anyone else, even better." [19]

Press speculation on the fight ahead led to rumors of a breach between Logan and various Republicans. That spring both Chester A. Arthur and Roscoe Conkling wrote to determine Logan's state of mind and to put such talk to rest. Arthur called the report "ignorant," and Logan assured "Lord Roscoe" he had never uttered unkind words about him.[20]

As usual Logan received his share of requests for speeches. For a presidential candidate, such appeals were welcome; and while they could not all be accepted, they did indicate that there had been no diminution in his drawing power. Iowa Senator William B. Allison sent several requests for Logan's assistance in his state. William E. Chandler hoped that Logan could come to New Hampshire, and another New Englander, trying to acquire Rutherford B. Hayes for an Independence Day gathering, advertised Black Jack's appearance in Connecticut. It was not possible for him to speak in the Northeast.[21]

In mid-April John and Mary Logan began a trip to Santa Fe, where for a time they cared for their grandson while Dollie and Will visited friends in Chicago. It was the beginning of a year of intensive western travel for Black Jack.[22] Until June the senator and his wife rested, enjoying their grandson, Logan Tucker, and the society of the Santa Fe post. A minor problem developed when Mary's sister, who also lived in Santa Fe, fell in love with Sergeant S.S. Enoch of the 22d Infantry. The soldier could not support a wife on army pay, and Logan wrote Robert Todd Lincoln and General Sherman asking for the sergeant's discharge. Logan told

Sherman, "My wife is greatly distressed." When he replied, Sherman agreed to the discharge and then outlined for the Military Affairs chairman his impending final grand tour prior to surrendering command to Phil Sheridan. Sherman would reach Santa Fe in September, but Logan would have already departed.[23]

In June, accompanied by a calvary escort, Logan rode to the Navajo Agency in search of further information on Indian affairs. It was "the most frightfully tiresome journey" he had ever taken. The following month the Logans left Major Tucker and Dollie, traveling to Denver together before going their separate ways. Mary went to Pennsylvania to spend three weeks with her son at his school. While there she received a letter from her husband asking her to tell young Logan he was "counting on him." The senator moved on to the Dakota Territory, where he was to join the commission, chaired by Senator Henry L. Dawes, selected to investigate conditions among the northern Sioux.[24]

The Dawes Commission traveled through the Northwest interviewing soldiers, civilian officials, and Indians. Chief Sitting Bull, just released from prison, was among those who appeared before the five legislators. Logan scolded the chief for breaking up the previous council, adding,

> you are not a great chief of this country . . . you have no following, no power, no control. You are on an Indian reservation merely at the suffrance of the government. . . . I merely say these things to you to notify you that you cannot insult the people of the United States of America. . . . The government feeds and clothes and educates your children now, and desires to teach you to become farmers, and to civilize you, and make you as white men.[25]

While in the area they went to Yellowstone Park, which Black Jack proclaimed "very wonderful indeed." The senator had long been interested in the park and in western surveys. He had supported the work of explorer-surveyor Frederick V. Hayden, who called Logan his "best friend" and hailed the Illinois senator as "the founder of the Geological Survey as it is now." After he discovered Logan had seen the park, Hayden wanted to talk to him to press his hope that no one be permitted to "meddle" with Yellowstone's natural beauty. By September, Logan was back in Chicago, where he joined Mary for a few days' rest before taking the stump.[26]

Before joining John in Chicago, Mary supervised her son's entrance into the United States Military Academy. Young Logan was determined to become an army officer, and through West Point lay his only path to a commission and a military career. The September 1883 entrance of fourth classman John A. Logan, Jr., son of the long-time foe of the professional military, contained within it the deepest elements of irony.

With his entrance into the academy, young Logan wanted to change his name. "Manning insists that he will not be called Manning any more but John A. Logan, Jr.," his mother wrote to Dollie that August. Mary Logan also corresponded often with West Point superintendent Wesley Merritt prior to her son's arrival. The general promised to do all in his power to assist the young man.[27]

Iowans heard John A. Logan, Sr.'s voice that September. Republican Senator Allison had written often to plead for Logan's voice in his behalf and the Illinoisan responded, making an address at Davenport. As the autumn passed, Logan spoke in Illinois and Ohio. Mary accompanied him to Cleveland but returned to Chicago before the general, who went instead to the Army of Cumberland reunion in Cincinnati. Shortly after his Ohio trek the senator, a member of the Select Committee on Navigational Improvements on the Mississippi River, entrained for New Orleans to gather evidence for a report.[28]

The family's greatest personal concern that winter was John A. Logan, Jr. "About the 13th of October Manning [despite their son's wishes both parents continued to use the name Manning] began to let down in his interest at West Point, he has steadily declined since, and we are thoroughly discouraged about him," Mary informed Dollie. She added that the disappointed senator said "he knew he would fail." Illness was part of the problem, and Mary hurried to the academy in early December only to find him recovered. The tyro cadet admitted his grades were not very good but he told his concerned mother, "I'll come out all right, don't you fear."[29] His grades did climb slightly in December and General Merritt, who surely did not carry on a regular correspondence with every cadet's parents, tried to reassure the senator. The senator paid his son a Christmas visit and informed a worried mother that "Manning" was doing very well and would pass if he improved his "thoughtless and careless" study habits. In the worst kind of parental excuse-making Logan wrote: "These old professors are in for life and they think it to show their impartiality by letting boys of known promise not pass. The rebels never fail an exam, somehow they get through Butlers and Hamptons, but I am sure Merritt will put Manning through if he can." Cadet Logan "enjoyed" his father's visit to a place Manning considered the "first place in the world."[30]

The December opening of the Forty-eighth Congress began an important term since Logan's record could have an impact on his presidential chances. The senior senator from Illinois introduced a large number (forty-three) of private relief and pension bills. He also had 152 petitions read into the record. This was a far larger number than most members introduced and seemed to indicate Logan's desire to satisfy any petitioning citizen. Most pleas were either from individual veterans or G.A.R. units, and most begged for an increase in benefits. December was a slack legislative month with little business and many truncated meetings. For Logan the entire first session was one of low productivity and low profile. Except for one or two issues his remarks were far less voluminous than usual. Logan seemed to be determined not to lose with congressional oratory what his party's delegates might bestow on him that coming June. He did vote for George Edmunds, also a contestant for the Republican nomination, as president pro tem.[31]

Pension and public school bills concerned Logan in this session. He introduced a measure to provide pensions for Union troops held in rebel prisons and another calling for an increase in benefits for amputees. These and other pension measures found an increasingly hostile reception, particularly from the heavily Democratic House. Late in the term Black Jack secured Senate passage, with almost no debate, of a bill providing full general's pay to the retired Ulysses S. Grant.[32] Long interested in federal support for public education, the Illinoisan sent a bill into the hopper to spend $50 million from internal revenue taxes and sales of public land for that purpose. As the debate proceeded Black Jack proposed an amendment to give no funds to any state that practiced discrimination based on race or color. It passed. Negroes, thought Logan, were the nation's largest illiterate group, and this measure was the only way to educate those blacks "to whom we owe a great obligation." As he had in the past, Logan fought distributing funds on any basis other than population. To do otherwise would encourage southern states to cut back their already paltry educational appropriations. If illiteracy rates were used, Logan believed only those persons from 5 to 20 should be counted. No matter what the formula he remained suspicious that southern whites would "use the black man to get the appropriations, and then . . . give it to the white man." Senate Bill 228 eventually passed by a bipartisan vote of

33 to 11 with the Illinois Stalwart voting in the affirmative.[33]

One legislative subject Logan could assault without fear of losing ground with his most devoted constituents was the Porter relief bill. Sewell brought up the bill again and Logan hit it hard in remarks that included long exerpts of testimony from the original trial. At the conclusion of his remarks Logan said:

> The conscientious feeling that I have performed my duty acceding to my honest convictions to my country, to the honor of our now faithful little Army, to my comrades in arms during the war, to the living and the dead that took part in the judgement of the court, to the loyal people that loved this country and helped to save it, shall be in my own breast through life my reward for my action in this case.

Few, if any, were influenced by such words. Sewell's bill passed 36 to 25. In May a House-Senate conference had to be named to iron out differences in the two bills. Logan was asked to serve but declined, saying he could not support a bill in any form. For the first time in the endless ordeal Congress passed a Porter relief bill. It restored Porter to the army without pay. But the general was to be frustrated again. President Arthur, who had pardoned Porter, vetoed the measure on grounds that it was an invasion of executive power and because he was unwilling to set aside the "solemn" deliberations of the court-martial. The Senate vote to override failed 27 to 27.[34]

On New Year's Day, as she had done so often, Mary Logan stood in the receiving line at President Arthur's annual White House reception. She wore a black velvet brocaded dress and diamonds. During this ceremony Mrs. Logan, noticing that former Senator Blanche Bruce's wife was being ignored, quietly escorted the black woman along the line, introducing her to each woman present.[35]

In January, one legislative fight sounded like an echo from the past. Alleged election violence in Virginia and Mississippi brought a proposal to create an investigatory committee. It passed by a 33-to-29 party-line vote. On February 8 the senator proposed a commission to investigate the "material, industrial, and intellectual progress" of Negroes since 1865. This commission, however, was not funded. Nevertheless, the proposal was styled by a black newspaper "an act of kindness . . . ever to be remembered by the colored race." [36]

The final area of legislative concern for Logan in this first session of the Forty-eighth Congress was military spending. As in the previous session no extended controversy surrounded army funding. Phil Sheridan, the new army commander, was gaining "experience in this station," and it was not his "intention to trouble Congress at this session by any suggestions on the matter of army reorganization." Nevertheless, if the legislative branch took up reorganization the blunt general promised to "candidly give my views." [37] Logan served on the House-Senate conference that reconciled the conflicting appropriations bills. He also was a conferee on the appropriations for West Point, John, Jr.'s college, whose funding was again decreased slightly. Thus the salaries and operating capital of the men who would determine if John A. Logan, Jr., was fit to remain at the academy came under the close scrutiny of the father, who had been an avowed enemy of the place for twenty years. Logan did have one amendment to the academy bill. He found Senate agreement for his provision that any cadet expelled for hazing could never be reappointed to West Point. Logan had fought hazing for years before his son entered the place, and he told the chamber when he made his proposal that the idea was supported by Superintendent Merritt and many professors. [38] The new year found young Logan showing improvement at the academy over which his father hovered. He passed a vital math examination, reporting to his father he had "maxed it." To his mother, with whom he was always more relaxed, the cadet wrote: "Great guns but the exam was hard, but this child didn't get scortched. Now he is good for 6 months more of wearing out Uncle Sam's clothes." Logan's influence at West Point brought occasional requests for support in gaining admission. That winter General John Pope, at the suggestion of Secretary of War Lincoln, solicited the senator's aid in securing an appointment for his son, John. [39]

When Congress took up bills affecting the Military Academy, Cadet Logan sent his father his opinion. West Point needed "shaking up," felt the eighteen-year-old, who had been there for just five months. His older professors, secure in their safety, thought they could do just what they pleased. The Board of Visitors, he wrote, saw only "the varnished surface . . . held up to them," not the real academy. Cadet Logan recommended "Congress ought to clean some of these old roosters out." In

March the young man was in the hospital with eye trouble. General Merritt suggested a sick leave, and John A. Logan, Jr., joined his family in Washington in the spring. It was the most important spring of his father's political career.[40]

While Congress droned on through the winter, the 1884 political storm blew in. One reason for Logan's lack of legislative activity was his incessant work to secure the nomination. The Illinois senator believed his long years of faithful service gave him a good claim to first place on the ticket. He was experienced in politics, had a large and vocal following, and was truly a "household word" across the North. He had far more political experience than either Grant or Arthur before they assumed office and as much as Hayes and Garfield. With the exception of Grant, no president since the Civil War had been better known before he took office. Nevertheless, while he faced some dark horse candidates in 1884, his two chief competitors were men better known than he. They were the presidential incumbent Chester A. Arthur and James G. Blaine—a man whose record for party regularity made him a model for most Republicans. And yet in 1876 and again in 1880 the favorites had been thrust aside in favor of men with less first-ballot support. Senator Logan could only hope that pattern would continue.

CHAPTER 13

Logan for President

THE CRY "Logan for President" was not new to post–Civil War politics. The politician turned general turned politician had been mentioned for president or vice-president in every election since the war. Not until after 1880 did this movement become more than a passing footnote to each presidential contest. After Garfield's death the Logan candidacy grew steadily. Each year brought more letters, editorials, and G.A.R. resolutions pressing Black Jack as a man who not only could be nominated but could also vanquish the Democrats. The senator did his best to promote his cause. He traveled thousands of miles making speeches and devoting himself to the interests of the veterans, who were his largest and most visible base of support. As 1883 ended he was encouraged by such evidence of success as a letter Mary received from Republican moneybags Levi P. Morton. The New York Stalwart wrote: "I should so much like to see your husband leading the column in the next campaign." [1]

For the first third of 1884 John and Mary stepped up the campaign's tempo. They both traveled to Illinois in mid-March with the senator spending a few days in Chicago and Springfield before returning to Washington. In the first three months of the year the Prairie State press followed Logan's candidacy and debated his chances. Springfield's *State Journal* and the *Chicago Evening Journal* were friendly; the former was filled daily with word of the growth of the Logan "boom." The newspaper predicted a solid Logan delegation from Illinois and in February even quoted Blaine as saying Black Jack was in the lead for the nomination. The *Chicago Tribune* agreed that the senator was the overwhelming popular choice of Illinois Republicans and reported Grant's endorsement calling Logan "a man of the people" and the most "available" contestant. Although the powerful *Chicago Tribune* did not editorially endorse

171

Logan, its columns were friendly. Not so the *Inter-Ocean*. Nixon regretted Grant's endorsement and dismissed the "boom" as a few muted "tom-tom beatings."[2]

When Logan returned to Washington in March, his wife, who was his most trusted political aide, stayed in Chicago on the pretense of renting their Calumet Avenue home. She reported getting along well with her "persecutors"—the press—but despite hard work was dismayed by the rumors and charges flying around Chicago. By March 22 she had rented the house and the senator urged her to join him as soon as she could. Plans were changed, however, and she stayed on.[3]

The candidate solicited assistance from his friends, and Grant was one of the first to fall in line when he endorsed Logan for the nomination. While pleased with the endorsement, Black Jack thought the old soldier had been a trifle "indiscreet" in making a confidential overture of friendship to Carl Schurz with whom he had little in common. By April 6 his quest for support had him disgruntled. His attempts to influence delegates from outside Illinois had brought few votes, but he thought he might still win if he went to the convention with a solid Illinois delegation at his back. Since the convention was meeting in Chicago he wanted no discordant notes from his home. "I am afraid of Chicago," he admitted; "it will beat me or nominate me."[4]

Mary was still in Cook County in April, and her work caused gossip in both Illinois and Washington. In a time when women played little role in politics and candidates' wives, following the example of Lucy Hayes, remained sedately in the background, Mary Logan was controversial. She and her husband worked closely together to advance his political career. Mary's widespread correspondence with prominent Republicans was carried out at John's behest. Her Leland Hotel salons in 1871, 1877, and 1879 had drawn unfavorable comment, and in 1884 her visibility was even greater than before. John A. Logan, Jr., embarrassed by the talk, asked her to come home:

> I think although you may be helping Father at home you are hurting him elsewhere as I hear it at all the hotels about John Logan's wife being at home trying to run the machine for him. Everyone knows the house has been rented and you have no excuse for staying longer. I have said nothing to Father about it on account of worrying him.

At least one Illinois woman disagreed with the whispers of improper behavior. "I would like to see [Mrs. Logan] in the White House, she is so good, and wise, and thoughtful of everyone. She would be very popular I know," wrote Sarah Ada Bailhache of Springfield. She added, "I think Logan would make a splendid president."[5] Whether her son's letter influenced her is not known, but Mary returned to Washington shortly after receiving it.

The Logans could hope that most Illinoisans would share Mrs. Bailhache's feelings, but the state seethed with both support and opposition that spring. Emory A. Storrs, an influential Cook County attorney, claimed Logan would win the endorsement of men who had been hostile in 1880, and Logan's man in the state auditor's office saw the Blaine fever cooling as Logan's support grew. John M. Hamilton, the lieutenant governor who had served out Cullom's gubernatorial term when he resigned to take the Senate seat, loudly proclaimed loyalty to Logan.[6]

A one-time ally and later bitter enemy, Richard Oglesby, was making a political comeback that year. He had his eye on the governor's mansion, but Black Jack's men were not certain Oglesby did not covet Logan's Senate seat, which was up in January 1885. An assurance that he only wanted to be governor would ensure Oglesby's nomination for that office. Oglesby made that assurance in a February address to the state central committee in which he spoke favorably of the man who had driven him from the Senate. That speech enraged anti-Logan forces across the prairies. Oglesby received word that his own cause had been injured and that "the fight in Cook on Logan is going to be very bitter and will continue until after a Senator is elected." A particularly disgusted citizen deplored "Jack Logan's audacity in pressing his 'claim' for the nomination. . . . It is unaccountable. L. is *not* the people's man, he is the Illinois politician's man and they hate him. Their hatred is only equalled by their craven fear of him."[7]

Shelby Cullom remained firmly in the Logan camp, although *Inter-Ocean* editor Nixon urged the senator not to become too closely identified with the Logan movement. He grudgingly admitted Logan's boom was growing but he thought he knew why: "There is nothing to get in the way and it is the same fellows all the time that are halooing."[8]

David Davis, who had been Republican, Democrat, and Independent and was now out of office, was courted by a number of different parties, factions, and individuals. Logan leaders leaked stories without Davis's approval that the former senator would also be an Illinois national convention delegate pledged to him. One of Judge Davis's close friends begged him not to support Logan, who had only the strength of a "military organization and some political machinery" behind him. Postmaster General Walter Q. Gresham also cautioned Davis. He reported Logan had no eastern support and that he had incurred the wrath of editor George W. Curtis and most eastern business leaders. Gresham believed that "Blaine has succeeded in capturing Logan," one of the earliest forecasts of a Blaine-Logan deal. The Maine senator was "simply using Logan to club Arthur down," explained the postmaster general. Furthermore, despite Arthur's estrangement from Logan, Grant, and Conkling, Gresham felt Arthur was steadily gaining strength. Sherman, he saw, was an outsider who might seize a deadlocked convention and gain the laurels. Returning to Logan, Gresham had found much hostility toward him from Chicago Republicans and he also sensed a lukewarm attitude on Shelby Cullom's part. "I do not think Cullom will wear crepe when Logan is defeated," he stated. As for himself, Logan had been very friendly, in spite of their wide differences. Black Jack for once was trying to alienate no one.[9]

Across the nation Republican leaders maneuvered for delegate votes and assayed the potential candidate's strength. Ohio Congressman William McKinley talked to Joseph Medill and found the *Chicago Tribune* editor "earnest" in his belief that Blaine should lead the ticket. Blaine remained the acknowledged front-runner, although many questioned his ability to win. Vermont Senator Justin S. Morrill feared his fellow Vermonter George S. Edmunds as did many members of the party's reform wing. When Philadephia banker Wharton Barker mentioned Edmunds but doubted his popularity in the West, Rutherford B. Hayes demurred, stating flatly that the New Englander would do as well there as anyone. Barker doubted Arthur's ability to win, as did Morrill. Some mentioned Indiana Senator Benjamin Harrison or Postmaster General Gresham as dark horse possibilities. Also mentioned was Robert Todd Lincoln, but Barker, who thought the secretary of war might win, was alarmed at his possible control by Logan and Grant. Lincoln's name was also used by those who wanted to keep Logan off of the ticket. Carl Schurz wrote Logan that "there is in the Republican ranks an almost unanimous voice in favor of nominating Lincoln for the vice-presidency."[10]

Both Shermans, John and William Tecumseh, were possible choices. Before he unequivocally took himself out of contention the former general received letters predicting an easy victory if he chose to run. The senator warned his brother to endorse no one, especially not Arthur, whose nomination was "sure defeat." General Sherman agreed. He was bitter toward parties and politicians, telling his politician brother: "All political parties are the same. . . . When the Republicans were in a vast majority they attacked and insulted the very army which rescued them from destruction . . . and reduced my pay. . . . I owe the Republican Party nothing and shall not sacrifice myself for it." Senator Sherman reported his own policy was one of "silence and neutrality" but that he "would gladly take [the nomination] as an honorable closing of 30 years of political life." [11]

Although neither Sherman showed any liking for Logan and refused to endorse him, they both thought he might win. On January 29 John Sherman predicted a Logan victory. The senator felt that General Sherman's withdrawal opened the way for Logan since a military man would add appeal to the ticket. Still he maintained "a strong prejudice" against Black Jack because of his treatment of the general. William Tecumseh Sherman agreed and remembered "Logan acted like a dog to me in 1870 in the Army reduction." However, "Logan has since in several ways shown a change and I must not say a word to his prejudice." Despite the past, the general believed his old foe would make a "good, fair executive." [12]

Other Republicans did not agree. Senator Nelson Aldrich was told by an eastern Republican that soldiers had told him Logan could not command as many veteran votes as several other contenders. Morrill and Barker were both certain the Illinois Stalwart could not be elected, and Illinoisan Elihu B. Washburne was opposed to Logan's "schemes." Former president Hayes called New York the pivotal state, and fear that Logan had no chance there severely limited his availability. [13]

Yet there were those who thought Logan's power in his party's midwestern heartland was so great it might be decisive. A member of the Ohio State Republican Committee and the editor of the *Indianapolis Journal* found large Logan followings in Ohio and Indiana. James H. McNeely, editor of the *Evansville Journal*, leaned toward Logan, whom he had found to be "warm-hearted and in comparison with [Benjamin Harrison], is like a volcano to an iceberg." [14]

Even though it would do him little good either among his party's power brokers or among the mass of the American people, Logan commanded great support among American Negroes. Black newspaper editors hailed Logan as a friend and much preferred him to Blaine, who they felt had betrayed them. The *New York Globe* consistently referred to the Illinoisan as the most available candidate. On January 12 the *Globe* endorsed Logan and gave its reasons: his Civil War record, his honesty, and his battle for veterans' benefits. But the chief factor was his continued support of a "fuller emancipation" of black men when other supposed friends "turned their backs upon the path of duty." The senator was hailed for taking as his guide the Constitution, not conciliation, and for his defense of popular education for Negroes.[15]

The *Washington Bee* ran Logan's name over its masthead as its presidential pick. Logan and Robert Todd Lincoln, wrote the *Bee,* were the two men most honored by Negroes. When the Colored National Executive Committee met in the capital, the *Bee* canvassed its members and found them largely for Logan. The paper also praised Mrs. Logan as a person of refinement who would bring dignity to the White House where she would be a "star." Two other Washington Negro journals, the *People's Advocate* and *Grit,* campaigned for Black Jack. The former called Logan the candidate of the people and reported an interview with Frederick Douglass in which the best known American Negro praised the Illinoisan as one who would run a campaign in which "enthusiasm, unity, and pure Republicanism" would be foremost. Black men would profit by a Logan victory, concluded Douglass. *Grit* came out for Logan over Lincoln, explaining it did so because Logan had done great deeds while Lincoln merely had a great name. The *Baltimore Vindicator* and the *Huntsville (Alabama) Gazette* also supported Logan as the best choice for black people.[16]

Almost every noted Negro leader endorsed the Illinoisan. Frederick Douglass was joined by Blanche K. Bruce, Julian H. Rainey, Robert Smalls, and Professor Richard T. Greener. All of these men agreed with Douglass's reply when asked why blacks favored Logan: "He has backbone." The Negro leader continued: "He is a brave man and does not fear to do right, even though he is surrounded by the most overwhelming opposition. John A. Logan has spread around the Negro the network of the laws."[17]

By May, Logan needed support anywhere he could find it. He had gained almost no backing in the East; Halfbreeds everywhere were going to stick to the end with Blaine, and the Schurz-Edmunds reformers viewed him as a boss hopelessly mired in machine corruption. In commenting on the Logan candidacy, *Nation* clearly stated the case of these eastern "best men" against the Illinois senator. Logan had reached his party position by "perseverance, self-confidence, good-fellowship, and active wire-pulling." The magazine did admit that "personally he is hearty, jovial and engaging." Yet in conclusion *Nation* revealed its elitist bias by proclaiming Black Jack's deficiency in "education, training, solidity of parts, and mental grasp." His nomination would be "looked upon in the eastern states as something altogether outré."[18] The veteran vote and his Civil War record remained his greatest claims to availability. Even though Logan remained a contender, on convention eve his prospects appeared to be declining. Many estimates placed him third, well behind Blaine and Arthur.

That spring a Robert Todd Lincoln boom threatened Logan's place on the ticket. Many Republicans began talking of young Lincoln as an excellent choice for second spot. If he won that, Logan could not possibly be the presidential nominee. Some even continued to mention Lincoln as a presidential contender, a proposal equally damaging to Black Jack. Nevertheless, the party in Illinois remained loyal to Logan. The Republican State Convention cheered Cullom's speech praising him and the body eagerly endorsed Black Jack as its favorite son. At least Illinois would be solid on the first ballot.[19]

For several months prior to the convention, rumors persisted that Logan would engineer a vote trade with one of the two leaders, garnering second place for himself. The Logan camp denied these reports, but they continued. Blaine was more and more singled out as the man with whom Black Jack was bargaining. William Penn Nixon reported Blaine money going to Logan's campaign to make inroads into Arthur's southern delegations. David Davis found a large number of Illinois' convention delegates pledged to Logan until released, whereupon they would quickly switch to the Halfbreed from Maine. Stephen B. Elkins of West Virginia and New Mexico urged Logan to "stick" with Blaine. He felt sure the Arthur and Sherman forces were fighting both Blaine and Logan. "They say beating Blaine beats Logan," Elkins told Black Jack. The wealthy, young G.O.P. leader found no help from Don Cameron, who was for either Arthur or Sherman. With Conkling in retirement and Logan and Cameron divided, the 1880 triumvirate had been broken forever.[20]

One of the most persistent sources of reports of a preconvention

Blaine-Logan deal was the *Chicago Tribune.* For six months before the convention the paper hinted at that combination. In January, Jerome Chaffee was quoted on the subject, and one month later a *Chicago Tribune* correspondent discovered indications that Blaine and Logan "are warm friends, if not indeed, political allies." The contention was denied by a leading Logan advocate. But the story surfaced again in April, and by May the Chicago newspaper was willing to make a flat prediction of eventual cooperation between Logan and Blaine. The Illinoisan had a "dark horse" plan to work hard for the presidency, but, if not nominated, then to say Blaine was his second choice all along and swing to him. On the eve of the convention the *Chicago Tribune* discovered the disposition of some Logan Stalwarts to fight to the end and warned against that tactic as foolish. The paper predicted an early chance for Logan's votes to nominate the Maine Halfbreed and urged the senator's men to act when the time arrived.[21]

The eighth Republican convention was to open on June 3 and politicians began to fill Chicago in late May. A.M. "Long" Jones, Logan's convention floor leader, established the first presidential candidate's headquarters in the city. When journalists continued to ask about the rumored bargain, Jones vowed to fight to the end for Logan. He predicted that neither Blaine nor Arthur could win and that the party would turn to a third man. The hometown advantage was counted in Logan's favor. Yet while a number of Illinois newspapers endorsed Logan, Chicago's most prestigious, the *Tribune,* proclaimed Blaine as its choice. To partially counter the *Tribune,* Springfield's *State Journal* sent a correspondent to give Logan wide coverage. He solicited from Mary "any points . . . that I can use to advantage here." Large crowds were to be marshaled for Logan, and his workers prepared to deluge the city with pamphlets and pictures.[22]

But the biggest story as the delegates gathered was Logan's rumored sellout to Blaine. It was estimated that Black Jack's votes would be just enough to give Blaine the nomination. The *New York Times* reported that on June 2 William Walter Phelps had telegraphed Logan an offer of second place on a Blaine-led ticket. "Long" Jones refused to acknowledge the telegram's existence while promising "I can assure you that Senator Logan will not accept the second place on any ticket." Logan, it was said, had expressed preference for his Senate seat to the vice-presidency.[23]

In the nineteenth century it was considered unseemly for presidential aspirants to attend conventions so Logan remained in Washington in close touch by wire with his son, Jones, and Cullom, who took his banner to Chicago. On the second, young Logan found everyone working "like fiends" and believed inroads were being made among Negro delegates pledged to Arthur. When the meeting opened on Tuesday, June 3, the reformers won the first skirmish when they elected a black Mississippian, John R. Lynch, temporary chairman over Blaine's man, Powell Clayton. Logan wired Cullom and Jones for firsthand information and discovered his fellow senator buoyed by the development. Cullom thought Arthur and Blaine were on the wane, and he had "increased confidence" in Logan's chances. Chicago gambling odds that night were 5 to 1 against Blaine and the president.[24]

Nixon of the *Inter-Ocean,* an Arthur man, encouraged Postmaster General Gresham to attempt a last-minute alliance between Logan and the chief executive. He discovered the Illinois delegates "disturbed and excited" and believed they would abandon Logan after several ballots. Logan, therefore, needed an early victory as much as did Arthur. Gresham, who steadfastly refused to be a candidate as long as Arthur was in the field, continued to labor for the president, but neither he nor anyone else was able to win Logan to Arthur's cause.[25]

On June 4 the delegates battled over platform and rules. The latter struggle attempted to enforce the unit rule during the convention and demanded an oath of loyalty binding all delegates to support the party's nominee after adjournment. George William Curtis, editor of *Harper's,* told those assembled, "A Republican and a free man I will go out of this convention," and the unit rule and loyalty oath failed.[26] That day Logan's managers began sending him regular bulletins as well as other more personal communications. Jones reported that New Hampshire's Senator Edward Rollins was considering Logan but was hesitant because of the rumored Blaine deal. The senator shot back, "Rollins ought to be my friend, he ought to know that I make no pledges to anyone." Logan urged hard work among eastern delegates and recommended abandoning the effort to lure Stephen Elkins away from Blaine before the roll call made it evident Blaine could not win. He heard talk that Illinois delegates were considering designating a second choice, and he angrily denounced the idea. Logan saw such a move as the first step in his defeat and encouraged his leaders to block the proposal.[27]

Excitement grew on the fifth, the day of the nominations. Logan was still encouraged when he asked former Congressman Burton Cook, his proxy vote, to telegraph him his assessment of the situation at the conclusion of the day's business. His managers assured him no time was being lost in working among eastern and southern delegates. However, all was not harmonious in the Logan camp. Reported bickering was disconcerting to the senator one thousand miles from the scene. One Illinoisan, who overconfidently felt "only mismanagement can beat you," believed Jones had "lost his head" and reported hostility between the floor manager and Richard Whiting, another Logan regular. In addition, some of the senator's loyalists suspected Cullom of his own ambitions for a vice-presidential nomination or of wanting to shunt Logan into second place and out of the Senate.[28]

At an evening session on the fifth, John A. Logan was placed in nomination by Senator Cullom. He recited Black Jack's long and distinguished military and political record and emphasized Logan as a man of the people. Then the senator turned to the greatest rationalization for a Logan nomination. He asked the delegates to choose Logan "in behalf of the hundreds of thousands of brave soldiers, who are . . . waiting to know whether that gallant leader of the volunteer soldiers of this country is to receive the nomination at your hands." A tremendous roar greeted the conclusion as the galleries sounded their approval of Illinois' favorite son. When Cullom had finished, he wired the man he had nominated: "I have got you before this convention. . . . My fight is to hold the power and finally secure your nomination." Late that evening Jones's Bulletin No. 18 predicted that the length of the nominating speeches would prevent a ballot until the following morning.[29] He was correct, and by the time Connecticut's Joseph Hawley, Arthur, Sherman, Edmunds, and Blaine had been presented it was so late that adjournment was agreed upon. Most of the nomination oratory had been standard fare, but Blaine's speaker, Judge William H. West of Ohio, the famous "Blind Orator," had lifted the delegates from their stupor and been echoed by shouts of "Blaine! Blaine! The Man from Maine!" Jones's Bulletin No. 19 outlined the Blaine ovation and estimated, "If all the delegates who are on chairs waving handkerchiefs are Blaine men he will be nominated."[30] After trying so often, James G. Blaine at last seemed on the verge of receiving his party's accolade.

Next morning Logan warned his managers to say nothing about his intentions before the balloting began. The first bulletin the candidate received on the sixth announced the *New York Times*'s opinion that neither Blaine nor Arthur could be nominated on the first ballot and that Blaine was trying to combine with Logan. To that point, said the *Times*, Logan had refused. Reports of an Arthur-Edmunds combine also circulated.[31]

Late the previous night the Illinois delegation had caucused, and with "everybody at sea" Arthur men tried to force a second choice together with a unit rule binding all delegates to vote for Arthur when Logan pulled out. The attempt was beaten down. Suspicions of Cullom's motivation remained alive, and Jerome Chaffee wired Logan that Black Jack's friends suspected the junior senator of "infidelity" and of overtures to Arthur. Burton Cook and "Long" Jones also had the wires crackling that Saturday morning. Cook told the senator of the possible Arthur-Edmunds alliance and feared if neither of those men could win they might shift to Lincoln. Cook's first ballot prediction named Blaine the leader with "not quite enough. I think!" Jones sent assurances that Logan had solid second-ballot strength in the Oregon delegation; nevertheless, Blaine's leaders were already "treating us as if we must do their bidding and all go in for him at once." In the face of all the talk of combination Logan replied, "I hope Illinois will stand by me no matter who Arthur and Edmunds combine on. . . . Do not let our friends get alarmed and stampeded."[32] When the roll call of the states began it was evident Blaine would run ahead with Arthur a strong second. At the first ballot's conclusion the Maine Halfbreed had 334½ of the 411 necessary to win, Arthur had 278, Edmunds 93, Logan 63½, Sherman 30, Hawley 13, with 6 scattered. Forty of Logan's votes were from Illinois and ten were from Missouri. From one to three votes were cast by delegates from Alabama, Kansas, Kentucky, Louisiana, North Carolina, Pennsylvania, Tennessee, Texas, and Virginia. The second ballot pushed Blaine's total to 349 while Arthur had 276, Edmunds 85, and Logan, losing two Missouri votes, 61½. On the third roll call Blaine jumped to 375, Arthur held at 274, Edmunds dropped to 69, and Logan, with defections in Missouri and five southern states, dropped to 53. A key point had been reached. Blaine was steadily climbing toward nomination. Logan's managers wired in Bulletin No. 68, "Indications strong that Blaine will be nominated on next ballot." The votes Logan still claimed could easily give Blaine his victory.[33]

Logan, receiving a state-by-state rundown on each ballot, was well aware of the situation and of the nuances of timing. He quickly sent Cullom a dispatch: "The Republicans of the States that must be relied upon to elect the President having so strongly shown a preference for Mr. Blaine, I deem it my duty not to stand in the way of the people's choice and recommend my following to assist in his nomination." An accompanying wire asked that the withdrawal be read to the convention, but permission was denied. Just after he wired Cullom, Logan informed Chaffee, "Have just sent Cullom request to cast vote for B." Even though Cullom was not able to read Logan's telegram the news rapidly circulated among the delegations amid great excitement. When the clerk reached Illinois on the fourth ballot Cullom withdrew Logan's name and cast thirty-four votes for the man from Maine. The bandwagon was rolling, and by the end of the roll call Blaine had 541 votes and his party's nomination. One Logan worker expressed the obvious facts: "Your telegram led the break and has placed him under lasting obligation to you." [34]

A Logan-for-vice-president cry went up even before the ballot had ended. However, many delegates were checked by a feeling Logan would not accept. Jones wired that such an offer would be forthcoming and that at the very least Blaine would consult the Logan managers before naming anyone. Since that consultation would take place immediately after adjournment Jones asked Logan to "answer quick." Although Jones did not know it, Walter Q. Gresham was receiving pleas that he take the second spot. Old-time Logan enemy Bluford Wilson wired the postmaster general that Illinois would unanimously back Gresham. Logan did receive a note from Chaffee predicting Lincoln's nomination unless Logan acted. He strongly preferred Logan and asked that Black Jack act at once. In the midst of these appeals the Illinoisan received a telegram from Blaine leader Robert R. Hitt. Hitt, speaking for Blaine friends Whitelaw Reid, William W. Phelps, and Stephen B. Elkins, wired "you can have anything you want but beg you to decline the vice presidency in telegram immediately to Phelps." This mysterious communication is clarified nowhere in the Logan manuscripts. Perhaps Chaffee was right that Blaine wanted Robert Lincoln's name on the ticket. Logan paid no attention to Hitt's appeal, and when Cullom, Cook, and Clark Carr wired "Will you accept nomination for vice-president. Pennsylvania offers it, we think we can carry it," he sent back, "The convention must do what they think best under the circumstances." [35]

That night the roll call reached Illinois and cheering filled the hall as Cullom presented Logan and then yielded to Kansas whose Senator Preston B. Plumb placed Black Jack in nomination. After a number of seconding speeches, including one by a North Carolina Negro, Logan was nominated by acclamation. Then it was pointed out that the rules prescribed a roll call. Amid great cheering the Illinois Stalwart got every vote except those of seven die-hard New Yorkers.[36]

At the end of the fight Logan telegraphed Shelby Cullom his "sincere gratitude" for his support. From Santa Fe, Dollie expressed surprise that her father had accepted second place and that his votes had given Blaine the top spot. For his support of Blaine, Dollie praised her father's "generosity" especially toward "a man who has been *false* to you from the first." She wrote resignedly, "I suppose one must expect such things in politics."[37]

"Such things" might have included a preconvention deal between Blaine and Logan. There is no conclusive evidence that a bargain was made. Neither the Logan collections, the Blaine papers, the standard Blaine biography, nor recent studies of national party politics in this period offer proof of a plot. Furthermore, the hour-by-hour bulletins and telegrams from the senator to his aides are filled with the feeling that Logan hoped lightning might still strike. A deal might have been talked about, but these communications indicate it had not been consummated. The unexplained Hitt telegram established doubt that any Blaine promise of the vice-presidency existed. Logan confidant Jerome B. Chaffee wrote the senator on the night of the sixth to protest Logan's loss of the presidential nomination through "treachery." He especially accused Missouri's Chauncey I. Filley of failing to keep his delegates in line. Of course, Chaffee might not have been privy to any deal, but he was an important advisor in close contact with the Logan managers as well as with the senator.[38] Finally there is the simple logic of Logan's nomination. Both geographically and factionally the Illinois Stalwart balanced the Maine Halfbreed. Then too, for the first time since the Civil War the G.O.P. presidential nominee had no military record. No Republican could retain the allegiance of voters influenced by bloody-shirt issues and the mystique of the uniform any better than John A. Logan.

But the *New York Times* carried a story of Logan's admission that Cullom had gone to Chicago with instructions to give the Illinois votes to Blaine when the time was ripe. There was also Logan's cryptic telegram on the morning of the sixth sent to both C.A. Logan and John A. Logan, Jr.: "Do not say anything about what I may do. Let the convention judge." Postconvention letters by long-time Republicans William Henry Smith and Leonard Swett both gave reports of a deal. Smith had seen that development well before the convention and had warned Whitelaw Reid and Murat Halstead that putting Logan on the ticket "would intensify the objection to Blaine." Reid, according to Smith, simply replied that the "bargain had to be consummated." Swett's information was more circumstantial, but he had been so confident of its accuracy that he wired David Davis on Tuesday evening that the ticket would be Blaine and Logan. The Chicago attorney saw such a well-orchestrated Blaine effort that he was convinced a deal had been included. Blaine forces, he wrote Davis, had the convention under control like a "lassoed steer." One Logan biographer has found Logan's willingness to surrender rather than fight to the bitter end, as he had in 1877 and 1880, an indication of some kind of prior arrangement.[39] Yet in both his Senate fight and the Grant third-term bid his cause was close to victory, only a few ballots from the top in a long deadlock. This time he was a dark horse far behind a popular leader whose vote total was rapidly mounting.

One explanation for Logan's actions came from the senator himself. Shortly after his nomination a *Chicago Tribune* reporter interviewed Logan at his "modest boarding house." Sitting beside a telegraph, surrounded by bundles of dispatches, the Illinoisan began with, "Well Blaine is nominated at last after the third trial and I am glad of it." He continued:

I could have told you this morning . . . that I should telegraph to my friends at Chicago at the proper time that it was my wish that they should cast their votes for Blaine. I had already written to Burton C. Cook to that effect, so that the letter might be used in the event that there should be any difficulty in communicating by wire, but I preferred that the letter should not be used too early for two reasons—first, I wanted a fair test of my own chances; and second, I did not wish to have the letter used as a basis of combinations which might defeat my purpose, and today directly the second ballot came clicking in here over this wire and I saw that Mr. Blaine had gained, I at once telegraphed Mr. Cullom.[40]

Deal or not, John A. Logan had been nominated for vice-president of the United States. The night after his selection the senator wrote to his son: "It is all right and I am satisfied with the result." Before he put down "satisfied" Logan had written "delighted" and then crossed it out.[41]

CHAPTER 14

Plumed Knight and Black Eagle

THE REACTION to the Blaine-Logan slate was mixed. Most Halfbreeds and Stalwarts began to organize the presidential campaign. Reformers, however, were alienated by both men. Blaine's connection with the Mulligan letters and Logan's reputation as one of the nation's leading machine bosses caused the defection of Republican reformers such as Carl Schurz and George W. Curtis, who led a faction that Charles A. Dana of the *New York Sun* called "Mugwumps." The word was Indian meaning "big chief," and Dana thought it fitting because the Mugwumps thought themselves superior to other party members. The Mugwumps announced that they would endorse any Democrat with a reputation for honesty. Friends of New York Governor Grover Cleveland, who was considered acceptable to the Mugwumps, were certain Blaine's nomination boosted the governor's chances. When Cleveland received the nomination the reformers gave him their allegiance. *Nation* and *Harper's Weekly* led the vanguard followed by the *New York Times, New York Herald, New York Post,* and *Boston Herald. Harper's* denounced party allegiance at any price, called the election a battle of personalities, and endorsed Cleveland. From Illinois, Lyman Trumbull, the old Liberal Republican, deplored the Republican choices, predicting their victory would mean a continuation of "partisanship, abuses, and corruption" that would ultimately endanger Republican government.[1]

In the days following the nomination, Logan received dozens of congratulatory messages, including many which, while offering best wishes, thought the ticket should have been reversed. Blaine wired, "I am proud and honored by being associated with you in the national campaign." A little later he informed Logan he was about to publish his letter of acceptance, and he wanted Logan's to come out at about the same time. "If

186

mine is out first, you can adjust so that we shall not have any sharp conflicts," wrote Blaine. He concluded, "slight differences of view are not objectionable and are, I suppose, quite inevitable." Former Wisconsin Governor Lucius Fairchild told Logan his choice strengthened the ticket; Chauncey I. Filley denied Schurz could control the Missouri German voters and promised to win them over. Stephen B. Elkins thought prospects were good but declined appointment as national committee chairman in favor of the wealthy B.F. Jones of Pennsylvania.[2]

As the days passed letters continued to arrive by the bale. Logan's brother sent his congratulations and said he guessed now he would have to vote for Blaine; but a Cairo Republican, while offering his assistance to Logan, admitted "I can't go Blaine." Explorer F.V. Hayden saw a victory for the West if Logan won and proclaimed Mugwump Carl Schurz a "dead duck." Negro Republicans solicited Logan's appearance at a national gathering of black citizens, and Frederick Douglass offered his voice in Logan's behalf. From the South, solidly Democratic in 1880, came several pleas for assistance before the Republican party disappeared forever from that "slavery cursed" section. Logan talked confidently of taking North Carolina and Florida in spite of predicted outrages against Republicans there.[3]

The reaction of Illinois Republicans to the ticket was predictably divided. Most party leaders seemed pleased, and few Mugwumps surfaced in the Prairie State. Trumbull and Davis had long since been out of power; their reservations might not be serious. Acting Governor John M. Hamilton was completely satisfied with the slate. Since he hoped to succeed Logan in the Senate, Hamilton had a great interest in a Republican victory. Cullom worked hard but worried about others putting "their shoulders to the wheel" in the quest for funds. William Henry Smith was depressed by the national Mugwump defection, which he thought was serious. The lack of enthusiasm among the traditionally Republican German electorate was also disturbing to him. Smith had tried vainly to swing George W. Curtis into John Sherman's camp, feeling Edmunds had no chance. Now he thought the price of Curtis's refusal to follow his advice was the Blaine-Logan combination. Smith was not pleased with the ticket nor was he sanguine as to its chances for success.[4]

Rutherford B. Hayes certainly agreed with Smith. He regarded the Republican choice as a "blunder and misfortune," saw little hope of taking New York, and was not encouraged. However, he would support

Blaine and Logan, for a Democratic victory would be a "serious calamity." In their convention postmortems several reformers deplored the failure of Mugwumps to join behind Arthur, thus halting the Blaine tide. Benjamin Bristow labeled the Curtis-Schurz forces "idiots," and David Davis called them "stupid" for their failure. A Kentucky Independent echoed the thought of many when he estimated that Logan's selection could only solidify the support of those already loyal while it would not influence borderline areas or groups.[5]

All Republicans did not agree. Leaders of the Rhode Island G.O.P. informed Nelson Aldrich they were pleased and would exert themselves for the "Plumed Knight and the Black Eagle." Veteran Vermont Senator Justin Morrill applauded the party for choosing Logan, always a patriot and ever victorious. Even David Davis, although he expressed reservations, believed Blaine was a better man than Garfield. Negro Republicans, though cautious of Blaine, were exultant at Logan's nomination. "Hon. John A. Logan on the ticket means victory," predicted the *Washington Bee*. Blacks across the North supported the Republican ticket and organized Blaine-Logan clubs, which worked enthusiastically for votes.[6]

One disappointed contestant for the nomination who was not pleased with Logan was John Sherman. He thought Blaine's nomination "a good one," but exclaimed, "I don't like Logan." The Ohioan branded Black Jack as "coarse, suspicious, and revengeful" and unfit to preside over the Senate. He was convinced the Illinoisan hated both him and his brother "with a venom that will only end in the grave." Nevertheless, the senator announced his support of his party's chosen leaders. The general was so relieved at not being chosen himself that he "would approve anything." But he thought the convention had been filled with the "deviltry and dishonesty" that made him more determined than ever to remain out of the arena. "Cump" accused Logan of "crowing too loud" and criticized newspaper stories of Logan's Civil War career. In the end, however, he could not blame Black Jack for everything written by partisan journalists. But the general could never forget Logan's army bill, which had reduced his pay. To his brother he excoriated "you Senators" for tamely submitting to Logan—"for which reason I mistrust all politicians." In spite of all this, Sherman believed Republicans *"must"* stand by the ticket "even if Logan be the devil himself." The general promised his brother to do and say nothing that would impair Logan's chances. Sherman also sent to Blaine an estimate of his running mate. He characterized Black Jack as "ardent, brave, enthusiastic," and an able military leader. He reminded the Maine senator that Logan had been a bitter Sherman foe in the 1860s and 1870s but he added, "Logan has spasms of generosity as well as hatred and I will be too happy to aid his chances by being in full witness to his really good qualities."[7]

Publishers soon contacted Logan in search of material for the standard campaign biographies. Thomas W. Knox, J.W. Buel, and Byron Andrews, as well as George F. Dawson, wrote partisan, unbalanced laudatory studies with an eye to electoral success, not accuracy. Dawson sent out five hundred complimentary copies for use in the campaign and others to book dealers. He told Mary he was not interested in making money but he was "anxious that it should have a large circulation for the general's sake." From Washington, Hinton R. Helper asked for photographs of the Logan family for inclusion in Buel's work. Finally, Edward W. Currier and James M. Ives, the noted artists, asked for Logan's signature so that they might include its facsimile on the official campaign portrait they were making.[8]

The platform on which Blaine and Logan ran was a collection of platitudes, some waving of the bloody shirt, and a firm stand on protection. Not much was said about veterans. Blaine developed the economic issues, securely wrapping the tariff in the flag, while to Black Jack was left the appeal to veterans and to all those who still found solace in the bloody shirt. The Democrats denounced Republican dishonesty, pledging to restore honest government to the nation. The party straddled the tariff issue.[9]

The 1884 election was a battle of personalities as well as of issues. It was a duel of charges made against both the personal and public lives of the standard-bearers. Blaine was assailed as a corruptionist who had accepted bribes from railroads. Midway through the contest a Republican newspaper charged Cleveland with fathering an illegitimate child and the cry, "Ma, Ma, Where's My Pa?" hung over the last two months of the election. The New York Democrat admitted the charge to the dismay of his Mugwump backers. Nevertheless, they stuck with him, reasoning that a man of public honesty and private immorality was better suited to the White House than one whose values were reversed. The vice-presidential candidates, Logan and Indiana's Thomas Hendricks, came in for a lesser share of mudslinging. Hendricks was branded a traitorous Copperhead and a dangerous inflationist. Democrats revived stories that Logan had supported the Confederacy in 1861 and that he was a member of the whisky ring. While Thomas Nast's cartoons in *Harper's* viciously portrayed Blaine, they rarely included his running mate.

Before he could devote his full time to the campaign trail, Logan had to return to Congress. The first session had rambled on through the conventions and was grinding to an end in early July. Logan was very inactive in the last months, but he did rise on July 4 to make a personal explanation. Congressman William McAdoo of New Jersey dubbed Logan a "land grabber" involved in an illegal scheme to take over 80,000 acres in New Mexico from the Zuni Indians. On this land he and his confederates supposedly grazed 30,000 head of cattle. Will Tucker and several of his fellow officers were also implicated. Logan, commenting on this picture of affluence, told the Senate, "I wish this were true, but there is no foundation for the statement." He called the charges malicious and read letters from the Geological Survey chief in New Mexico and from Secretary of the Interior Henry M. Teller absolving the Illinoisan of any wrongdoing. He stridently rose to Will Tucker's defense with a challenge: "When any one thinks I have not manhood enough to defend openly any of my family or friends when wrongfully assailed, he mistakes me." [10]

Logan was exhausted by his efforts and he had no time to rest when the session ended. Mary reported he was working under great strain and was "beset from every quarter." She moaned that she had "not a dollar with which to do anything" and told Dollie her father was "keeping up bravely." John Logan, Jr., despite a warning from General Merritt that West Point's summer camp might exhaust him, went anyway. [11]

When Congress adjourned Logan began to respond to some of the great number of requests for speeches that he had received. His first junket was to Maine, where he made a few speeches and conferred with Blaine on campaign strategy. Then he traveled to the national G.A.R. encampment in Minneapolis, where he was warmly received by huge crowds. He returned worn out from shaking hands. Mary remained in Washington when Logan went to Minnesota and she wrote her daughter that she would join him on his next tour since "Papa is growing more dependent on me for *company*." [12]

In August the Logans went to New York for a week of speeches and meetings with the national committee. New York Senator Warner Miller believed that if the election was held in August the Republicans would carry his state by a large majority. Late that month Black Jack made a triumphant return to Chicago after a brief swing through Michigan. The candidate was pleased with the crowds, and Mary called the Cook County reception the "largest thing of the kind I ever saw," eclipsing Grant's reception there when he returned from his world tour in 1879.[13]

Logan ended August speaking at Rockford, Illinois. He joined Richard Oglesby, the gubernatorial candidate, on the platform. Logan applauded Oglesby's remarks but warned him to husband his strength for the long battle ahead. "We are not as young as we once were," cautioned the senator, who was alarmed at Oglesby's look of exhaustion when he finished his address. At the end of August, Logan received reports of Arthur's coolness and of an alarmingly high number of Germans allied with the Mugwumps. He also heard fears that John P. St. John's Prohibition party might siphon off votes from the Republicans. That month rumors were spread that St. John had told voters Logan was a drunkard and a gambler, but the dry candidate sent Logan a quick denial.[14]

To assist the ticket in Illinois, National Chairman B.F. Jones solicited support from Robert Ingersoll. The great orator found both candidates "a little tainted with original sin." He wrote, "It is a nasty business and the principle issues in the campaign will be fornication and adultery—great country!" But he did raise his voice once again for the Grand Old Party.[15]

On September 1 Logan addressed the Wisconsin Republican State Convention and remained in the state for several days before making a three-week tour of Ohio, Michigan, New York, Pennsylvania, and West Virginia. While in Chicago, Logan heard from B.F. Jones, who thanked him for his hopeful predictions about his native state. Jones was concerned about the apathy of overconfidence and he hoped Black Jack could rally the voters. The chairman forecast a victory in Maine and Vermont, states that voted in September. The two New England states did vote Republican, cheering the Logans with that news.[16]

The long September tour focused in particular on Ohio, considered a vital, but doubtful, state. Some Republican leaders reported a mass of Blaine and Logan clubs being organized there. Through the summer heat, which made it a "very hard trip," the vice-presidential candidate stumped Toledo, Sandusky, Youngstown, Akron, Wheeling, Columbus, Dayton, and Cincinnati. In one day he made seventeen speeches in a swing from Akron to Wheeling. At one stop he shared the platform with Maine's

Thomas B. Reed and Cassius M. Clay of Kentucky. After a brief return to Chicago, Logan resumed the trail in Indiana and Ohio. Once in late September his appearance before a large gathering of veterans threatened to draw people away from a nearby Blaine address and plans had to be altered. On September 29 the two candidates campaigned together in Cleveland.[17]

Another change of plan concerned a projected Logan trip to New England. Powerful northeastern Republicans asked Black Jack to visit their section. Henry Cabot Lodge, the Massachusetts state chairman, and Senators George F. Hoar, Nelson Aldrich, and Joseph R. Hawley sent requests. A large meeting to be addressed by Logan, Hoar, and Hawley was set for Pittsfield, Massachusetts; John and Mary were to stay with the Hoars while in the Bay State. However, plans were changed when it was decided Logan could be of more help in the West, especially in Ohio, Indiana, and Illinois. Lodge acquiesced in the change but hoped for a Logan appearance late in the contest. Except for his early trip to Maine, however, Black Jack did not go east of New York.[18]

On October 7 Logan reached Washington, where he rested for a day before retracing his path across Pennsylvania, West Virginia, Ohio, Indiana, and into Illinois. At Philadelphia he joined former Stalwart ally Don Cameron in addressing a crowd of thirty thousand. By the time Logan reached Ohio that state had held its state elections, which the Republicans won. A Canton Republican telegraphed the results to the Illinoisan thanking him for his efforts to which "we owe much." After Ohio's October results were in, the national committee believed its electoral votes were secure and urged concentration on the doubtful states of Indiana, New Jersey, New York, and Connecticut.[19]

Logan spoke in Illinois in late October before making a rapid sweep through Iowa. After a return to Illinois for a large gathering in Springfield addressed by Logan, Robert Todd Lincoln, and Oglesby, the senator spent the last few days of the campaign in Indiana, one of the doubtful states.[20]

Throughout the campaign John Logan's speeches sang a familiar tune. They were filled with an appeal to veterans and contained a sometimes muted, sometimes strident, bloody-shirt note. He supported the party platform's tariff plank in an effort to harmonize his views with the more strongly protectionist Blaine. Logan often defended his running mate, and once his biographer, George F. Dawson, wrote the vice-presidential candidate to suggest he stop defending Blaine and advocate a more positive program. "It should be assumed that Blaine needs no defense," was the advice from Dawson.[21]

Logan spoke in G.A.R. halls, city auditoriums, and from the rear platforms of trains. He sometimes gave a number of speeches in one day as he whistle-stopped the Middle West. Democrats did more than accuse the man they still regarded as an apostate of corruption; they hooted at him from the edge of crowds and mimicked his grammar and rough ways. The *New York Times* claimed a lifelong Irish Democrat told Logan he would vote for him because "you're the mon wot will murther the King's English, and for that rayson alon Oi intend to vote for ye."[22]

Relations between Logan and Blaine during their joint effort were distant at best. The more polished easterner had little in common with the blunt Illinoisan. Years of hostility as leaders of opposing Republican factions could not be wiped out by a few handclasps in the name of unity. The refusal of leading Stalwarts such as Conkling to campaign for the ticket increased the distance between the Plumed Knight and the Black Eagle. Logan's greed for publicity also disturbed both Blaine and the national committee. The Illinoisan complained that his speeches were not given enough coverage and that the campaign was not being waged aggressively enough. The sparsity of correspondence between the two men who were carrying the Republican banner is mute indication of the coolness between them. Logan's coolness toward Blaine coupled with Black Jack's supposed penchant for bad grammar led to an 1884 jingle: "We never speak as we pass by / Me to Jim Blaine nor him to I."[23]

The early victories in Maine, Vermont, and Ohio raised Republican hopes and centered the last-minute efforts of both parties on New York. Against the advice of several party leaders, including Logan, Blaine decided to make a late October appearance in New York City with the state hanging precariously between the two parties. He was welcomed to a meeting of Protestant ministers with a condemnation of the Democrats as the party of "Rum, Romanism, and Rebellion." Following that disastrous anti-Catholic slur Blaine attended a lavish feast to which Logan had been invited but, due to commitments in Indiana, was not able to attend. The Democrats dubbed this banquet "Belshazzar's Feast." On October 8 Dawson had written Logan that enough of the New York Irish vote, assiduously courted, would wind up in the Republican column so that the state would be safe in November. In one day that safe vote had been endangered.[24]

The influence of the Mugwumps, concentrated as it was in the Northeast, threatened to make the last-minute Republican blunders in New York more serious than they would have been originally. Carl Schurz, who thought that "thoughtful and patriotic men should recoil from a Blaine-Logan administration," spoke and wrote for Cleveland. Benjamin Bristow predicted a large group of stay-at-home Republicans would damage the G.O.P. as much as Mugwump defections.[25] In New York one of the stay-at-homes was Roscoe Conkling.

Ironically, the scholarly, genteel Mugwumps, convinced that they were "the upper house in the politics of the world," engaged in many of the partisan activities they so deplored in Blaine and Logan. They formed exclusive organizations, published inflammatory pamphlets, sent out rabble-rousing speakers, and slanted their news reporting. Finally, these reformers never seemed to recognize that their own narrow class interests influenced their political actions.[26]

On election eve Blaine wired his running mate urging him to prod members of the national committee to one final push. Blaine voted at his home in Augusta while Black Jack cast his ballot in Chicago. That night the Logan party awaited the returns and read the dozens of telegrams congratulating the senator on his elevation to the vice-presidency. Illinois was counted in the Republican column early as was Ohio. Indiana returns were slow coming in, and as they did John New telegraphed doubts about Republican victory. New York was a similar story. George F. Dawson, Stephen B. Elkins, and Samuel Fessenden reported a close tally but all three were confident of carrying the Empire State. Logan also received a number of appeals from party faithful asking for information on New York returns and warning against Democratic frauds there. These communications continued to come in until the early hours of the sixth.[27]

By the morning of November 6 returns from the contested states had begun to turn against Blaine and Logan. New, citing votes purchased with the Democrats' "abundant money" as the cause, feared the loss of the Hoosier State. Dawson persisted in his optimism, giving New York to the G.O.P. by just over 1,000 votes. Late on the sixth an anxious Dollie wired her parents in search of the final count. Two days after the election John New regretfully told Logan that Indiana had been lost and reports from New York now predicted a 1,000-vote Democratic plurality. Yet the *New York Tribune* still claimed victory for Blaine, the G.O.P. demanded a recount, and the *Chicago Tribune* told its readers that Logan remained confident of victory. Future Republican vice-president Garret Hobart assured Logan, "we . . . are protecting every point from fraud." [28]

As the count wore on, despite continual Republican cries of trickery and fraud, there was no material change from the early report of a Democratic triumph. With New York's vote excluded, Cleveland led Blaine 183 to 182 in the electoral college. The Empire State recount gave Cleveland a 1,143-vote plurality out of the 1,167,000 votes cast. Nationwide Cleveland won a narrow 4,911,017 to 4,848,334 victory. Prohibitionist St. John garnered 150,369 votes and Logan's old Radical comrade Ben Butler polled 175,370 votes as the candidate of the Antimonopoly-Greenback party. [29] Even after the results were finally tallied some Democrats feared desperate measures by the opposition. One New York Democrat sensed a plot to obstruct Cleveland's inauguration the following March. [30]

Logan's coattails helped to pull his ticket through in Illinois by a 25,000-vote plurality. Oglesby won the governor's race, but the general assembly was so closely divided that the upcoming Senate race seemed in doubt. Black Jack had devoted so much time to the national contest that he had not been able to put in his usual time and mileage in the Prairie State. After losing the vice-presidency Logan was in peril of losing his seat in the Senate. [31]

"There would now be no doubt about the result if our ticket had been the other end up," wrote G.A.R. leader Mortimer D. Leggett after the election. There were many such statements from Logan partisans. The *Washington Bee* continued to praise the Illinoisan as "the friend of the Negro," adding that a Democratic victory could have been avoided by placing Logan first on the ticket. [32]

Bitter Republicans had a legion of excuses for defeat. Shelby Cullom believed his party had been "crushed out by cranks on the one side, whisky on the other." Whitelaw Reid saw the tide turned "by a wretched accident" in New York. Philadelphian Wharton Barker sent regrets for his defeat but urged Logan to put aside past mistakes and go on to new efforts to enact a Republican legislative program in spite of the Cleveland presidency. Robert Ingersoll saw the election as a crushing blow to Blaine's career, but he felt Logan's stock was still high. The latter sentiment was shared by many of Logan's friends. Ever since his vice-presidential nomination Black Jack had received letters from those who were certain he would be the G.O.P. presidential nominee four years later. Logan biographer Byron Andrews sounded the call: "Let's get ready for 1888." [33]

John A. Logan's addition to the Republican ticket in 1884 probably pleased the veterans, but it did not bring all the Stalwarts into line. Roscoe Conkling's hatred of Blaine could not be overcome by Logan's influence. When asked to campaign for the Maine Halfbreed, "Lord Roscoe" grumpily replied: "I do not engage in criminal practice." It is impossible to determine John Logan's effect on the voters, although some estimates place the Democratic veteran vote at its highest mark since the Civil War. The bloody shirt's appeal had waned, and Logan's technique, while gathering cheering crowds, did not effect results as it had in the past. [34]

Yet perhaps Logan's nomination *was* a determining factor in the outcome. He appealed to party factions that were already intensely loyal, but his record made him anathema to independent and reform Republicans. He could not bring in any elements that Blaine had not already captured. The nomination of Robert Todd Lincoln or Walter Q. Gresham might have prevented the defections that contributed to the razor-thin margin of defeat. On the other hand, Blaine alone could have so alienated the potential defectors and stay-at-homes that no running mate could have changed the result. In the end the race was so close and hung on such slender threads that perhaps no satisfactory explanation of the outcome is possible.

It is possible that both Republicans and Democrats in 1884 and historians since have assigned too much importance to the effect of Blaine's record and therefore of the Mugwump movement. A look at voting trends in the years following the Civil War indicates a gradual decline in Republican percentages after 1872. Yet the 1884 vote saw a smaller Republican decline than had been the case in the two previous elections or would be the case in the two subsequent contests. In New York the Republican ticket actually made considerable gains over the midterm election of 1882. Cleveland did far better running for governor in 1882 than running for president in 1884. [35]

National economic conditions also must be taken into account. In 1882 a recession set in, and by the spring of 1884 the depression of the mid-eighties had brought hard times to many Americans. A reaction against the Republican administration in office as the economy faltered could have swung votes to the Democrats.

Furthermore, recent studies indicate that except for sectionalism, party affiliations were rooted in family tradition, religion, and local issues. Historian Robert Marcus has written: "Questions that voters of the Gilded Age found salient revolved almost exclusively about local cultural conflicts: native versus immigrant, Protestant versus Catholic, evangelical temperance-oriented church groups versus liturgical tradition-oriented Lutherans." These local-oriented political influences make the understanding of close national elections even more difficult.[36]

Democrats were unconcerned about the reasons they had won their first presidential election since 1856. One Democratic journal reviewed the facts and laughingly reported:

THE WORLD SAYS THE INDEPENDENTS DID IT
THE TRIBUNE SAYS THE STALWARTS DID IT
THE SUN SAYS BURCHARD DID IT
BLAINE SAYS ST. JOHN DID IT
THEODORE ROOSEVELT SAYS IT WAS THE SOFT SOAP DINNER
WE SAY BLAINE'S CHARACTER DID IT
BUT WE DON'T CARE WHAT DID IT
IT'S DONE.[37]

When Black Jack was asked his feelings about losing, he told a story more often attributed to another Illinoisan—Abraham Lincoln. "I feel," said Logan, "like the man who stubbed his toe and replied to a sympathetic neighbor, 'I'm too big too cry, and it hurts too bad for me to laugh.'"[38]

CHAPTER 15

The Logan Machine and the "Still Hunt"

THE SECOND session of the Forty-eighth Congress did not detain John A. Logan for long. The senator had not lavished his usual close personal care on Illinois politics in 1884, and he felt he must now compensate for that failure. He would shortly have to contend with an assembly whose one-vote Republican majority in the upper house was balanced by a one-vote Democratic majority in the lower chamber. Furthermore, Logan would have to wage his reelection battle without the powerful promise of patronage behind him. Whitelaw Reid wrote in November sounding out the former general on the possibility of writing his reminiscences of the Civil War. The *New York Tribune* editor thought "a little literary work might furnish an agreeable diversion." Facing the Senate struggle Logan did not need a diversion, agreeable or otherwise, and even Reid's promise of money could not lure Black Jack. He did promise a series of articles but warned Reid of the gravity of the impending fight. The editor agreed and promised any help the *New York Tribune* could give. He concluded on a note that could not have consoled the already depressed senator: "Sincerely hope the outlook there is more cheerful than some of the newspapers indicate."[1]

In his twenty-two-day attendance in the Senate, Black Jack did little. He was named one of the thirteen Senate members of a committee to open the New Orleans Exposition. In addition, the Illinoisan increased the staff of the Military Affairs Committee, which he stated had considered 37 percent of the Senate's business during the previous session. Finally, he voted with the majority as a bill passed enabling the Dakota Territory to apply for statehood.[2]

Off the floor, the Republicans' last patronage days brought an effort by Walter Q. Gresham to obtain confirmation as U.S. circuit judge at Chicago. Cullom endorsed Gresham, but the outgoing postmaster general was unsure of Logan. "I have no reason to suppose that Senator Logan will be unfriendly but you know that he is sometimes a little singular," wrote Gresham. Logan played his own patronage game in Illinois and finally admitted to newly elected Governor Richard Oglesby, in a very cordial letter, that he was tired of pleading: "this is a good man and qualified for any place you may see fit . . . or words to that effect." [3]

John A. Logan, Jr., who had returned to West Point the past summer, left the academy for good that winter, and the Tuckers came from New Mexico to spend the winter in Chicago. The senator wanted Will to aid him in Springfield in what Mary forecast as a "very long contest." In spite of the November defeat and the tension ahead, the Logans spent a festive holiday season. Mary, dressed in a "dark embossed velvet train, with front of pink plush under duchesse lace," assisted at the presidential reception. The senator was present "in his happiest mood and was at all times . . . surrounded by friends." After the president's affair the Logans entertained at a large reception in their newly rented home at 3 Iowa Circle. It was proclaimed one of the most brilliant parties of the day. Just after New Year's Day, Black Jack left for Chicago, but Mary remained in Washington. [4]

By the time the incumbent arrived in Illinois speculation was already swirling around the Senate fight. Governor John M. Hamilton believed Charles Farwell would support Logan only to lie in wait and claim the seat when Logan failed. On January 1 the *Chicago Tribune* reported that Farwell had endorsed Logan. The *Tribune*, which strongly supported the senator's reelection, also claimed Logan had written his friends in the legislature that the caucus should not nominate him unless its members were "determined to stand by him to the end." *Nation* forecast Logan's defeat, but it surprisingly urged the party to stick by him since he had loyally served the party as vice-presidential nominee in 1884; to abandon Logan would produce widespread demoralization. Oglesby was confident Logan would eventually win, but Logan, vowing to remain alert to trickery, thought a choice in "a tied legislature is doubtful." Prominently mentioned Democrats were John M. Palmer, J.D. Black, Carter Harrison, and an old Logan associate from Egypt, William Ralls Morrison. Men on both sides suggested David Davis, the perpetual compromise man. [5]

The early skirmishing indicated that Independent Elijah Haines, a seven-term representative, might be a key figure. Haines had opposed

Logan in 1877 and 1879 and announced he wanted "anybody" but Logan in 1885. He might vote for another Republican, if there was a chance that the incumbent might be unseated. However, another rumor had it that Haines, who wanted to be speaker, might trade Logan's election for the speakership. In the 1885 duel the *Chicago Tribune* solidly supported Black Jack while William Penn Nixon's *Inter-Ocean,* critical of the senator, urged him to put party above self and, alluding to 1877, editorialized, "A good fighter knows when he is beaten." The opposition *State Register* predicted a Logan defeat.[6]

On January 7 the Republicans organized the Senate by their one-vote margin, 26 to 25. The House attempted to organize, but Haines's ambitions and the close division prevented final action. Logan reached Springfield on the eighth to find his rooms at the Leland thronged with members of both parties paying their respects. Next morning he breakfasted with Black and Morrison, and the three chatted pleasantly. More and more press reports surfaced predicting that Logan would eventually be chosen by Oglesby after the deadlock had rendered an assembly victory impossible. The *Inter-Ocean* felt that the senator did not really think he would be elected. Hovering over the session from its first gavel was Charles Farwell, a traitor waiting to strike, according to the *Tribune,* a loyal Republican who could draw Democratic votes and win, according to the *Inter-Ocean.*[7]

Logan was enraged at Farwell's duplicity, but he told Mary he would "fight it out, no matter how long it takes." "I *will be elected* . . . or else no one else will be," he swore. He complained often of the costs of a long stay in Springfield and fatalistically wondered if he was not "doomed to misfortune."[8]

As January passed, the House remained unorganized until the twenty-ninth when Haines was finally selected and Governor Oglesby was at last sworn in. Rumors that three House Democrats might break ranks to vote for Farwell circulated but were condemned as groundless by Logan men. Relations between the senatorial candidates of both parties were friendly. A party given for them on the fifteenth produced a "good natured wrangle over their prospective chances for election," and on Sunday, the eighteenth, Logan, Morrison, and Palmer met in the Leland to "exchange cigars and yarns." One of Logan's greatest problems was Republican Representative Eugene Sittig, who, it was rumored, had said he would refuse to vote for Black Jack no matter what promises were made.[9]

A constant side feature of the Springfield deadlock was the internecine journalistic war between the *Chicago Tribune* and the *Inter-Ocean*. Farwell was clearly the latter's choice. Reading these two newspapers made the Logan-Farwell contretemps seem far more intense than that between Black Jack and the Democrats. The *Tribune* hailed Logan as a man of "strong feelings, indomitable energy, and good judgement, his influence has always been counted a positive weight in the right direction." [10]

To the end of the month Logan held on, his hopes of a quick solution rapidly dwindling. He was upset because so few of his old friends showed up to join him. The senator thought he knew the reason—a lack of patronage to offer them. He wrote Mary, "you know what a crowd was here when I was elected before, we had the patronage then, now no one is here." He credited the defection to human nature, but revenge rose in him again when he promised, "I will be all right, or there will be several heads go with mine." Logan blended a dose of cynicism with his emotional mixture of revenge and fatalism when he wrote Elihu Washburne that "trickery" was rampant, and no man could win without it. [11]

In the enemy camp William Morrison was given the inside track to the caucus nomination. Called "Horizontal Bill" after his proposal for a general horizontal 20 percent reduction of tariff duties, Morrison had been the House's leading antitariff spokesman for a decade. One Morrison supporter feared that since he was in Congress from a district to which no other Democrat could be elected, he might be passed over. Another reported labor union opposition because of Morrison's low-tariff views. On January 23 John C. Black, a Morrison rival, requested that a legislative supporter remove his name from consideration so that a united front might be presented. [12]

On February 4 the Democratic caucus picked Morrison, "a lifelong and sterling Democrat," by a vote of 67 to 19. The following evening Logan was chosen by acclamation in what appeared to be a harmonious gathering. His nomination was moved by Richard Whiting and seconded by William Morris, the representative from Logan's old legislative district, a private in Logan's 31st Illinois Infantry Regiment and later regimental historian. "Hold this spot to the last man," roared Morris just before the caucus broke into "Marching Through Georgia." Logan's acceptance speech was a rouser, urging the 102 Republicans to stay together until victory. Eight Republicans were not on hand, including Sittig, who was known to be hostile, and Thomas MacMillan, a member of the *Inter-Ocean*'s editorial staff. MacMillan refused to reveal how he would vote, but the *Tribune* called him "the *Inter-Ocean* legislator who was sent there for no other purpose than to put a knife in between Mr. Logan's ribs." Nixon hotly denied the charge, informing critics that MacMillan represented his district and not the newspaper. Grover Cleveland was introduced early in February into Illinois politics with the report that the president-elect was anxious that Black Jack be retired.[13]

As the Senate contest dragged on, Edward McPherson, for many years clerk of the U.S. House of Representatives and renowned as "the walking political cyclopedia," told the press that the Illinois situation was "absolutely without parallel in all the legislative history of this country." Little did McPherson know when he made his February assessment just how true his words would be. With both houses organized and the caucus nominations made, balloting was slated for February 10, but nature took a hand. A severe blizzard swept southward from Lake Michigan and kept about one-half of the assemblymen from reaching Springfield. Drifts piled up and railroads halted service as the temperature plummeted to eighteen degrees below zero. The frigid blasts paralyzed the state for almost a week. Not until the eighteenth (the session's forty-fourth day) was the first ballot taken—Logan led Morrison 101 to 94. Seven votes scattered, and the incumbent, just short of a majority, was not elected. Although not yet victorious, Logan was pleased.[14]

The General Assembly acted under the rule that victory came to the candidate who gained a majority of those voting and constituting a quorum, not a majority of all elected members. Each party had 102 members; therefore if one Republican was absent and all remaining legislators voted the Democrats would win. Both parties feared one absence could spell defeat so the tactic both adopted was to refuse to vote if there was even one absentee. This would deny a quorum and prevent a roll call. Leaders on both sides labored to ensure discipline so as to make the strategy work.[15]

In Washington, Mary gave an afternoon reception on Lincoln's birthday while keeping one eye on the martyred president's hometown. John wrote, "There never was such a legislature got together in this state" and complained about the weather and the absenteeism. He was still hopeful and told Mary he was applying pressure on the "*Inter-Ocean* member," MacMillan; he had despaired of moving Sittig into line. On the seventeenth he wished Mary was with him but he advised her "you could do no good as no one could." [16]

One man that might help was James G. Blaine. Alerted to his running mate's problems the Maine senator called his victory "of the utmost importance to all sound political interests." He advocated a "hearty and united" effort to influence public opinion. Whitelaw Reid also sent encouragement along with his request for the Civil War articles Logan had outlined. Another Logan correspondent that month was suffragist Susan B. Anthony. "I regret beyond words that you cannot be present when our bill comes before the Senate," she wrote, "for I relied on your good word as well as vote to help us." [17]

As the Illinois contest proceeded Sittig and MacMillan continued to refuse to vote for the caucus nominee. The *Chicago Tribune* saw Mac-Millan's obstinance influenced directly by Nixon, who was seeking revenge for Logan's refusal to support his appointment as Chicago collector in 1881. The *Inter-Ocean* replied to the *Chicago Tribune* and *Illinois State Journal* with the explanation "we do not own him." Then on February 26 the situation was dangerously altered. The Capitol elevator was out of order and fifty-seven year old Republican legislator Robert F. Logan insisted on walking the four flights to the chamber. He collapsed and died a few minutes later. Logan's 19th District, made up of Whiteside and Lee counties, was solidly Republican, but at the very least the Senate choice would be delayed until after a March 21 special election could be held. The incumbent felt the assemblyman's death "complicates matters greatly," and he told Mary that if the dead man had voted that morning he would have been elected—a doubtful supposition. [18]

While Republicans sniped at each other, Morrison held most of the Democratic vote. But he had his own bolters, and Illinois Democrats worked to rally these independents behind the congressman. On February 24 Morrison received word from an aide of Grover Cleveland that the president-elect was closely following the race and hoped for a Morrison victory. [19]

Prolongation of the election beyond March 4 meant that the Forty-ninth Congress was organized without Logan. When committees were set the Illinoisan lost his chairmanship of the Military Affairs Committee as well as his important seats on the Judiciary and Appropriations committees.

For most of March the legislature debated its regular business while the people of the 19th District campaigned and the state speculated. Morrison took advantage of the break to attend Cleveland's inauguration, returning with a promise of some patronage assistance. But a Morrison victory depended in part upon Haines and former Greenbacker Alson J. Streeter, and both persisted in their opposition on grounds that Morrison could not win. Haines's opposition provoked a fistfight on the House floor between two Democrats. On the other side, the *Inter-Ocean* forecast a break away from Logan and headlined, "New Nominees Wanted, Both Political Parties at Springfield Tiring of the Caucus Candidates." [20]

One day before the 19th District selected Robert Logan's successor, Democratic Senator Frank Bridges died. Bridges's district had turned in a 2,100-vote Democratic majority in 1884 and the *Chicago Tribune* conceded his successor would be a Democrat. On the twenty-first, Republican Dwight S. Spafford was elected in the 19th District, but now the assembly had to await the 37th Senatorial District's special election on April 11. Within days eleven Democrats qualified for Bridges's seat. One weekend in late April Logan went to Carlinville, in the 37th, to campaign for a Republican. [21]

Through March, Black Jack vacillated between despair and confidence. He denied the *Illinois State Journal* article predicting his friends would shortly desert him, but he warned Mary that there were few men in Springfield whom he could trust. He was even afraid Cullom wanted him beaten so that he could head the G.O.P. in the Prairie State. Logan feared Farwell and Cullom might be in league. Mary, however, talked to Cullom and found him enthusiastically in favor of Logan's reelection. One day Logan had "great hopes" of imminent victory only to complain the next day of dreariness and suspense. Mary praised his patience and "self-discipline," cautioned him against too much smoking, and in frustration exclaimed, "I wish we were well out of the political world." She saw money behind everything and feared the country was approaching "degenerate times that characterized the fall of the Roman Senate." If her husband lost, Mary would be consoled by his chance to write his memoirs while he was in good health rather than on his deathbed like Grant. [22]

On March 25 Sittig cast his first vote for Logan, but MacMillan held aloof and the Democrats refrained from voting. Black Jack polled 101 votes, again just short. On the twenty-seventh he went to Chicago for a long weekend away from the turmoil. He rested, appearing at only one public gathering where he was cheered as "our next president." [23]

Morrison spent that weekend bringing pressure to bear on Streeter. A Mugwump and a Greenbacker acted to convince the holdout that he should back Morrison. One of the arguments used was the old refrain, "anybody is better than Logan." [24]

As the *Chicago Tribune* roasted legislators for drawing their pay while refusing to vote, the incredible deadlock continued into April. The *Illinois State Journal* referred to the assembly as "The Springfield Nuisance," and when former president Andrew Jackson got one vote the *Chicago Tribune* blasted the "Broad Farce." Fistfights, votes for dead men, and chronic absenteeism made Illinois a national disgrace, added the Chicago journal. [25]

"The senatorial matter is just where it was," John wrote Mary on April 1. Despairing of victory in the legislature, the senator reminded his wife that Oglesby could appoint him. However, that solution would involve another fight at the next session and was to be avoided if possible. When the Logans' Chicago home became vacant Mary came to Illinois to rent it again and to see her husband and her son. [26]

On April 11 Democrat Robert S. Davis was easily elected to Bridges's place and the balance was unchanged. Then the next day death struck the Democrats again. J. Henry Shaw of the 34th House District was found dead at his Springfield hotel. Once again the previous fall's election returns were examined and the Democrats' 1,700-vote margin in the district made up of Cass, Mason, Menard, and Schuyler counties was deemed sufficient to return another Democrat. A special election was called for May 6. [27]

When Shaw died the legislature almost ceased trying to find a senator. A few votes were taken with MacMillan voting for Logan for the first time, but the Democrats boycotted to prevent a quorum. Morrison went to Washington again in search of further assistance and Logan traveled to Chicago to see Mary off on her return to Washington. While there, the senator was interviewed by the *Chicago Tribune* on the possibility of his stepping aside:

They are at liberty to call a new caucus, but the fact of the matter is that the Republicans in the legislature understand two things. First, that so long as there is a tie of the membership . . . it may not be possible for the Republicans to elect anybody. And second, that if the Republican ranks were to be broken, the probability is that a Democrat would be elected. It is the latter fact that no doubt influences the actions of my friends. No Democrat shall succeed me in the United States Senate if I and my friends can prevent it.

In late April *Chicago Tribune* editor Joseph Medill heard rumors of a legislative plot between several Democrats and whisky interests to vote for Logan in return for eased alcohol taxes. The story had no foundation; no Democrats crossed party lines. For months the Chicago newspaper had been attacking assembly members for defrauding the state by their refusal to vote. In early May forty-four legislators took a junket to New Orleans, drawing the ire of the *Chicago Tribune*, which printed their names in a blacklist.[28]

When Logan vowed no Democrat would succeed him he meant just that, and Shaw's death gave him the opportunity to keep his vow. To replace Shaw the Democrats of the 34th nominated Arthur Leeper to sustain the deadlock. Republicans in this Democratic district northwest of Springfield appeared to be going to default; they nominated no one. However, Logan's friends had not given up plans to capture the seat. A few days after Shaw's death Henry Craske, a Republican from the 34th, wrote Logan asking him to create an organizational framework that would honeycomb each county, ensuring a heavy turnout of Republican voters. While the party nominated no one publicly, its leaders would agree in private on a candidate and pass the word through the information network. Craske would print all Republican ballots in his own office. On April 17 Logan answered in the affirmative and, outside of the district, began to raise the $1,000 that Craske deemed necessary to carry out the so-called still hunt. In the last week of April Logan, "Long" Jones, Dan Shepard, and representatives from each of the four counties met at the Leland Hotel to select a candidate. They settled on William H. Weaver, an insurance salesman who could travel the district without drawing unusual notice. In addition, trusted Republicans disguised as stock buyers or sewing machine salesmen were sent into the 34th to distribute the ballots and keep the voters informed. All Republicans contacted were told to show no interest in the result, appearing to have acquiesced in Leeper's certain victory. No G.O.P. voters were to approach the polls until after 3 P.M.[29]

One look at the *Chicago Tribune* headline on May 8 revealed that the "still hunt" had worked perfectly. "A Famous Victory," blared the paper, continuing, "Illinois Republicans Score Splendid Triumph in a Bourbon Stronghold." With so little interest, few Democrats bothered to vote and when the enemy began to deluge the polls it was too late in the day for the Democrats to rally. Weaver won by 336 votes out of the 6,700 cast. He carried Schuyler and his home county, Menard, while Leeper led in Cass and Macon.[30]

Republican legislators were so overjoyed one suggested painting the Capitol dome red in honor of the victory. From Washington, Morrison telegraphed to learn the result and was told his chance of going to the Senate was dead. Many Democrats blamed Morrison's absence and over-confidence for the setback. One disagreed, however, and, calling Morrison's effort a "manly and noble fight," found fault with some Republican "sons of bitches and the sleepy democrats of the 34th district." The *Illinois State Register* also faulted local Democrats for their "political crime."[31]

Logan told the press he was "much pleased," but he joyously told Mary, "all feel happy since electing Weaver. Nothing was ever done so slick since the landing of Columbus. I was afraid to write to you of our plans for fear the letter might miscarry." Manning, who was with his father, excitedly described the scene, telling his mother, "The Republicans are verily painting the town red. The Democrats are very blue." Not all Republicans were pleased. Lyman Trumbull condemned the tactics as "sharp practice" and declared he believed in honest and fair elections, not trickery.[32] Doubtless many in the Prairie State thought the act typical of Logan the machine boss.

As soon as Weaver reached Springfield and took the oath the Republicans would have a majority. But the Democrats intended to fight the election results and Weaver's certification. They first said the Republican ballots were not printed according to law, but this attack was dropped. Delay was also advocated since county clerks did not have to report the returns for twenty days. Morrison returned, called the "still hunt" unfair, and reported a similar proposal had been made to him earlier which he had rejected. The *Chicago Tribune* believed the only reason the Democrats had not tried it was Republican alertness. Haines called the contests immoral and asked Logan to agree to set it aside. The senator cut him short with a warning that such tactics would not be tolerated. Then the Demo-

crats tried to force a vote before Weaver arrived, but the Republicans refused to participate.[33] In the end there was no way the Democrats could
set aside Weaver's election; the best they could do was to delay a legislative vote until the nineteenth. With one week to go Manning wrote Mary:
"Poor father is about worn out and shows it very much." [34]

With Weaver in his seat would Sittig and MacMillan stay in line to
make victory certain? The *Chicago Tribune* headlined "Now Elect Logan!" calling on all G.O.P. members to end the farce at once. "Any
skulkers will be smoked out of their holes," cautioned the journal. There
was talk that the Democrats, urged on by the White House, might switch
to Farwell in an attempt to lure Republicans into breaking ranks, but these
reports were branded "fruitless scheming" by the *Tribune*.[35]

On May 19, with all 204 members seated, the 120th ballot began. The
galleries were packed; Logan stood, hat in hand, at the rear of the chamber while Morrison sat in the Democratic benches. The Senate roll call
brought Democratic abstentions but a solid Republican vote. When
Haines began the House roll the same tactic was followed. A hush fell
over the chamber as the roll reached MacMillan's name. When the Cook
County assemblyman voted for Logan the chamber erupted with applause
that was quieted by Logan "with a wave of the hand." When Sittig's
name was reached he did not vote. Democrats wildly applauded as Republicans sat in silence. At the end of the roll the clerk announced 102
votes for the incumbent and began to call the abstentions. When he
reached Sittig the representative, manuscript in hand, rose and was recognized. He had once said he would vote for Logan if it would elect the
senator and now he had his chance. Sittig denounced the binding caucus
nomination and Logan's demand for "blind, unquestioning and docile
support." He found Logan's methods "galling" and deplored the pressure
on himself and his family. In the end Sittig said he could not injure his
party and he concluded: "in obedience to the Republicans . . . who sent
me here as their trusted servant and officer (but under my personal protest) I vote for John A. Logan." Republicans cheered, threw hats and
newspapers in the air, slapped Logan on the back, and shook Sittig's
hand. Democrats canceled their abstentions and began voting for Farwell
in hope that some Republicans would join them to defeat Black Jack. But
all Republicans, including Farwell's partisans, held their ground and after
171 days and 120 ballots John A. Logan was returned to the Senate. Ten

minutes of applause followed the final tally before Logan could speak. He expressed his gratitude, praised Morrison as a worthy opponent, and in magnificent understatement, called the contest "unusually close and heated." [36]

John immediately wired Mary the result and she was the first to send congratulations ending with "Thank God you were successful." Logan made a notebook listing congratulatory notes that came from persons in thirty-one states and territories. It bears an inscription in his hand: "This book is of great value to me, and must be returned no matter whose hands it may fall into." Listed are David Davis, Wharton Barker, George Boutwell, William McKinley, William B. Allison, William Evarts, Russell Alger, Whitelaw Reid, and General James Longstreet, among others. Logan filed the 518 telegrams he received in bound volumes. [37]

Some of his old friends were simply elated at his success, others saw it as a victory of national importance following so closely the 1884 Republican defeat, while still others saw the triumph as a first step to the 1888 presidential nomination. Chauncey I. Filley thought Logan's victory was a vindication of party regularity and unity. Blaine called the contest "unprecedented," and Hamilton Fish philosophized, "all's well that ends well." Benjamin Harrison, the man who would win the presidency in 1888, wired, "Indiana Republicans are shouting," and Joseph B. Foraker reported, "all Ohio Republicans rejoice." Virginia Senator Harrison Riddleberger was pleased with Logan's success since he would "have been sadly missed in the Senate." George F. Hoar wired from Washington, "Your election is regarded here as one of the important turning points in our political history." John Hay agreed, calling it a "victory of the greatest national importance and value." *Harper's Weekly*, which lauded both Logan and Morrison for the clean race, went on to praise the victor as "a man of high personal honor . . . and of long political experience." But the New York weekly added: "He is called a splendid leader in the sense of political management and party tactics, not of the control which springs from mental and moral ascendancy, which is true leadership." [38]

Shelby Cullom, so often suspected of duplicity by Logan and his agents, sent wholehearted congratulations and some advice:

It is a grand triumph by patience and good management. . . . I do not need to tell you that you were never so strong before as now throughout the entire country. All you want to do now is to be a little careful and you are on the high road to the achievement of your highest ambitions with almost a clear track.

Cullom's allusions to national strength and future ambitions were echoed by many of those sending best wishes. George F. Dawson called the vote another Donelson and believed the 1888 nomination would be another Appomattox. Kansas Congressman Lewis Hanback mentioned Logan as the logical choice for 1888 as did William Pitt Kellogg and dozens of others. Illinois legislator Simon Greenleaf, one of the "loyal 103," was sure the Senate triumph was the first step to the 1888 nomination which Logan would win "if kind providence spares your life." [39]

On the night of May 19 the Leland Hotel swarmed with festive Republicans and some of Logan's telegrams were read to the throng by a legislator standing on a steam heater in the lobby. Everywhere the senator went he drew cheers, and that evening a torchlit parade came to the hotel to call for Logan. He made a brief speech and joined the crowd watching fireworks streak through the spring sky. Similar parades were held all over Illinois, and G.A.R. posts in Madison (Wisconsin), Utica (New York), Topeka, and Cincinnati organized marches of triumph. In Washington many callers went to Iowa Circle to congratulate Mary. In New York, Whitelaw Reid's *New York Tribune* believed the Illinois senator stood higher than ever as a man of "skill, courage, and sagacity." [40]

On the twenty-third Logan went by rail to Chicago. Crowds thronged platforms at every stop and on his arrival at the Grand Pacific a salute of 103 guns boomed out along the lakefront. A reception committee wore badges proclaiming Logan "Our leader for 1888." The senator shook hands with three thousand people. The triumphant week ended with a banquet at Chicago's Union Club where *Chicago Tribune* editor Joseph Medill mentioned Logan as a leading candidate for 1888. The one discordant note in the Republican celebrations came from Charles Farwell, who said he had supported Black Jack throughout the canvass despite abuse from the senator and his men. Asked if he resented Logan, Farwell replied: "No I do not. But when a man acts the hog, and the dog-in-the-manger, I don't like him much, that's all." [41]

Mary joined John in Chicago in time to accompany him to a Memorial Day ceremony at Bloomington. The couple went on to Springfield, back to Chicago, and then to Washington. John A. Logan, Jr., whom they still consistently called "Manning," remained behind to handle family business in Egypt. In Washington another round of festivities brought the reelected Logan back to the capital. The special session of the Senate had ended and the couple spent their days accepting congratulations and writing notes acknowledging letters and telegrams. One of the groups to serenade the Logans was composed of over five thousand Negroes. A black speaker hailed Logan as a man of "humane and courageous" spirit who had fought to free his people. "They know that the black race has but few to champion their cause at the present time, but in you they recognize a strong defender of their rights," he told the Illinoisan. When Logan responded he swore: "as long as I have energy and strength to raise my voice in the halls of legislation, I will earnestly devote my powers to place each and every man beneath the stars and stripes upon an equality before the law." Later that summer, in an Independence Day speech at Woodstock, Connecticut, Logan reiterated this theme by demanding equal rights for all citizens.[42]

In June two of Logan's old Civil War comrades were in the news. General Sherman had revised his memoirs and this second edition "omitted much that gave rise to criticism." Ulysses S. Grant, dying in the summer of 1885, asked to see his old corps commander. John and Mary Logan went to New York to visit Grant with the two generals reviving old memories as well as comparing notes on their books about the conflict. Grant showed Logan some parts of his *Personal Memoirs.* The Logans went on to Portland, Maine, for the national G.A.R. encampment late in the month, while in New England, Rhode Island Senator Nelson Aldrich, an increasingly friendly colleague, invited Logan to a clambake at which he would meet many of the state's leading businessmen. With a view to extending his following in the East, where he had always been weak, Logan accepted. The *Chicago Tribune,* which often alluded to Logan as a candidate in 1888, proudly reported, "Our Black Jack is still East. They like him."[43]

When the Logans returned from New England they decided, after years of renting, to buy a home. With a secure six years ahead Mary wrote Dollie they would pay a little down and the rest on time. After a brief search they located a two-story brick house fifty or sixty years old that had been used as a hospital during the Civil War. It had eight rooms and a large hall, which could be converted into an office, and was surrounded by one and a half acres. The home, owned by John Sherman, was just outside of the city in a section called Columbia Heights and sat on a hill giving an excellent view of the city. The couple named it "Calumet Place." Through the summer Mary worked to complete preparations; by September they were comfortably settled so that Mary could tell her daughter, "We have at last got a lovely place."[44]

Although there was some time to rest and to write that summer and fall, the senator remained active. He was appointed by the Senate to be one of its official representatives at Grant's funeral in early August. The senator went to New York along with Sherman, Sheridan, and former Confederate General Joseph E. Johnston as a pallbearer. Logan also promised Joseph B. Foraker to come to Ohio in September to speak in behalf of his Senate candidacy. After a quiet August in Washington, Logan attended the eighteenth reunion of the Society of the Army of the Tennessee at the Grand Pacific on September 9 and 10. He politicked a bit in Springfield before returning through Ohio, where he spoke for Foraker.[45]

By October, John Logan was back in Washington spending most of his time writing. Mary wanted him to rest so as to completely recuperate before the session began in December, but he worked on, drawing from her the fear that he would "break down before he finished all he has on hand."[46]

Manning had gone from Illinois to New York, where he had a job in the James B. Eads engineering firm. He reported visiting the Grant family and preparing for his father's visit in mid-October. Dollie and Will were still in New Mexico and both wanted to be transferred east to either Atlanta or Washington. Mary advised the couple a transfer might take months, especially since the senator "has to *get his committee back first before he has a leverage.*" That October, situated in her new home and facing "a nice comfortable *certain* salary and so many pleasant friends and surroundings and sure *promotion* in the future," Mary told Dollie: "I tell Papa every day that I have never felt so light hearted and hopeful for the future in all these long 30 years of drudgery and vexation and anxiety through which we have pulled together."[47] With prospects of Senate security and increasing talk of "Logan for president," the couple viewed the future with confidence after two years of failure, disappointment, and struggle for political survival.

CHAPTER 16

The Last Snowfall

JUST BEFORE the Forty-ninth Congress met, Vice-President Thomas Hendricks died. Friends urged Logan to accept the position as president pro tem of the Senate now that he was without a chairmanship. The Republican caucus endorsed Logan by acclamation. Blaine urged his running mate to take the slot: "It is yours by right of claims which cannot be successfully disputed nor safely ignored." The thought entered Logan's mind that some Republicans wanted to shunt him into this relatively quiet position, thus dimming his presidential hopes. Whether or not that was the motivation the Illinoisan believed he could far more effectively keep his name before the nation as an active participant in debate. He thanked his colleagues for the honor but declined. Logan's daughter applauded his decision since "active life on the floor is more suited to his tastes." Republican leader Stephen B. Elkins agreed with Logan's reasons for turning down the post and congratulated him on being accorded the honor of the offer.[1]

John Sherman was chosen president pro tem, and Logan snidely told Elkins, "I dislike to stand in the way of any good man, and as Senator Sherman was so anxious on the subject much as he felt this would be a stepping-stone for him to the presidency, and feeling assured *that the whole people were* 'hankering' for him, I thought it was right for a little fellow like myself to give way." He informed Elkins that the new session was "swimming into shape."[2]

On December 7 Logan answered the roll call for the new session and one week later William J. Sewell of New Jersey stepped aside as chairman of the Military Affairs Committee, allowing Black Jack to resume his old place. Logan was also placed on the Privileges and Elections Committee and the Appropriations Committee. Few of the men who had

213

been in the Senate when Logan had first arrived were still there. The veteran Vermont duo of George Edmunds and Justin Morrill was on hand as was John Sherman, but many new faces would appear in debate. The wealthy Californian Leland Stanford, former Secretary of the Interior Henry M. Teller, Johnson's impeachment attorney William Evarts, and Democratic wheelhorse Arthur P. Gorman of Maryland were among this group.[3]

As the year ended Logan was working hard to finish the book he had been writing through most of 1885. The editor of the *North American Review* knew it was almost finished and asked for an advance chapter to include in his publication. Mary helped her husband push the project to fruition. Every moment he could spare from legislative business found Logan making final corrections. Mary was sure it would be "a great improvement on Grant's in which we were greatly disappointed." This verdict was on the first volume of *Personal Memoirs;* the second volume she was certain would "fall flat." The Tuckers were still in Santa Fe as the year ended, and Manning was beginning a new job. Working out of New York he traveled through the East and Midwest selling supplies to railroads. The skeptical Dollie hoped this time he would make up his mind to work. Finally, it was a slow social season in the capital. Mary reported there was no one to entertain for bachelor Cleveland.[4]

When Congress reassembled on January 5 Logan again introduced a bill to create a commission to investigate the "material, industrial, and intellectual" progress made by Negroes since the Civil War. This bill, applauded by the *Washington Bee,* which hailed its author as "the Negroes' friend, the Enemy's Foe, and a Defender of the Right," again died in committee. Late in the month the Illinois senator joined discussions of problems among the Sioux. He demanded that men in the Interior Department stop encouraging Indians to make claims against the government. Education, he believed, would stop Indian wars. He also demanded that the government stop selling guns to "wild savages."[5]

In January major debate concerned pension legislation. Faced by a hostile president whose philosophy toward veterans' benefits was conservative, the Republican Senate continued its liberal policy. Logan attacked the removal of wounded pension agents by the Cleveland administration. However, he denied any hostility toward John C. Black, one of his opponents in the 1885 Senate race and Cleveland's new pension commissioner. Black Jack advocated increasing benefits for disabled veterans, but his amendments were beaten. When Delaware's Eli Saulsbury denounced Republicans for paying for votes in their pension measure, an angry Logan shot back that wounded soldiers were due the support whether or not they voted: it was a debt of honor. Later that session a broad dependent pension bill, granting benefits to any disabled veteran regardless of the reason for his disability, passed—only to be vetoed by the president.[6]

The admission of Dakota to statehood came to the floor in February with Logan outspoken in support of it. When Butler of South Carolina said the territory was controlled by a "political clique," Logan countered by arguing that it was easy and irresponsible to brand opponents with the emotional word "clique." Black Jack and Benjamin Harrison were the bill's chief proponents as it passed.[7]

That winter the Logans' grandson, Logan Tucker, wrote his grandparents from Santa Fe. He told his grandmother that he would come to see her when it got warmer. "I go to school every day," he continued, adding, "I read and study arithmetic and geography." When the boy told his grandfather he had some baby puppies who were blind, the senator replied they "must be *democrats* or they could see."[8]

After one year of gathering material and writing, John A. Logan published *The Great Conspiracy* early in 1886. The senator joined a long list of Civil War participants, from North and South, who wrote either personal memoirs or general histories of the conflict. Grant, Sherman, and Blaine led the former group while Logan followed Alexander H. Stephens, Henry Wilson, and Jefferson Davis in the latter category. To prepare himself Logan read Blaine's *Twenty Years of Congress* and admitted that the work was "well written." He found Blaine had used lengthy quotes and decided that overquoting would not meet with public approval. George F. Dawson read the manuscript of *The Great Conspiracy* and gave his advice throughout.[9]

Writing absorbed Logan all summer and fall. While Mary supervised house preparations Logan labored with his book. Mary was concerned that the senator's long hours would force a "break down." In late October Mary, who copied much of the manuscript, told Dollie that her father had "written so constantly and so many hours day and night that he has grown as nervous as a cat and . . . is very irritable." By November, Mary was relieved that *The Great Conspiracy* was within sight of completion. Logan hoped to finish before the Senate convened, but last-minute revisions prevented publication until early in the new year.[10]

Logan's history of the United States from the origins of the Civil War through Reconstruction is summed up in the title. The author saw a deeply developed conspiracy by the leaders of southern political and economic life. While this conspiracy concerned itself with the defense of slavery, it also had a broad economic base. Southern leaders were determined to maintain free trade and engaged in "ingenious methods of 'firing the Southern heart' " in opposition to any tariff. Logan's concentration on differences over the tariff as a major cause of the war was a departure from most histories written to that point. Earlier works had concentrated on slavery almost to the exclusion of anything else, and Black Jack was one of the first to develop a broader economic basis as a cause for the conflict.[11]

The Great Conspiracy was one of those works that develop a devil theory of history. Yet Logan's "devils" were not only Calhoun and Jefferson Davis; they were also those Americans who continued to advocate a reduced tariff and other policies contrary to those of Logan and the Republican leadership. *The Great Conspiracy,* though a history, was also written with an eye on national politics in 1886 and to the development of an issue for the election of 1888. Where the past conflicted with what Logan wanted to say to his contemporaries, he conveniently glossed over past events. An Illinois biographer summed up Logan's failings in *The Great Conspiracy* when he wrote: "The truth is that he lacked the judicial mind and temperament requisite to an historian. He wrote his history from a partisan standpoint and in the style of his political speeches." In its review, *Nation* blasted the author for a lack of either original research or original ideas. *The Great Conspiracy,* thought the reviewer, "is not a history. . . . It is rather what might be called a narrative stump speech." John Hay also criticized the senator's work, commenting, "I don't count John Logan as company for historians."[12]

The 810-page book was published by A.R. Hart & Co. of New York. Logan was disappointed in its sale, especially in the first months after publication. By November, seventeen thousand copies had been sold and the senator had been assured by Hart that he was stepping up sales efforts and hoped for an increase that winter. Logan expected the first royalties to come in that December.[13]

While Logan awaited the public's reception of *The Great Conspiracy* he participated in intense debates in March and April over a federal education bill and his own measure to increase army efficiency. The former, known as the Blair Bill after its sponsor, Henry W. Blair of New Hampshire, was aimed at ending illiteracy in the United States. Logan supported the general concept, but as he had in the past, he opposed distribution of funds to states on an index of illiteracy alone. He again accused the South of claiming funds to educate blacks and using the money solely for whites. If illiteracy was to be the index used, Black Jack favored using illiterates between ages ten and twenty-one as a base. No matter how the ratio was established, the Illinoisan wanted a commissioner to see that the states properly distributed the money without regard to race. Logan tried to amend the bill to increase funds from the proposed $77 million to $136 million. The amendment was defeated. He did succeed in getting an amendment adopted which set aside $2 million to build schools in sparsely settled districts. When he demanded guarantees so as to ensure that the money would go to Negro schools he predicted:

> If this money should be used as it ought to be used, for the benefit of the colored people, you will find the time will come . . . when there will be songsters and poets in their midst. . . . There is in the colored race an element of music, of poetry, of oratory, that is seldom found anywhere else when we give them the advantages that the white race have had. Let them have that advantage, and if they can outstrip us in the race of life, in God's name let them have the chance. I do not know why the white man with all his advantages and all the privileges that he has had in this government in times past should fear the colored man. He should rather reach out his hand to him and say, "While you are struggling down in that pit of ignorance and despair I will, with what strength I have, take your hand and lift you up to the plane where we should both stand, having an equal and fair chance in life." [14]

In the course of this debate Logan received suggestions on the education bill. He also continued to receive support from the black press. Former President Hayes thought the bill was the only chance for an efficient southern school system; trying to encourage a journalist friend to endorse the measure he used as his argument that "reliable and able" Republicans such as Sherman and Logan had dropped their objections and announced support. On March 5 the Illinois senator voted "aye" as the bill passed. [15]

On March 18 Senate Bill 777 to increase the efficiency of the Army reached the floor. For the next two weeks the solons fought over its provisions. When Logan presented the bill he gracefully accepted a number of minor amendments. The most controversial point in the bill was an increase in troop strength from 25,000 to 30,000. Logan pointed out that the entire 5,000-man increase would be in the enlisted ranks and that, although there was no threat of war at the time, this force was needed as a cadre to form the basis of a defense force in case of future hostilities. Early in the debate Logan read the Senate a letter from General John M. Schofield labeling the measure "excellent in all its features." Schofield also said the provisions showed a "master's hand," but Black Jack deleted those words. Logan also read a letter from Sheridan supporting S 777.[16]

Some senators argued that with the end of Indian strife and two peaceful boundaries there was no need for an increase, if, indeed, there were even any need for an army. Sounding the tocsin of preparedness Logan said war had been with man from the beginning of time and the nation must prepare for war in peacetime. Applause rang in the galleries as Logan said the country should be able to say if attacked: "Lay on, Macduff; and damn'd be him that first cries, 'Hold enough!'" Henry M. Teller of Colorado opposed the bill and drew a heated response from Logan. The Coloradan replied in kind: "We all know that the Senator from Illinois was in the Army. We are not likely to forget it, for if the Senator should fail to remind us of it on every occasion, the very . . . method of threatening us in the Senate would call our attention sharply to the fact." For days Teller and Logan sniped at each other. Preston Plumb of Kansas joined Teller in attacking the bill. There were some implications that the measure was an attempt by Logan to increase his popularity, thus assisting his 1888 presidential effort. One of Logan's correspondents mentioned that the Illinoisan had "cleaned the Colorado man's clock in a very workmanlike manner." He added that Logan stock was rising and Black Jack would take the country "in '88 by spontaneous combustion." On April 7 Logan's bill lost by a 31-to-19 vote. Most Republicans supported S 777 but John Sherman along with James Wilson of Iowa joined Teller and Plumb in opposition.[17]

Logan was behaving more and more like a presidential candidate. He accompanied Michigan Senator Thomas Palmer to Detroit for a Republican party Washington's Birthday celebration and went to Chicago in mid-April for a speech. The press constantly mentioned Logan as a leading contender for 1888, and his Detroit speech received wide publicity. Laboring to increase his visibility, Logan angrily charged Blaine, Sherman, and Harrison, three men he saw as his most dangerous rivals, with trying to "put me on the shelf." He received a great deal of mail that spring in support of his ambitions. Michigan Governor Russell A. Alger told him "we are all Logan men." Another project aimed at keeping his name before the public was a second book. Joining *The Great Conspiracy* would be a study of the role of the nonprofessional soldier, tentatively entitled *The Volunteer Soldier of America.*[18]

Manning had gone on to another job by April, returning to Chicago to work for a street-paving company. He did not like the job and told his mother he was not doing well. The spoiled young man wrote Mary: "I am on my feet all day and walk some 12–15 miles every day over these sidewalks and it uses me all up. I want to do something that will be a permanent business for me and that I can make some money and that will not require me to be a drummer or solicitor." He also announced in April that he had become engaged to Edith Andrews of Youngstown, Ohio. Mary was busy that spring managing a charity ball for the Garfield Hospital fund.[19]

During the last two months of the first session Logan was much less active than he had been earlier. Illness, work on his new book, and travel kept him out of the chamber for long intervals in the period from May through the August adjournment. Logan did not vote for the Cullom Act creating the Interstate Commerce Commission, and he warned the junior senator the bill would ruin him. Logan spoke against the proposal to end free railroad passes for politicians. He opposed interference in a private enterprise's right to "haul me without charge" if it wanted to. Logan was a man of modest means who often traveled on passes, and his real reason for opposition was transparently clear.[20]

Logan served as a House-Senate conferee on the lower chamber's Army appropriations bill and successfully managed the passage of the Military Academy appropriation. He spoke out for Illinois projects in the rivers and harbors bill but was unsuccessful in his attempts to amend the measure for the benefit of his native state. His charge of unfairness toward Illinois by the Commerce Committee and general "spite" against the Prairie State brought a sharp rebuttal from George Edmunds, who said Logan had a "chip on each shoulder." When Cleveland's pension vetoes returned to the Senate, Logan was not on hand. His vote would not have made possible an override in any case.[21]

Logan's greatest effort in the session's waning months was his final tilt with the Porter relief bill. There was absolutely nothing new to be said. Logan defended the court-martial, denied Congress's constitutional power to restore Porter as a colonel, and again mentioned Lincoln's feeling that the general should have been shot. Several long portions of these remarks were read from *The Great Conspiracy,* an act that caused *Nation* to chide Logan for using *The Congressional Record* to gain free publicity. He tried to add an amendment that all men wounded at Second Bull Run should be retired at the rank they held when wounded. The amendment was beaten. On June 25 the Porter bill passed 30 to 17. This time the House agreed and a Democratic president signed the bill into law; after twenty-four years Porter had finally won.[22]

Eighteen years after Logan had first ordered Memorial Day celebrations, the practice was more widespread than ever. This year Black Jack's oration was delivered at Grant's Tomb in New York. He glorified his old commander and resorted to spread-eagle oratory, a style on the decline among national politicians. It was a style that some still relished while others were disgusted by its excesses. Ward H. Lamon, Abraham Lincoln's old friend, read the words with "pride and admiration." After praising the memories of Lincoln and Grant, Lamon told Logan he hoped Illinois had not exhausted its supply of chief executives. The senator promised at once to send Lamon a copy of his speech. On the other hand, Shelby Cullom received a note from a Prairie State Republican who attacked Logan's remarks as the "d_____dest performance I ever saw." He asked, "What is the matter with the man?" and concluded: "Such ghastly rubbish would disgrace a freshman in a Western college." When Logan finished his New York visit he went to Indiana to join Benjamin Harrison in addressing a G.A.R. assembly.[23]

In June, Logan received an appeal for aid in the fall elections from powerful Cincinnati editor Murat Halstead. He also received advice for 1888 from old comrade Jerome B. Chaffee. David Davis died that month, and Logan sent condolences to his widow. The deceased was "a man of great ability and honesty of purpose . . . a patriot in the truest sense of the term," stated the man defeated by Davis in 1877.[24]

The following month John and Mary Logan boarded Governor Alger's private railroad car for a trip to the national G.A.R. encampment in San Francisco. In addition to his appearance before the veterans, Logan wanted to test his presidential appeal in the Mountain and Pacific states.

He was gone for six weeks and in that time spoke at Lawrence and Ottawa, Kansas, at Omaha, Denver, Oakland, Portland, Tacoma, Seattle, and Salt Lake City. At Lawrence on a blistering afternoon, a young journalist named Arthur Capper, later on an able Republican senator from Kansas, listened to one of the last classic examples of bloody-shirt oratory. While her parents toured the West, Dollie Tucker and her family arrived in Washington; the senator had been able to get Will a transfer.[25]

After a brief rest in Chicago on his return from California, Logan took the stump across the Middle West. At Moline, Illinois, he spoke in a downpour and sat for a time in his wet clothes. From that exposure he became chilled and was bedridden in mid-September with what Mary called "a bilious attack aggravated by a cold." But he recovered in time to speak to a large group of veterans in St. Louis and an enthusiastic group of Republicans in Pittsburgh. To the former soldiers he made the enlightened suggestion that aged veterans be permitted to bring their wives to soldiers' homes, a practice not then allowed. At another veterans' encampment, that of the Society of the Army of the Tennessee, the general became embroiled in a controversy. When Illinois General Augustus Chetlain, citing the rise of political radicalism, advocated property qualifications for voting, the senator rose immediately to reply. He could never countenance a limitation on the right to vote, roared Logan, as he vigorously supported universal manhood suffrage. Just before election day, Logan swung back into Illinois, making some of his last campaign speeches in Egypt. These appearances were in support of Republican House candidates, but they were also intended to keep the senator's name in the newspapers and his voice before the public. The November results were cheering because Republicans ran well, especially in the Prairie State, where Logan pronounced the Democrats "utterly broken."[26]

John A. Logan might also have described himself as being "utterly broken down." The senator had reached sixty the previous February, and his Senate work, his constant travel, and long hours of writing coupled with his autumn illness had seriously weakened him. Mary urged her husband to go to Hot Springs, Arkansas, where treatment had once before restored his health, but pleading the urgency of the Senate session and his work on *The Volunteer Soldier,* Logan promised to go during the Christmas recess.[27]

By December, Senator Logan had almost finished *The Volunteer Soldier of America.* Published after his death, it contained an autobiographical sketch of the general's Civil War career. However, most of the work was a history of the military situation in the United States, together with comments on the contemporary scene and suggestions for the future. From George Washington through the Civil War, Logan believed volunteers, not professionals, had defended the nation and brought an endless string of victories. He viewed a professional army as a danger.

It was no surprise that *The Volunteer Soldier* was hostile to West Point. Logan wrote that political influence filled the academy with snobs and men not capable of truly distinguished military service. The giants, such as Grant, who had emerged from West Point, finished well down in their classes and were, in Logan's view, soldiers in spite of, not because of, their academy training. His long-held opinion that West Point deeply imbedded aristocratic notions in the heads of its graduates was fully developed in this book. One of the most persistent themes of Logan's second book was the protest against automatic elevation of regular officers over volunteers without consideration of fitness or ability. Between the lines Logan cried, "Look at my case." [28]

Looking to the future, Logan proposed an end to political influence in all of the academy's affairs. Class favoritism should also be eradicated and admission and progress at the academy and through the army should be based on merit alone. As he had done earlier in Congress, Logan proposed courses of military education for universities across the nation, whose graduates would be the equals of West Pointers. Thus the source of officer selection would be broadened and the danger of placing too much power in the hands of an aristocratic clique would be lessened. Furthermore, Logan wanted all those admitted to either service academy to pass a nationally competitive examination. [29]

The Volunteer Soldier of America seems to have had little effect on the military system. The professionals, long used to Logan's badgering, were not open to his suggestions. Many readers regarded the work as little more than a polemic in which the political general's prejudices often overcame accuracy and fairness. Published posthumously, it did not have the thrust it might have developed had Logan lived.

As Logan worked to complete his book the Forty-ninth Congress began its second session. Despite a severe attack of rheumatism he answered the December 6 roll call. The following day he voted with the majority against a Columbia River improvement bill and two days later he introduced a petition calling for the improvement of New York's Harlem

River. These were his only appearances of this session. On the afternoon of the ninth, Logan suffered a severe attack while in the Capitol. He was taken home that afternoon and confined to bed with what seemed to be his usual end-of-the-year bout with rheumatism. From his corner bedroom Logan could see the Capitol dome in the distance. It was a murky December with an unusual amount of snow. When the pain did not subside the weakened senator told his family, "I wish the snow would go. Snow always gives me rheumatism." Logan's usual pair, Matt Ransom of North Carolina, indicated paired votes through the term's second week. On the seventeenth he wrote the Illinoisan to discover if he wanted to retain the pair. Word of his illness had reached the press, this time with a greater note of seriousness than heretofore.[30]

On December 22 Logan's condition worsened. He was struck with terrible pains in the arms and chest. Three physicians attempted to ease the pain, but the exhausted body steadily weakened and the senator became semiconscious. It was a sad holiday season, for by the twenty-sixth it was clear Logan was dying. Just after 2 P.M. that afternoon he rallied long enough to recognize Mary. Then he lapsed into unconsciousness. His family and his physicians, together with Shelby Cullom, Green B. Raum, and General Phil Sheridan, were at his bedside when at 3:15 the Illinois soldier-politician died.[31]

Word of John A. Logan's death was spread across the United States in black-edged columns of the press. Three-fourths of the always loyal *Illinois State Journal* was devoted to the senator's death, "the most shocking to the nation since Lincoln's because Black Jack died in his prime, before his time." The once hostile *Inter-Ocean* joined the mourners as did his bitter foe, the *State Register.* "Another active, eventful and useful life is closed," thought the latter. The *Chicago Tribune,* which called Logan's death an "irreparable national loss," emphasized Logan's honesty and Mary's deep devotion in its lengthy tribute.[32]

A military honor guard watched over Logan's body at Calumet Place until December 30. Illinois associates, Civil War heroes, and his fellow senators called to offer their condolences. After brief home services the catafalque was transferred to the Capitol rotunda, where a G.A.R. detachment mounted guard. Thousands of mourners passed the bier before it was moved to the Senate chamber for funeral services on the morning of Friday, December 31. Shelby Cullom was in charge of arrangements, including the assembly of distinguished guests and pallbearers. Logan's long-time antagonist General Sherman replied to Cullom, "Will come of course," and Logan's fellow Stalwart Roscoe Conkling advised Cullom, "I will attend funeral as bearer." Logan's funeral would be the only time "Lord Roscoe" entered the Senate chamber after his resignation. After the Senate ceremony General Sheridan led a long funeral procession to Rock Creek Cemetery. It was a raw, icy day, but a huge crowd lined the route of the procession. Just before entering the park the cortege passed several hundred veterans from the Old Soldiers Home. Standing with heads bared in the cold, they tendered their final salute to the man who had led them in war and fought for their interests in peace.[33]

When the Senate reassembled on January 4 Cullom announced Logan's "unexpected" death to the chamber. Congress adjourned out of respect for "one of the bravest and noblest of men." In February thirty-four House members and fourteen senators eulogized the deceased Illinoisan. As expected, Logan's military prowess was emphasized, but he was also hailed as a "true man of the people," who had died before reaching the "zenith of his usefulness." William McKinley remembered Black Jack as a forceful debater and a nonpareil orator on the "popular hustings." "Uncle Joe" Cannon, soon to be a much reviled Speaker, told the House that "by placing his fingers upon his own pulse he was enabled to count the heartbeats of the whole people." Several of his colleagues called Logan "self-made," a man with little formal education who was "born poor and died poor." He learned readily, worked hard, and rose through the force of his own abilities and his close touch with the people. Inevitably Gray's "Elegy," Mark Antony's funeral oration, and a surfeit of florid Victorian sentiment filled the chambers.[34]

Shelby Cullom said death was a surprise since Black Jack seemed "tough as the sturdy oak." The Illinois senator also alluded to Logan's poverty and said it was due to his honesty and refusal to use his office as a means of becoming wealthy. Logan had "bitter enemies," said Cullom, but he pointed out that a man without such foes was "not a positive force. Logan was a positive force." John T. Morgan and Wade Hampton, two of those "bitter enemies," followed Cullom. Morgan hailed his former adversary as a candid, sincere, and resolute man. He also called Logan a man who was "more than almost any man in my rememberance, the typical American of the Western States." Hampton recalled Black Jack's zeal and efficiency as chairman of the Military Affairs Committee. Joseph Hawley might have surprised some listeners when he called Logan a "tender" man, but he surprised no one when he said: "He was classed as a political general. I do not know that it was altogether an unfriendly remark. . . . It was a political war; and he was as strong in one field of battle as the other; the political generals did double duty." The final Senate remarks were given by the man who succeeded John A. Logan. "He was the bravest of soldiers, an able statesman, and an honest man," said Charles Farwell.[35]

Almost all obituaries of the senator made mention of his particular style, that of a rough-hewn, unlettered, sometimes rowdy westerner. Speaking to such comments, the editors of the *Chicago Tribune* were certain that

> It will be a sad day for Americans when polish takes the place of homespun bluntness. The purity of American public life will not be advanced by an infusion of dilettantism, a feeble accuracy of speech. The more honest, virile, and sincere our public men are the better; and it is not important that their language shall be elegant.[36]

Those words might have been written by John A. Logan.

Far from the seat of power a small Negro newspaper spoke for the people Logan had defended until his death. "But few deaths in many years past so touched the public heart," reported the *Huntsville Gazette*.[37]

Mary Logan survived her husband by thirty-seven years. When she died in 1923 the congressman from Logan's old district in Egypt paid tribute to the eighty-four-year-old widow as "one of the nation's great characters." Character she was. Mary Logan remained devoted to the cause of the veteran and was in great demand at G.A.R. meetings. Once it was even proposed that she be named pension commissioner, an amazing proposal in the days before women's suffrage. She served for a time as a companion for George Pullman's daughters and traveled widely in Europe. Later the senator's widow founded *Home Magazine,* which published for six years under her editorial guidance. After the magazine's failure, she wrote for years for William Randolph Hearst's publications. She also wrote several books, including her *Reminiscences of a Soldier's Wife*. Active in the struggle for women's suffrage, Mary Logan was also named president of the American Red Cross in the early twentieth century. She constantly glorified the name of her husband and spent the remainder of her life polishing what one biographer called Logan's "mail of untarnished integrity." [38]

Many of Logan's contemporaries did not recognize him as a man of "untarnished integrity." They saw him instead as a power broker, as a politician who refused to let the wounded nation heal, and as a person who used his office for personal—and perhaps illegal—gain. His critics pointed the accusing finger at the boss of a powerful Illinois machine who used and abused patronage to stay in power. They cringed when, well after Reconstruction, the enduring Radical orator continued to wave the bloody shirt, and they questioned what sort of public servant this Logan was who shamelessly promoted the senatorial salary grab and who seemed to have so many ties to the whisky ring.

The "best men" of American politics scorned him as an example of American political life at its worst. "Politics as a vocation was never truly 'legitimate work'," writes historian Robert Wiebe of this period. He continues: "Most successful politicians continued to designate themselves lawyers or businessmen or generals, as if they were temporarily on leave from their real occupations." Although Logan was almost always called "general" rather than "senator," he came closer than most to acknowledging that he was a "politician." [39]

At the other end of the spectrum were those who idolized John Logan. They saw the old Confederacy as the source of the nation's ills and, long after Appomattox, felt Logan's scoring of the South as no more than the traitorous section deserved. Logan's bloody-shirt rhetoric took these partisans back to a time when good and bad and right and wrong were as easily distinguishable as blue and gray. These admirers of the man known as the Black Eagle refused to believe the charges leveled at him, refused to believe that he was anything less than what they had known him to be—the man on horseback who led them well.

Logan was often charged with being one of the new breed of Radicals who, little concerned with principle, used the Negro and Reconstruction as issues to maintain themselves in office. No historical evidence supports the theory that Logan's efforts for black Americans were disingenuous. Certainly black Americans of Logan's day did not believe him to be anything but their ally in high place; within the black community harsh and perceptive observers such as Frederick Douglass were not so easily fooled, even by a politician of Logan's skills.

Somewhere between condemnation and adulation lies a more judicious appraisal of John A. Logan. His change of party after the war was a result not only of expediency but also of conviction brought on by the years of conflict. A better question than why Logan became a Republican following the war is how he could have remained a Democrat after his experiences on the battlefield. As a member of Congress for eighteen years Logan used patronage to maintain himself in office, and his battles for office were, unlike the careers of many affluent late-nineteenth-century politicians, struggles to provide an income for his family. Because so many of Logan's business ventures failed, throughout his public life the issues of holding office, using patronage to stay in office, and the sustenance of himself and his family were vitally interdependent.

John A. Logan was preeminently the political general and the idol of Union veterans. He was most closely identified with Memorial Day, the Grand Army of the Republic, and soldiers' pensions. The Illinois Radical-Stalwart was one of the most popular and well-known figures of his time. In 1879 a Union veteran requesting Logan's autograph told him, "I would bequeath it to my chidren along with our family Bible and my discharge papers." [40] His large mustache, his fiery oratory, and his forthright positions on national issues were all highly visible. A man of action, often precipitate action, Logan fought in the political arena with the ferocity he had exhibited on the battlefield. His career defies the neat classification sometimes accorded him. Logan was called a Radical, yet he clashed with fellow Radicals and often opposed them. He was linked with President Grant's inner circle, yet he engaged in many political battles with his old commander. John A. Logan was profoundly influenced by the political and social changes wrought by the Civil War and Reconstruction. More than most late-nineteenth-century American politicians he battled for full equality for all citizens and continued this battle in spite of abundant evidence that it was not politically profitable. Yet the Illinoisan was otherwise a pragmatic politician constantly motivated in his choice of tactics by self-preservation. It is this combination of political pragmatism and staunch idealism that gives John A. Logan a distinctive place in the political life of post–Civil War America.

Notes

Chapter 1. Radical Reinforcement

1. U.S., Congress, Senate, *Congressional Globe*, 36th Cong., 1st sess., pt. 1:86.

2. James G. Blaine, *Twenty Years in Congress, 1861–1881*, 2:287; Shelby M. Cullom, *Fifty Years of Public Service: Personal Recollections*, p. 182. For Logan's career to 1867, see James P. Jones, *"Black Jack:" John A. Logan and Southern Illinois in the Civil War Era*.

3. John A. Logan to Mary Logan, Jan. 9, 1867, John A. Logan mss, Library of Congress. The Logans are hereafter cited as JAL and ML, the Library of Congress as LC.

4. JAL to Edwin D. Morgan, Jan. 23, 1867, Morgan mss, New York State Library, Albany; JAL to Henry Wilson, Feb. 23, 1867; JAL to ML, Mar. 5, 1867, Logan mss, LC; Michael Les Benedict, *The Impeachment and Trial of Andrew Johnson*, p. 10. The term "bloody shirt" has been generally applied to the strident oratory of Republican politicians who sought to keep war issues alive into Reconstruction and after. It has been used in a derogatory manner by southerners who used their own strident "bloody shirt" rhetoric for their own political purposes. The phrase is not used in this study in a derogatory sense. It is used to identify the oratorical style used by Logan throughout his post–Civil War career.

5. *Illinois State Journal* (Springfield), Mar. 7, 1867; *Alton Telegraph*, Mar. 15, 1867; *Chicago Times*, Mar. 4, 1867. The year before the *Chicago Times*'s editor Wilbur F. Storey, angered by Logan's party change, had compared him to a Chicago streetwalker. Justin E. Walsh, *To Print the News and Raise Hell! A Biography of Wilbur F. Storey*, p. 218.

6. *Carbondale New Era*, Feb. 7, 1867; *Illinois State Register* (Springfield), Mar. 11, 1867; John Sherman to William T. Sherman, Mar. 7, 1867, William T. Sherman mss, LC.

7. Kenneth M. Stampp, *The Era of Reconstruction, 1865–1877*, p. 119–20; Hans Trefousse, *Benjamin Franklin Wade: Radical Republican from Ohio*, p. 283; Albert V. House, "Northern Congressional Democrats as Defenders of the South during Reconstruction," *Journal of Southern History* 6(1940):48.

8. *Cong. Globe*, 40th Cong., 1st sess., pp. viii, 1, 4.

9. Ibid., pp. 17, 21–22, 67. On March 6 Logan had joined Butler and Robert Schenck in a secret caucus to speed the impeachment process. The effort failed. Benedict, *Impeachment*, p. 23.

10. *Cong. Globe*, 40th Cong., 1st sess., pp. 87–89.

11. Ibid., pp. 213, 236, 257–58, 282. The racist Democratic press of Egypt assailed Logan as a man "who gives millions to the 'almighty nigger,' but not one cent to the white man." *Jonesboro Gazette*, Mar. 30, 1867.

12. *Cong. Globe*, 40th. Cong., 1st sess., p. 314.

13. Ibid., pp. 126–27.

14. Ibid., pp. 391, 451, 463; Oliver P. Morton to Murat Halstead, Mar. 20, 1867, Halstead mss, Rutherford B. Hayes Library, Fremont, Ohio.

15. Shelby M. Cullom to Ozias M. Hatch, Feb. 16, 1867, Hatch mss, Illinois State Historical Library, Springfield; J.W. Shaffer to Benjamin F. Butler, Mar. 22, 1867, Butler mss, LC. The Illinois State Historical Library is hereafter cited as ISHL.

16. *Carbondale New Era*, Mar. 28, 1867; *DuQuoin Tribune*, Mar. 28, 1867; *Freeport Weekly Journal*, Mar. 27, 1867.

17. Henry Bennett to T.L. Tullock, Apr. 30, 1867, John Covode mss, LC.

18. *Illinois State Register*, Apr. 3, 9, 1867; *Chicago Times*, Mar. 22, 1867.

19. JAL to Richard Yates, Apr. 8, 1867, Yates mss, ISHL; *Illinois State Journal*, Mar. 27, Apr. 19, 1867.

20. JAL to ML, Apr. 3, 1867, Logan mss, LC; Maxwell Woodhull to Benjamin F. Butler, May 3, 1867, Butler mss, LC.

21. *Carbondale New Era*, Apr. 11, 25, 1867; *DuQuoin Tribune*, Apr. 18, 1867; *Freeport Weekly Journal*, Apr. 3, 1867. The *Cairo Democrat* scoffed at the Logan-for-president talk with "Pshaw! The joke is a flat one," in its issue of July 26, 1867. Yet across the country the *New York Tribune*, Mar. 20, 1867, ran a story on Logan as a potential candidate.

22. Robert G. Ingersoll to Ebon C. Ingersoll, May 22, 1867, Robert G. Ingersoll mss, LC; Robert Schenck to Zachariah Chandler, May 8, 1867, Zachariah Chandler mss, LC.

23. JAL to ML, July 6, 1867, Logan mss, LC; George W. Julian to Laura Julian, July 8, 1867, Julian mss, Indiana State Library, Indianapolis.

24. Henry Stanbery to Orville H. Browning, June 30, 1867, Browning mss, ISHL.

25. *DuQuoin Tribune*, July 18, 1867.

26. *Cong. Globe*, 40th. Cong., 1st sess., pp. 469, 471–72, 478–79, 501. See Jones, "*Black Jack*," chap. 5, for treatment of Logan's supposed disloyalty.

27. JAL to ML, July 3, 7, 1867, Logan mss, LC.

28. *Chicago Times*, July 6, 1867; *Illinois State Register*, July 5, 13, 1867; *Cairo Democrat*, July 18, 1867; Gideon Welles, *The Diary of Gideon Welles*, ed. Howard K. Beale, 2:129.

29. *Carbondale New Era*, July 11, 1867; *Illinois State Journal*, July 12, 1867; *Chicago Tribune*, July 6, 10, 1867.

30. JAL to ML, Feb. 17, 1867, Logan mss, LC.

31. *Cong. Globe*, 40th. Cong., 1st sess., appendix, pp. 13–16.

32. George W. Julian to Mollie Giddings, July 17, 1867, Julian mss, Indiana State Library.

33. *Cong. Globe*, 40th. Cong., 1st sess., p. 747; *Chicago Tribune*, July 26, 1867.

34. Ulysses S. Grant to Edwin M. Stanton, July 20, 1867, Stanton mss, LC.

35. *Cong. Globe*, 40th. Cong., 1st sess., pp. 695, 725.

36. *Illinois State Journal*, July 29, 1867; *Chicago Tribune*, July 16, 1867; *DuQuoin Tribune*, Aug. 1, 1867; *Carbondale New Era*, Aug. 1, 1867.

37. S.S. Marshall to John McClernand, July 27, 1867, McClernand mss, ISHL.

38. JAL to ML, July 10, 22, 1867, Logan mss, LC.

39. *Chicago Tribune*, Sept. 7, 1867. Michael Les Benedict in "The Rout of Radicalism: Republicans and the Election of 1867," *Civil War History*, 18(1972):334–44, emphasizes the importance of this election since Ohio was the only populous northern state where voters could directly ballot on black suffrage. The anti-Logan *Chicago Times*, Nov.

1, 1867, wrote that Logan campaigned in Ohio only because he was paid $6,000 for doing so. Logan's friend, the *DuQuoin Tribune*, Oct. 24, 1867, wrote, however: "The statement that Gen. John A. Logan was paid $6,000 for stumping Ohio is a Copperhead lie. He not only received no pay, but a part of the time paid his own traveling expenses."

40. *Carbondale New Era*, Sept. 26, 1867.

41. *Carbondale New Era*, Sept. 26, 1867; *Cincinnati Gazette*, Sept. 13, 1867.

42. *Illinois State Journal*, Sept. 24, 1867.

43. Martin E. Mantell, *Johnson, Grant, and the Politics of Reconstruction*, p. 5.

44. *Miami Union* (Troy, Ohio), Aug. 31, Sept. 7, 1867; *Illinois State Journal*, Sept. 20, 1867. While Logan's chief wartime command was the xv Corps, the xvii Corps served under him briefly in Georgia.

45. *Chicago Tribune*, Sept. 25, 1867.

46. *Chicago Tribune*, Sept. 30, 1867; *DuQuoin Tribune*, Sept. 26, 1867; *Elyria Independent Democrat*, Sept. 31, 1867.

47. *Miami Union*, Aug. 31, 1867; *Portage County Democrat* (Ravenna, Ohio), Oct. 2, 1867; *Elyria Independent Democrat*, Oct. 2, 1867; *Allen County Democrat* (Lima, Ohio), Sept. 25, 1867.

48. *Chicago Times*, Sept. 12, 1867; Richard Yates to Henry Wilson, Oct. 7, 1867, Wilson mss, LC; Schuyler Colfax to John A.J. Creswell, Sept. 28, 1867, Colfax mss, Hayes Library.

49. *Chicago Tribune*, Oct. 1–12, 1867. Wade's biographer believes that the unpopularity of black suffrage made the senator's fight for reelection an "uphill battle" and cost him the election. However, the senator refused to temporize on the issue since he felt that "Ohio ought to set an example for the nation." Trefousse, *Wade*, pp. 289–90.

50. *Carbondale New Era*, Oct. 17, 1867. Martin Mantell writes: "Many moderates . . . welcomed the defeats feeling that it was just as well that the losses had come in a series of minor elections, giving the party time to make the changes necessary for victory in 1868." Mantell, *Johnson, Grant*, p. 67.

51. JAL to ML, Apr. 3, 1867, Logan mss, LC; ML to Richard Oglesby, Mar. 17, 1867, Oglesby mss, ISHL.

52. Egypt is the southern tier of counties in Illinois. For derivation of the name see Jones, *"Black Jack,"* chap. 1.

53. I.N. Haynie to JAL, Apr. 5, 1867, Logan mss, LC; *Alton Telegraph*, Feb. 1, 1867; *Centralia Sentinel*, Jan. 31, 1867.

54. ML to JAL, Dec. 16, 1866, Logan mss, LC; *Carbondale New Era*, Apr. 18, 1867.

55. *Carbondale New Era*, June 6, 13, 1867; *DuQuoin Tribune*, June 20, 27, 1867; *Illinois State Register*, June 19, 1867.

56. JAL to Richard Oglesby, June 19, 1867, Oglesby mss, ISHL.

57. *Carbondale New Era*, Aug. 9, Sept. 19, 1867; *Cairo Democrat*, Sept. 14, 1867; *Illinois State Journal*, Aug. 15, Sept. 5, 1867; *Chicago Times*, Sept. 5, 1867.

58. Mary Logan, *Reminiscences of a Soldier's Wife*, p. 205. A revealing look at Logan's worth came in a tax statement prepared by Logan's brother in Illinois. The list includes: 6 horses–$500; 1 cow–$15; 2 carriages–$175; 2 watches–$200; money–$7,000; unenumerated–$1,000. Undated, 1867, Logan mss, LC.

59. *Illinois State Journal*, Oct. 30, 1867; JAL to Richard Oglesby, Nov. 9, 1867, Oglesby mss, ISHL; JAL to General Kingsbury, Nov. 5, 1867, Eldridge mss, Box 36, Huntington Library, Pomona, California. So virulent was the political journalism of the era that rather than eliciting sympathy, Logan's illness brought from the *Cairo Democrat*,

Nov. 2, 1867: "Gen. Logan is said to be suffering from inflammation of the lungs. The howling of red hot negro suffrage harangues seems to bring its punishment. *Information* of the *brain* is, we believed, a disease to which the General is not subject."

60. Bluford Wilson to Elihu B. Washburne, Oct. 24, 1867; D.W. Lusk to Elihu B. Washburne, Oct. 24, 1867; Thurlow Weed to Elihu B. Washburne, Nov. 22, 1867, Washburne mss, LC.

61. D.W. Munn to JAL, Nov. 12, 1867, Logan mss, LC; John M. Palmer to John Mayo Palmer, Oct. 16, 1867, John Palmer mss, ISHL; Robert G. Ingersoll to Richard Oglesby, Sept. 21, 1867, Oglesby mss, ISHL.

62. *DuQuoin Tribune*, Dec. 5, 1867; *Illinois State Register*, Dec. 3, 1867; *Cong. Globe*, 40th Cong., 1st sess., p. 785.

63. Horace White to Elihu B. Washburne, Nov. 27, 1867, Washburne mss, LC.

64. Notebook, undated, 1867, Logan mss, ISHL. The congressman also purchased a signature and stamping box for ten dollars. Note, Nov. 12, 1867, Logan mss, LC.

Chapter 2. Steering the Boat

1. *Cong. Globe*, 40th. Cong., 2d sess., pt. 1:viii–ix, 12.

2. Benedict, *Impeachment*, p. 76.

3. *Cong. Globe*, 40th Cong., 2d sess., pt. 1:68; George W. Julian to Laura Julian, Dec. 8, 1867, Julian mss, Indiana State Library; *Illinois State Journal*, Dec. 9, 1867; *Chicago Tribune*, Dec. 8, 1867. The *Jonesboro Gazette* on Dec. 14, 1867, said that the next move would be Logan's trial for "aiding and abetting the rebellion." Michael Les Benedict points out that the impeachment movement was deeply involved in Republican party politics. In some quarters it was seen as a move to elevate President Pro-tem Ben Wade to the presidency, aiding the Ohioan's chances for the nomination in 1868. Thus it was for some an anti–Grant move since "many radicals regarded the likelihood of Grant's nomination with despair." Logan did not share that view and supported Grant's presidential bid. Benedict, *Impeachment*, pp. 69, 72.

4. *Cong. Globe*, 40th Cong., 2d sess., pt. 1:209.

5. John Cochrane to Elihu B. Washburne, Dec. 5, 1867, Washburne mss, LC.

6. JAL to ML, Jan. 6, 1868, Logan mss, LC.

7. *Cong. Globe*, 40th Cong., 2d sess., pt. 1:353.

8. Ibid., pp. 489, 664.

9. See Jones, *"Black Jack,"* pp. 273–75.

10. Mary R. Dearing, *Veterans in Politics: The Story of the Grand Army of the Republic*, pp. 115–16.

11. Norman B. Judd to Lyman Trumbull, July 16, 1866, Trumbull mss, LC.

12. Dearing, *Veterans*, pp. 115–16.

13. Mary Logan, *Reminiscences*, p. 148; *Chicago Tribune*, Jan. 28, 1868.

14. B.F. Stephenson to JAL, Jan. 30, 1868, Logan mss, LC; Robert B. Beath, *The History of the Grand Army of the Republic*, pp. 78, 83; Dearing, *Veterans*, pp. 132–34.

15. JAL to W.E. Chandler, Sept. 19, 1868, Chandler mss, LC.

16. Dearing, *Veterans*, pp. vii–viii; Beath, *Grand Army*, pp. 95, 109–11, 117–18; B.F. Stephenson to JAL, Jan. 30, 1868, Logan mss, LC; Mary Logan, *Reminiscences*, p. 148. Mary R. Dearing, in estimating the G.A.R.'s power, wrote: "Although the commonly heard statement that Union Civil War veterans virtually ruled the country for thirty years is exaggerated, the Grand Army of the Republic did wield great political power. At

the height of their influence . . . former soldiers were able to command benefits which cost the federal government more than one-fifth of its total revenue.

17. Paul H. Buck, *The Road to Reunion, 1865–1900*, p. 116.

18. Mary Logan, *Reminiscences*, pp. 171–74; Beath, *Grand Army*, p. 90; *Chicago Tribune*, June 1, 1868.

19. Buck, *Road*, p. 117.

20. N.A. Gray and A.P. Gray to JAL, July 6, 1868, W.T. Sherman mss, Ohio Historical Society, Ohio State Museum, Columbus. Eventually verses such as this appeared in large numbers in the *Great Republic*, the G.A.R.'s magazine. It was published weekly and, in 1867, cost three dollars a year. *Centralia Sentinel*, May 9, 1867.

21. *Cong. Globe*, 40th Cong., 2d sess., pt. 1:735, 780; Joseph Medill to John Sherman, Jan. 7, 1868, John Sherman mss, LC.

22. J.C. Webster to JAL, Jan. 25, 1868; I.N. Haynie to JAL, Feb. 14, 1868; S.A. Hurlbut to JAL, Feb. 6, 1868; D.W. Lusk to JAL, Feb. 7, 1868; James Rea to JAL, Feb. 3, 1868, Logan mss, LC; *Chicago Tribune*, Feb. 10, 20, 1868; Richard Oglesby to R.H. Sturgess, Feb. 10, 1868, Oglesby mss, ISHL. The *Centralia Sentinel*, Feb. 6, 1868, endorsed Logan for governor. The *Illinois State Journal*, Feb. 3, 1868, denied that Logan would run for governor, but on January 31, mentioned talk of a "new radical" ticket with Logan for president. The *Illinois State Register*, Jan. 6, 1868, laughed at Logan as a potential governor in a story headed "Radicals, Niggers, and Cannibals."

23. JAL memorandum, Feb. 10, 1868, Logan mss, LC; Drake DeKay to Benjamin F. Butler, Jan. 23, 1868, Butler mss, LC; Mary Logan, *Reminiscences*, p. 157.

24. Charles S. Spencer to JAL, Feb. 12, 1868, Logan mss, LC; JAL to Conrad Baker, Feb. 16, 1868, Baker mss, W.H. Smith Library, Indianapolis, Indiana.

25. *Chicago Times*, Dec. 28, 1867; Charles Francis Adams to Thomas Jenckes, Jan. 11, 1868, Jenckes mss, LC.

26. *Cong. Globe*, 40th Cong., 2d sess., pt. 1:987–90.

27. James Fishback to JAL, Feb. 23, 1868, Logan mss, LC; Charles Sumner to Edwin M. Stanton, Feb. 21, 1868, Stanton mss, LC; Johnson's appointment of Thomas violated the Constitution. With the Senate in session all appointees had to be confirmed before taking office.

28. JAL to N.P. Chipman, Feb. 22, 1868, Logan mss, LC; Mary Logan, *Reminiscences*, pp. 154–55; Sister Mary Karl George, *Zahariah Chandler: A Political Biography*, p. 154; *Illinois State Journal*, Feb. 22, 1868; *Illinois State Register*, Feb. 22, 1868; Benjamin P. Thomas and Harold M. Hyman, *Stanton: The Life and Times of Lincoln's Secretary of War*, p. 594.

29. Benedict, *Impeachment*, p. 104; Mantell, *Johnson, Grant*, p. 4.

30. George W. Julian to Laura Julian, Feb. 21, 22, 1868, Julian mss, Indiana State Library; W.A. Pile to James A. Garfield, Feb. 24, 1868, Garfield mss, LC; William T. Sherman to John Sherman, Feb. 25, 1868, William T. Sherman mss, LC.

31. *Cong. Globe*, 40th Cong., 2d sess., pt. 1:1351–53. Copies of this address were run in the Illinois press. See *DuQuoin Tribune*, Mar. 5, 1868; *Illinois State Journal*, Mar. 6, 1868.

32. *Cong. Globe*, 40th Cong., 2d sess., pt. 1:1401–2; George W. Julian to Laura Julian, Feb. 24, 1868, Julian mss, Indiana State Library.

33. Benedict, *Impeachment*, p. 114.

34. Thaddeus Stevens to Benjamin F. Butler, Feb. 28, 1868, Butler mss, LC; *Cong.*

Globe, 40th Cong., 2d sess., pt. 1:1427, 1616–19, 1642, 1647. The vote in the House for managers was: Bingham, 114; Boutwell, 113; Wilson, 112; Butler, 108; Williams, 107; Logan, 106; Stevens, 105. Samuel S. Cox, *Three Decades of Federal Legislation, 1855– 1885,* p. 586.

35. *Harper's Weekly,* Mar. 14, 21, Apr. 11, 1868; George W. Julian to Laura Julian, Feb. 29, 1868, Julian mss, Indiana State Library; William P. Kellogg to Benjamin F. Wade, Feb. 28, 1868; B. Gratz Brown to Benjamin F. Wade, Mar. 2, 1868, Wade mss, LC.

36. Joseph Medill to JAL, Mar. 6, 1868, Logan mss, LC; *Cong. Globe,* 40th Cong., 2d sess., pt. 2:1641. Since the twenty-first the *Chicago Tribune* had called for impeachment labeling Johnson's defenses "miserable subterfuges." When the additional charges were added, the influential journal attacked them as "side issues" that were regrettable. However, the newspaper continued to endorse impeachment. *Chicago Tribune,* Feb. 26, 28, Mar. 1, 2, 3, Apr. 19, 1868.

37. *Cong. Globe,* 40th Cong., 2d sess., Supplement for the Impeachment of Andrew Johnson, pp. 23–24; Joseph Medill to JAL, Mar. 18, 1868, Logan mss, LC.

38. Edwin M. Stanton to Benjamin F. Butler, Apr. 1, 1868, Butler mss, LC.

39. George W. Julian to Laura Julian, Apr. 27, 1868, Julian mss, Indiana State Library.

40. *Cong. Globe,* 40th Cong., 2d sess., Supplement, pp. 251–406; Richard Yates to John D. Strong, May 4, 1868, Strong mss, ISHL; Benedict, *Impeachment,* p. 168.

41. *Cong. Globe,* 40th Cong., 2d sess., Supplement, pp. 251–68. In spite of his lesser public role, Shelby Cullom wrote that Logan "did his full share as one of the managers." Cullom, *Fifty Years,* p. 182.

42. *Chicago Tribune,* Apr. 24, 1868; Blaine, *Twenty Years,* 2:370; Stephen Hurlbut to JAL, Apr. 26, 1868, Logan mss, LC; Mary Logan, *Reminiscences,* p. 155. Mrs. Logan reported doing much of her husband's research into impeachment. In the Logan mss, ISHL, are a number of items used by Logan in preparing his argument. They include commentaries by Justice Story, notes from *The Federalist,* numbers 33, 34, 48, 65, 66, and 77, and notes on the trial of Warren Hastings. The *Illinois State Register,* Apr. 1, 1868, thought Logan was of no value as a manager and called him a "fifth wheel."

43. George W. Julian to Laura Julian, May 11, 1868, Julian mss, Indiana State Library; John Cook to Richard Yates, Mar. 14, 1868, Yates mss, ISHL.

44. John F. Kennedy, *Profiles in Courage,* p. 119; *Cong. Globe,* 40th Cong., 2d sess., Supplement, pp. 411–12. One of the dissenting Republicans was Lyman Trumbull, who had earlier branded the impeachers as "excited demagogues." Lyman Trumbull to William Jayne, Dec. 6, 1868, Jayne mss, ISHL.

45. Elihu B. Washburne to Henry L. Dawes, May 17, 1868, Dawes mss, LC.

46. JAL to ML, May 26, 1868, Logan mss, LC. At the Chicago convention "the fury against Trumbull is unprecedented," wrote an Illinois Republican. Jesse O. Norton to Orville H. Browning, May 18, 1868, Browning mss, ISHL.

47. *Chicago Tribune,* May 16, 20, 1868; Cullom, *Fifty Years,* p. 128; William T. Sherman to John Sherman, Mar. 14, 1868, William T. Sherman mss, LC.

48. Mantell, *Johnson, Grant,* p. 4; *Chicago Tribune,* May 21, 1868; *Proceedings of the Republican National Convention, 1868,* pp. 64, 82.

49. *Chicago Tribune,* May 22, 1868; *Illinois State Journal,* May 22–23, 1868. Blaine remembered Logan's speech as "vigorous and eloquent." Blaine, *Twenty Years,* 2:389. *Proceedings, 1868,* p. 90.

50. Trefousse, *Wade,* p. 305; William P. Kellogg to Benjamin F. Wade, May 6, 1868,

Wade mss, LC; JAL to ML, May 23, 26, 1868, Logan mss, LC; Schuyler Colfax to "My Dear Sir," Apr. 29, 1868, Colfax mss, LC.

51. Robert G. Ingersoll to Ebon Ingersoll, Mar. 2, 13, 24, 29, 1868, Ingersoll mss, LC; Ebon Ingersoll to Robert G. Ingersoll, Apr. 6, 1868, Ingersoll mss, ISHL.

52. D.L. Phillips to JAL, Mar. 29, Apr. 20, 1868; Giles A. Smith to JAL, Apr. 15, 1868; D.W. Lusk to JAL, Apr. 17, 1868, Logan mss, LC.

53. *Chicago Tribune,* Apr. 16, 1868; *Illinois State Journal,* May 7, 1868; *DuQuoin Tribune,* May 14, 21, 1868; *Quincy Daily Herald,* Sept. 4, 8, 1868; *Illinois State Register,* Apr. 16, 1868.

54. JAL to ML, June 1, 11, 1868, Logan mss, LC.

55. *Cong. Globe,* 40th Cong., 2d sess., pt. 3:2971; pt. 4:3132, 3174.

56. William T. Sherman to Jacob M. Howard, Jan 29, 1868, William T. Sherman mss, LC; *Cong. Globe,* 40th Cong., 2d sess., pt. 1:967.

57. *Cong. Globe,* 40th Cong., 2d sess., pt. 1:1019, 1021, 1050.

58. *Cong. Globe,* 40th Cong., 2d sess., pt. 1:1278–79, 1282, 1306–7; *Chicago Tribune,* Feb. 21, 1868; *Illinois State Journal,* Feb. 21, 1868.

59. *Cong. Globe,* 40th Cong., 2d sess., pt. 4:3950, 3970, 3972; William T. Sherman to John Sherman, July 30, 1868, William T. Sherman mss, LC.

60. *Cong. Globe,* 40th Cong., 2d sess., pt. 5:4136–40; John A. Logan, "Speech of General John A. Logan, Principles of the Democratic Party, July 16, 1868," pamphlet in Logan mss, LC; George F. Dawson, *The Life and Services of General John A. Logan as Soldier and Statesman,* p. 136; Charles H. Coleman, *The Election of 1868: The Democratic Effort to Regain Control,* p. 205.

61. *Cong. Globe,* 40th Cong., 2d sess., pt. 5:4479.

62. Memorandum, June 20, July 10, 1868, Logan mss, LC; JAL to ML, July 21, 1868, Logan mss, LC.

63. JAL to ML, Aug. 1, 1868, Logan mss, LC; James G. Blaine to Elihu B. Washburne, July 11, 1868, Washburne mss, LC; JAL to ML, Aug. 8, 1868; ML to JAL, Aug. 17, 1868, Logan mss, LC.

64. Dawson, *Logan,* p. 154; Byron Andrews, *A Biography of General John A. Logan: With an Account of His Public Services in Peace and War,* pp. 561, 565; JAL to ML, Sept. 6, 1868; ML to JAL, Sept. 6, 1868, Logan mss, LC; *DuQuoin Tribune,* Sept. 10, 1868; *Illinois State Register,* Apr. 27, Sept. 4, 1868.

65. ML to JAL, Sept. 6, 1868, Logan mss, LC; ML to William T. Sherman, Sept. 14, 1868; William T. Sherman to John Sherman, Sept. 23, 1868, William T. Sherman mss, LC.

66. Jay Cooke to W.E. Chandler, Sept. 29, 1868, W.E. Chandler mss, LC; Jay Cooke to JAL, Sept. 29, 1868, Logan mss, LC; JAL to W.E. Chandler, Oct. 5, 1868, W.E. Chandler mss, New Hampshire Historical Society.

67. Dawson, *Logan,* pp. 154–59; *DuQuoin Tribune,* Oct. 8, 1868; *Chicago Tribune,* Sept. 8, 10, 26, 30, 1868; *Centralia Sentinel,* Sept. 10, Oct. 8, 15, 1868; *Illinois State Journal,* Sept. 4, 9, Oct. 8, 21, 22, 1868.

68. David W. Lusk, *Politics and Politicians of Illinois, 1856–1884,* pp. 205–7; Charles A. Church, *The Republican Party in Illinois, 1854–1912,* p. 104; *Illinois Fact Book and Historical Almanac,* p. 90.

Chapter 3. Scourge of the Regular Army

1. *Cong. Globe,* 40th Cong., 3d sess., pt. 1:1, 7, 183.

2. William Schouler to Henry L. Dawes, Nov. 24, 1868, Dawes mss, LC; James G. Blaine to JAL, Nov. 20, 1868, Logan mss, LC; Mary Logan, *Reminiscences*, p. 182.

3. Godlove Orth to Schuyler Colfax, Nov. 9, 1868, Orth mss, Indiana State Library; *Cong. Globe*, 40th Cong., 3d sess., pt. 1:262–67; *Chicago Tribune*, Jan. 9, 1869.

4. *Quincy Weekly Whig and Republican*, Jan. 23, 1869; J.K.C. Forest to Richard Yates, Jan. 11, 1869, Yates mss, ISHL; Robert G. Ingersoll to Richard Oglesby, Jan. 11, 1869, Oglesby mss, ISHL.

5. William T. Sherman to John Sherman, Oct. 30, Nov. 23, Dec. 8, 20, 1868, Jan. 6, 1869; John Sherman to William T. Sherman, Nov. 18, 1868, Jan. 8, 1869, William T. Sherman mss, LC; William T. Sherman to James G. Blaine, Nov. 13, 1868, Blaine mss, LC.

6. *Cong. Globe*, 40th Cong., 3d sess., pt. 2:925–27.

7. Ibid., pp. 1146, 1148; Mary Logan, *Reminiscences*, pp. 162–64. The *Chicago Tribune*, Feb. 13, 1869, praised Logan's defense of Wade.

8. *Cong. Globe*, 40th Cong., 3d sess., pt. 2:1428; Dawson, *Logan*, pp. 176–78. In his work, *The Right to Vote: Politics and the Passage of the Fifteenth Amendment*, pp. 68–71, William Gillette writes: "John A. Logan, a wily Republican politician from anti-Negro southern Illinois, wanted to scrap the Negro officeholding guarantee, no doubt accurately reflecting the will of his constituency, where opinion against Negro officeholding ran strong." Logan, of course, did not represent southern Illinois; his constituency was the entire state. Furthermore, there is little evidence that the man who fought for Negro suffrage in Ohio in 1867 was hostile to Negro officeholding.

9. *Cong. Globe*, 40th Cong., 3d sess., pt. 3:1707–8.

10. Robert G. Ingersoll to Ebon C. Ingersoll, Mar. 3, 1869, Ingersoll mss, LC; *Cong. Globe*, 41st Cong., 1st sess., pt. 1:2, 19.

11. *Cong. Globe*, 41st Cong., 1st sess., pt. 1:75–77.

12. Ibid., p. 198.

13. Ibid., pp. 708–10; Augustus L. Chetlain, *Recollections of Seventy Years*, pp. 237–38.

14. JAL to ML, Apr. 5, 10, 17, 26, 1869, Logan mss, LC; JAL to John Sherman, Apr. 21, 1869, Richard Yates mss, ISHL; John Olney to Lyman Trumbull, June 15, 1869, Trumbull mss, LC.

15. Richard Yates to Simon Cameron, May 25, 1869, Cameron mss, LC.

16. JAL to ML, May 1, 1869, Logan mss, LC; *Cairo Bulletin*, May 17, June 3, 1869; ms of a speech by JAL, undated, 1869, Dr. John Logan mss, ISHL; ms of a speech by JAL, May 30, 1869, Logan mss, LC; *DuQuoin Tribune*, May 13, June 10, 1869.

17. Richard Jensen, "The Religious and Occupational Roots of Party Identification: Illinois and Indiana in the 1870's," *Civil War History* 16(1970):325–43; Paul Kleppner, *The Cross of Culture: A Social Analysis of Midwestern Politics, 1850–1900*, pp. 21, 35, 63, 99.

18. JAL to ML, June 7, 1869, Logan mss, LC; George T. Brown to Lyman Trumbull, June 30, 1869, Trumbull mss, LC.

19. *Chicago Republican*, Aug. 16, 1869; JAL to B.H. Chever, Oct. 12, 1869, Chever mss, Western Reserve Historical Society, Cleveland, Ohio.

20. John Palmer to Richard Oglesby, Sept. 21, 1869, Oglesby mss, ISHL.

21. Mary Logan, *Reminiscences*, p. 192.

22. *Cong. Globe*, 41st Cong., 2d sess., pt. 1:9, 293, 342.

23. Ibid., pp. 362, 401–2, 432–33, 492.

24. Ibid., p. 720; Shelby M. Cullom to Ozias M. Hatch, Jan. 19, 1870, Hatch mss, ISHL.

25. *Cong. Globe,* 41st Cong., 2d sess., pt. 1:679–85, 973, 1264–68; Mary Logan, *Reminiscences,* p. 201.

26. Whitelaw Reid to JAL, Feb. 27, 1870, Logan mss, LC; *Cong. Globe,* 41st Cong., 2d sess., pt. 2:1469–73, 1522–33, 1544–47, 1616–22, 2002, 2036.

27. *Cong. Globe,* 41st Cong., 2d sess., pt. 3:2189–90.

28. John M. Palmer to JAL, Feb. 12, 1870, Logan mss, LC; Jesse H. Moore to Richard Oglesby, Feb. 28, 1870, Oglesby mss, ISHL.

29. William T. Sherman to John Sherman, Oct. 29, 1869; Philip H. Sheridan to William T. Sherman, Dec. 6, 1869, Jan. 14, 1870, William T. Sherman mss, LC; Philip H. Sheridan to JAL, Jan. 22, 1870; William W. Belknap to JAL, Jan. 21, 1870, Logan mss, LC.

30. *Cong. Globe,* 42d Cong., 2d sess., pt. 2:1848–54, Appendix, pp. 146–54; Mary Logan, *Reminiscences,* pp. 203–4.

31. *New York Times,* Mar. 21, 1870; *New York Evening Mail,* Mar. 12, 1870.

32. See James P. Jones, "The Battle of Atlanta and McPherson's Successor," *Civil War History* 7(1961):393–405.

33. *New York Herald,* Mar. 21, 1870; William T. Sherman to John Sherman, Mar. 21, 1870, William T. Sherman mss, LC. Yet even the usually hostile *Cairo Bulletin,* Feb. 10, 1870, applauded the reduction bill.

34. *Cong. Globe,* 41st Cong., 2d sess., pt. 3:2275–80; William T. Sherman to John Sherman, Mar. 21, 1870, William T. Sherman mss, LC. Secretary of the Navy A.E. Borie wrote Sherman to thank him for the letter that attacked "demagoguism in Congress." Borie to William T. Sherman, Mar. 28, 1870, William T. Sherman mss, LC. Logan was encouraged by support from the *Chicago Republican,* Mar. 10, 1870, and from letters such as the one he received on April 6 thanking him "as a constituent and citizen." J.D. Ward to JAL, Apr. 6, 1870, Logan mss, LC; Arthur Ekirch, *The Civilian and the Military,* p. 13.

35. Lloyd Lewis, *Sherman, Fighting Prophet,* pp. 602–8; Henry Wilson to JAL, May 13, 1870, Logan mss, LC; Mary Logan, *Reminiscences,* p. 204.

36. See Jones, "Battle of Atlanta," pp. 393–405.

37. E.O.C. Ord to William T. Sherman, June 17, 1870; William T. Sherman to John Sherman, July 27, Aug. 5, 1870; Ulysses S. Grant to William T. Sherman, July 31, 1870, William T. Sherman mss, LC; William T. Sherman to John McClernand, July 29, 1870, McClernand mss, ISHL.

38. *Cong. Globe,* 41st Cong., 2d sess., pt. 5:3927, pt. 6:4734.

39. Ibid., pt. 3:2768, pt, 4:3002–3, 3079, 3130.

40. Joseph Medill to JAL, Mar, 6, 1870; Horace White to JAL, Mar. 6, 1870, Logan mss, LC; see also Joseph Logsdon, *Horace White, Nineteenth Century Liberal,* pp. 178–79.

41. *Cong. Globe,* 41st Cong., 2d sess., pt. 4:3628, 3771–72, pt. 5:4442; *New York Tribune,* June 16, 1870. Logan wrote Mary that Illinois newspapers had not done him justice on the Cuba speech, but that the New York press had been kinder. JAL to ML, June 18, 1870, Logan mss, LC.

42. Dawson, *Logan,* pp. 183, 187; Joseph R. Hawley to JAL, May 8, 1870; Montgomery Meigs to JAL, May 13, 1870, Logan mss, LC.

43. Mary Logan, *Reminiscences,* p. 207; JAL to ML, May 26, June 2, 13, 18, 1870, Logan mss, LC.

44. *Cong. Globe*, 41st Cong., 2d sess., pt. 5:4588–89, 4669, 4674.
45. JAL to ML, June 28, July 4, 1870, Logan mss, LC.

Chapter 4. A High Place in the World

1. Schuyler Colfax to H.B. Anthony, Aug. 7, 1870, Colfax mss, LC; Journal of George W. Julian, June 26, 1870, Julian mss, Indiana State Library; Horace White to JAL, May 6, 1870, Logan mss, LC. There were those who did not agree with Julian. The Washington correspondent of the *Sioux City Daily Journal*, July 26, 1870, called Logan "the most honest politician in America."
2. Jesse H. Moore to Richard Oglesby, Dec. 11, 1869, Oglesby mss, ISHL; Horace White to JAL, May 6, 1870, Logan mss, LC; Anne W. Martin to John M. Palmer, June 30, 1870, Palmer mss, ISHL; *Freeport Journal*, Apr. 20, 1870; *Cairo Egyptian Sun*, May 4, 1870.
3. JAL to ML, Aug. 4, 5, 8, 16,1870; ML to JAL, Aug. 30, 1870, Logan mss, LC.
4. JAL to ML, Aug. 8, 1870, Logan mss, LC; William T. Sherman to John Sherman, Oct. 23, 1870, William T. Sherman mss, LC; Lyman Trumbull to William Jayne, Nov. 18, 1870, Jayne mss, ISHL.
5. R. Berry to JAL, Aug. 3, 1870; JAL to ML, Aug. 16, 1870, Logan mss, LC; A. Chester to Lyman Trumbull, Aug. 11, 1870, Trumbull mss, LC.
6. *Illinois State Register*, Aug. 30, Sept. 2, 1870; *Chicago Tribune*, Sept. 2, 3, 1870; *Illinois State Journal*, Sept. 1, 2, 1870.
7. Benjamin F. Butler to JAL, Aug. 20, Sept. 2, 1870, Logan mss, LC.
8. JAL to ML, Sept. 3, 4, 5, 1870, Logan mss, LC; John M. Palmer to Richard Oglesby, Sept. 8, 1870; David Davis to Richard Oglesby, Sept. 13, 1870, Oglesby mss, ISHL. The practice of canvassing the state to secure support of county conventions and legislative candidates was pioneered by Logan and Oglesby. Some Republican newspapers deplored the vote-seeking and condemned the candidates. See Ernest L. Bogart and Charles M. Thompson, *The Industrial State, 1870–1893*.
9. JAL to ML, Sept. 17, 23, 1870, Logan mss, LC; *Illinois State Register*, Sept. 15, 1870; *Cairo Bulletin*, Sept. 10, 1870; *Quincy Daily Herald*, Sept. 17, 1870.
10. F.V. Hayden to JAL, Sept. 21, 1870; F.V. Hayden to ML, Oct. 1, 1870, Logan mss, LC.
11. Stephen Hurlbut to JAL, Sept. 13, 1870; JAL to ML, Oct. 2, 1870, Logan mss, LC; Lyman Trumbull to William Jayne, Oct. 9, 1870, Jayne mss, ISHL.
12. JAL to ML, Oct. 2, 4, 5, 8, 16, 1870, Logan mss, LC.
13. JAL to ML, Oct. 4, 1870, Logan mss, LC.
14. Andrews, *Logan*, p. 585; *Des Moines Register*, Oct. 11, 1870; *New York Sun*, Oct. 18, 1870.
15. JAL to ML, Oct. 16, 28, 1870, Logan mss, LC; *Illinois State Journal*, Sept. 24, Oct. 17, 1870.
16. *Golconda* (Illinois) *Herald*, Nov. 3, 1870; *Quincy Daily Herald*, Sept. 26, 1870; *Illinois State Register*, Oct. 6, 15, 1870.
17. Lusk, *Politics and Politicians*, pp. 215–17; Church, *Republican Party*, p. 108; *Illinois State Register*, Nov. 26, 1870. In Egypt, Logan ally Daniel Munn lost the southern Illinois House seat to Democrat John Crebs, a sign, thought the hostile *Cairo Bulletin*, Nov. 11, 1870, of "Black Jack's" declining power.
18. JAL to ML, Nov. 13, 18, 21, 25, 1870, Logan mss, LC.

19. *Cong. Globe,* 41st Cong., 3d sess., pt. 1:25, 67, 153; *Harper's Weekly,* Dec. 31, 1870.

20. JAL to ML, Dec. 12, 17, 18, 1870; Jeremiah Davis to JAL, Dec. 26, 1870, Logan mss, LC.

21. *Illinois State Register,* Aug. 24, 1870.

22. Lyman Trumbull to William Jayne, Nov. 18, 1870, Jayne mss, ISHL; John M. Palmer to Richard Oglesby, Dec. 4, 1870; Richard Oglesby to John M. Palmer, Dec. 4, 1870; Jesse H. Moore to Richard Oglesby, Dec. 24, 1870, Jan. 4, 1871; David Davis to Richard Oglesby, Dec. 12, 1870; Richard Oglesby to J.K.C. Forest, Dec. 21, 1870, Oglesby mss, ISHL.

23. Gustave P. Koerner, *Memoirs of Gustave P. Koerner,* 2: 519–21.

24. Scrapbook, 1870–71, container 88, Logan mss, LC. On January 9, 1871, a member of the McKendree College faculty wrote supporting Logan "because he is not ashamed to be a Christian and a Methodist." Robert Allyn to James Robarts, Jan. 9, 1871, Logan mss, LC. One of the best examples of the Democratic press onslaught against Logan was the *Illinois State Register*'s front-page editorial of Nov. 23, 1870, entitled "Tearing off Logan's Mask."

25. *Davenport* (Iowa) *Daily Gazette,* Jan. 13, 1871; Mary Logan, *Reminiscences,* pp. 208–9. In *The Search for Order, 1877–1920,* Robert Wiebe, writing of the verities of American life in the Gilded Age, spoke of the "advantage of a wife who stayed home and kept a good house" (p. 4). Mary Logan was not exactly that kind of wife.

26. Koerner, *Memoirs,* 2:522. Koerner added a later look at Mary Logan: "Since the death of her husband, Mrs. Logan has become a kind of patron saint of the Grand Army of the Republic. After her death I should not be surprised if she were canonized as such, like Santa Barbara, who in all Catholic countries is considered the patroness of heavy artillery. . . . She continues to dabble in politics, and is present at the Republican National Convention trying her hand, though thus far unsuccessfully, at nominating politicians of her own choice for President. My opportunities were too limited to judge of her intellectual capacities. But be her gifts what they may, a dashing female worker in politics ought not to be approved, much less admitted." The *Quincy Daily Herald,* Jan. 15, 1870, also condemned Mrs. Logan's politicking but advised that "Black Jack" would never be president because he could not use Mary as effectively on the national level. Also see Bogart and Thompson, *Industrial State,* pp. 62–63.

27. Wiebe, *Search for Order,* pp. 27–29. See also Keith Ian Polakoff, *The Politics of Inertia: The Election of 1876 and the End of Reconstruction.*

28. C.A. Haviland to John M. Palmer, Jan. 7, 1871; A.J. McFarland to Richard Yates, Jan. 1, 1871, Yates mss, ISHL; Jesse H. Moore to Richard Oglesby, Jan. 26, 1871, Oglesby mss, ISHL; *Illinois State Register,* Jan. 16, 1871.

29. Joseph Medill to Richard Oglesby, Jan. 11, 1871, Oglesby mss, ISHL.

30. Church, *Republican Party,* p. 109; *Illinois State Register,* Jan. 14, 17, 1871; *Illinois State Journal,* Jan. 14, 18, 1871; *Appleton's Cyclopedia, 1871,* p. 386; Koerner, *Memoirs,* 2:522. The *Centralia Sentinel,* Jan. 19, 1871, hailed Logan's "surprising strength" in the caucus and called his victory a "happy augury for the future."

31. C.A. Haviland to John M. Palmer, Jan. 7, 1871, Palmer mss, ISHL; A.J. McFarland to Richard Yates, Jan. 1, 1871, Yates mss, ISHL; Jesse H. Moore to Richard Oglesby, Jan. 26, 1871, Oglesby mss, ISHL; *Illinois State Register,* Jan. 16, 1871.

32. Lyman Trumbull to William Jayne, Jan. 8, 1871, Jayne mss, ISHL.

33. See, for example, Headquarters, Department of New Jersey to JAL, Jan. 25, 1871, Logan mss, LC.

34. *Cong. Globe*, 41st Cong., 3d sess., pt. 2:1230–33, 1239–40, 1319–20.

35. Ibid., pp. 858–61, 1069–70.

36. Ibid., pt. 3:1856, 1928–29, 1940.

Chapter 5. The Senator Stands for Grant

1. *Cong. Globe*, 42d Cong., 1st sess., pt. 1:v, 1, 33–34.

2. J.G. Nicolay to Ozias M. Hatch, Feb. 26, 1871, Hatch mss, ISHL; I.T. Eccles to Richard Yates, Feb. 5, 1871, Yates mss, ISHL; *New National Era* (Washington, D.C.), Feb. 2, 1871.

3. *Cong. Globe*, 42d Cong., 1st sess., pt. 1:46–47; Moorfield Storey, *Charles Sumner*, p. 395; W.S. Wilkinson to JAL, Mar. 15, 1871, Logan mss, LC; John Sherman to *Springfield Republican*, Apr. 24, 1871, John Sherman mss, LC; Thomas A. Scott to Simon Cameron, Mar. 14, 1871, Cameron mss, LC; *Chicago Tribune*, Mar. 11, 13, 1871.

4. *Cong. Globe*, 42d Cong., 1st sess., pt. 1:90, 110, 276–77.

5. Ibid., pt. 2:709, 779, 831.

6. Lyman Trumbull to William Jayne, Apr. 9, 1871, Jayne mss, ISHL.

7. JAL to ML, Apr. 16, 20, May 3, 14, 27, 1871, Logan mss, LC.

8. JAL to ML, June 16, July 15, Aug. 7, 19, 1871; ML to JAL, Aug. 9, 29, 1871, Logan mss, LC; Mary Logan, *Reminiscences*, p. 214.

9. JAL to ML, Sept. 1, 20, 1871, Logan mss, LC; R.H. Sturgess to Richard Oglesby, Aug. 26, 1871, Oglesby mss, ISHL.

10. Mary Logan, *Reminiscences*, pp. 214–16; Philip H. Sheridan to W.W. Belknap, Nov. 13, 1871, Sheridan mss, LC; A.W. Luther to James Luther, Dec. 17, 1871, James Luther mss, Indiana State Library; *Chicago Tribune*, Oct. 16, 1871.

11. ML to Dollie Logan, Oct. 20, Nov. 6, 12, 27, 1871, Logan mss, LC.

12. See Mary Logan, *Reminiscences*.

13. *Cong. Globe*, 42d Cong., 2d sess., pt. 1:4, 482–83, 521, 548–64, 954, 1795–1804, 1823–28; *Chicago Tribune*, Jan. 17, 23, Mar. 19, 21, 28, 1872; *Chicago Times*, Feb. 17, Mar. 21, 29, 1872.

14. *Cong. Globe*, 42d Cong., 2d sess., pt. 1:41–42.

15. Ibid., pt. 3:1935.

16. Ibid., pt. 1:161, 1460, 1505; Oliver P. Morton to Simon Powell, Dec. 19, 1871, Morton mss, Indiana State Library.

17. *Cong. Globe*, 42d Cong., 2d sess., pt. 1:170–71, 185.

18. Ibid., pp. 818, 839–40; Zeb Vance to JAL, Jan. 12, 1872, Logan mss, LC.

19. *Cong. Globe*, 42d Cong., 2d sess., pt. 3:1974, 2002.

20. Ibid., pt. 5:3902, 3904, 4078.

21. Ibid., pt. 3:2638; pt. 4:3470.

22. Ibid., pt. 5:4155; appendix, pp. 522–30.

23. JAL to ML, June 1, 1872, Logan mss, LC; John Pope to Ulysses S. Grant, June 8, 1872, Grant mss, Hayes Library, Fremont, Ohio; *Harper's Weekly*, June 22, 1872. The *Chicago Times*, June 2, 1872, assailed Logan's effort as "venomous," but the *Illinois State Journal*, June 3, 1872, said all Americans would reply "amen" to Black Jack's remarks.

24. Lyman Trumbull to William Jayne, Mar. 24, 1871, Jayne mss, ISHL.

25. D.W. Wood to Lyman Trumbull, Dec. 12, 1871; W.C. Flagg to Lyman Trumbull,

Jan. 25, 1872; Gustave P. Koerner to Lyman Trumbull, Feb. 19, 1872; Lyman Trumbull to Horace White, Jan. 27, 1872, Trumbull mss, LC.

26. Oliver P. Morton to Simon Powell, Feb. 26, 1872, Morton mss, Indiana State Library; Lyman Trumbull to Gustave P. Koerner, Mar. 9, 1872; Horace White to Lyman Trumbull, Mar. 9, 1872, Trumbull mss, LC; Lyman Trumbull to C. Bryant, May 10, 1872, Trumbull mss, ISHL.

27. S.D. Phelps to JAL, Mar. 6, 18, 1872; Horace White to JAL, Apr. 9, 1872, Logan mss, LC; Lusk, *Politics and Politicians*, pp. 227–29; D.L. Phillips to John M. Palmer, Oct. 24, 1872, Palmer mss, ISHL; *Chicago Tribune*, May 21, 30, 1872; Logsdon, *Horace White, Nineteenth Century Liberal*, p. 217.

28. A.W. Schiart to Lyman Trumbull, Apr. 29, 1872, Trumbull mss, LC.

29. Jesse K. Dubois to Lyman Trumbull, May 12, 1872, Trumbull mss, LC.

30. JAL to ML, May 15, 25, June 7, 9, 1872, Logan mss, LC; William B. Hesseltine, *Ulysses S. Grant, Politician*, p. 277; *Proceedings of the Republican National Convention, 1872*, pp. 10, 57.

31. Ulysses S. Grant to Roscoe Conkling, July 15, 1872, Conkling mss, LC.

32. *Inter-Ocean* (Chicago), July 5, 1872; *Illinois State Journal*, July 27, 1872; A.J. Grover to Lyman Trumbull, July 14, 1872, Trumbull mss, ISHL; Silas Bryan to Lyman Trumbull, Sept. 11, 1872, Trumbull mss, LC.

33. James G. Blaine to JAL, July 15, 1872; Simon Cameron to JAL, July 6, 1872; Horace Porter to JAL, July 24, 1872, Logan mss, LC.

34. JAL to ML, July 13, 22, 25, 1872, Logan mss, LC.

35. JAL to ML, Aug. 15, 19, 1872; W.W. Belknap to JAL, Aug. 15, 27, 1872, Logan mss, LC; Mary Logan, *Reminiscences*, pp. 232–33.

36. ML to JAL, Sept. 11, 14, 1872; JAL to ML, Sept. 5, 6, 7, 15, 1872; Edward S. McCook to ML, Sept. 20, 1872, Logan mss, LC; *The Diary of James A. Garfield*, ed. Harry J. Brown and Frederick D. Williams, 2:92.

37. JAL to Dollie Logan, Sept. 17, 1872, Logan mss, LC; Rutherford B. Hayes to Lucy Hayes, Sept. 22, 1872, Hayes mss, Hayes Library; John Sherman to William T. Sherman, Sept. 29, 1872, William T. Sherman mss, LC. John Sherman said of Grant: "He has weakened us in so many ways, not in matters of principle, but in innumerable small things."

38. JAL to ML, Oct. 4, 1872; W.E. Chandler to ML, Oct. 7, 1872, Logan mss, LC; ML to W.E. Chandler, Oct. 13, 1872, W.E. Chandler mss, New Hampshire Historical Society; Scrapbook, 1867–1891, container 87, Logan mss, LC; *Illinois State Register*, Oct. 5, 8, 1872, called Logan's efforts "a failure" and reported that he paid people to attend his meetings; *Chicago Times*, Oct. 15, 1872.

39. Hamilton Fish to Simon Cameron, Oct. 9, 1872, Cameron mss, LC; Church, *Republican Party*, p. 117; *Chicago Tribune*, Nov. 18, 1872; *Illinois Fact Book and Historical Almanac*, p. 90. Lyman Trumbull's prediction that Greeley would be a strong candidate in Illinois was a serious miscalculation. Matthew T. Downey, "Horace Greeley and the Politicians: The Liberal Republican Convention in 1872," *Journal of American History* 53(1967):727–30, 750.

40. *Cong. Globe*, 42d Cong., 3d sess., pt. 1:1, ix, 347, 427; *Inter-Ocean*, Jan. 16, 1873, supported Logan's stand against the sale of arms.

41. *Cong. Globe*, 42d Cong., 3d sess., pt. 2:1359; pt. 3:1759–71; David D. Porter to William T. Sherman, May 7, 1872, William T. Sherman mss, LC.

42. U.S., Congress, *Congressional Record*, 43d Cong., special session, pp. 1, 48. Be-

ginning with this session, the name of the official report of debates is changed from *Globe* to *Record*. William Windom to Schuyler Colfax, Mar. 18, 1873, Colfax mss, Hayes Library.

43. *San Francisco Elevator,* Mar. 29, 1873.

44. JAL to ML, Mar. 20, Apr. 25, June 19, 1873; ML to JAL, Mar. 11, 28, 1873, Logan mss, LC; Mary Logan, *Reminiscences,* p. 245.

45. JAL to ML, July 24, 28, Aug. 17, 1873, Logan mss, LC; JAL to W.E. Chandler, Aug. 22, 1873, W.E. Chandler mss, New Hampshire Historical Society. Mary Logan, *Reminiscences,* p. 245, gives the address as 2119 Calumet Avenue.

46. Handbill, Society of the Army of the Tennessee, Aug. 20, 1873, John M. Palmer mss, ISHL; *Chicago Tribune,* Oct. 15, 1873; *Chicago Times,* Oct. 17, 1873; JAL to ML, Sept. 5, Oct. 4, 1873, Logan mss, LC.

47. JAL to L.D. Marchant, Sept. 11, 16, 1873, Gratz Collection, Historical Society of Pennsylvania.

48. *Chicago Times,* Sept. 19, 1873; JAL to ML, Nov. 28, Dec. 2, 1873, Logan mss, LC.

Chapter 6. The Paper Money Trinity

1. *Cong. Record,* 43d Cong., 1st sess., pt. 1:361–62, 477–78; Richard S. West, Jr., *Lincoln's Scapegoat General: A Life of Benjamin F. Butler, 1818–1893,* p. 330. Allan Peskin, *Garfield,* pp. 363–68. Robert Wiebe in *The Search for Order* calls the "salary grab" "a reasonable, if mishandled effort to raise Congressmen's stipends" (p. 5).

2. George, *Zachariah Chandler,* p. 200; David M. Jordan, *Roscoe Conkling of New York: Voice in the Senate,* pp. 190–91.

3. William B. Parker, *The Life and Public Services of Justin Smith Morrill,* pp. 243–44; JAL to ML, Dec. 4, 7, 10, 1873, Logan mss, LC.

4. JAL to ML, Jan. 6, Feb. 12, 1874, Logan mss, LC; *Cong. Record,* 43d Cong., 1st sess., pt. 1:362. The *Illinois State Register,* Apr. 26, 1873. called Logan a "salary stealer," and the equally hostile *Chicago Times,* June 26, 1873, branded him one of the "unrepentant thieves."

5. Grayson Kirk, "The Crédit Mobilier Scandal," *American Mercury* 32(1934):352; Matthew Josephson, *The Politicos,* pp. 180–87.

6. U.S., Congress, House of Representatives, 42d Cong., 3d sess., *Reports of Committees of the House of Representatives,* Report No. 77, "Crédit Mobilier," p. 346; typescript of Logan's testimony on Crédit Mobilier, Logan mss, LC; JAL memorandum, Feb. 10, 1868, Logan mss, LC.

7. *New York Tribune,* Jan. 29, 1873; Fernando Jones to JAL, Feb. 8, 1873, Logan mss, LC; *Chicago Tribune,* Jan. 28, 29, 1873. Colfax, forced out of office by his role in the scandal, seemed resigned to retirement and wrote Mary: "All well and enjoying home life and freedom from all responsibility for public affairs hugely." Schuyler Colfax to ML, May 6, 1873, Logan mss, LC.

8. JAL to ML, Dec. 4, 7, 12, 1873, Logan mss, LC; James Tanner to JAL, n.d., 1873, D.D. Pratt mss, Indiana State Library.

9. JAL to ML, Dec. 4, 16, 1873, Logan mss, LC.

10. *Cong. Globe,* 40th Cong., 2d sess., pt. 1:70.

11. Ibid., 3d sess., pt. 3:1536; Irwin Unger, *The Greenback Era: A Social and Political History of American Finance, 1865–79,* p. 228.

12. *Cong. Globe,* 41st Cong., 2d sess., pt. 2:1460; Unger, *The Greenback Era,* says that for many midwestern politicians "it seemed expedient to ride the soft money current" (p. 234).

13. Unger, *Greenback Era,* pp. 213–15.

14. *Cong. Record,* 43d Cong., 1st sess., pt. 1:2; pt. 3:2680. The repeal was strongly backed by the *Inter-Ocean,* Dec. 3, 6, 1873.

15. Schuyler Colfax to H. Anthony, Apr. 4, 1874, Colfax mss, LC; William E. Chandler to ML, Apr. 17, 1874, Logan mss, LC.

16. *Cong. Record,* 43d Cong., 1st sess., pt. 1:187, 258, 304–5, 663.

17. JAL to ML, Jan. 9, 10, 13, 14, 17, 1874, Logan mss, LC; *Chicago Times,* Jan. 6, 1874; *Chicago Tribune,* Jan. 8, 11, 1874. The Illinois legislature also passed a resolution condemning the salary grab. Copies were sent to Logan. *Chicago Tribune,* Jan. 11, 1874.

18. John Sherman to Ulysses S. Grant, Feb. 11, 1873; Edwards Pierrepont to John Sherman, Jan. 18, 1874, John Sherman mss, LC; Pierrepont wrote: "The Republican Party depends upon its ability to wisely manage the finances of the country." *Cong. Record,* 43d Cong., 1st sess., pt. 1:752–60, 866.

19. JAL to ML, Jan. 21, 23, 28, 1874, Logan mss, LC.

20. *Illinois State Journal,* Jan. 21, 29, 31, 1874; *Inter-Ocean,* Jan. 21, 26, 1874; *Chicago Tribune,* Jan. 20, 26, Feb. 12, 1874; *Chicago Times,* Jan. 20, 1874; E. Bruce Thompson, *Matthew Hale Carpenter,* p. 210.

21. *Chicago Evening Journal,* Mar. 24, 1874; JAL to ML, Feb. 21, 1874, Logan mss, LC. While Logan and Morton stood together, eastern Republicans like Roscoe Conkling, usually allies of the Indiana and Illinois senators, furiously fought inflation. Jordan, *Conkling,* p. 207.

22. *Chicago Times,* Feb. 20, Mar. 4, 18, 20, 1874; JAL to ML, Feb. 21, 25, 28, 1874, Logan mss, LC.

23. Unger, *Greenback Era,* p. 235.

24. Carl Schurz to Manton Marble, Feb. 1, 1874, Marble mss, LC; *Cong. Record,* 43d Cong., 1st sess., pt. 3:2440, 2484; Walter T.K. Nugent, *Money and American Society, 1865–1880,* pp. 223–24.

25. *Cong. Record,* 43d Cong., 1st sess., pt. 3:2516. Unger in *The Greenback Era,* p. 219, writes of the eastern-western confrontation in Congress that easterners felt they must defend the "'national honor' against the ignorant country members."

26. William J. Kunhs to JAL, Mar. 27, 1874, Logan mss, LC; H.C. Woods to Carl Schurz, Mar. 3, 1874, Schurz mss, LC; *Inter-Ocean,* Mar. 6, 1874.

27. JAL to ML, Mar. 3, 7, 25, 1874, Logan mss, LC.

28. Ibid., Mar. 13, 1874.

29. ML to JAL, Feb. 15, Mar. 16, 26, 1874, Logan mss, LC.

30. Unger, *Greenback Era,* pp. 241–42; JAL to ML, Apr. 18, 1874, Logan mss, LC.

31. *Illinois State Journal,* Apr. 23, 1874; *Illinois State Register,* Apr. 23, 1874; JAL to ML, Apr. 27, 1874; ML to JAL, Apr. 22, 27, May 1, 1874, Logan mss, LC. The *Chicago Tribune,* Apr. 23, 1874, reported that when Grant's veto was read "Morton seemed stupified and Logan sat gnawing his black mustache with great nervousness." On the following day the *Tribune* told its readers "Logan has been foaming and fretting all day like a mad bull." Walter T.K. Nugent, *Money and Society,* p. 225, writes: "With a single veto message, the President smashed most of what was left of Sherman's patient effort since 1869 to create Republican harmony on the money question."

32. *Cong. Record,* 43d Cong., 1st sess., pt. 4:3426, 3433.

33. Ibid., p. 3436.

34. J.T. Deweese to JAL, Apr. 24, 1874; J. Gillespie to JAL, Apr. 24, 1874; Daniel Mark to JAL, Apr. 24, 1874; B. Arnold to JAL, Apr. 23, 1874, Logan mss, LC.

35. Erastus Collins to Joseph Hawley, Apr. 18, 1874; Charles D. Warner to Joseph Hawley, Apr. 26, 1874, Hawley mss, LC; William Grosvenor to Carl Schurz, Apr. 25, 1874, Schurz mss, LC.

36. JAL to ML, May 7, 17, 24, 1874, Logan mss, LC.

37. William E. Chandler to ML, Apr. 17, May 11, 1874, Logan mss, LC; ML to William E. Chandler, May 4, 1874, W.E. Chandler mss, New Hampshire Historical Society.

38. E.O.C. Ord to William T. Sherman, May 4, 1874, William T. Sherman mss, LC; W.W. Belknap to Simon Cameron, Mar. 3, 1874, Cameron mss, LC; William T. Sherman to Stephen Hurlbut, May 26, 1874; William T. Sherman to JAL, June 2, 1874, Logan mss, LC; *Cong. Record,* 43d Cong., 1st sess., pt. 3:2307, 2312–13.

39. *Cong. Record,* 43d Cong., 1st sess., pt. 4:3839–40; ML to Dollie Logan, May 27, 1874, Logan mss, LC.

40. Koerner, *Memoirs,* 2:583; Gustave P. Koerner to Carl Schurz, June 1, 1874, Schurz mss, LC; JAL to ML, May 17, 24, 1874; ML to JAL, May 7, 1874, Logan mss, LC; *Nation,* June 25, 1874, predicted that Republican division between hard money advocates and Logan's forces would throw the Prairie State to the Democrats (p. 404).

41. JAL to ML, May 24, 1874, Logan mss, LC; *Illinois State Journal,* June 18, 1874; *Inter-Ocean,* June 19, 1874; Unger, *Greenback Era,* p. 285.

42. *Inter-Ocean,* July 6, 1874.

43. ML to JAL, July 28, Aug. 11, 16, 1874; JAL to ML, July 23, 25, Aug. 11, 13, Sept. 23, 1874; Scrapbook, 1877, pp. 50–51, container 89, Logan mss, LC; Mary Logan, *Reminiscences,* p. 248.

44. Dawson, *Logan,* p. 208.

45. Horace White to James G. Blaine, Nov. 17, 1874, Blaine mss, LC.

46. William T. Sherman to John Sherman, Aug. 28, Oct. 23, 1874, William T. Sherman mss, LC.

47. JAL to Richard Oglesby, Nov. 13, 1874, Oglesby mss, ISHL; Burton J. Williams, *Senator John James Ingalls: Kansas' Iridescent Republican,* p. 85; *Cong. Record,* 43d Cong., 2d sess., pt. 1:v, 2. At last the *Record* listed Logan's residence as Chicago.

48. Unger, *Greenback Era,* pp. 252–53; Allen Weinstein, *Prelude to Populism: Origins of the Silver Issue, 1867–1878,* p. 42.

49. Unger, *Greenback Era,* pp. 252–53; *Nation,* Dec. 31, 1874, pp. 427, 432.

50. *Cong. Record,* 43d Cong., 2d sess., pt. 1:208; *Chicago Tribune,* Dec. 23, 1874; George, *Zach Chandler,* p. 209; Jordan, *Conkling,* pp. 218–19. See also Nugent, *Money and American Society,* pp. 226–28.

51. Weinstein, *Prelude to Populism,* pp. 42–44.

52. *Cong. Record,* 43d Cong., 2d sess., pt. 1:242–43, 422–30, 449–55.

53. H.W. Blodgett to JAL, Jan. 18, 1875, Logan mss, LC; John M. Palmer to Carl Schurz, Jan. 16, 1875; Gustave P. Koerner to Carl Schurz, Jan. 28, 1875, Schurz mss, LC; *Inter-Ocean,* Jan. 15, 1875; *Chicago Tribune,* Jan. 14, 1875; *Illinois State Register,* Jan. 20, 1875. See also Don C. Barrett, *The Greenbacks and Resumption of Specie Payments, 1862–1879,* pp. 182–87.

54. W.P. Kellogg to Oliver P. Morton, Jan. 17, 1874, Morton mss, Indiana State Library; *Cong. Record,* 44th Cong., 1st sess., pt. 1:21–22.

55. Gene Smith, *High Crimes and Misdemeanors: The Impeachment and Trial of Andrew Johnson*, p. 301.

56. JAL to ML, Mar. 31, Apr. 11, 14, 22, 1875, Logan mss, LC.

57. JAL to ML, Apr. 20, 24, 28, 30, May 3, 6, 7, 1875, Logan mss, LC.

58. JAL to Richard Oglesby, May 13, 1875, Oglesby mss, ISHL; JAL to ML, Apr. 28, 1875, Logan mss, LC.

59. JAL to ML, May 21, 28, 31, June 1, 8, 23, July 3, 6, 1875, Logan mss, LC; Dawson, *Logan*, p. 217.

60. JAL to ML, July 15, 26, 31, Aug. 11, 1875, Logan mss, LC.

61. JAL to ML, Aug. 7, 1875, Logan mss, LC.

62. ML to Dollie Logan, Nov. 4, 1875, Logan mss, LC; JAL to ML, Sept. 8, 13, 1875, Logan mss, LC; J.M. Dalzell to Rutherford B. Hayes, Aug. 6, 1875, Hayes mss, Hayes Library.

63. William T. Sherman to John Sherman, May 25, 1875, William T. Sherman mss, LC.

64. William T. Sherman, *Memoirs of General William T. Sherman*, 2:85–86, 145.

65. John Sherman to William T. Sherman, May 23, Dec. 10, 1875, William T. Sherman mss, LC.

66. Ulysses S. Grant to William T. Sherman, Jan. 29, 1876; Grenville M. Dodge to William T. Sherman, July 25, 1875, William T. Sherman mss, LC. For a discussion of the Sherman-Logan clash at Atlanta see Jones, "Battle of Atlanta," pp. 393–405.

67. William T. Sherman to Roscoe Conkling, Nov. 1, 1875, Conkling mss, LC.

68. ML to Dollie Logan, Dec. 4, 1875; S.D. Phelps to ML, Nov. 30, 1875; Thomas Ferry to ML, Dec. 1, 1875, Logan mss, LC; ML to Richard Oglesby, Dec. 13, 1875, Oglesby mss, ISHL; *Inter-Ocean*, Dec. 1, 4, 6, 13, 1875.

Chapter 7. The Organization Is Defeated

1. Hesseltine, *Grant*, p. 380; *Illinois State Register*, Nov. 15, 1875; *Inter-Ocean*, Dec. 2, 13, 1875.

2. Bluford Wilson to William K. Rodgers, May 29, 1877, Hayes mss, Hayes Library; Scrapbook, 1876, container 89, Logan mss, LC; *Chicago Tribune*, Dec. 14, 15, 16, 1875.

3. *Chicago Evening Journal*, Aug. 11, 1875; JAL to ML, Aug. 7, 1876; Shelby Cullom to JAL, Apr. 19, 1876; C.H. Fowler to JAL, Apr. 19, 1876, Logan mss, LC; William C. Searles, "Governor Cullom and the Pekin Whisky Ring Scandal," *Journal of the Illinois State Historical Society* 51(1958):28–41. Cullom's biographer believes "there seemed to be some ground, however slight, for connecting Cullom with the Pekin whisky ring." James W. Neilson, *Shelby M. Cullom, Prairie State Republican*, p. 40. See also Ross Webb, *Benjamin Helm Bristow: Border State Politician*, pp. 208–10.

4. ML to Dollie Logan, Jan. 11, 1876, Logan mss, LC; *Cong. Record*, 44th Cong., 1st sess., pt. 1:187, 273.

5. *Cong. Record*, 44th Cong., 1st sess., pt. 1:992; pt. 2:1216, 1256, 1328, 1606.

6. Ibid., pt. 2:1283–86, 1341–42.

7. Ibid., pp. 1545–52; James Haskins, *Pinckney Benton Stewart Pinchback*, pp. 220–21.

8. William Windom to Schuyler Colfax, Apr. 15, 1876, Colfax mss, Hayes Library.

9. Charles A. Dana to John M. Palmer, Mar. 29, 1876, Palmer mss, ISHL.

10. Thomas C. Platt, *The Autobiography of Thomas Collier Platt*, p. 71; Shelby

Cullom to JAL, Apr. 19, 1876, Logan mss, LC; John Hay to James G. Blaine, Jan. 27, 1876, Blaine mss, LC; William Henry Smith to R.B. Hayes, Jan. 26, 1876, Hayes mss, Hayes Library.

11. *Cong. Record,* 44th Cong., 1st sess., appendix (Trial of William W. Belknap), pp. 345, 348, 350, 353, 356; *Chicago Tribune,* Jan. 3, Feb. 22, 1876; *Illinois State Journal,* May 26, 1876.

12. *Proceedings of the Republican National Convention, 1876,* pp. 7–10, 16–21; *Inter-Ocean,* June 15, 1876; *Chicago Tribune,* June 15, 1876.

13. *Chicago Tribune,* June 6, 12, 1876; *Inter-Ocean,* June 13, 1876; Jordan, *Conkling,* p. 238; Webb, *Bristow,* p. 249.

14. *Appleton's Cyclopedia, 1876,* p. 392; John Hay to James G. Blaine, May 26, 1876, Blaine mss, LC; William Henry Smith to R.B. Hayes, May 27, 1876, Hayes mss, Hayes Library; Chauncey I. Filley to Oliver P. Morton, May 21, 1876, Morton mss, Indiana State Library.

15. James M. Comly to R.B. Hayes, June 15, 1876, Hayes mss, Hayes Library.

16. *Proceedings of the Republican National Convention,* 1876, pp. 84, 100–6, 108–9.

17. JAL to ML, June 19, 1876, Logan mss, LC. Logan's biographer Byron Andrews wrote that Logan might have been nominated when a deadlock occurred at Cincinnati. But Logan refused since "he had not entered the lists before the convention and the Illinois delegation had been instructed for Blaine" (*Logan,* p. 608). There is no indication of this. Andrews was writing in 1884 in an attempt to create more cordial relations between Blaine and Logan. The Illinois delegation cast 38 of its 42 votes for Blaine on the first ballot and stuck to him throughout. *Proceedings of the Republican National Convention,* 1876, pp. 84, 87, 108–9. Bristow's biographer believes the "decisive factor" in the Kentuckian's defeat was his alienation of Conkling, Cameron, Logan, and Morton, who thought Hayes gave them a better chance of continuing Grantism. Webb, *Bristow,* pp. 209–10, 249.

18. *Cong. Record,* 44th Cong., 1st sess., pt. 4:3906–11, 3922, 3951.

19. Ibid., pp. 4057, 4324; Ulysses S. Grant to R.B. Hayes, July 4, 1876, Grant mss, Hayes Library.

20. *Cong. Record,* 44th Cong., 1st sess., pt. 4:4139, 4144, 4909; pt. 5:5012–14, 5138, 5566, 5657.

21. Ibid., pt. 4:4208; pt. 5:5096; Weinstein, *Prelude to Populism,* pp. 100–1, 107–8. Senator Logan had earlier attended the opening of the exposition. Mary Logan, *Reminiscences,* p. 268.

22. *Cong. Record,* 44th Cong., 1st sess., pt. 5:5254–57; JAL to ML, Aug. 2, 1876, Logan mss, LC.

23. Charles Nordhoff to R.B. Hayes, July 10, 1876, Hayes mss, Hayes Library; JAL to Dollie Logan, Sept. 11, 23, 1876, Logan mss, LC; Logan's many Illinois orations were hailed by Republican newspapers as "vigorous" and attacked by the opposition as "foul mouthed and abusive." *Chicago Tribune,* Sept. 11, Oct. 24, 31, 1876; *Illinois State Journal,* Oct. 2, 12, 1876; *Illinois State Register,* Sept. 19, 27, Oct. 1, 1876. Logan also served on the executive committee of the Republican National Congressional Committee. *Proceedings of the Republican National Convention,* 1876, p. 57.

24. Zachariah Chandler to R.B. Hayes, Sept. 12, 1876; Marshall Jewell to Zachariah Chandler, Sept. 17, 1876; William E. Chandler to Zachariah Chandler, Oct. 4, 1876, Zachariah Chandler mss, LC.

25. Shelby Cullom to JAL, Nov. 1, 1876; ML to JAL, Sept. 25, 1876; Hermann Raster to JAL, Sept. 12, 1876, Logan mss, LC; William H. Green to John M. Palmer, Sept. 8, 1876, Palmer mss, ISHL. Cullom had been linked to the Whisky Ring and though he denied any connection, the Democrats used the issue. Republican division over currency also weakened the party in the Prairie State. Polakoff, *The Politics of Inertia*, p. 177.

26. *The Great Campaign* (Chicago), July 18, 25, 1876.

27. Ibid., Aug. 1, 8, 15, 1876. Editor of *The Great Campaign* was a maverick named Mark "Brick" Pomeroy. See Richard M. Doolen, "'Brick' Pomeroy and the Greenback Clubs," *Journal of the Illinois State Historical Society* 65(1972):434–50.

28. JAL to Zachariah Chandler, Oct. 19, 1876, Zachariah Chandler mss, LC.

29. William Henry Smith to R.B. Hayes, Oct. 5, 30, Nov. 4, 1876, Hayes mss, Hayes Library; Rutherford B. Hayes, *The Diary and Letters of Rutherford B. Hayes, Nineteenth President of the United States,* ed. Charles R. Williams, 3:365; Polakoff, *The Politics of Inertia*, p. 176.

30. *Appleton's Cyclopedia, 1876,* p. 392; *Illinois State Register,* Dec. 30, 1876; *Chicago Tribune,* Dec. 28, 1876; *Illinois Fact Book and Historical Almanac,* p. 90.

31. Ulysses S. Grant to JAL, Nov. 10, 1876; Zachariah Chandler to JAL, Nov. 10, 1876; J.M. Edmunds to JAL, Nov. 11, 1876; D.H. Chamberlain to JAL, Nov. 12, 1876; P.B.S. Pinchback to JAL, Nov. 12, 1876, Logan mss, LC; William Henry Smith to R.B. Hayes, Nov. 10, 1876, Hayes mss, Hayes Library.

32. JAL to ML, Nov. 10, 1876, Logan mss, LC; Theodore C. Smith, *The Life and Letters of James A. Garfield* 1:616–19; *Chicago Tribune,* Nov. 12, 1876, says Logan and Edmunds declined while Evarts, John Sherman, Garfield, and Benjamin Harrison were to go.

33. *Cong. Record,* 44th Cong., 2d sess., pt. 1:338, 343,; JAL to ML, Dec. 6, 7, 1876, Logan mss, LC; William Henry Smith to R.B. Hayes, Dec. 30, 1876, Hayes mss, Hayes Library; Donald B. Chidsey, *The Gentleman from New York: A Life of Roscoe Conkling,* p. 225.

34. JAL to J.H. Oakwood, Nov. 20, 1876, David Davis mss, ISHL; *Chicago Tribune,* Dec. 15, 1876; *Illinois State Register,* Dec. 30, 1876.

35. JAL to ML, Dec. 6, 7, 12, 14, 15, 1876; Hermann Raster to JAL, Dec. 12, 1876; Ulysses S. Grant to JAL, Dec. 17, 1876, Logan mss, LC; *Inter-Ocean,* Dec. 21, 1876; *Illinois State Journal,* Dec. 21, 1876.

36. Scrapbook, 1877, container 89, Logan mss, LC. The always hostile *Illinois State Register,* Jan. 2, 1877, maintained that Logan had "pitched his camp" at the Leland Hotel ready to buy the election with ample funds supplied by the Republican National Committee. The newspaper lashed out at him daily, continuing to accuse him of complicity in both the Whisky Ring and the Crédit Mobilier.

37. *Chicago Tribune,* Jan. 1, 2, 3, 1877.

38. Ibid., Jan 4, 5, 8, 1877.

39. Ibid., Jan 9, 11, 12, 1877; *Inter-Ocean,* Jan. 4, 5, 6, 15, 1877; *Illinois State Journal,* Jan. 2, 10, 1877. Greenbackers recruited more voters from the Democrats than from the Republicans. In statewide popular vote races this situation aided Republican candidates, but in the legislature Greenbackers were far more likely to rally with the Democrats than with the Republicans. Paul Kleppner, *The Cross of Culture: A Social Analysis of Midwestern Politics, 1850–1900,* p. 15.

40. W.C. Goudy to David Davis, Jan. 10, 12, 1877, Davis mss, ISHL.

41. Willard L. King, *Lincoln's Manager, David Davis,* p. 292; David Davis to William

H. Hidell, Apr. n.d., 1884, Davis mss, ISHL; Polakoff, *The Politics of Inertia*, p. 280.
   42. *Illinois State Register*, Jan. 16, 1877; *Chicago Tribune*, Jan. 17, 1877.
   43. J.P. Dugan to John M. Palmer, Jan. 17, 1877, Palmer mss, ISHL; Orville H. Browning, *The Diary of Orville H. Browning*, ed. James G. Randall, 2:471.
   44. *Chicago Tribune*, Jan. 18–20, 1877; *Inter-Ocean*, Jan. 24, 1877.
   45. Oliver P. Morton, Hannibal Hamlin, and John Sherman to JAL, Jan. 22, 1877; James G. Blaine to JAL, Jan. 22, 1877; Green B. Raum to JAL, Jan. 22, 1877, Logan mss, LC.
   46. *Chicago Tribune*, Jan. 23–25, 1877.
   47. Ibid., Jan. 24–27, 1877; *Journal of the House of Representatives of the 30th General Assembly of the State of Illinois*, pp. 149–50. In her *Reminiscences*, Mary Logan accuses Logan's opponents of bribing legislators (see pp. 276–77). There is no evidence supporting her charges.
   48. *Chicago Times*, Jan. 11, 25, 1877; Polakoff, *The Politics of Inertia*, pp. 280–83.
   49. Edwin M. Clarke to Oliver P. Morton, Jan. 30, 1877, Morton mss, Indiana State Library; George W. Julian to Laura Julian, Feb. 23, 1877, Julian mss, Indiana State Library; Walter Q. Gresham to Thomas E. Slaughter, Feb. 1, 1877, Gresham mss, LC; H. Chrisman to John C. Bagby, Jan. 27, 1877, Bagby mss, ISHL.
   50. William Henry Smith to R.B. Hayes, Jan. 29, 1877, Hayes mss, Hayes Library; *Illinois State Register*, Jan. 24, 1877.
   51. JAL to ML, Jan. 31, 1877, Logan mss, LC; JAL to J.H. Oakwood, Jan. 27, 1877, David Davis mss, ISHL.
   52. *Cong. Record*, 44th Cong., 2d sess., pt. 2:1623–25, 2205, 2157–58; Weinstein, *Prelude to Populism*, pp. 195–96.

Chapter 8. "The Fiery Furnace"

   1. ML to JAL, Feb. 4, 1877; JAL to ML, Feb. 1, 1877, Logan mss, LC; JAL to J.P. Newman, Feb. 19, 1877, Logan miscellaneous mss, Hayes Library.
   2. Jerome B. Chaffee to R.B. Hayes, Feb 16, 1877; John Beveridge to R.B. Hayes, Feb. 19, 1877; Richard Oglesby, et al., to R.B. Hayes, Feb. 26, 1877; Twenty-four Republican Members of the House to R.B. Hayes, n.d., 1877; Shelby Cullom to R.B. Hayes, Feb. n.d., 1877, Hayes mss, Hayes Library; *Illinois State Register*, Feb. 21, Mar. 1, 1877.
   3. William Henry Smith to Richard Smith, Feb. 19, 1877; Joseph Medill to Richard Smith, Feb. 17, 1877; William M. Dickson to R.B. Hayes, Feb. 19, 1877; Carl Schurz to R.B. Hayes, Jan. 30, 1877; John Sherman to R.B. Hayes, Feb. 18, 1877, Hayes mss, Hayes Library. Also see John G. Sproat, *The Best Men: Liberal Reformers in the Gilded Age*. The *Chicago Tribune*, Mar. 5, 1877, condemned the pro-Logan effort as "bulldozing" and felt that Logan, an enemy of civil service reform, should not be named to the cabinet.
   4. Hayes, *Diary*, Feb. 19, 1877; Kenneth E. Davison, *The Presidency of Rutherford B. Hayes*, p. 94.
   5. Richard Oglesby, et al., to R.B. Hayes, Mar. 2, 1877; F.W. Palmer to R.B. Hayes, Mar. 4, 1877, Hayes mss, Hayes Library; *Diary of James A. Garfield*, ed. Brown and Williams, 3:448, 453; J.M. Beardsley to JAL, Mar. 3, 1877; ML to JAL, Mar. 4, 1877, Logan mss, LC. Hayes, interested in naming a southerner to his cabinet, considered Confederate General Joseph E. Johnston for secretary of war; General Sherman supported the idea. But with the refusal to send Logan to the War Department, Hayes decided that nam-

ing a leading Confederate would create a loud and hostile reaction. Thomas Donaldson, "Memoirs," pp. 191, 193, Donaldson mss, Hayes Library. McCrary's appointment was partly engineered by Senator William B. Allison, Iowa Republican boss, who wanted to remove the popular McCrary from Iowa politics. Davison, *The Presidency of Rutherford B. Hayes,* p. 102. Perhaps one reason Hayes was reluctant to name Logan to the War Department was that the new secretary would have to reassign the last troops in the Reconstruction South. Logan, a Radical opposed to the end of Reconstruction, might not have carried out the presidential orders.

6. ML to JAL, Mar. 4, 1877; JAL to ML, Mar. 8, 11, 1877, Logan mss, LC; Mary Logan, *Reminiscences,* p. 277.

7. JAL to R.B. Hayes, Mar. 12, 1877, Ward Lamon mss, Huntington Library.

8. Joseph J. Kelly to JAL, Mar. 13, 1877; J.M. Beardsley to JAL, Mar. 14, 1877, Logan mss, LC; O.H. Browning to William Evarts, Mar. 10, 1877, Evarts mss, LC; Jordan, *Conkling,* p. 266. Hayes's appointment of old foes such as Evarts and Schurz to the cabinet antagonized Logan, Conkling, and Cameron. See Stanley P. Hirshson, *Farewell to the Bloody Shirt,* p. 27.

9. JAL to ML, Apr. 6, 24, 1877, Logan mss, LC; *New York Tribune,* Apr. 6, 1877.

10. ML to R.B. Hayes, May 11, 1877; William Henry Smith to R.B. Hayes, May 9, 1877; R.B. Hayes to William Henry Smith, May 13, 1877, Hayes mss, Hayes Library. In her *Reminiscences,* Mary Logan conveniently forgot her 1877 supplications and told her readers, "We were both too proud to make any sign," to Hayes (p. 278).

11. R.B. Hayes to JAL, May 18, 1877; JAL to R.B. Hayes, May 26, 1877, Logan mss, LC.

12. JAL to Edward McPherson, May 5, 1877, McPherson mss, LC.

13. Green B. Raum to JAL, May 2, 1877, Logan mss, LC; J.S. Reynolds to E.F. Noyes, May 10, 1877, Hayes mss, Hayes Library; John H. Wickizer to David Davis, June 3, 1877, Davis mss, ISHL.

14. G.W. McMullen and O.F. Willard to R.B. Hayes, May 23, 1877; William Henry Smith to R.B. Hayes, May 28, 1877; Bluford Wilson to William K. Rodgers, May 29, 1877, Hayes mss, Hayes Library.

15. JAL to R.B. Hayes, May 27, 1877; William Henry Smith to R.B. Hayes, May 28, 1877; Richard Oglesby to John Sherman, Apr. 27, 1877, Hayes mss, Hayes Library.

16. JAL to Richard W. Thompson, May 28, 1877, Thompson mss, Indiana State Library.

17. ML to JAL, June 28, July 7, 1877; JAL to ML, July 1, 24, 25, 27, 1877, Logan mss, LC.

18. JAL to ML, July 24, 25, 1877, Logan mss, LC.

19. JAL to ML, Aug. 1, 8, 15, 20, 1877; ML to JAL, Aug. 19, 31, 1877, Logan mss, LC.

20. JAL to ML, Aug. 21, 28, Sept. 14, 1877, Logan mss, LC.

21. R.B. Hayes to William Henry Smith, Sept. 4, 1877, Hayes mss, Hayes Library; JAL to ML, Oct. 18, 20, 23, 1877, Logan mss, LC.

22. Green B. Raum to ML, Oct. 31, Nov. 2, 1877; JAL to ML, Oct. 23, 27, 1877, Logan mss, LC.

23. JAL to ML, Oct. 31, Nov. 2, 1877; Dollie Logan to JAL and ML, Dec. 15, 29, 1877, Logan mss, LC; Mary Logan, *Reminiscences,* p. 364; *Chicago Tribune,* Nov. 25, 28, 1877.

24. R.B. Hayes to William Henry Smith, Nov. 10, 1877, Hayes mss, Hayes Library;

Jeremiah Evarts to William Evarts, Nov. 21, 1877, Evarts mss, LC; JAL to Richard Oglesby, Nov. 24, 1877, Oglesby mss, ISHL; Shelby Cullom to JAL, Nov. 21, 1877, Logan mss, LC.

25. William Henry Smith to John Sherman, n.d., 1877, John Sherman mss, Ohio Historical Society, Ohio State Museum, Columbus.

26. Shelby Cullom to JAL, Feb. 20, 1878; ML to Dollie Logan, Jan. 2, 7, 9, Feb. 4, Mar. 3, 1878; JAL to Will Tucker, Feb. 1, 1878, Logan mss, LC. Once again Mary Logan's *Reminiscences* paint a very different picture. Logan, she claimed, was shortly making more money than he had as a senator and the two years out of office "were by no means the most unhappy years of our lives" (pp. 363, 364, 370). Mrs. Logan's rose-colored nostalgia had forgotten the "fiery furnace."

27. JAL to ML, Apr. 8, 13, 19, 1878; JAL to Will Tucker, May 11, 1878, Logan mss, LC; John A. Logan and W.W. Wilshire, *A Claim of the State of Illinois With Other Western and Southern States Based Upon the 5% Clause of the Act of Admission Into the Union.* Washington, 1878.

28. JAL to ML, May 23, 1878, Logan mss, LC; Mary Logan, *Reminiscences,* pp. 363–64.

29. JAL to ML, Apr. 19, May 20, 1878, Logan mss, LC; JAL to J.H. Oakwood, Mar. 26, 1878, Logan personal miscellaneous mss, Indiana State Library; Cullom, *Fifty Years,* pp. 199–200.

30. JAL to ML, June 16, July 5, 1878; ML to JAL, June 17, 1878, Logan mss, LC.

31. M.H. Chamberlain to Richard Oglesby, July 31, 1878, Oglesby mss, ISHL; Isaac R. Hitt to R.B. Hayes, July 26, 1878, Hayes mss, Hayes Library.

32. JAL to ML, Sept. 27, Oct. 21, Nov. 13, 1878, Logan mss, LC; William Henry Smith to R.B. Hayes, Oct. 30, Nov. 12, 1878, Hayes mss, Hayes Library; *Inter-Ocean,* Oct. 1, 11, 15, Nov. 2, 1878; *Illinois State Journal,* Oct. 8, 10, 1878.

33. J.B. McCullough to JAL, Dec. 9, 1878; Richard Butler to JAL, Dec. 23, 1878; Clark E. Carr to JAL, Nov. 17, 1878, Logan mss, LC; New Orleans *Weekly Louisianan,* Dec. 21, 1878.

34. C.M. Lyon to Richard Oglesby, Nov. 25, 1878; Richard Oglesby to W.H. Robinson, Dec. 10, 1878; Richard Oglesby to Joseph Medill, Dec. 14, 1878, Oglesby mss, ISHL; *Chicago Tribune,* Dec. 10, 21, 26, 1878.

35. Church, *Republican Party,* p. 133.

36. Scrapbook, 1878, container 90, Logan mss, LC; *Illinois State Register,* Dec. 11, 18, 1878, Jan. 18, 1879.

37. John Budlory to JAL, Jan. 10, 1879; James A. Gregory to JAL, Jan. 7, 1879; W. Beckwith to JAL, Jan. 10, 1879, Logan mss, LC.

38. Green B. Raum to JAL, Jan. 7, 1879, Logan mss, LC; William Henry Smith to R.B. Hayes, Jan. 11, 16, 1879, Hayes mss, Hayes Library; *Chicago Tribune,* Jan. 3–18, 1879.

39. *Illinois State Register,* Jan. 18, 22, 1879; *Illinois State Journal,* Jan. 18, 1879; *Inter-Ocean,* Jan. 18, 22, 1879; Lusk, *Politics and Politicians,* p. 273. In frustration and anger, the *Chicago Tribune,* Jan. 18, 1879, protested the outcome "in behalf of intelligence, principle, and public interest."

40. Stephen Hurlbut to JAL, Jan. 18, 1879; John P. St. John to JAL, Jan. 21, 1879; Green B. Raum to JAL, Jan. 28,1879; F.V. Hayden to JAL, Jan. 23, 1879; Matthew H. Carpenter to JAL, Jan. 18, 1879; Potter Palmer to JAL, Jan. 18, 1879; Godlove Orth to

JAL, Jan. 23, 1879; Schuyler Colfax to ML, Jan. 28, 1879, Logan mss, ISHL; JAL to Orville Babcock, Feb. 14, 1879, Babcock mss, Newberry Library, Chicago; JAL to Frederic E. Lockley, Feb. 16, 1879, Lockley mss, Huntington Library.

41. George H. Ward to Richard Oglesby, Jan. 18, 1879; J.M. Kelly to Richard Oglesby, Jan. 21, 1879, Oglesby mss, ISHL.

42. William Henry Smith to R.B. Hayes, Jan. 22, 1879, Hayes mss, Hayes Library. In partial confirmation of the *Inter-Ocean* story Logan was contacted by the newspaper's owner in May, 1878, and offered stock. There is no record in the Logan mss of any $40,000 investment. After Black Jack was elected to the Senate Nixon wired congratulations and added: "Hope you are satisfied with the part the *Inter-Ocean* has taken in the fight." JAL to ML, May 22, 1878; William Penn Nixon to JAL, Jan. 18, 1879, Logan mss, LC.

43. Mary Logan, *Reminiscences*, p. 372.

44. Writing of popular identification with party and faction in late nineteenth-century America, Robert Wiebe says: "Factional names like Stalwart, Half Breed, and Mugwump carried the kind of emotion that determined who could and who could not become a man's intimates" (*The Search for Order*, p. 27).

Chapter 9. Return of the Stalwart

1. JAL to ML, Feb. 23, 1879, Logan mss, LC; Mary Logan, *Reminiscences*, p. 375; Dawson, *Logan*, p. 238.

2. ML to JAL, Feb. 9, 1879; JAL to ML, Feb. 10, 1879; Green B. Raum to JAL, Feb. 8, 1879, Logan mss, LC.

3. M.L. Joslyn to JAL, Feb. 22, 1879; E.H. Hodges to JAL, Feb. 5, 1879; JAL to ML, Feb. 23, 25, 27, 1879, Logan mss, LC.

4. JAL to Dollie Logan, Mar. 29, 1879, Logan mss, LC.

5. *Cong. Record,* 46th Cong., 1st sess., pt. 1:1, 15, 32–33.

6. Ibid., pp. 381–84.

7. Ibid., pp.435–42.

8. Ibid., pp. 907–13.

9. Shelby Cullom to R.B. Hayes, May 5, 1879, Hayes mss, Hayes Library; Richardson Vasey to David Davis, May 1, 1879, Davis mss, ISHL; *Inter-Ocean,* Apr. 16, 1879; *Illinois State Register,* Apr. 16, 1879.

10. J.C. Brown to JAL, Apr. 29, 1879; Augustus Chetlain to JAL, Apr. 16, 28, 1879; S.M. Bowman to JAL, Apr. 28, 1879, Logan mss, ISHL; John Logan to JAL, Apr. 16, 1879; R.P. Baker to JAL, Apr 23, 1879; ML to Dollie and Will Tucker, May 6, 1879, Logan mss, LC; Andrews, *Logan*, pp. 628, 639; *New Orleans Weekly Louisianan,* May 10, 1879; *Illinois State Journal,* Apr. 30, 1879; *Inter-Ocean,* Apr. 26, 28, 1879; the *Chicago Tribune,* so recently a Logan foe, praised his "good sense" in handling Lowe. In its April 27 issue it stated that the Illinois senator "curtly replied that if Lowe were a sufficiently blooming idiot to march out to the field of honor at an hour in the morning when sensible people prefer to snooze, he was not going to make an ass of himself by doing so."

11. *Cong. Record,* 46th Cong., 1st sess., pt. 1:1114–17; pt. 2:1460.

12. Ibid., pt. 2:2212, 2346–47.

13. JAL to A.K. McClure, Apr. 17, 1879, Gratz mss, Historical Society of Pennsylvania; ML to Dollie Tucker, May 13, June 2, 1879, Logan mss, LC.

14. ML to Dollie Tucker, June 8, 1879, Logan mss, LC; Shelby Cullom to R.B.

Hayes, June 9, 1879; William Henry Smith to R.B. Hayes, Apr. 5, 21, 1879, Hayes mss, Hayes Library. The political alliance between Logan and Cullom was tightened in 1879 and 1880. The senator endorsed Cullom's bid for the governor's mansion while Cullom worked for the Grant nomination. A Logan-Cullom force was being opposed by such Illinois G.O.P. leaders as Oglesby, Farwell, and perhaps Elihu Washburne. See Cullom to JAL, Jan. 19, 1880, Logan mss, LC.

15. Personal memoranda of William Henry Smith, May 26, 1879; William Henry Smith to R.B. Hayes, Apr. 21, 1879, Hayes mss, Hayes Library; JAL to William Henry Smith, July 12, 1879, William Henry Smith mss, Ohio Historical Society.

16. John Sherman to William Henry Smith, May 10, 1879, Smith mss, William Henry Smith Library, Indianapolis.

17. William Henry Smith to R.B. Hayes, Apr. 21, 1879; personal memoranda of William Henry Smith, May 26, 1879, Hayes mss, Hayes Library; John Sherman to William Henry Smith, May 10, 1879, Smith mss, Smith Library.

18. H.E. Griswold to R.B. Hayes, July 1, 1879, Hayes mss, Hayes Library; JAL to ML, July 31, Sept. 15, 23, 1879, Logan mss, LC.

19. John Sherman to William Henry Smith, Sept. 2, Nov. 13, 1879, Smith mss, Smith Library; Bluford Wilson to Richard Oglesby, Aug. 19, 1879, Oglesby mss, ISHL.

20. William Henry Smith to R.B. Hayes, Oct. 20, 1879, Smith mss, Smith Library; William Henry Smith to R.B. Hayes, Nov. 1, 1879, Hayes mss, Hayes Library; W.J. Gilbert to Elihu B. Washburne, Nov. 24, 1879; John McNulta to Elihu B. Washburne, Nov. 17, Dec. 8, 1879; Casper Bretz to Elihu B. Washburne, Dec. 24, 1879, Washburne mss, LC. By the fall McNulta had shifted focus and was urging Washburne to announce for governor.

21. JAL to Elihu B. Washburne, Dec. 10, 1879, Washburne mss, LC; Elihu B. Washburne to JAL, Dec. 29, 1879, Logan mss, LC; William Henry Smith to R.B. Hayes, Nov. 1, 1879, Hayes mss, Hayes Library.

22. JAL to William Henry Smith, Dec. 13, 1879, Smith mss, Ohio Historical Society.

23. *Cong. Record*, 46th Cong., 2d sess., pt. 1:124, 337, 407, 1175, 1467, 1919; JAL to Frederic E. Lockley, Feb. 16, 1879, Lockley mss, Huntington Library.

24. *Cong. Record*, 46th Cong., 2d sess., pt. 1:565–66; *Chicago Tribune*, Nov. 1–3, 1879.

25. See Otto Eisenschiml, *The Celebrated Case of Fitz-John Porter*, for a defense of Porter. On the other hand, Kenneth P. Williams, *Lincoln Finds a General*, 2:785–89, presents evidence that Porter was guilty as charged.

26. Fitz-John Porter to J.C. Bullitt, Feb. 27, 1879; Theodore F. Randolph to Fitz-John Porter, Nov. 28, 1879; Fitz-John Porter to Theodore F. Randolph, Dec. 1, 30, 1879, Porter mss, LC; Fitz-John Porter to James G. Blaine, Nov. 24, 1879, Blaine mss, LC.

27. Fitz-John Porter to J.C. Bullitt, Dec. 15, 1879; Fitz-John Porter to Richard Oglesby, Jan. 7, 1880; Fitz-John Porter to Theodore F. Randolph, Jan. 6, 1880; Theodore F. Randolph to Fitz-John Porter, Jan 9, 16, 1880, Porter mss, LC.

28. *Cong. Record*, 46th Cong., 2d sess., pt. 1:536–37, 803; Fitz-John Porter to Theodore F. Randolph, Jan. 28, 1880, Porter mss, LC.

29. J.K. Herbert to JAL, Feb. 10, 1880, Logan mss, LC.

30. J.A. McMahon to J.C. Bullitt, Feb. 4, 1880; Theodore F. Randolph to Fitz-John Porter, Feb. 5, 1880; W.B. Franklin to Fitz-John Porter, Feb. 17, 1880, Porter mss, LC.

31. *Cong. Record*, 46th Cong., 2d sess., appendix, pp. 47–92; Mary Logan, *Reminiscences*, pp. 395–97.

32. John Pope to JAL, Mar. 8, 1880; Elihu B. Washburne to JAL, Apr. 5, 1880; Robert Todd Lincoln to JAL, Apr. 8, 1880; Manning Force to JAL, Mar. 29, 1880; Stephen Hurlbut to JAL, Mar. 8, 1880; Benjamin Prentiss to JAL, Mar. 19, 1880; Irvin McDowell to JAL, Mar. 26, 1880; Charles B. Campbell to JAL, Mar. 11, 1880; Spencer Donnegan to JAL, Mar. 23, 1880, Logan mss, LC.

33. Theodore F. Randolph to Fitz-John Porter, Mar. 7, 17, 1880; Theodore F. Randolph to J.C. Bullitt, Mar. 17, 1880, Porter mss, LC.

34. John Schofield to William T. Sherman, Mar. 13, 1880, William T. Sherman mss, LC.

35. *Illinois State Register*, Jan. 13, Mar. 4, 12, 1880; *Chicago Tribune*, Jan. 22, Mar. 4, 13, 1880; *Illinois State Journal*, Jan. 27, Feb. 2, 20, Mar. 5, 1880. *Harper's Weekly*, Mar. 27, 1880, ran an excellent Nast cartoon of Logan, Randolph, and Porter.

36. *Cong. Record*, 46th Cong., 2d sess., pt. 2:1228, 1360, 1371–74, 1377–79, 1429–31.

37. Theodore F. Randolph to Fitz-John Porter, Apr. 5, 12, 1880; Fitz-John Porter to Theodore F. Randolph, Apr. 3, 10, 1880; Junius Simons to W.A.D. Cochrane, Apr. 24, 1880, Porter mss, LC.

Chapter 10. The Immortal 306

1. Thomas B. Reed to Martin Townsend, May 21, 1878, Reed miscellaneous mss, Hayes Library.

2. *Chicago Tribune*, Nov. 6, 12, 14, 1879; *Inter-Ocean*, Nov. 12–15, 19, 1879; Mary Logan, *Reminiscences*, pp. 385–87. In spite of his presence at the Grant fetes, Cullom remained aloof from the Stalwart push for Grant. Neilson, *Cullom*, p. 55.

3. JAL to William Henry Smith, Dec. 13, 1879, Smith mss, Ohio State Historical Society; William E. Chandler to Mrs. James G. Blaine, Dec. 13, 1879, Jan. 17, 1880, Blaine mss, LC; *Chicago Tribune*, Dec. 24, 1879.

4. Elihu B. Washburne to JAL, Jan. 16, 17, 20, 25, 1880, Logan mss, LC; John Sherman to William Henry Smith, Jan. 26, 1880, Smith mss, Smith Library; Chetlain, *Recollections of Seventy Years*, p. 182.

5. M.L. Joslyn to JAL, Feb. 26, 1880; F.W. Palmer to JAL, Feb. 26, 1880, Logan mss, LC; *Inter-Ocean*, Jan. 27, 1880; *Chicago Tribune*, Feb. 10, 13, 20, 25, 26, 1880. The *Illinois State Register*, Jan. 29, 1880, greeted Logan's announcement of support as the death gasp of the third-term movement. Also see Robert G. Ingersoll, *The Works of Robert G. Ingersoll*, 8:28. Careful not to alienate any of the other contenders, Logan told a *Chicago Daily News* reporter: "No man has heard me say a cruel or unjustifiable word about Mr. Blaine, Mr. Sherman, or indeed any of the gentlemen whose names have been mentioned as candidates" (Dawson, *Logan*, p. 285).

6. Eilhu B. Washburne to JAL, Feb. 10, 20, 24, 1880, Logan mss, LC.

7. Thurlow Weed to Elihu B. Washburne, Feb. 27, 1880; John Coburn to Elihu B. Washburne, Feb. 17, 1880; T.C. Cronin to Elihu B. Washburne, Feb. 27, 1880; J. Milliken to Elihu B. Washburne, Feb. 4, 1880, Washburne mss, LC. Throughout the spring the *Chicago Tribune* urged Washburne to remain in the contest. Herbert J. Clancy, in *The Presidential Election of 1880*, writes: "If Grant had retired, it was felt by many that his strength would have gone to Washburne" (p. 43).

8. George A. Hook to William E. Chandler, Mar. 5, 1880; Jerome B. Chaffee to William E. Chandler, Mar. 7, 1880, W.E. Chandler mss, LC.

9. William Penn Nixon to JAL, Mar. 7, 1880; JAL to William Penn Nixon, Mar. 11, 1880, Logan mss, LC.

10. Jessie Spalding to JAL, Apr. 6, 1880; ML to Will Tucker, Apr. 7, 1880; Elihu B. Washburne to JAL, Apr. 10, 1880; Dollie Tucker to ML, Apr. 14, 17, 1880, Logan mss, LC; *Chicago Tribune*, Apr. 13, 16, 1880; Mary Logan, *Reminiscences*, p. 399; *New York Times*, Apr. 27, 1880.

11. Dollie Tucker to ML, Apr. 17, 1880; JAL to ML, Apr. 19, 1880; Dan Shepard to JAL, Apr. 26,1880; J.W. Nichols to JAL, Apr. 28, 1880; Elihu B. Washburne to JAL, Apr. 30, 1880, Logan mss, LC; *Illinois State Journal,* May 5. 1880.

12. JAL to H.W. Draper, Apr. 29, 1880, Logan mss, LC.

13. R.W. Townshend to Charles Lanphier, Apr. 1, 1880, Lanphier mss, ISHL; John Sherman to William Henry Smith, Apr. 19, 1880; A.C. Hawley to John Sherman, Apr. 24, 1880, Smith mss, Smith Library; James G. Blaine to Carl Schurz, Apr. 28, 1880, Hayes mss, Hayes Library; Thurlow Weed to Simon Cameron, Apr. 29, 1880, Cameron mss, LC; Thurlow Weed to Elihu B. Washburne, Apr. 30, 1880, Washburne mss, LC; *Illinois Staats-Zeitung* (Chicago), May 7, 1880.

14. *Chicago Tribune,* May 10, 1880; JAL to ML, May 4, 6, 8, 9, 10, 1880, Logan mss, LC; William Henry Smith to R.B. Hayes, May 5, 1880, Hayes mss, Hayes Library; *Illinois State Register,* May 18, 20, 1880.

15. JAL to ML, May 10, 11, 1880; JAL to Don Cameron, May 10, 11, 1880, Logan mss, LC. The Logan bolt was called a "grab-and-gouge game" in the *Chicago Tribune,* May 13, 1880.

16. *Chicago Tribune,* May 21, 1880; JAL to ML, May 16, 1880, Logan mss, LC; *Illinois State Journal,* May 19, 20, 1880.

17. *Chicago Tribune,* May 22, 23, 1880. The paper labeled third term tactics "usurpation" and a "high-handed outrage."

18. *Illinois State Register,* May 21–23, 1880; Church, *Republican Party,* pp. 136–37; *Chicago Tribune,* May 22, 23, 1880; *Nation,* May 27, 1880, ran a long editorial decrying presidential nominating by bosses. It concentrated on Logan and Illinois as the prime example.

19. JAL to ML, May 21, 1880; A.M. Jones to ML, May 21, 1880, Logan mss, LC.

20. William Henry Smith to R.B. Hayes, May 5, 15, 21, 1880, Hayes mss, Hayes Library. Both the *Chicago Tribune,* May 22, 23, 1880, and the *Illinois Staats-Zeitung* (Chicago), May 22, 1880, regarded the state party as wholly the captive of "Boss" Logan. The *Illinois State Journal,* May 29, 1880, countered by writing that if Illinois had to have a "boss" Logan was better than any other possibility.

21. John Sherman to William Henry Smith, May 15, 1880, Smith mss, Smith Library.

22. George Jones to Elihu B. Washburne, May 14, 1880; J.B. McCullagh to Elihu B. Washburne, May 18, 1880, Washburne mss, LC.

23. George Jones to Elihu B. Washburne, May 14, 1880; Emery A. Storrs to Elihu B. Washburne, Apr. 6, 1880, Washburne mss, LC; William Henry Smith to R.B. Hayes, Nov. 1, 1879, Hayes mss, Hayes Library; Adam Badeau, *Grant in Peace,* p. 322.

24. J.P. Emmet to C.B. Farwell, May 24, 1880; W.H. Mason to William E. Chandler, May 28, 1880, W.E. Chandler mss, LC.

25. Horace White to Murat Halstead, May 22, 1880, Halstead mss, Hayes Library.

26. Smith, *Garfield,* 2:960.

27. Clancy, *Election of 1880,* pp. 83–84; Thomas C. Reeves, *Gentleman Boss: The Life of Chester Alan Arthur,* p. 168.

28. Leon B. Richardson, *William E. Chandler, Republican*, pp. 251–52; *Proceedings of the Republican National Convention, 1880*, p. 160; *Chicago Tribune*, June 2, 3, 1880; *Harper's Weekly*, May 29, June 12, 1880.

29. *Inter-Ocean*, May 31, June 1, 1880; *Illinois State Journal*, June 1, 1880; *Chicago Tribune*, June 1, 1880.

30. *Proceedings of the Republican National Convention, 1880*, pp. 170, 198, 202–71, 294; *Chicago Tribune*, June 4–7, 9, 1880. During the week of balloting Grant dispatched a letter to the triumvirate authorizing the withdrawal of his name if they deemed it wise. Mrs. Grant intercepted the letter and told the general's managers "if General Grant were not nominated then let it be so, but he must not withdraw his name—no never." Julia Dent Grant, *The Personal Memoirs of Julia Dent Grant*, ed. John Y. Simon, p. 321.

31. *Proceedings of the Republican National Convention, 1880*, pp. 202–71, 296; *Chicago Tribune*, June 5, 1880. *Harper's Weekly*, June 19, 1880, scoffed at Logan's remarks after a convention he had attempted to control by "foul play."

32. Platt, *Autobiography*, pp. 120–23; James A. Beaver to ML, Apr. 21, 1893, Beaver mss, ISHL. In late 1880 the Stalwarts published a pamphlet called *The Roll of Honor* (Boston, 1880), which contained the names of the 306 as well as Conkling's nomination speech. In addition, Chauncey I. Filley had "Grant" medals struck off for distribution to each of the 306. Alfred Conkling, *The Life and Letters of Roscoe Conkling*, p. 609; Reeves, *Gentleman Boss*, p. 169.

33. William Henry Smith to R.B. Hayes, June 15, 1880, Hayes mss, Hayes Library.

34. Mary Logan, *Reminiscences*, p. 406; ML to JAL, June 29, 1880, Logan mss, LC.

35. Howard Knowles to JAL, July 12, 1880; James A. Garfield to JAL, July 23, 1880, Logan mss, LC; JAL to James A. Garfield, July 20, 1880, Hayes mss, Hayes Library; William B. Allison to Edward McPherson, July 21, 1880, McPherson mss, LC. The *Illinois State Journal*, July 16, 1880, reported that at Murphysboro Logan opened the campaign with a "vigorous arraignment" of the Democrats.

36. JAL to James A. Garfield, July 15, 1880, Garfield mss, LC.

37. James A. Garfield to JAL, Aug. 1, 1880; JAL to ML, Aug. 6, 10, 1880; ML to JAL, Aug. 10, 1880; Ulysses S. Grant to JAL, Aug. 12, 1880, Logan mss, LC; *Inter-Ocean*, Aug. 6, 14, 1880; *Illinois State Journal*, Aug. 7, 11, 1880. Garfield's political intimate Charles E. Henry had suggested that Logan be invited both to heal the party's factional wounds and to have someone along to help with whistlestop speeches. James D. Norris and Arthur H. Shaffer, eds., *Politics and Patronage in the Gilded Age*, p. 285.

38. Marshall Jewell to JAL, Sept. 29, 1880; C.B. Farwell to S.W. Dorsey, Aug. 2, 1880, Logan mss, LC; *Inter-Ocean*, July 2–3, 1880; *Illinois Fact Book and Historical Almanac*, p. 90. Greenback party candidate James B. Weaver polled 26,358 votes in Illinois. Reeves, *Gentleman Boss*, p. 188; Clancy, *Election of 1880*, p. 170.

39. JAL to ML, Sept. 5, 1880; James A. Garfield to JAL, Sept. 20, 1880; Chester A. Arthur to JAL, Oct. 7, 1880; John C. New to JAL, Oct. 24, 1880; JAL to J.T. Raleigh, Oct. 25, 1880, Logan mss, LC; *Illinois State Journal*, Sept. 10, 1880.

40. M. Woodhull to JAL, Oct. 17, 1880; Luther L. Mills to JAL, Nov. 4, 1880, Logan mss, LC; JAL to William Henry Smith, Nov. 18, 1880, Smith mss, Smith Library.

Chapter 11. A Hornet's Nest in the Senate

1. J. Donald Cameron to ML, Nov. 28, 1880, Logan mss, LC; JAL to William Henry Smith, Nov. 18, 1880, Smith mss, Ohio State Historical Society; *Illinois State Journal*, Dec. 1, 4, 1880; Mary Logan, *Reminiscences*, p. 409.

2. ML to Will and Dollie Tucker, Dec. 12, 1880, Logan mss, LC; *Cong. Record,* 46th Cong., 3d sess., pt. 1:14–15, 88.

3. *Cong. Record,* 46th Cong., 3d sess., pt. 1:93, 96–98, 125, 130; *Harper's Weekly,* Jan. 1, 1881.

4. Frederick Douglass to Roscoe Conkling, Dec. 21, 1880; Ulysses S. Grant to JAL, Dec. 27, 1880, Logan mss, LC.

5. *Cong. Record,* 46th Cong., 3d sess., pt. 1:477, 810, 870–73, 901–2; pt. 2:1096–97; *Chicago Tribune,* Dec. 14, 1880, Jan. 11, 25, 1881; *Illinois State Journal,* Jan. 18, 21, 1881; *Inter-Ocean,* Jan. 11, 17, 1881.

6. William T. Sherman to John Sherman, Jan. 31, 1881, Hayes mss, Hayes Library; William T. Sherman to JAL, Feb. 5 1881; Ulysses S. Grant to JAL, Feb. 9, 1881, Logan mss, LC; William T. Sherman to R.B. Hayes, May 12, 1881, Hayes mss, Hayes Library.

7. Robert T. Lincoln to JAL, Jan. 10, 1881; JAL to Ulysses S. Grant, Jan. 31, 1881; Joseph Medill to JAL, Jan. 27, 1881, Logan mss, LC; Edmund M. Smith to William E. Chandler, Mar. 15, 1881, W.E. Chandler mss, LC; Ulysses S. Grant to Roscoe Conkling, Mar. 5, 1881, Conkling mss, LC. The *Inter-Ocean,* Dec. 20, 1880, took a poll to ask its readers who should be put in Garfield's cabinet and Logan finished third behind Grant and William T. Sherman. Robert Todd Lincoln's biographer writes, "There can be little doubt that Logan originated the idea of Lincoln's being in the cabinet." John S. Goff, *Robert Todd Lincoln: A Man in His Own Right,* pp. 112–13. See also Cullom, *Fifty Years,* pp. 124–25.

8. John Cessna to JAL, Jan. 5, 1881; Shelby Cullom to JAL, Feb. 25, 1881, Logan mss, LC; William Henry Smith to R.B. Hayes, Jan. 8, 31, 1881; R.B. Hayes to William Henry Smith, Jan. 27, 1881, Hayes mss, Hayes Library; George A. Hook to William E. Chandler, Jan. 26, 1881, W.E. Chandler mss, LC.

9. ML to Dollie Tucker, Feb. 8, 25, Mar. 20, 28, 1881, Logan mss, LC; ML and JAL to R.B. and Lucy Hayes, Feb. 15, 1881, Hayes mss, Hayes Library.

10. Oliver O. Howard to JAL, Jan. 31, Feb. 15, 1881, Logan mss, LC; JAL to Oliver O. Howard, Feb. 2, 7, 1881, Howard mss, Bowdoin College Library. See also Jones, "*Black Jack.*"

11. *Cong. Record,* 46th Cong., 3d sess., pt. 1:477, 564, 584; pt. 2:1204–5; JAL to William Henry Smith, Jan. 20, 1881, Smith mss, Ohio State Historical Society.

12. *Cong. Record,* 46th Cong., 3d sess., pt. 2:1099–1100, 1104, 1245–50, 1291–97; pt. 3:1925–34.

13. Carl Schurz to JAL, Feb. 1, 1881; ML to Will and Dollie Tucker, Feb. 25, 1881, Logan mss, LC; *Cong. Record,* 46th Cong., 3d sess., pt. 3:1059, 2117.

14. *Cong. Record,* 47th Cong., special sess., p. 5; *New York Times,* Mar. 6, 12, 16, 1881; *Harper's Weekly,* Apr. 2, 1881.

15. *New York Times,* Mar. 17, 19, 25, 1881; *Cong. Record,* 47th Cong., special sess., pp. 47–48.

16. *Cong. Record,* 47th Cong., special sess., pp. 132–33; *New York Times,* Mar. 26, 31, 1881; Dawson, *Logan,* p. 288; *Chicago Tribune,* Mar. 26, 31, 1881; *Illinois State Journal,* Mar. 13, 31, Apr. 2, 1881; *Illinois State Register,* Apr. 7, 1881.

17. *Cong. Record,* 47th Cong., special sess., pp. 169–73; *New York Times,* Apr. 2, 1881.

18. *Cong. Record,* 47th Cong., special sess., pp. 33–335; *New York Times,* Apr. 20, 1881; L.Q.C. Lamar to JAL, Apr. 14, 1881, Logan mss, LC. Alabama Senator J.L. Pugh

endorsed the letter at the bottom. *Chicago Tribune,* Apr. 20, 1881; *Illinois State Journal,* Apr. 20, 21, 1881.

19. *Cong. Record,* 47th Cong., special sess., p. 33; *New York Times,* May 10, 17, 21, 1881; Joseph Medill to JAL, May 2, 1881, Logan mss, LC.

20. *New York Times,* May 17, 1881; George F. Howe, *Chester A. Arthur: A Quarter-Century of Machine Politics,* pp. 138–39; Robert G. Caldwell, *James A. Garfield, Party Chieftain,* pp. 347–48. The anti-Stalwart *Harper's Weekly,* June 4, 1881, said the resignations were followed by a "universal smile."

21. Howe, *Chester A. Arthur,* p. 139. Caldwell, *Garfield,* p. 342; JAL to ML, May 6, 16, 1881, Logan mss, LC; *Chicago Tribune,* May 20, 1881; *Illinois State Register,* Apr. 13, 1881.

22. James A. Garfield to R.B. Hayes, May 22, 1881, Smith mss, Smith Library.

23. Mc to JAL, Mar. 23, Apr. 13, 1881, Logan mss, LC; William Henry Smith to R.B. Hayes, Apr. 7, 1881, Hayes mss, Hayes Library; D.C. Fitzmaurice to David Davis, July 4, 1881, Davis mss, ISHL; *Chicago Tribune,* Mar. 16, 19, 23, 1881; *Illinois State Journal,* Mar. 29, 1881; Cullom, *Fifty Years,* p. 128.(See note 48 below for explanation of "Mc.")

24. ML to Dollie Tucker, Apr. 24, 1881; JAL to ML, Apr. 30, May 8, 16, June 3, 8, 1881, Logan mss, LC.

25. Robert T. Lincoln to JAL, July 2, 3, 5, 6, 1881; Green B. Raum to JAL, July 2, 1881, Logan mss, LC.

26. See Charles Rosenberg, *The Trial of the Assassin Guiteau,* pp. 7, 37, 38. Logan stated "unhesitatingly" to the press "that no normal person could have committed so pointless a crime." Rosenberg, *Guiteau,* p. 76. Also see *Chicago Tribune,* July 3–5, 1881, Nov. 25, 1881; *Illinois State Register,* July 4, 1881; *Harper's Weekly,* July 23, 1881.

27. JAL to ML, July 29, Aug. 17, 19, 24, 26, 29, Sept. 6, 17, 1881, Logan mss, LC.

28. JAL to ML, Sept. 20, 1881, Logan mss, LC. At Cleveland Logan was the house guest of rising Republican politician Mark A. Hanna. *Chicago Tribune,* Sept. 26, 1881.

29. JAL to ML, Sept. 30, Oct. 4, 21, 1881, Logan mss, LC; Rosenberg, *Guiteau,* pp. 78–79.

30. James E. Harvey to David Davis, Aug. 18, Davis mss, ISHL; G.A. Pierce to JAL, Oct. 18, 1881; William Penn Nixon to JAL, Oct. 15, 16, Nov. 18, 1881; Samuel H. Elbert to JAL, Nov. 24, 1881, Logan mss, LC.

31. *Chicago Tribune,* Dec. 19, 20, 27, 29, 1881; *Inter-Ocean,* Dec. 20–28, 1881.

32. Jerome B. Chaffee to JAL, Oct. 11, 13, Nov. 25, 1881, Logan mss, LC; *Chicago Tribune,* Sept. 28, 1881; Reeves, *Chester A. Arthur,* p. 259.

33. Jerome B. Chaffee to JAL, Dec. 1, 9, 12, 14, 1881, Logan mss, LC.

34. Wharton Barker to Charles C. Smith, Dec. 27, 1881, Barker mss, LC; Warner M. Bateman to William E. Chandler, Dec. 10, 1881, W.E. Chandler mss, LC.

35. *Cong. Record,* 47th Cong., 1st sess., pt. 1:1, 4, 76; pt. 2:1285–94, 1376.

36. Ibid., pt. 1:79, 146, 609; pt. 7:6876.

37. Ibid., pt. 1:266; pt. 2:1950–56; Frank Burns to JAL, Apr. 17, 1882, Logan mss, LC.

38. Joseph Medill to JAL, Jan. 20, 1882, Logan mss, LC; Joseph Medill to JAL, Feb. 22, 1882, Logan mss, ISHL; *Chicago Evening Journal,* Apr. 1, 1882; John A. Logan,

"National Aid to Public Schools," *North American Review* 136(1883):337–44; *Huntsville (Alabama) Gazette*, Mar. 31, 1883; *Chicago Tribune*, Jan. 10, 14, 19, 1882; *Inter-Ocean*, Feb. 21, 1882.

39. Ulysses S. Grant to Chester A. Arthur, Dec. 22, 1881, Simon Cameron mss, LC; *Cong. Record*, 47th Cong., 1st sess., pt. 5:4350; *Chicago Tribune*, Jan. 5, 1882; Ulysses S. Grant to Chester A. Arthur, Jan. 23, 1882, Arthur mss, LC.

40. Joseph Medill to JAL, Jan. 20, 1882; Thomas D. Mosscrop to JAL, May 22, 1882; Maurice J. McGrath to JAL, Jan. 9, 1882; Oliver Sabin to JAL, June 2, 1882, Logan mss, LC; Joseph Medill to JAL, Jan. 12, 1882, Logan mss, ISHL; *Chicago Tribune*, Jan. 6, 16, Feb. 14, 1882; *Illinois State Journal*, Jan. 7, 1882; *Illinois State Register*, Jan. 12, 1882; *Quincy Herald*, Feb. 5, 1882.

41. JAL to ML, Jan. 29, 1882, Feb. 21, 1882, Logan mss, LC.

42. *Cong. Record*, 47th Cong., 1st sess., pt. 5:4410, 4515–22, 4526, 4565–76, 5340–41; William T. Sherman to Philip H. Sheridan, June 19, 1882, Logan mss, LC; John M. Bacon to William T. Sherman, May 5, 1882, William T. Sherman mss, LC.

43. JAL to Dollie Tucker, Apr. 14, 1882; H.B. Anthony to ML, Apr. 5, 1882, Logan mss, LC; *Illinois State Journal*, Feb. 9, 20, Mar. 31, Apr. 1, 2, 1882; May 20, 1882.

44. William B. Allison, JAL, Samuel J.R. McMillan, Thomas Henderson, S.L. Farwell, William M. Springer, George C. Hazleton to Oliver Spaulding, Mar. 20, 1882, Spaulding mss, University of Michigan, Michigan Historical Collections.

45. *Cong. Record*, 47th Cong., 1st sess., pt. 6:5712–21, 5775–77, 5950; pt. 7: 6770–71.

46. Ibid., pt. 6:6024, 6090–93.

47. Ibid., pt. 7:6509–18, 6545–46, 6553, 6612, 6676.

48. Oliver Sabin to JAL, May 18, June 2, 1882; Edwin Henry to JAL, May 14, 1882; J.K. Yager to JAL, May 22, 1882; Richard S. Tuthill to JAL, Apr. 25, 1882; Jerome B. Chaffee to JAL, Feb. 13, 1882, Logan mss, LC. On July 1 and 21, 1882, Logan received pencil written messages from "Mc" marked "private." They came from Springfield and the actions of most Illinois Republican leaders were discussed. Mc was one of the senator's best sources of home-state developments. He was especially hostile to Charles Farwell, but he watched the state party for signs of any opposition to Logan. See Mc to JAL, July 1, 21, 1882, Logan mss, LC.

49. Jacob Wheeler to JAL, Feb. 23, 1882; J.D. Harvey to JAL, Apr. 18, 1882; M.E. Stone to JAL, Jan. 13, 1882, Logan mss, LC.

50. A.M. Jones to JAL, June 9, 14, 1882; Jacob Wheeler to JAL, June 30, 1882; Mc to JAL, June 9, 1882; Jesse Spalding to JAL, July 15, 1882, Logan mss, LC; *Inter-Ocean*, June 15, 27, 1882.

51. A.M. Jones to JAL, July 21, 1882; Dan Shepard to JAL, July 21, 1882; J.H. Magee to JAL, July 19, 1882; Benjamin O. Jones to JAL, July 15, 1882; M.L. Joslyn to JAL, July 2, 1882, Logan mss, LC.

Chapter 12. A Household Word

1. Mc to JAL, July 21, 1882, Logan mss, LC.

2. M.L. Joslyn to JAL, Oct. 3, 1882, Logan mss, LC.

3. Pennsylvania Military Academy Report to JAL, Dec. 22, 1882, Logan mss, LC.

4. ML to Dollie Tucker, Oct. 24, 1882; ML to Will and Dollie Tucker, Oct. 28, 1882;

JAL to Will and Dollie Tucker, Nov. 3, 1882; ML to Dollie Tucker, Nov. 8, 1882; A.M. Jones to JAL, Nov. 22, 1882, Logan mss, LC.

5. *Cong. Record,* 47th Cong., 2d sess., pt. 1:1, 18, 35–37, 101; Chester A. Arthur to ML, Dec. 27, 1882, Logan mss, LC.

6. *Cong. Record,* 47th Cong., 2d sess., pt. 1:211, 246, 590, 615, 657, 661; *Illinois State Journal,* Dec. 16, 1882.

7. *Cong. Record,* 47th Cong., 2d sess., pt. 1:416; pt. 4:3556, 3574.

8. Ibid., pt. 1:173–74.

9. Ulysses S. Grant, "An Undeserved Stigma," *North American Review* 125(1882): 536–46; *Chicago Tribune,* Nov. 26, 1882.

10. *Cong. Record,* 47th Cong., 2d sess., pt. 1:671, 692–701, 715–36, 752–80; pt. 2:1091–97; *Chicago Tribune,* Dec. 12, 1882.

11. John Pope to JAL, Nov. 28, 1882, Jan. 16, 1883; Augustus Brandegee to JAL, Jan. 28, 1883; Mortimer D. Leggett to JAL, Jan. 5, 1883; E.T. Roe to JAL, Jan. 4, 1883; J.R. Lorimer to JAL, Jan. 12, 1883; S.C. Van Tassel to JAL, Jan. 24, 1883, Logan mss, ISHL; Andrew Shuman to JAL, Jan. 11, 1883, Logan mss, LC; *Illinois State Journal,* Jan. 4, 5, Feb. 3, 1883. The *Illinois State Register,* Jan. 4, 1883, called Logan's Porter speech his most "discreditable" act.

12. ML to Dollie Tucker, Jan. 24, 1883, Logan mss, LC.

13. *Cong. Record,* 47th Cong., 2d sess., pt. 1:820, 1005; pt. 3:2333, 2335.

14. Ibid., pt. 3:2547; pt. 4:3171, 3385, 3398, 3488.

15. ML to Dollie Tucker, Feb. 18, 1883, Logan mss, LC.

16. *Cong. Record,* 47th Cong., 1st sess., pt. 3:2342.

17. Ibid., 2d sess., pt. 3:2439, 2486, 2789, 2927–30, 2962, 2992; pt. 4:3586.

18. Z. Eastman to R.B. Hayes, Jan. 12, 1883, Hayes mss, Hayes Library; ML to Dollie Tucker, Apr. 8, 1883, Logan mss, LC; *New York Times,* Sept. 6, 1882; *Chicago Tribune,* Jan. 16, 1883; *Illinois State Journal,* May 10, 1883; Cullom, *Fifty Years,* p. 313. See also Bogart and Thompson, *Industrial State,* pp. 138–39. When Cullom joined Logan in the Senate he stood out in vivid contrast to the senior senator. Cullom's biographer writes of his subject: "He appeared sometimes taciturn, even self-effacing. . . . He lacked the brilliance and dash of John A. Logan." Neilson, *Cullom,* pp. v, 11.

19. A.T. Wood to JAL, Feb. 16, 1883; M.L. Joslyn to JAL, Apr. 20, 1883; J.B. Chaffee to JAL, June 3, 1883, Logan mss, LC.

20. Chester A. Arthur to JAL, May 8, 1883; Roscoe Conkling to JAL, June 3, 1883, Logan mss, LC.

21. William B. Allison to JAL, May 26, June 9, 1883; William B. Allison to ML, Sept. 25, 1883; William E. Chandler to JAL, Sept. 19, 1883, Logan mss, LC; Henry C. Bowen to R.B. Hayes, Mar. 5, 1883, Hayes mss, Hayes Library.

22. ML to Dollie Tucker, Apr. 8, 1883, Logan mss, LC.

23. JAL to William T. Sherman, June 7, 1883, William T. Sherman mss, LC; William T. Sherman to JAL, June 18, 1883, Logan mss, LC.

24. Special Orders No. 66, Headquarters District of New Mexico, Santa Fe, June 16, 1883; Henry L. Dawes to JAL, Apr. 26, 1883; JAL to ML, July 25, 1883, Logan mss, LC; JAL to Stephen B. Elkins, July 4, 1883, Elkins mss, West Virginia University Library; ML to Chester A. Arthur, June 2, 1883, Arthur mss, LC.

25. Dee Alexander Brown, *Bury My Heart at Wounded Knee: An Indian History of the*

American West, pp. 395–400; U.S., Cong., 48th Cong., 1st sess., *Senate Report 283,* pp. 79–81.

26. JAL to Dollie Tucker, Aug. 19, 1883; F.V. Hayden to ML, Dec. 23, 1883, Logan mss, LC; JAL to William E. Chandler, Sept. 18, 1881, W.E. Chandler mss, New Hampshire Historical Society; *Illinois State Journal,* Aug. 22, 1883.

27. ML to Dollie Tucker, Aug. 15, 1883; Wesley Merritt to ML, July 20, 1883, Logan mss, LC. Mary returned to Chicago thanks to railroad passes. Prior to the 1907 Hepburn Act politicians were often given free rides. Mary reported passes on the Burlington and Santa Fe while Grenville M. Dodge, former general and Republican congressman, sent her a Union Pacific pass on July 21. Grenville M. Dodge to ML, July 21, 1883, Logan mss, LC.

28. William B. Allison to JAL, Sept. 15, 1883; ML to Dollie Tucker, Sept. 20, Oct. 23, 1883, Logan mss, LC; JAL to D.F. Murphy, June 11, 1883, Gratz mss, Historical Society of Pennsylvania; JAL to William E. Chandler, Sept. 18, 1883, W.E. Chandler mss, New Hampshire Historical Society; *Illinois State Journal,* Sept. 22, 1883; *Chicago Tribune,* Oct. 10, 15, 1883.

29. ML to Dollie Tucker, Oct. 23, 1883; JAL to ML, Nov. 20, 1883; JAL, Jr., to ML, Dec. 5, 1883, Logan mss, LC.

30. JAL, Jr., to JAL, Dec. 16, 1883; JAL, Jr., to ML, Dec. 9, 30, 1883; JAL to ML, Dec. 26, 1883; Wesley Merritt to JAL, Dec. 21, 1883, Logan mss, LC.

31. *Cong. Record,* 48th Cong., 1st sess., pt. 1:1, 49.

32. Ibid., pt. 1:13, 228; pt. 2:1110; pt. 4:4096.

33. Ibid., pt. 1:18; pt. 3:2066, 2469, 2641–42, 2712, 2724.

34. Ibid., pt. 1:602; pt. 2:1829–65; pt. 4:3952; pt. 6:5935; Robert S. Gash to Nelson Aldrich, Mar. 26, 1884; William Fredericks to Nelson Aldrich, Apr. 7, 1884, Aldrich mss, LC: *Illinois State Journal,* Mar. 4, 1884; *Chicago Tribune,* Mar. 12, 14, 1884. Logan was not the only senator to receive requests for his newest speech in the battle against Fitz-John Porter. Newly seated Rhode Island Republican Nelson Aldrich sent several copies to constituents who endorsed the volunteer soldier's latest effort.

35. *Illinois State Journal,* Jan. 2, 1884; *Illinois State Register,* Jan. 8, 1884.

36. *Cong. Record,* 48th Cong., 1st sess., pt. 1:712, 718; pt. 2:1420; *Washington Bee,* Feb. 16, 1884; Jonathan T. Dorris, *Pardon and Amnesty under Lincoln and Johnson,* p. 385.

37. Philip H. Sheridan to William S. Rosecrans, Jan. 14, 25, 1884, Sheridan mss, LC.

38. *Cong. Record,* 48th Cong., 1st sess., pt. 2:1582–83, 1772; pt. 3:2104; pt. 5:5477; pt. 6:5717.

39. JAL, Jr., to JAL, Jan. 4, 1884; JAL, Jr., to ML, Jan. 7, 1884; Wesley Merritt to ML, Jan. 9, 1884; John Pope to ML, Jan. 9, 1884, Logan mss, LC.

40. JAL, Jr., to JAL, Feb. 24, Mar. 6, 1884; Wesley Merritt to JAL, Mar. 7, 1884, Logan mss, LC.

Chapter 13. Logan for President

1. Levi P. Morton to ML, Dec. 17, 1883, Logan mss, LC.

2. *Illinois State Journal,* Jan. 13, 18, Feb. 8, 12, 18, 1884; *Chicago Evening Journal,* Jan. 11, 1884; *Inter-Ocean,* Mar. 8, 10, 1884; *Chicago Tribune,* Jan. 10, Feb. 1, 11, 14, 1884. One possible reason for *Tribune* friendship is that a Logan-Blaine deal was in the works. The *Tribune* did mention such a deal on Jan. 18, Feb. 12, and Feb. 18, 1884.

3. ML to JAL, Mar. 19, 1884; JAL to ML, Mar. 21, 1884, Logan mss, LC.

4. JAL to ML, Mar. 22, Apr. 1, 6, 1884, Logan mss, LC; JAL to Carl Schurz, Feb. 28, 1884, Schurz mss, LC. The story of Grant's endorsement was a sensational journalistic exclusive broken in the *New York World*. George Juergens, *Joseph Pulitzer and the "New York World,"* p. 34.

5. JAL, Jr., to ML, Apr. 6, 1884, Logan mss, LC; Sarah Ada Bailhache to Mary Brayman, Jan. 22, 1884, Bailhache-Brayman mss, ISHL.

6. Emory Storrs to JAL, Jan. 26, Mar. 5, 1884; Mc to JAL, Apr. 26, 1884, Logan mss, LC.

7. A.M. McIntosh to Richard Oglesby, Jan. 21, 1884; H. Hilliard to Richard Oglesby, Feb. 5, 1884; Richard Oglesby to J.M. Kelly, Feb. 21, 1884; Richard Oglesby to George B. Leonard, Feb. 25, 1884; A.C. Babcock to Richard Oglesby, Mar. 7, 1884; Henry D. Dement to Richard Oglesby, Mar. 9, 1884; M.H. Chamberlain to Richard Oglesby, Mar. 20, 1884, Oglesby mss, ISHL; *Inter-Ocean*, Feb. 13, Mar. 10, 1884.

8. William Penn Nixon to Shelby Cullom, Feb. 3, 1884, Cullom mss, ISHL.

9. James E. Harvey to David Davis, Mar. 11, 26, 29, Apr. 4, 1884; L.H. Reavis to David Davis, Apr. 6, 1884; Walter Q. Gresham to David Davis, Feb. 11, Mar. 7, 1884, Davis mss, ISHL.

10. Justin S. Morrill to Redfield S. Proctor, Apr. 26, 1884, Morrill mss, LC; Wharton Barker to R.B. Hayes, Apr. 22, 1884; R.B. Hayes to Wharton Barker, Apr. 24, 1884, Hayes mss, Hayes Library; William Henry Smith to George W. Curtis, May 3, 1884, Curtis mss, Hayes Library; Carl Schurz, *Speeches, Correspondence and Political Papers of Carl Schurz*, ed. Frederic Bancroft, 4:194–95.

11. William T. Sherman to John Sherman, Nov. 28, 1883; John Sherman to William T. Sherman, Nov. 24, 1883, Mar. 7, 1884; Blanton Duncan to William T. Sherman, Apr. 29, 1884, William T. Sherman mss, LC.

12. John Sherman to William T. Sherman, Nov. 24, 1883, Jan. 29, Mar. 7, 1884; William T. Sherman to John Sherman, Feb. 24, May 7, 1884, William T. Sherman mss, LC.

13. Anson Smith to Nelson Aldrich, Apr. 3, 1884, Aldrich mss, LC: Justin S. Morrill to Redfield Proctor, Apr. 26, 1884, Morrill mss, LC; Elihu B. Washburne to Ninian Edwards, Dec. 6, 1883, Washburne mss, ISHL; Wharton Barker to R.B. Hayes, Apr. 22, May 3, 1884; R.B. Hayes to Wharton Barker, Apr. 24, 1884, Hayes mss, Hayes Library.

14. John F. Ogelvee to A.L. Conger, Feb. 9, 1884, Conger mss, Hayes Library; John C. New to JAL, Apr. 30, 1884, Logan mss, LC; J.H. McNeely to F.S. Howell, Mar. 2, 1884, Benjamin Harrison mss, LC.

15. *New York Globe*, Nov. 24, 1883, Jan. 5, 12, Apr. 12, 1884.

16. *The People's Advocate* (Washington), Feb. 23, Mar. 15, 1884; *Washington Bee*, Dec. 22, 1883, Jan. 19, 26, Feb. 23, Mar. 1, Apr. 5, 1884; *Washington Grit*, Dec. 21, 1883, Jan. 26, Feb. 2, 1884; *Baltimore Vindicator*, Jan. 10, 1884; *Huntsville Gazette*, Feb. 9, May 3, 1884.

17. *Illinois State Journal*, Jan. 24, Feb. 22, Mar. 17, 1884; *Chicago Tribune*, Apr. 10, 1884.

18. *Nation*, Apr. 3, 1884.

19. Schuyler Colfax to Richard Oglesby, May 21, 1884, Oglesby mss, ISHL; A. Cowles to Horace White, May 17, 1884, White mss, ISHL; *Chicago Tribune*, Apr. 11, 17, 1884.

20. William Penn Nixon to Walter Q. Gresham, May 27, 1884; David Davis to Walter

Q. Gresham, May 14, 1884, Gresham mss, LC; Stephen B. Elkins to JAL, May 19, 24, 25, 1884, Logan mss, LC.

21. *Chicago Tribune,* Jan. 18, Feb. 12, 18, Apr. 10, 17, May 3, 17, 23, 31, 1884; Robert D. Marcus, *Grand Old Party; Political Structure in the Gilded Age, 1880–1896,* pp. 68–69, 78–80.

22. A.M. Jones to JAL, Apr. 24, 1884; L.N. Reavis to JAL, May 16, 1884; Paul Selby to ML, May 4, 1884, Logan mss, LC; A. Cowles to Horace White, May 17, 1884, White mss, ISHL; *New York Times,* May 28, 29, 1884.

23. *New York Times,* May 21, June 2, 3, 1884.

24. JAL, Jr., to JAL, June 2, 1884, Logan mss, LC; JAL to Shelby Cullom, June 3, 1884; JAL to A.M. Jones, June 3, 1884; Shelby Cullom to JAL, June 3, 1884; William H. Harper to JAL, June 3, 1884, Logan mss, ISHL. Illinois cast 28 votes for Clayton and 16 for Lynch. Cullom voted for the latter. *Proceedings of the Republican National Convention, 1884,* p. 18.

25. William Penn Nixon to Walter Q. Gresham, June 2, 1884; Walter Q. Gresham to John W. Foster, June 2, 1884, Gresham mss, LC.

26. *Proceedings of the Republican National Convention, 1884,* pp. 3–10, 38; H. Wayne Morgan, *From Hayes to McKinley: National Party Politics, 1877-1896,* p. 202.

27. A.M. Jones to JAL, June 4, 1884; JAL to A.M. Jones, June 4, 1884; JAL to C.A. Logan, June 4, 1884; JAL to Richard Whiting, June 4, 1884, Logan mss, ISHL.

28. C.A. Logan to JAL, June 5, 1884; E.P. Brooks to JAL, June 5, 1884; JAL to Burton C. Cook June 5, 1884, Logan mss, ISHL.

29. Bulletin No. 18 to JAL, June 5, 1884; Shelby Cullom to JAL, June 5, 1884, Logan mss, ISHL; *Proceedings of the Republican National Convention, 1884,* pp. 97–128, 135; *Chicago Tribune,* June 6, 1884.

30. *New York Times,* June 6, 1884; Bulletin No. 19 to JAL, June 5, 1884, Logan mss, ISHL.

31. JAL to JAL, Jr., June 6, 1884, Logan mss, LC; JAL to C.A. Logan, June 6, 1884; Bulletin No. 1 to JAL, June 6, 1884, Logan mss, ISHL.

32. C.A. Logan to JAL, June 6, 1884; Jerome B. Chaffee to JAL, June 6, 1884; Burton C. Cook to JAL, June 6, 1884; A.M. Jones to JAL, June 6, 1884; JAL to Burton C. Cook, June 6, 1884, Logan mss, ISHL. Long before the convention the *Illinois State Register,* Apr. 13, 1884, had warned Logan to watch Cullom, remembering how Garfield had betrayed John Sherman in 1880.

33. *Proceedings of the Republican National Convention, 1884,* pp.141–42, 146–48, 149–50; Bulletin No. 68 to JAL, June 6, 1884, Logan mss, ISHL.

34. JAL to Shelby Cullom, June 6, 1884; JAL to Jerome B. Chaffee, June 6, 1884; C.A. Logan to JAL, June 6, 1884, Logan mss, ISHL; Cullom, *Fifty Years,* p. 187; *Proceedings of the Republican National Convention, 1884,* pp. 157–58; *Chicago Tribune,* June 7, 1884. The final Illinois vote was Blaine 34, Logan 7, Arthur 3.

35. A.M. Jones to JAL, June 6, 1884; Jerome B. Chaffee to JAL, June 6, 1884; Robert R. Hitt to JAL, June 6, 1884; Shelby Cullom, Burton C. Cook, and Clark E. Carr to JAL, June 6, 1884; JAL to Shelby Cullom, Burton C. Cook, and Clark E. Carr, June 6, 1884, Logan mss, ISHL; Bluford Wilson to Walter Q. Gresham, June 6, 1884; Walter Q. Gresham to John W. Foster, June 6, 1884, Gresham mss, LC; Cullom, *Fifty Years,* p. 188. On June 11 Cullom explained his overture to Gresham. "The delegation from Illinois was in hopes Logan would not accept or consent to the use of his name. It was not thought best

for him nor for the party; and there was a general feeling that the Arthur side should be represented on the ticket, and you were the man whose name was in everyone's mouth. If General Logan had said no, you would have been nominated."

36. *Proceedings of the Republican National Convention, 1884*, pp. 177–78; *Illinois State Journal*, June 7, 1884; *Chicago Tribune*, June 6, 7, 1884. Logan's nomination was especially well received by Chicagoans. Bessie L. Pierce *A History of Chicago*, 3:358.

37. JAL to Shelby Cullom, June 6, 1884, Logan mss, ISHL; Dollie Tucker to JAL, June 6, 1884; Dollie Tucker to ML, June 7, 1884, Logan mss, LC.

38. Jerome B. Chaffee to JAL, June 6, 1884, Logan mss, ISHL; David S. Muzzey, *James G. Blaine, A Political Idol of Other Days*, pp. 256–86; Morgan, *From Hayes to McKinley*, pp. 201–4.

39. *New York Times*, June 8, 1884; JAL to C.A. Logan, June 6, 1884, Logan mss, ISHL; JAL to JAL, Jr., June 6, 1884, Logan mss, LC; William Henry Smith to R.B. Hayes, June 9, 1884, Hayes mss, Hayes Library; Leonard Swett to David Davis, July 10, 1884, Davis mss, ISHL; William Gene Eidson, "John A. Logan: Hero of the Volunteers," Ph.D. dissertation, Vanderbilt University, 1967, p. 337.

40. *Chicago Tribune*, June 7, 1884.

41. JAL to JAL, Jr., June 6, 1884, Logan mss, ISHL.

Chapter 14. Plumed Knight and Black Eagle

1. Allan Nevins, *Grover Cleveland: A Study in Courage*, p. 157; Muzzey, *Blaine*, p. 298; Morgan, *From Hayes to McKinley*, p. 198; Lyman Trumbull to Samuel J. Tilden, June 7, 1884, Trumbull mss, ISHL; William Bushmill to Grover Cleveland, June 9, 1884, Cleveland mss, LC; *Harper's Weekly*, June 21, 28, July 19, 1884. George Edmunds, the defeated "reform" candidate, called Logan's nomination "the best thing that could possibly be done." *Washington Post*, June 7, 1884. Dana's *New York Sun* endorsed Ben Butler.

2. A.T. Bissell to JAL, June 7, 1884; Chauncey I. Filley to JAL, June 13, 1884, Logan mss, ISHL; Stephen B. Elkins to JAL, June 15, 1884; James G. Blaine to JAL, June 7, July 13, 1884; Lucius Fairchild to JAL, June 7, 1884, Logan mss, LC; JAL to A.L. Conger, June 13, 1884, Conger mss, Hayes Library.

3. J.V. Logan to JAL, June 12, 1884; F.V. Hayden to JAL, June 7, 1884; William Williams to JAL, June 20, 1884; Editor-in-Chief, *Florida Journal* to JAL, June 22, 1884, Logan mss, ISHL; George Charles and Charles Charles to JAL, July 9, 1884; Frederick Douglass to JAL, July 3, 1884, Logan mss, LC; Thomas Settle to JAL, June 16, 1884; JAL to Thomas Settle, June 19, 1884, Settle mss, Southern Historical Collection, University of North Carolina, Chapel Hill.

4. Lyman Trumbull to Samuel J. Tilden, June 7, 1884, Trumbull mss, ISHL; John M. Hamilton to Joseph F. Fifer, June 11, 1884, Fifer mss, ISHL; JAL to Mason Brayman, June, n.d., 1884, Bailhache-Brayman mss, ISHL; Shelby Cullom to JAL, July 31, 1884, Logan mss, LC; William Henry Smith to George W. Curtis, May 3, 1884, Curtis mss, Hayes Library; William Henry Smith to R.B. Hayes, June 9, 1884, Hayes mss, Hayes Library.

5. R.B. Hayes to G.H. Grosvenor, June 13, 1884; R.B. Hayes to William Henry Smith, June 12, 1884, Hayes mss, Hayes Library; David Davis to Walter Q. Gresham, June 9, 1884; John Mason Brown to Walter Q. Gresham, June 8, 1884; Benjamin Harrison to Walter Q. Gresham, June 9, 1884, Gresham mss, LC.

6. Robert S. Gash and Clark H. Burdick to Nelson Aldrich, June 9, 1884, Aldrich

mss, LC; Justin S. Morrill to Boston *Traveler,* June, n.d., 1884, Morrill mss, LC; David Davis to Walter Q. Gresham, June 25, 1884, Gresham mss, LC; *Washington Bee,* June 7, 14, 1884; Leslie Fishel, Jr., "The Negro in Northern Politics, 1870–1900," *Mississippi Valley Historical Review* 42(1955):466–89.

7. John Sherman to William T. Sherman, June 11, 19, 1884; William T. Sherman to John Sherman, June 7, 15, 21, 1884, William T. Sherman mss, LC; William T. Sherman to James G. Blaine, June 7, 1884, Blaine mss, LC.

8. A. Barnum to JAL, June 7, 1884; A. Barnum to ML, June 12, 1884; Currier and Ives to JAL, June 11, 1884, Logan mss, ISHL; Hinton R. Helper to JAL, June 25, 1884; George F. Dawson to JAL, Sept. 11, 1884, Logan mss, LC.

9. Kirk H. Porter and Donald B. Johnson, *National Party Platforms, 1840–1964,* pp. 66–68; *Proceedings of the Republican National Convention, 1884,* pp.91–94.

10. *Cong. Record,* 48th Cong., 1st sess., pt. 6:6042–44. A bitter enemy, *Harper's Weekly,* July 19, 1884, vindicated Logan from any complicity in the land grab.

11. ML to Dollie Tucker, July 1, 4, 1884; Wesley Merritt to ML, July 1, 1884; JAL, Jr., to ML, July 8, 1884, Logan mss, LC.

12. *Illinois State Journal,* June 17, 18, 1884; *Chicago Tribune,* June 20, 23, 1884; ML to Dollie Tucker, July 20, 29, 1884, Logan mss, LC. The Logan manuscripts, both in Washington and Springfield, contain hundreds of telegrams and letters asking him to speak. Many came from G.A.R. or other military societies asking for appearances at reunions. Other manuscript collections contain examples of Logan's letters of thanks and regret. See for example JAL to Col. H.J. Johnson, Aug. 1, 1884, Clara J.J. Morrow mss, Duke University Library, Durham, North Carolina.

13. ML to Dollie Tucker, July 20, Aug. 27, 1884; JAL to Dollie and Will Tucker, Aug. 28, 1884; Warner Miller to JAL, July 26, 1884, Logan mss, LC; *Chicago Tribune,* Aug. 15, 16, 1884.

14. JAL to Richard Oglesby, Aug. 29, 1884, Oglesby mss, ISHL; S.C. Pomeroy to JAL, Aug. 28, 1884; Stephen B. Elkins to JAL, Aug 29, 1884; John P. St. John to JAL, Aug. 7, 1884, Logan mss, LC; Jerome B. Chaffee to A.L. Conger, Aug. 10, 1884, Conger mss, Hayes Library.

15. B.F. Jones to Robert Ingersoll, Aug. 23, 1884; Robert Ingersoll to "Dear Clint," Aug. 13, 1884, Ingersoll mss, LC.

16. B.F. Jones to JAL, Sept. 2, 1884; ML to Dollie Tucker, Sept. 9, 1884; Russell Alger to JAL, Sept. 1, 1884, Logan mss, LC; JAL to George F. Hoar, Sept. 18, 1884, Hoar mss, Massachusetts Historical Society, Boston; *Chicago Tribune,* Sept. 13, 16, 17, 1884.

17. John Ogelvee to Samuel Fessenden, Aug. 10, 1884; George R. Haynes to A.L. Conger, Sept. 12, 1884, Conger mss, Hayes Library; *Youngstown* (Ohio) *News,* Aug. 31, 1884; J.F. Orr to JAL, Sept. 30, 1884, Logan mss, LC; JAL to George F. Hoar, Sept. 18, 1884, Hoar mss, Massachusetts Historical Society, Boston; *Illinois State Journal,* Sept. 25, 1884; *Chicago Tribune,* Sept. 27, Oct. 1, 1884.

18. JAL to George F. Hoar, Sept. 18, 1884, Hoar mss, Massachusetts Historical Society, Boston; H.C. Lodge to JAL, Sept. 13, Oct. n.d., 1884; Joseph R. Hawley to JAL, Sept. 18, 1884; Nelson Aldrich to JAL, Sept. 27, 1884; ML to Dollie Tucker, Sept. 25, 1884, Logan mss, LC.

19. C. Aultman to JAL, Oct. 15, 1884; John F. Ogelvee, Joshua K. Brown, and D.K. Watson to JAL, Oct. 14, 1884; B.F. Jones to JAL, Oct. 19, 1884, Logan mss, LC; *Harper's Weekly,* Oct. 25, 1884, believed "Ohio speaks for itself not for the country."

20. *Illinois State Journal,* Oct. 25, 1884; Mary Logan, *Reminiscences,* p. 421; *Chicago Tribune,* Oct. 9, 23, 30, 1884. To welcome Black Jack to the capital the *Illinois State Register,* Oct. 24, 1884, ran an editorial which dredged up all of the long-reported charges of pro-Confederate activity in 1861.

21. George F. Dawson to JAL, Oct. 8, 1884, Logan mss, LC; Mary Logan, *Reminiscences,* p. 423.

22. *New York Times,* Sept. 3, 1884.

23. B.F. Jones to JAL, Aug. 28, 1884, Logan mss, LC; Muzzey, *Blaine,* pp. 306–7; Mary Logan, *Reminiscences,* pp. 421–23; Cullom, *Fifty Years,* p. 188; Fred A. Shannon, *The Centennial Years: A Political and Economic History of America from the Late 1870's to the Early 1890's,* p. 134.

24. Muzzey, *Blaine,* p. 318; Nevins, *Cleveland,* p. 182; George F. Dawson to JAL, Oct. 8, 1884; Horace Porter to JAL, Oct. 25, 1884, Logan mss, LC.

25. Thomas Bayard to Carl Schurz, June 29, 1884, Schurz mss, LC: Brooks Adams to Grover Cleveland, Oct. 28, 1884, Cleveland mss, LC; Benjamin Bristow to Walter Q. Gresham, Oct. 22, 1884, Gresham mss, LC.

26. John Tomsich, *A Genteel Endeavor: American Culture and Politics in the Gilded Age,* pp. 89, 92; John M. Dobson, *Politics in the Gilded Age; A New Perspective on Reform,* p. 164. Dobson suggests that the Mugwumps made little impact on reform; rather the independents who stayed with the Republican party were those who eventually produced meaningful change (pp. 164, 188).

27. James G. Blaine to JAL, Nov. 3, 1884; John C. New to JAL, Nov. 5, 1884; Stephen B. Elkins to JAL, Nov. 5, 1884; Samuel Fessenden to JAL, Nov. 5, 1884; C.R. Spore to JAL, Nov. 5, 1884; R.H. Sturgiss to JAL, Nov. 5, 1884, Logan mss, LC.

28. John C. New to JAL, Nov. 6, 7, 1884; Dollie Tucker to JAL, Nov. 6, 1884; George F. Dawson to JAL, Nov. 6, 1884; M.H. Marston to JAL, Nov. 7, 1884; Garrett A. Hobart to JAL, Nov. 8, 1884, Logan mss, LC; *Chicago Tribune,* Nov. 7, 1884.

29. Stephen B. Elkins to JAL, Nov. 14, 1884; Samuel Fessenden to JAL, Nov. 8, 1884, Logan mss, LC; Walter D. Burnham, *Presidential Ballots, 1836–1892,* pp. 247, 249.

30. A.G. Browne to D.S. Lamont, Nov. 7, 1884; Charles F. Button to Grover Cleveland, Nov. 7, 1884, Cleveland mss, LC.

31. Church, *Republican Party,* pp. 154–55; *New York Times,* Nov. 8, 1884. The Illinois vote was Blaine 337,469; Cleveland 312,351; St. John 12,074. *Illinois Fact Book and Historical Almanac,* p. 90.

32. Mortimer D. Leggett to JAL, Nov. 8, 1884, Logan mss, LC; *Washington Bee,* Nov. 22, Dec. 6, 1884.

33. Shelby Cullom to JAL, Nov. 7, 1884; Whitelaw Reid to JAL, Nov. 20, 1884; Wharton Barker to JAL, Nov. 17, 1884; L.M. Reavis to JAL, May 11, 1884, Logan mss, LC; A.M. Jones to JAL, Dec. 12, 1884; Byron Andrews to JAL, June 6, 1884; J.V. Logan to JAL, June 12, 1884, Logan mss, ISHL; Robert Ingersoll to "Dear Clint," Nov. 8, 1884, Ingersoll mss, LC.

34. Dearing, *Veterans,* pp. 297, 306–7.

35. Lee Benson, "Research Problems in American Political Historiography," in *Common Frontiers of the Social Sciences,* ed. Mirra Komarovsky, pp. 113–83.

36. Marcus, *Grand Old Party,* pp. 5–11.

37. Morgan, *From Hayes to McKinley,* p. 234. The Blaine-Logan ticket and the party as a whole had run a strong campaign. In addition to wiping out Cleveland's huge majority

from 1882, the Republicans gained 22 House seats and would control the new Senate.

38. *Huntsville Gazette,* Dec. 6, 1884. Late in the year Logan, in New York, when interviewed, said he believed the Burchard speech more than any other single factor accounted for the Republican loss. *Illinois State Journal,* Nov. 29, Dec. 1, 1884. Mary Logan, *Reminiscences,* p. 423, says the loss to Hendricks, a Civil War Copperhead, was "pretty tough" for her husband to bear.

Chapter 15. The Logan Machine and the "Still Hunt"

1. Whitelaw Reid to JAL, Nov. 20, Dec. 21, 1884, Logan mss, LC.

2. *Cong. Record,* 48th Cong., 2d sess., pt. 1:1, 35, 101, 103, 233.

3. Walter Q. Gresham to Shelby Cullom, Nov. 28, 1884, Cullom mss, ISHL; JAL to Richard Oglesby, Dec. 6, 1884, Oglesby mss, ISHL.

4. ML to Dollie Tucker, Dec. 7, 1884; ML to Will Tucker, Dec. 22, 1884, Logan mss, LC; *Cong. Record,* 48th Cong., 2d sess., pt. 1:430; *Inter-Ocean,* Jan. 2, 1885; *Chicago Tribune,* Jan. 2, 1885; Mary Logan, *Reminiscences,* p. 424.

5. John M. Hamilton to JAL, Dec. 22, 1884, Logan mss, LC; Richard Oglesby to JAL, Dec. 3, 1884; JAL to Richard Oglesby, Dec. 6, 1884, Oglesby mss, ISHL; C.C. Post to David Davis, Sept. 27, 1884; Charles Shackleford to David Davis, Nov. 23, 1884, Davis mss, ISHL; *Chicago Tribune,* Dec. 20, 1884, Jan. 1, 1885; *Inter-Ocean,* Jan. 2, 1885; *Nation,* Jan. 29, 1885; Joseph Medill to JAL, Dec. 11, 1884, Logan mss, LC.

6. *Inter-Ocean,* Jan. 3, 6, 7, 1885; *Chicago Tribune,* Jan. 4, 1885; *Illinois State Journal,* Jan. 3, 12, 16, 1885; *Illinois State Register,* Jan. 15, Feb. 4, 1885.

7. *Chicago Tribune,* Jan. 8–10, 13, 1885; *Inter-Ocean,* Jan. 11, 1885.

8. JAL to ML, Jan. 11, 17, 29, 1885, Logan mss, LC.

9. *Inter-Ocean,* Jan. 14, 19, 1885; *Chicago Tribune,* Jan. 21, 1885.

10. Inter-Ocean, Jan. 19, 24, 1885; *Chicago Tribune,* Jan. 27, 1885.

11. JAL to ML, Jan. 21, 25, 31, 1885, Logan mss, LC.

12. J.F. Snyder to William R. Morrison, Jan. 1, 1885; B. Arntzen to William R. Morrison, Jan. 2, 1885, Morrison mss, ISHL; John C. Black to E.R.E. Kimbrough, Jan. 23, 1885, Black mss, ISHL; Tom E. Terrill, "David A. Wells, The Democracy and Tariff Reduction, 1877–1894," *Journal of American History* 56(1969):540–55.

13. *Chicago Tribune,* Feb. 3, 5, 6, 1885; *Inter-Ocean,* Feb. 2, 4, 6, 7, 1885; David W. Lusk, *History of the Contest for United States Senator, before the 34th General Assembly of Illinois, 1885,* pp. 6, 12; *Illinois State Journal,* Feb. 16, 21, 1885; *Illinois State Register,* Feb. 5, 1885.

14. Lusk, *Contest for United States Senator,* pp. 29–51; *Chicago Tribune,* Feb. 6, 12, 13, 19, 1885; *Inter-Ocean,* Feb. 7, 13, 19, 1885; *Illinois State Journal,* Feb. 12, 1885.

15. Lusk, *Contest for United States Senator,* pp. 29–51; *Chicago Tribune,* Feb. 13, 1885.

16. *Chicago Tribune,* Feb. 13, 1885; JAL to ML, Feb. 5, 6, 7, 10, 12, 17, 1885, Logan mss, LC.

17. James G. Blaine to R.C. Kerns, Feb. 24, 1885; Whitelaw Reid to JAL, Feb. 28, 1885; Henry Anthony to JAL, Feb. 1, 1885, Logan mss, LC.

18. *Chicago Tribune,* Feb. 21, 27, 1885; *Inter-Ocean,* Feb. 26, 27, 1885; JAL to ML, Feb. 21, 26, 1885, Logan mss, LC.

19. Charles T. Marsh to William R. Morrison, Feb. 3, 1885; J.H. Jones to William R. Morrison, Feb. 3, 1885; J.H. Hungate to William R. Morrison, Feb. 20, 1885; John H. Oberly to William R. Morrison, Feb. 24, 1885, Morrison mss, ISHL.

20. *Chicago Tribune*, Mar. 4, 5, 7, 10, 13, 1885; *Inter-Ocean*, Mar. 11, 1885; JAL to ML, Mar. 4, 1885, Logan mss, LC.

21. *Chicago Tribune*, Mar. 21–25, 1885.

22. JAL to ML, Mar. 2, 3, 14, 24, 1885; ML to JAL, Mar. 15, 19, 20, 29, 1885, Logan mss, LC. Cullom's biographer writes that Logan's fellow senator was "most anxious for his return" (Neilson, *Cullom*, p. 75).

23. JAL to ML, Mar. 28, 31, 1885, Logan mss, LC; *Chicago Tribune*, Mar. 26–28, 31, 1885.

24. A.J. Grover to William R. Morrison, Apr. 1, 1885; A.J. Grover to Alson Streeter, Mar. 31, 1885; R.N. Davis to William R. Morrison, Mar. 28, 1885; J.T. Johnston to William R. Morrison, Apr. 18, 1885, Morrison mss, ISHL.

25. *Chicago Tribune*, Apr. 1, 3, 4, 1885.

26. *Chicago Tribune*, Apr. 8, 1885; JAL to ML, Apr. 1, 6, 1885; ML to JAL, Mar. 29, 1885, Logan mss, LC; William R. Morrison to Charles Lanphier, Apr. 28, 1885, Lanphier mss, ISHL.

27. Lusk, *Contest for United States Senator*, pp. 30–31; *Chicago Tribune*, Apr. 13, 1885.

28. ML to Dollie Tucker, Apr. 27, 1885, Logan mss, LC; *Illinois State Journal*, Apr. 23, 1885; *Chicago Tribune*, Apr. 18, 26, May 2, 1885; Joseph Medill to Richard Oglesby, Apr. 20, 1885, Oglesby mss, ISHL.

29. Henry Craske, *A Complete and Authentic History of the Campaign*, pp. 27–38; *Chicago Tribune*, May 8, 1885; *Illinois State Journal*, May 8, 1885. The latter newspaper blared: "The Sleepy Bourbons Beaten With Their Hands in Their Breeches Pockets."

30. Craske, *A Complete and Authentic History of the Campaign*, pp. 1–21. See also Bogart and Thompson, *Industrial State*, p. 157, for a discussion of the origin of the "still hunt" or "gum-shoe" campaign as it was called in the state press.

31. Warren N. Wilson to William R. Morrison, May 20, 1885, Morrison mss, ISHL; *Illinois State Register*, May 8, 1885.

32. *Chicago Tribune*, May 8, 1885; JAL to ML, May 9, 1885; JAL to ML, May 7, 1885, Logan mss, LC. During the Senate battle the *Chicago Daily News* called young Logan "sort of a half dude." One of the Republican assemblymen denounced the slur and praised Manning at great length. W.E. Mason to ML, May 29, 1885, Logan mss, ISHL.

33. Lusk, *Contest for United States Senator*, pp. 32–33; *Chicago Tribune*, May 9–13, 1885.

34. JAL, Jr., to ML, May 12, 1885, Logan mss, LC.

35. *Chicago Tribune*, May 15, 16, 19, 1885.

36. Ibid., May 20, 1885. The *St. Louis Globe-Democrat*, May 16, 1885, found Logan's ability to hold his supporters in line without patronage or a personal fortune to be truly amazing.

37. JAL to ML, May 19, 1885; JAL, Jr., to ML, May 19, 1885; ML to JAL, May 19, 1885; Bound Volumes and Scrapbooks, 1885, Logan mss, ISHL. The Logans wrote responses to most of those sending congratulations. See JAL to Henry J. Johnson, June 10, 1885, Clara J.J. Morrow mss, Duke University Library.

38. Chauncey I. Filley to JAL, May 19, 1885; James G. Blaine to JAL, May 19, 1885; Hamilton Fish to JAL, May 19, 1885; Benjamin Harrison to JAL, May 19, 1885; Harrison H. Riddleberger to JAL, May 22, 1885; George F. Hoar to JAL, May 28, 1885; John Hay to JAL, May 19, 1885, Logan mss, ISHL; Joseph Foraker to JAL, May 19, 1885, Foraker mss, Cincinnati Historical Society; *Harper's Weekly*, May 30, 1885.

39. Shelby Cullom to JAL, May 21, 1885; George F. Dawson to JAL, May 19, 1885; Lewis Hanback to JAL, May 21, 1885; William Pitt Kellogg to JAL, May 19, 1885; Simon Greenleaf to JAL, May 26, 1885, Logan mss, ISHL. The day before Logan won, Cullom met Rutherford B. Hayes and expressed a fear that "bribery of Republican members from Chicago will lose Logan his seat." No such charges were made. Hayes, *Diary,* 4:210.

40. *Chicago Tribune,* May 20, 21, 1885; *New York Tribune,* May 19, 1885; the *Illinois State Journal,* May 20, 1885, attributed victory to Logan's "indomitable pluck and perseverance."

41. Dawson, *Logan,* p. 369; *Chicago Tribune,* May 21, 24, 27, 1885.

42. *Chicago Tribune,* May 31, June 1, 2, 1885; *Washington Bee,* June 20, 1885; JAL to Henry J. Johnson, June 10, 1885, Clara J.J. Morrow mss, Duke University Library; *New York Tribune,* July 5, 1877.

43. Dawson, *Logan,* pp. 373–74; ML to Dollie Tucker, June 29, 1885; Nelson Aldrich to JAL, June 29, 1885, Logan mss, LC; William T. Sherman to John Sherman, June 23, 1885, William T. Sherman mss, LC; *Illinois State Journal,* June 30, 1885; *Chicago Tribune,* July 1, 1885.

44. ML to Dollie Tucker, July 14, Aug. 31, Sept. 2, 1885, Logan mss, LC; Mary Logan, *Reminiscences,* p. 427; *Chicago Tribune,* July 28, 1885. The home was at the corner of Thirteenth and Clifton streets.

45. W.P. Canaday to JAL, July 25, 1885; JAL to ML, Sept. 14, 1885, Logan mss, LC; JAL to Joseph B. Foraker, July 10, 12, 1885, Foraker mss, Cincinnati Historical Society; Richard S. Tuthill to R.B. Hayes, July 7, 1885, Hayes mss, Hayes Library; *Illinois State Journal,* July 31, Aug. 9, 1885; *Chicago Tribune,* July 25, 28, Aug. 9, 1885.

46. ML to Dollie Tucker, Oct. 2, 9, 1885, Logan mss, LC.

47. ML to Dollie Tucker, Oct. 21, 1885; Will Tucker to JAL, Oct. 9, 1885; JAL, Jr., to JAL, Oct. 11, 1885; JAL, Jr., to ML, Oct. 19, 1885, Logan mss, LC.

Chapter 16. The Last Snowfall

1. James G. Blaine to JAL, Nov. 29, 1885; Stephen B. Elkins to JAL, Nov. 27, Dec. 5, 1885; Dollie Tucker to ML, Dec. 12, 1885, Logan mss, LC; *Illinois State Journal,* Dec. 5, 1885, joined *Harper's Weekly,* Dec. 19, 1885, in hailing Black Jack's "lofty patriotism" in declining the office. But the *Illinois State Register,* Dec. 5, 1885, saw the senator's motivation in his yearning for the presidency in 1888. The presidency of the Senate would have buried him, thought the *Register.*

2. JAL to Stephen B. Elkins, Dec. 11, 1885, Elkins mss, West Virginia Collection, West Virginia University Library, Morgantown.

3. *Cong. Record,* 49th Cong., 1st sess., pt. 1:104, 167; *Chicago Tribune,* Nov. 23, 1885.

4. A.J. Rice to JAL, Dec. 8, 1885; ML to Dollie Tucker, Dec. 18, 1885; Dollie Tucker to ML, Dec. 12, 1885, Logan mss, LC.

5. *Cong. Record,* 49th Cong., 1st sess., pt. 1:402, 971–72; *Washington Bee,* Jan. 30, 1886.

6. *Cong. Record,* 49th Cong., 1st sess., pt. 1:499–500; pt. 5:4584–90, 4669–72, 4680; John C. Black to Mrs. John C. Black, Aug. 2, 1885, Black mss, ISHL; *Illinois State Journal,* Jan. 8, 1886.

7. *Cong. Record,* 49th Cong., 1st sess., pt. 1:307, 1088; pt. 2:1157–61, 1171. See Harry J. Sievers, *Benjamin Harrison, Hoosier Statesman* 2:282–83.

8. Logan Tucker to ML, Jan. 21, 1886; JAL to Logan Tucker, Feb. 28, 1886, Logan mss, LC. Mary also received a February letter from Miss Maggie Irving of Louisville. The girl asked for the Logans' autographs, telling Mary her father had fought under Black Jack. She pleaded: "Please don't get angry and call me an autograph feind [sic] 'cause I ain't one of them either." Maggie Irving to ML, Feb. 22, 1886, Logan mss, ISHL.

9. JAL to ML, Apr. 27, May 2, 1885, Logan mss, ISHL; JAL to ML, Apr. 29, 1885, Logan mss, LC.

10. ML to Dollie Tucker, June 19, Sept. 2, Oct. 9, 21, 1885, Logan mss, LC.

11. John A. Logan, *The Great Conspiracy, Its Origin and History,* pp. 13–30; Thomas J. Pressly, *Americans Interpret Their Civil War,* pp. 38–44; Howard K. Beale, "What Historians Have Said About the Causes of the Civil War," *Theory and Practice in Historical Study: A Report of the Committee on Historiography of the Social Science Research Council,* Bulletin No. 54, pp. 60, 69.

12. Joseph Wallace, "A Biography of John A. Logan," unpublished manuscript in ISHL, pp. 40–41; *Nation,* June 3, 1886; William R. Thayer, *The Life and Letters of John Hay* 2:31. Eighty years after *The Great Conspiracy* was published, Roy Frank Nichols wrote: "We are reviving another once widely held concept, that mysterious cloak-and-dagger concept of conspiracy. . . . Gen. John A. Logan gave the idea wide publicity in his book" ("A Hundred Years Later: Perspectives on the Civil War," *Journal of Southern History* 33(1967):154–62).

13. Wallace, "Biography," pp. 40–41; JAL to ML, Nov. 15, 1886, Logan mss, LC. The *Chicago Tribune,* May 8, 1886, did its best to help sales by including a lengthy quote from the volume.

14. *Cong. Record,* 49th Cong., 1st sess., pt. 2: 1993–97, 2033–35.

15. JAL to Charles N. Hunter, Dec. 7, 1885, Hunter mss, Duke University Library; *Washington Bee,* Mar. 7, 1886; R.B. Hayes to J.M. Comly, Mar. 27, 1886, Hayes mss, Hayes Library; *Cong. Record,* 49th Cong., 1st sess., pt. 2:2105; *Chicago Tribune,* Mar. 6, 1886. See Daniel W. Crofts, "The Black Response to the Blair Education Bill," *Journal of Southern History* 38(1971):41–65. Although the Blair Bill passed the Senate, it failed in the House. Crofts indicates that 75 percent of the money would have gone to the South, and that it might have benefitted whites as much as blacks. Crofts concludes, however: "Had the Blair Bill been enacted, irregularities in distributing its benefits would almost certainly have occurred in view of the obvious opposition or indifference of many Southern whites to black education."

16. *Cong. Record,* 49th Cong., 1st sess., pt. 3:2480, 2610–14; John M. Schofield to JAL, Feb. 22, 1886, Logan mss, LC; *Inter-Ocean,* Mar. 31, 1886. The *Inter-Ocean* supported the bill and generally supported Logan throughout 1886.

17. *Cong. Record,* 49th Cong., 1st sess., pt. 3:2866, 2906, 2940–42, 3116, 3194–95; Scorce to JAL, Apr. 2, 1886, Logan mss, ISHL.

18. ML to Dollie Tucker, Feb. 21, May 1, 1886; JAL to ML, Apr. 12, 1886; W.N. Taft to JAL, May 21, 1886, Logan mss, LC; C.A. Logan to JAL, June 24, 1886; Russell A. Alger to JAL, Apr. 26, 1886, Logan mss, ISHL; *Illinois State Journal,* Feb. 3, 1886; *Chicago Tribune,* Feb. 23, 1886; *Illinois State Register,* Feb. 24, 1886; *Harper's Weekly,* Mar. 13, 1886.

19. JAL, Jr., to ML, Apr. 28, May 7, 1886; Dollie Tucker to ML, Apr. 8 1886, Logan mss, LC; *Illinois State Register,* Apr. 13, 1886.

20. *Cong. Record,* 49th Cong., 1st sess., pt. 5:4539, 4423; ML to Dollier Tucker, May 1, 1886, Logan mss, LC; Cullom *Fifty Years,* p. 319.

21. *Cong. Record,* 49th Cong., 1st sess., pt. 5:4681–82; pt. 6:5747, 5665–67; pt. 7:7029–31; *Chicago Tribune,* Apr. 7, 21, 1886.

22. *Cong. Record,* 49th Cong., 1st sess., pt. 6:6082–86, 6106–20, 6126–28; *Chicago Tribune,* June 26, 1886; *Nation,* July 1, 1886.

23. ML to Dollie Tucker, June 3, 1886, Logan mss, LC; Ward H. Lamon to JAL, June 2, 1886; JAL to Ward H. Lamon, June 10, 1886, Lamon mss, Huntington Library; Isaac N. Phillips to Shelby M. Cullom, July 14, 1886, Cullom mss, ISHL.

24. Murat Halstead to JAL, June 11, 1886; Jerome B. Chaffee to JAL, June 23, 1886, Logan mss, LC; JAL to Adeline Burr Davis, June 23, 1886, Adeline B.D. Green mss, Duke University Library.

25. Dawson, *Logan,* pp. 430–36; Homer E. Socolofsky, *Arthur Capper, Publisher, Politician, Philanthropist,* p. 23; Russell A. Alger to JAL, Apr. 26, 1886, Logan mss, ISHL; Mary Logan, *Reminiscences,* pp. 427–28. The *Illinois State Register,* June 29, 1886, reported rumors that Leland Stanford of California preferred Logan for 1888. *Nation,* Sept. 2, 1886, told its readers that Black Jack's 1888 presidential hopes had been jarred when the G.A.R. "snubbed his attempt to 'run' the convention."

26. ML to Dollie Tucker, Sept. 19, 1886; ML to Will and Dollie Tucker, Oct. 17, 1886; JAL to ML, Nov. 3, 1886, Logan mss, LC; *Inter-Ocean,* Sept. 5, Oct. 23, 1886; *Illinois State Journal,* Oct. 13, 29, 30, 1886; *Chicago Tribune,* Sept. 17, 1886.

27. ML to Dollie Tucker, Sept. 26, 1886, Logan mss, LC; Mary Logan, *Reminiscences,* p. 429.

28. John A. Logan, *The Volunteer Soldier of America,* pp. 583–84.

29. Ibid., pp. 598–612.

30. *Cong. Record,* 49th Cong., 2d sess., pt. 1:1, 23, 55, 177; Joseph R. Hawley to JAL, Dec. 17, 1886, Logan mss, LC; Matt Ransom to JAL, Dec. 17, 1886, Ransom mss, Southern Historical Collection, University of North Carolina; *Illinois State Register,* Dec. 21, 1886; *Illinois State Journal,* Dec. 18, 1886; *Inter-Ocean,* Dec. 27, 1886; Mary Logan, *Reminiscences,* pp. 428–29.

31. Dawson, *Logan,* p. 448; Mary Logan, *Reminiscences,* pp. 429–30; Doctor McMillan to William T. Sherman, Dec. 26, 1886, William T. Sherman mss, LC. In his telegram to Sherman the doctor called Logan's death a "distressing scene." *Inter-Ocean,* Dec. 27, 1886.

32. *Illinois State Journal,* Dec. 27, 1886; *Inter-Ocean,* Dec. 27, 1886; *Illinois State Register,* Dec. 27, 1886; *Chicago Tribune,* Dec. 27, 28, 1886.

33. JAL, Jr., to William T. Sherman, Dec. 28, 1886, William T. Sherman mss, LC; Philip H. Sheridan to ML, Dec. 27, 1886, Sheridan mss, LC; William T. Sherman to Shelby M. Cullom, Dec. 27, 1886; Simon Cameron to Shelby M. Cullom, Dec. 27, 1886; Roscoe Conkling to Shelby M. Cullom, Dec. 27, 1886, Cullom mss, ISHL; Chidsey, *Conkling,* p. 370; Mary Logan, *Reminiscences,* pp. 430–31. Logan's remains were deposited in the mausoleum of a friend until a monument could be erected in the Soldier's Home Cemetery. When that was done the casket was moved there.

34. *Cong. Record,* 49th Cong., 2d sess., pt. 1:348; pt. 2:1823–52. In his memoir, Cullom said he believed Logan would have been elected president had he lived. Cullom, *Fifty Years,* p. 185.

35. *Cong. Record,* 49th Cong., 2d sess., pt. 2:1532–45.

36. *Chicago Tribune,* Dec. 28, 1886.

37. *Huntsville Gazette,* Jan. 8, 1887. Frederick Douglass agreed and in his autobiogra-

phy bemoaned the passage of Sumner, Wade, Morton, Conkling, Stevens, and Logan from positions of leadership in the Republican party. Frederick Douglass, *Life and Times of Frederick Douglass,* p. 555.

38. Jones, *"Black Jack,"* p. xvi; Mary Logan, *Reminiscences,* pp. 289–93; *Cong. Record,* 67th Cong., 4th sess., pt. 4:4319.

39. Wiebe, *Search for Order,* p. 6.

40. F.M. Hayes to JAL, May 3, 1879, Logan mss, ISHL.

BIBLIOGRAPHY

Primary Materials

Collections of Letters and Manuscripts

Nelson Aldrich Papers, Library of Congress
Chester A. Arthur Papers, Library of Congress
Orville Babcock Papers, Newberry Library, Chicago
John C. Bagby Papers, Illinois State Historical Library, Springfield
Bailhache-Brayman Papers, Illinois State Historical Library, Springfield
Conrad Baker Papers, William Henry Smith Library, Indianapolis
Wharton Barker Papers, Library of Congress
James A. Beaver Papers, Illinois State Historical Library, Springfield
John Charles Black Papers, Illinois State Historical Library, Springfield
James G. Blaine Papers, Library of Congress
Orville H. Browning Papers, Illinois State Historical Library, Springfield
Benjamin F. Butler Papers, Library of Congress
Simon Cameron Papers, Library of Congress
William E. Chandler Papers, Library of Congress
William E. Chandler Papers, New Hampshire Historical Society, Concord
Zachariah Chandler Papers, Library of Congress
B.H. Chever Papers, Western Reserve Historical Society, Cleveland
Grover Cleveland Papers, Library of Congress
Schuyler Colfax Papers, Hayes Library, Fremont, Ohio
Schuyler Colfax Papers, Library of Congress
A.L. Conger Papers, Hayes Library, Fremont, Ohio
Roscoe Conkling Papers, Library of Congress
John Covode Papers, Library of Congress
Shelby M. Cullom Papers, Illinois State Historical Library, Springfield
George W. Curtis Papers, Hayes Library, Fremont, Ohio
David Davis Papers, Illinois State Historical Library, Springfield
Henry L. Dawes Papers, Library of Congress
Thomas Donaldson Papers, Hayes Library, Fremont, Ohio
Eldridge Papers, Huntington Library, Pomona, California
Stephen B. Elkins Papers, West Virginia Collection, West Virginia University Library, Morgantown
William M. Evarts Papers, Library of Congress
Joseph Fifer Papers, Illinois State Historical Library, Springfield
Joseph Foraker Papers, Cincinnati Historical Society

273

James A. Garfield Papers, Library of Congress
Ulysses S. Grant Papers, Hayes Library, Fremont, Ohio
Gratz Papers, Historical Society of Pennsylvania, Philadelphia
Adeline B.D. Green Papers, Duke University Library, Durham, North Carolina
Walter Q. Gresham Papers, Library of Congress
Murat Halstead Papers, Hayes Library, Fremont, Ohio
Benjamin Harrison Papers, Library of Congress
Ozias M. Hatch Papers, Illinois State Historical Library, Springfield
Joseph Hawley Papers, Library of Congress
Rutherford B. Hayes Papers, Hayes Library, Fremont, Ohio
George F. Hoar Papers, Massachusetts Historical Society, Boston
Oliver O. Howard Papers, Bowdoin College Library, Brunswick, Maine
Charles N. Hunter Papers, Duke University Library, Durham, North Carolina
Ebon and Robert G. Ingersoll Papers, Illinois State Historical Library, Springfield
Robert G. Ingersoll Papers, Library of Congress
William Jayne Papers, Illinois State Historical Library, Springfield
Thomas Jenckes Papers, Library of Congress
George W. Juilian Papers, Indiana State Library, Indianapolis
Ward Lamon Papers, Huntington Library, Pomona, California
Charles Lanphier Papers, Illinois State Historical Library, Springfield
Frederic E. Lockley Papers, Huntington Library, Pomona, California
Dr. John Logan Papers, Illinois State Historical Library, Springfield
John A. Logan Miscellaneous Papers, Hayes Library, Fremont, Ohio
John A. Logan Papers, Illinois State Historical Library, Springfield
John A. Logan Personal Papers, Miscellaneous, Indiana State Library, Indianapolis
John A. Logan Papers, Library of Congress
James Luther Papers, Indiana State Library, Indianapolis
John McClernand Papers, Illinois State Historical Library, Springfield
Edward McPherson Papers, Library of Congress
Manton Marble Papers, Library of Congress
Edwin D. Morgan Papers, New York State Library, Albany
Justin S. Morrill Papers, Library of Congress
William R. Morrison Papers, Illinois State Historical Library, Springfield
Clara J.J. Morrow Papers, Duke University Library, Durham, North Carolina
Oliver P. Morton Papers, Indiana State Library, Indianapolis
Richard Oglesby Papers, Illinois State Historical Library, Springfield
Godlove Orth Papers, Indiana State Library, Indianapolis
John M. Palmer Papers, Illinois State Historical Library, Springfield
Fitz-John Porter Papers, Library of Congress
D.D. Pratt Papers, Indiana State Library, Indianapolis
Matt Ransom Papers, Southern Historical Collection, University of North Carolina Library, Chapel Hill
Thomas B. Reed Miscellaneous Papers, Hayes Library, Fremont, Ohio
Carl Schurz Papers, Library of Congress
Thomas Settle Papers, Southern Historical Collection, University of North Carolina Library, Chapel Hill
Philip H. Sheridan Papers, Library of Congress
John Sherman Papers, Library of Congress

John Sherman Papers, Ohio Historical Society, Ohio State Museum, Columbus
William T. Sherman Papers, Library of Congress
William T. Sherman Papers, Ohio Historical Society, Ohio State Museum, Columbus
William Henry Smith Papers, William Henry Smith Library, Indianapolis
Oliver Spaulding Papers, Michigan Historical Collections, University of Michigan Library, Ann Arbor
Edwin M. Stanton Papers, Library of Congress
John D. Strong Papers, Illinois State Historical Library, Springfield
Richard W. Thompson Papers, Indiana State Library, Indianapolis
Lyman Trumbull Papers, Illinois State Historical Library, Springfield
Lyman Trumbull Papers, Library of Congress
Benjamin F. Wade Papers, Library of Congress
Elihu B. Washburne Papers, Illinois State Historical Library, Springfield
Elihu B. Washburne Papers, Library of Congress
Horace White Papers, Illinois State Historical Library, Springfield
Henry Wilson Papers, Library of Congress
Richard Yates Papers, Illinois State Historical Library, Springfield

Government Documents

U.S., Congress, Senate, *Congressional Globe*, 36th Cong., 1859–60; 40th Cong., 1867–68, through 42nd Cong., 1871–72.
U.S., Congress, Senate, *Congressional Record*, 43d Cong., 1873–74, through 49th Cong., 1885–86.
U.S. Congress, *Reports and Documents*. 48th Cong. 1st sess., Senate Report No. 283; 42d Cong., 3d sess., House of Representatives Report No. 77, "Crédit Mobilier."
Illinois, General Assembly. *Journal of the House of Representatives of the 30th General Assembly of the State of Illinois.*

Newspapers and Periodicals

Allen County Democrat, Lima, Ohio
Alton Telegraph, Alton, Illinois
Baltimore Vindicator
Cairo Bulletin, Cairo, Illinois
Cairo Democrat, Cairo, Illinois
Cairo Egyptian Sun, Cairo, Illinois
Carbondale New Era, Carbondale, Illinois
Centralia Sentinel, Centralia, Illinois
Chicago Daily News
Chicago Evening Journal
Chicago Republican
Chicago Times
Chicago Tribune
Cincinnati Gazette
Davenport Daily Gazette, Davenport, Iowa
Des Moines Register
DuQuoin Tribune, DuQuoin, Illinois
Elyria Independent Democrat, Elyria, Ohio
Freeport Weekly Journal, Freeport, Illinois
Golconda Herald, Golconda, Illinois
The Great Campaign, Chicago
Great Republic, Washington, D.C
Harper's Weekly
Huntsville Gazette, Huntsville, Alabama
Illinois Staats-Zeitung, Chicago
Illinois State Journal, Springfield
Illinois State Register, Springfield
Inter-Ocean, Chicago
Jonesboro Gazette, Jonesboro, Illinois
Miami Union, Troy, Ohio
Nation
New National Era, Washington, D.C
New Orleans Weekly Louisianan
New York Evening Mail
New York Globe
New York Herald
New York Sun
New York Times

New York Tribune
New York World
The People's Advocate, Washington, D.C
Quincy Daily Herald, Quincy, Illinois
Quincy Weekly Whig and Republican, Quincy, Ill.

St. Louis Globe-Democrat
San Francisco Elevator
Sioux City Journal, Sioux City, Iowa
Washington Bee, Washington, D.C.
Washington Grit, Washington, D.C.

Books

Blaine, James G. *Twenty Years of Congress, 1861–1881.* 2 vols. Norwich, Conn.: Henry Bill Publishing Co., 1886.

Browning, Orville H. *Diary of Orville Hickman Browning.* Edited by James G. Randall. 2 vols. Springfield, Ill.: Illinois State Historical Library, 1938.

Burnham, Walter D. *Presidential Ballots, 1836–1892.* Baltimore: Johns Hopkins University Press, 1955.

Chetlain, Augustus. *Recollections of Seventy Years.* Galena, Ill.: Gazette Publishing Co., 1899.

Conkling, Alfred. *The Life and Letters of Roscoe Conkling.* New York: C.L. Webster and Company, 1889.

Cox, Samuel S. *Three Decades of Federal Legislation, 1855–1885.* Providence, R.I.: J.A. and R.A. Reid, 1885.

Craske, Henry. *A Complete and Authentic History of the Campaign in which the 'Mighty Sleeper' was Defeated in the 34th Senatorial District of Illinois, which Culminated in the Re-election of Honorable John A. Logan to the United States Senate.* Rushville, Ill.: Published by one of the fine workers, 1885.

Cullom, Shelby M. *Fifty Years of Public Service: Personal Recollections.* Chicago: A.C. McClurg, 1911.

Douglass, Frederick. *Life and Times of Frederick Douglass.* New York: Macmillan, 1962.

Garfield, James A. *The Diary of James A. Garfield.* Edited by Harry J. Brown and Frederick D. Williams. 3 vols. East Lansing, Mich.: Michigan State University Press, 1967–1973.

Grant, Julia Dent. *The Personal Memoirs of Julia Dent Grant.* Edited by John Y. Simon. New York: Putnam, 1975.

Hayes, Rutherford B. *Diary and Letters of Rutherford B. Hayes, Nineteenth President of the United States.* Edited by Charles R. Williams. 5 vols. Columbus, Ohio: Ohio State Archaeological and Historical Society, 1922–1926.

The Illinois Fact Book and Historical Almanac, 1673–1968. Carbondale, Ill.: Southern Illinois University Press, 1970.

Ingersoll, Robert G. *Works of Robert G. Ingersoll.* 12 vols. New York: Ingersoll Publishers, 1900.

Koerner, Gustave P. *Memoirs of Gustave P. Koerner.* 2 vols. Cedar Rapids, Iowa: Torch Press, 1909.

Logan, John A. *The Great Conspiracy, Its Origin and History.* New York: A.R. Hart, 1886.

Logan, John A. *The Volunteer Soldier of America.* Chicago and New York: R.S. Peale Co., 1887.

Logan, Mary S.C. *Reminiscences of a Soldier's Wife.* New York: Charles Scribner's Sons, 1913.

Lusk, David W. *History of the Contest for the U.S. Senator before the 34th General Assembly of Illinois.* Springfield, Ill.: H.W. Rokker, 1885.

Lusk, David W. *Politics and Politicians of Illinois, 1856–1884*. Springfield, Ill.: H.W. Rokker, 1884.

Platt, Thomas C. *The Autobiography of Thomas C. Platt*. New York: Dodge, 1910.

Porter, Kirk H., and Johnson, Donald B. *National Party Platforms, 1840–1964*. Urbana, Ill.: University of Illinois Press, 1966.

Proceedings of the Republican National Convention, 1868, 1872, 1876, 1880, 1884.

Schurz, Carl. *Speeches, Correspondence and Political Papers of Carl Schurz*. Edited by Frederic Bancroft. 6 vols. New York: Putnams, 1913.

Sherman, William T. *Memoirs of General William Tecumseh Sherman*. 2 vols. New York: D. Appleton Co., 1875.

Smith, Theodore Clarke, editor. *The Life and Letters of James Abram Garfield*. 2 vols. New Haven: Yale University Press, 1925.

Thayer, William R. *The Life and Letters of John Hay*. 2 vols. Boston: Houghton, Mifflin, 1908.

Welles, Gideon. *The Diary of Gideon Welles*. Edited by Howard K. Beale. 2 vols. New York: W.W. Norton, 1960.

Articles

Grant, Ulysses S. "An Undeserved Stigma," *North American Review* 125(1882):536–46.

Logan, John A. "National Aid to Public Schools" *North American Review* 136(1883): 337–44.

Secondary Materials

Books

Andrews, Byron. *A Biography of General John A. Logan: With an Account of His Public Service in Peace and War*. New York: H.S. Goodspeed, 1884.

Appleton's Cyclopedia and Register of Important Events. 1871, 1876.

Badeau, Adam. *Grant in Peace*. Hartford, Conn.: S.S. Scranton Co., 1887.

Barrett, Don C. *The Greenbacks and Resumption of Specie Payments, 1862–1879*. Cambridge: Harvard University Press, 1931.

Beath, Robert B. *History of the Grand Army of the Republic*. New York: Bryan, Taylor & Co., 1889.

Benedict, Michael Les. *The Impeachment and Trial of Andrew Johnson*. New York: W.W. Norton, 1973.

Bogart, Ernest L., and Thompson, Charles M. *The Industrial State, 1870–1893*. Springfield, Ill.: Illinois Centennial Commission, 1920.

Brown, Dee Alexander. *Bury My Heart at Wounded Knee: An Indian History of the American West*. New York: Bantam Books, 1971.

Buck, Paul H. *The Road to Reunion, 1865–1900*. Boston: Little, Brown, 1937.

Caldwell, Robert G. *James A. Garfield, Party Chieftain*. Hamden, Conn.: Archon Books, 1931.

Chidsey, Donald B. *The Gentleman from New York: A Life of Roscoe Conkling*. New Haven: Yale University Press, 1935.

Church, Charles A. *A History of the Republican Party in Illinois, 1854–1912*. Rockford, Ill.: Wilson Brothers Co., 1912.

Clancy, Herbert J. *The Presidential Election of 1880*. Chicago: Loyola University Press, 1958.

Coleman, Charles H. *The Election of 1868: The Democratic Effort to Regain Control*. New York: Octagon Books, 1971.

Davison, Kenneth E. *The Presidency of Rutherford B. Hayes*. Westport, Conn.: Greenwood Publishing Corp., 1972.

Dawson, George Francis. *The Life and Services of General John A. Logan as Soldier and Statesman*. Chicago and New York: Belford, Clarke Co., 1887.

Dearing, Mary R. *Veterans in Politics: The Story of the Grand Army of the Republic*. Baton Rouge: Louisiana State University Press, 1952.

Dobson, John M. *Politics in the Gilded Age: A New Perspective on Reform*. New York: Praeger Publishers, 1972.

Dorris, Jonathan T. *Pardon and Amnesty under Lincoln and Johnson*. Chapel Hill: University of North Carolina Press, 1953.

Eisenschiml, Otto. *The Celebrated Case of Fitz-John Porter: An American Dreyfus Affair*. Indianapolis and New York: Bobbs-Merrill, 1950.

Ekirch, Arthur. *The Civilian and the Military*. New York: Oxford University Press, 1956.

George, Mary Karl. *Zachariah Chandler: A Political Biography*. East Lansing: Michigan State University Press, 1969.

Gillette, William. *The Right to Vote: Politics and the Passage of the Fifteenth Amendment*. Baltimore: Johns Hopkins University Press, 1965.

Goff, John S. *Robert Todd Lincoln: A Man in His Own Right*. Norman: University of Oklahoma Press, 1969.

Haskins, James. *Pinckney Benton Stewart Pinchback*. New York: Macmillan, 1973.

Hesseltine, William B. *Ulysses S. Grant, Politician*. New York: Dodd, Mead and Company, 1935.

Hirshson, Stanley P. *Farewell to the Bloody Shirt: Northern Republicans and the Southern Negro, 1877–1893*. Chicago: Quadrangle Books, 1962.

Howe, George F. *Chester A. Arthur: A Quarter Century of Machine Politics*. New York: Dodd, Mead, 1934.

Jones, James P. *"Black Jack:" John A. Logan and Southern Illinois in the Civil War Era*. Tallahassee: Florida State University Press, 1967.

Jordan, David M. *Roscoe Conkling of New York: Voice in the Senate*. Ithaca, N.Y.: Cornell University Press, 1971.

Josephson, Matthew. *The Politicos*. New York: Harcourt, Brace, 1938.

Juergens, George. *Joseph Pulitzer and the "New York World."* Princeton N.J.: Princeton University Press, 1966.

Kennedy, John F. *Profiles in Courage*. New York: Pocket Books, 1957.

King, Willard L. *Lincoln's Manager, David Davis*. Cambridge, Mass.: Harvard University Press, 1960.

Kleppner, Paul. *The Cross of Culture: A Social Analysis of Midwestern Politics, 1850–1900*. New York: The Free Press, 1970.

Lewis, Lloyd. *Sherman, Fighting Prophet*. New York: Harcourt, Brace, 1932.

Logan, John A., and Wilshire, W.W. *A Claim of the State of Illinois with Other Western*

and Southern States Based Upon the 5% Clause of the Act of Admission Into the Union.
Washington: National Republican Publishing Co., 1878.

Logsdon, Joseph. *Horace White, Nineteenth-Century Liberal.* Westport, Conn.: Greenwood Publishing Co., 1971.

Mantell, Martin E. *Johnson, Grant and the Politics of Reconstruction.* New York: Columbia University Press, 1973.

Marcus, Robert D. *Grand Old Party: Political Structure in the Gilded Age, 1880–1896.* New York: Oxford University Press, 1971.

Morgan, H. Wayne. *From Hayes to McKinley: National Party Politics, 1877–1896.* Syracuse: Syracuse University Press, 1969.

Muzzey, David S. *James G. Blaine, A Political Idol of Other Days.* New York: Dodd, Mead and Company, 1935.

Neilson, James W. *Shelby M. Cullom, Prairie State Republican.* Urbana: University of Illinois Press, 1962.

Nevins, Allan. *Grover Cleveland, a Study in Courage.* New York: Dodd, Mead and Company, 1932.

Norris, James D., and Shaffer, Arthur H., editors. *Politics and Patronage in the Gilded Age.* Madison: State Historical Society of Wisconsin, 1970.

Nugent, Walter T.K. *Money and American Society, 1865–1880.* New York: The Free Press, 1968.

Parker, William B. *The Life and Public Services of Justin Smith Morrill.* Boston and New York: Houghton, Mifflin, 1924.

Peskin, Allan. *Garfield.* Kent, Ohio: Kent State University Press, 1978.

Pierce, Bessie L. *A History of Chicago.* 3 vols. New York: Alfred A. Knopf, 1937–1957.

Polakoff, Keith Ian. *The Politics of Inertia: The Election of 1876 and the End of Reconstruction.* Baton Rouge: Louisiana State University Press, 1973.

Pressly, Thomas L. *Americans Interpret Their Civil War.* Princeton, N.J.: Princeton University Press, 1954.

Reeves, Thomas C. *Gentleman Boss: The Life of Chester Alan Arthur.* New York: Alfred A. Knopf, 1975.

Richardson, Leon B. *William E. Chandler, Republican.* New York: Dodd, Mead and Company, 1940.

Rosenberg, Charles E. *The Trial of the Assassin Guiteau.* Chicago: University of Chicago Press, 1968.

Shannon, Fred A. *The Centennial Years: A Political and Economic History of America from the Late 1870's to the Early 1890's.* New York: Doubleday, 1967.

Sievers, Harry J. *Benjamin Harrison, Hoosier Statesman.* 3 vols. Chicago: Henry Regnery, 1952–1968.

Smith, Gene. *High Crimes and Misdemeanors: The Impeachment and Trial of Andrew Johnson.* New York: William Morrow, 1977.

Socolofsky, Homer E. *Arthur Capper, Publisher, Politician, Philanthropist.* Lawrence: Regents' Press of the University of Kansas, 1962.

Sproat, John G. *The Best Men: Liberal Reformers in the Gilded Age.* New York: Oxford University Press, 1968.

Stampp, Kenneth M. *The Era of Reconstruction, 1865–1877.* New York: Vintage Books, 1967.

Storey, Moorfield. *Charles Sumner.* Boston and New York: Houghton, Mifflin, 1900.

Thomas, Benjamin P., and Hyman, Harold M. *Stanton: The Life and Times of Lincoln's Secretary of War.* New York: Alfred A. Knopf, 1962.

Thompson, E. Bruce. *Matthew Hale Carpenter.* Madison: State Historical Society of Wisconsin, 1954.

Tomisch, John. *A Genteel Endeavor: American Culture and Politics.* Stanford: Stanford University Press, 1971.

Trefousse, Hans. *Benjamin Franklin Wade: Radical Republican from Ohio.* New York: Twayne, 1963.

Unger, Irwin. *The Greenback Era: A Social and Political History of American Finance, 1865–1879.* Princeton, N.J.: Princeton University Press, 1964.

Walsh, Justin E. *To Print the News and Raise Hell! A Biography of Wilbur F. Storey.* Chapel Hill: University of North Carolina Press, 1968.

Webb, Ross A. *Benjamin Helm Bristow: Border State Politician.* Lexington: University of Kentucky Press, 1969.

Weinstein, Allen. *Prelude to Populism: Origins of the Silver Issue, 1867–1878.* New Haven: Yale University Press, 1970.

West, Robert S. *Lincoln's Scapegoat General: A Life of Benjamin F. Butler, 1818–1893.* Boston: Houghton, Mifflin, 1965.

Wiebe, Robert H. *The Search for Order, 1877–1920.* New York: Hill and Wang, 1967.

Williams, Burton J. *Senator John James Ingalls: Kansas' Iridescent Republican.* Lawrence: Regents' Press of the University of Kansas, 1972.

Williams, Kenneth P. *Lincoln Finds a General.* 5 vols. New York: Macmillan, 1949–1959.

Articles

Beale, Howard K. "What Historians Have Said About the Causes of the Civil War," *Theory and Practice in Historical Study: A Report of the Committee on Historiography.* New York: Social Science Research Council Bulletin 54, 1946.

Benedict, Michael Les. "The Rout of Radicalism: Republicans and the Election of 1867," *Civil War History* 18(1972):334–44.

Benson, Lee. "Research Problems in American Political Historiography." In *Common Frontiers of the Social Sciences,* ed. Mirra Komarovsky, pp. 113–83. Glencoe, Ill.: The Free Press, 1957.

Crofts, Daniel W. "The Black Response to the Blair Education Bill," *Journal of Southern History* 38(1971):41–65.

Doolen, Richard M. "'Brick' Pomeroy and the Greenback Clubs," *Journal of the Illinois State Historical Society* 65(1972):434–50.

Downey, Matthew T. "Horace Greeley and the Politicians: The Liberal Republican Convention in 1872," *Journal of American History* 53(1967):727–50.

Fishel, Leslie H. "The Negro in Northern Politics, 1870–1900," *Mississippi Valley Historical Review* 42(1955):466–89.

House, Albert V. "Northern Congressional Democrats as Defenders of the South During Rerconstruction," *Journal of Southern History* 6(1940):46–71.

Jensen, Richard. "The Religious and Occupational Roots of Party Identification: Illinois and Indiana in the 1870s," *Civil War History* 16(1970):325–43.

Jones, James P. "The Battle of Atlanta and McPherson's Successor," *Civil War History* 7(1961):393–405.

Kirk, Grayson. "The Crédit Mobilier Scandal," *American Mercury* 32(1934):351–59.

Nichols, Roy Frank. "A Hundred Years Later: Perspectives on the Civil War," *Journal of Southern History* 33(1967):154–62.

Searles, William C. "Governor Cullom and the Pekin Whisky Ring Scandal," *Journal of the Illinois State Historical Society* 51(1958):28–41.

Terrill, Tom E. "David A. Wells, the Democracy and Tariff Reduction, 1877–1894," *Journal of American History* 56(1969):540–55.

Unpublished Materials

Eidson, William Gene. "John A. Logan: Hero of the Volunteers." Ph.D. dissertation, Vanderbilt University, 1967.

Wallace, Joseph. "A Biography of John A. Logan." Manuscript, Illinois State Historical Library, Springfield.

INDEX

University Presses of Florida is the central agency for scholarly publishing of the State of Florida's university system. Its offices are located at 15 NW 15th Street, Gainesville, FL 32603. Works published by University Presses of Florida are evaluated and selected for publication by a faculty editorial committee of any one of Florida's nine public universities: Florida A&M University (Tallahassee), Florida Atlantic University (Boca Raton), Florida International University (Miami), Florida State University (Tallahassee), University of Central Florida (Orlando), University of Florida (Gainesville), University of North Florida (Jacksonville), University of South Florida (Tampa), University of West Florida (Pensacola).

Library of Congress Cataloging in Publication Data

Jones, James Pickett.
  John A. Logan, stalwart Republican from Illinois.

  "A Florida State University book."
  Bibliography: p.
  Includes index.
  1. Logan, John Alexander, 1826–1886. 2. United States—Politics and government—1865–1883. 3. Legislators—United States—Biography. 4. United States. Congress—Biography. I. Title.
  E664.L83J64   973.8'092'4 [B]   82-2663
  ISBN 0–8130–0729–1   AACR2

The paper in this book meets the guidelines for permanence and durability of the Committee on Production Guidelines for Book Longevity of the Council on Library Resources.